366 Glimpses Of God

Getting To Know
The God
Who Knows You

By

Sharon Norris Elliott

STiAW rAtpX

366 Glimpses of God

Getting To Know The God Who Knows You

By

Sharon Norris Elliott

Published By:

ABM Publications
A division of HSBN Publishing.
PO Box 6811, Orange, CA 92868

www.hsbn.pub

ISBN: 978-1-931820-75-2

Dedication for *366 Glimpses of God*

This book is dedicated to the pastors who have fed me God's word over the years.

This book is dedicated first to my first pastor, my daddy, Rev. Dr. Vincent Isaiah Norris. Although I was a pastor's kid (a PK), I never felt like I was second to the churches he pastored. Daddy's first and most important congregation was us, his family, and he ministered love and grace to us every day of his life. The chorus of the song I wrote for him sums up my sentiments:

> I want to be like my dad, not for all he's provided us,
> I want to be like my dad, not for the wisdom that's guided us,
> But the example I see in him,
> Gives me reason to be like him,
> For my dad is so much like the Lord.

Daddy didn't tell us how to live, he lived his life to show us how to be Christians. Daddy has been in Glory for 24 earth-years already, but his legacy lives on in all his children, grand children, and great-grandchildren who continue to serve the God he so dearly loved. Daddy, we're still honoring God with our lives. We'll join you when He's finished with us down here.

To my current pastor, Rev. Welton Pleasant II: Your preached revelation of God's word week-after-week is my steady, healthy spiritual diet. My daily devotional blog, "A Heart for the Word," is a direct result of your insight when you stated, "When you open your Bible, God opens His mouth." That word moved me to want to hear God speak to me every day. Thank you.

To former pastors, Dr. Frederick Holmes and Rev. Ralph Williams: I thank you both for the influence you have had in my life, training me to "rightly divide" the Word, and giving me opportunities to practice ministry leadership. God bless you both.

To other pastor/mentors, Bishop Andrew Bills and Evangelist, Dr. Kazumba Charles: What an inspiration you have both been to me.

Bishop, you have encouraged me by believing in my ministry gifts and giving me an international platform through which to share them with the world. Dr. Kazumba, we are family. I guess it takes one to know one because you ignited the flame of missionary zeal in my heart. Who would have believed that your spontaneous invitation, "You must come preach to the women in Africa" would actually become a reality? Yet, we've been once and no doubt will return many times. Thank you for allowing God to let you see what He already had in store for me.

And to all the other men and women of God who have allowed me to preach in their pulpits and speak at their retreats and conferences, thank you for providing an outlet for all the splendors of God's revelations He allows me to see. As I know you know, sharing God's word is the best thing in the world! I am truly grateful, honored, and humbled to be a part of this amazing brotherhood and sisterhood.

Endorsements for *366 Glimpses of God*

In *366 Glimpses of God*, Rev. Sharon Elliott gives us both theological and practical insights into the ways and purposes of God. This book will not only increase your passion for Him, but will also give you wise, practical, and powerful strategies that are sure to deepen your relationship with Christ.

Pastor Welton Pleasant II
Senior Pastor of Christ Second Baptist Church, Long Beach, CA

■ ■

In *366 Glimpses of God*, Rev. Sharon Norris Elliott shines a bright light on the true nature of God. I was impressed with the solid Biblical teaching put forward and the accompanying insights about the nature of God. It is obvious the author has been taught by the Father and given this powerful revelation of who God really is and who He wants to be to us. This is a good and important book, full of practical insights that will benefit everyone who reads it. I heartily recommend it to you.

Evangelist, Dr. Kazumba Charles
Christ Passion Evangelistic Ministries, Canada

■ ■

Reverend Sharon Elliott is a powerful woman of God who walks the walk! Her book, *366 Glimpses of God: Getting to Know the God Who Knows You,* is full of revelation from a woman who knows not only the word of God but the heart of God. This book will draw you closer into an intimate walk with God the Father. If you are ready for a deeper walk, if you desire to hear is voice more clearly, then this is a must read! I highly recommend it.

Pastor Cathy Coppola
President of Cathy Coppola International Ministries
Pastor at House of Glory

■ ■

As a leader of leaders, having had an opportunity to sit and hear Rev. Sharon Norris Elliott teach in our one week Next Level Conference, I do recommend without hesitation this brilliant and sound piece of work. The devotional *366 Glimpses of God* is a must read eye opener as it will impact on your perspective of the spiritual dimensions God.

Bishop Dr. Julius Atsango
Presiding Bishop of Cornerstone Ministries & Churches & President of Eldoret Ministerial Association Kenya.

■■

Sharon Elliott writes and speaks from the truth of her life narrative as God lays it on her heart. Through her thoughtful reflections upon God's word and her own life experience, Sharon shares tender, challenging, and encouraging nuggets of truth for each and every day of the year. The light and love of Jesus shines through the words on these pages revealing God's glory and the desire of God's heart for our lives: hope, peace, love, and joy.

Pastor Bob Mooney
Messiah Lutheran Church, Yorba Linda, CA

■■

"There's the preacher!"

Rev. Dr. Vincent Isaiah Norris
Sharon's dad, spoken of her in 1978, 13 years before she recognized her call to the ministry of speaking, preaching, and writing.

Glimpses of God
Enter In

Enter into His gates with thanksgiving,
and into His courts with praise.
Be thankful to Him,
and bless His name.
For the LORD is good;
His mercy is everlasting,
and His truth endures to all generations.
Ps 100:4-5 (NKJ)

What will it be like to actually enter into God's gates and God's court? We will undoubtedly be overwhelmed by the majesty of Heaven. The golden streets, the pearly gates, and the tree of life: everything we've read about will be brilliant splendor. I even imagine there will be colors we've never seen before, harmonies we've never heard before, and sweet perfumes we've never before smelled. But aside from all the tremendous sights, sounds, smells, and sensations, the one highlight of all will be beholding the glory of the Lord our God.

The writer of an old hymn reflected:
Oh, I want to see Him, look upon His face,
There to sing forever of His saving grace;
On the streets of glory let me lift my voice,
Cares all past, home at last, ever to rejoice. [1]

Indeed, like you, I may be in no great hurry to leave this life, but I am excited to think about one day seeing God face-to-face. In the meantime, I'd like to get to know Him as best I can. After hearing my pastor say, "When you open your Bible, God opens His mouth," I decided to listen for God's voice and anticipate a revelation of Him every time I read my Bible. So as I worked my way through the Word one year, my goal was to discover something new or be reminded of something amazing about God every day.

You hold in your hands, or are viewing on your screen, the result of that year's enterprise. Read by the numbers or by the dates. Read one entry per day, or take your time to savor each

---

[1] "O I Want to See Him." Public Domain.

devotional for several days; perhaps reading it one day, journaling your reflections the next, and delving into the context of the highlighted verse on day three. Maybe you'll want to read each devotion as you read through the chapter of the Bible from where that devotion is taken. Or maybe you'll want to skip around according to which devotional titles interest you most.

In whatever manner in which you plan to use this devotional guide, thank you for entering in, for joining with me in this wonderful discovery of who God is. May your doubts about Him be erased, your understanding of Him enhanced, and your love for Him enriched as you enter in and experience these glimpses of God.

Part 1

Glimpses of God

In the

Books of Moses

And the

Books of History

(90 Devotions)

#1
January 1: A New Year, a New Focus, a New Challenge

Welcome to the new year! Beginnings always hold such promise. They are times to reflect and then make new plans. They are times to be honest with ourselves about both what we did wrong and what we did right. Beginnings are fresh and full of hope; great times to set goals and priorities.

As you get to know God better with these daily glimpses of Him, I challenge you to also focus on some personal spiritual theme for this year. For example, one year, my focus was on prayer. I used Nick Harrison's daily devotional entitled *Magnificent Prayer*, and read a short selection on the topic every day. Just that extra few minutes turned my prayer life around and made me anticipate and appreciate my communication moments with God more and more. Another year, my spiritual focus was on getting to know God better. I used J.I. Packer's books *Knowing God, God Has Spoken*, and *Evangelism and the Sovereignty of God*.

I also challenge you to choose a word for the year. For the past 18 years, I have chosen a word that is my personal affirmation for that year. In 1998, the first year I did this, I was facing some pretty hard trials, so my word was "stand." In the years since, I have concentrated on words like peace, trust, vision, and joy. One year, my word was "glory" and I made a special effort to give God glory and let the glory of the Lord shine through me. Another year, my word was "favor," because I was determined to watch closely to see how my magnificent Heavenly Father showered favor on me and on His people throughout the year.

The devotion you hold in your hands begins with the uplifting verse found in Psalm 149:4, "For the Lord takes pleasure in His people" (NKJ). As I wrote these devotions and read through my Bible again, I determined to look for facts and gems about God. The first day's fact is—He takes pleasure in us. In other words, God smiles when He thinks about us. I've heard that if God had a refrigerator, our picture would be on it.

So again, welcome to the new year. May these devotions kick start your quiet times with God for many years to come. Choose your own spiritual focus and your special word for each year, and join me in a quest that is a glorious journey: to get to know God better. Happy New Year!

Year   Spiritual Focus   Word for the Year

_____
_____
_____
_____
_____
_____
_____
_____
_____
_____

#2
January 2: Living Outside of Time

It tilts my brain to realize that God lives outside of time. Because of the finite nature of our minds and understanding, He had to introduce Himself to us using a "time" word when He opened His book saying, "In the beginning" (Genesis 1:1). To us, the word "beginning" indicates the starting point in time. What we need to comprehend, though, about God is that in order for Him to have been there "in the beginning," he had to exist before the beginning. And God did. He is eternal, meaning He had no beginning and will have no ending. God created time as a touchstone for us.

As the One who lives outside of time, God's perspective on things is much different from ours. Starts are just as immediate to Him as are finishes. He exists in a perpetual state of now. The question, "How will things turn out?" never even crosses God's mind because He already knows. For example, consider this: years only separate births and deaths to us, not to Him. Since there is no past or future with Him, we are all dying at different times, but we all get to Heaven at the same time. After all, since God is in Heaven and He lives outside of time, there can be absolutely no concept of time there.

This understanding of God's constant "now-ness" should enable us to more intelligently perceive the happenings or our time-locked existence. As long as we're in His hands, we can stop worrying about how things will turn out, because whatever will be,

God already sees, and we know His plans for us are good. We can stop visualizing our dead loved ones waiting for us because by Heaven's non-clock, they haven't been there any longer than we have. It's impossible to wait in a place where there's no past or future.

I know, I told you, this concept really is a mind tilt. That's okay. Who needs a God who can be totally contained in a finite brain? Now we can have a much better understanding of Romans 8:28 which says, "And we know that God causes all things to work together for good to those who love God, to those who are called according to {His} purpose (NAS). God is working outside of time causing everything to fall into place for the good for us, His loved ones, who are traveling through time.

God locked Himself into time for one 33-year stretch and it killed Him to have to deal with our sin. Now all we have to do is believe, and when we do, His first act in our lives is to release us from the time prison by making us heirs to everlasting life. That's what John 3:16 is all about. "For God so loved the world, that he gave his only begotten Son, that whosoever believeth in him should not perish, but have everlasting life." (KJV)

Ponder and then rejoice today over the fact that God lives outside of time.

#3
January 3: God in the Beginning

There is so much revealed about God in the first two chapters of Genesis that we can't really go into great detail, but we have all year to revisit many of these themes. Although we generally think of the start of Genesis as the story of how everything came into being, note that God has also opened His book with an introduction of Himself. Consider these 18 revelations of what God has already told us about who He is and what He's like:

1. "In the beginning God created..." God is the uncaused cause. He had no beginning; He always was. He is the originator of all that there is.
2. "...and the Spirit of God was hovering..." God always has been and always will be paying attention to everything that's going on.

3. "And God said..." God speaks.
4. "God saw..." God sees.
5. "...he separated..." God is responsible for separating things out. He is well able to differentiate that which needs to be unraveled and unscrambled.
6. "God called..." God is responsible for assigning purpose.
7. God commanded "the water under the sky [to] be gathered..." Just as He is responsible for separating things, God can cause things to be gathered together.
8. God commanded "the land produce vegetation..." God has the power to make anything productive.
9. God commanded that the lights in heaven "serve as signs..." God can speak to us through signs He sends our way.
10. "God set..." God places everything exactly where it should be.
11. God commanded "the water [to] teem with living creatures... [and] "the land [to] produce living creatures..." That which God creates, He has the right to command. And that which was created by God is under obligation to perform His word without question or hesitation.
12. "God blessed..." God's first blessings involved fruitfulness and multiplication. God's blessings always result in abundance.
13. "Then God said, 'Let us make man...and let them rule...'" God, His Spirit, and the Word (Jesus Christ – see John 1) were involved in the creation process. The Trinity declared that man's purpose was to rule on the earth.
14. "Then God said, 'I give you... food.'" God provides our daily sustenance.
15. "...the Lord God had planted a garden... [and] took the man and put him in the Garden of Eden to work it and take care of it." God is the source of employment, but He intends for us to participate in the fulfillment of our needs. (Notice that work was in God's plan for us even before sin entered the picture.)
16. "The Lord God said, '...I will make a helper suitable for [Adam].'" God is about the business of making sure we have all the help we need.
17. "Then the Lord God made a woman... and he brought her to the man." God designs for us and brings to us people who are perfect for us.

18. "By the seventh day God had finished… so on the seventh day he rested…" God is an example to us of how to make a plan, work a plan, complete a plan, and then rest and enjoy the fruit of our labors.

#4
January 4: God and the Miracle of Birth

The first words accompanying the first birth were words of praise and thanksgiving to God. Genesis 4:1 says, "Now Adam knew Eve his wife, and she conceived and bore Cain, and said, 'I have acquired a man from the LORD'" (NKJ). Without there ever being a history of other women having babies, somehow Eve realized that the birth of her baby was the work of God.

Eve had it right: the start of a new life should bring us to worship and wonder. When a baby is created, we need to realize that God has allowed us the awesome privilege of participating with Him in the creation process. Only God can "bara." "Bara" is the Hebrew word that means to create or make something out of nothing. When a man's sperm and a woman's egg come together, two strands of DNA combine to start a new life. Although this process takes the couple's participation, God made that DNA. Vine's Expository Dictionary of Biblical Words further explains bara creation by saying, "Though a precisely correct technical term to suggest cosmic, material creation from nothing, bara is a rich theological vehicle for communicating the sovereign power of God, who originates and regulates all things to His glory."

I remember the moment I realized I was pregnant with my first son. My life changed forever. Carrying and then birthing that life brought me closer to God. The sheer weight of the responsibility caused me to know I had to really live right from then on. But even more than feeling the enormity of my upcoming task of being somebody's mother, was my sense of awe at having this new life in my womb. I felt him move for the first time on my birthday, six months before he was born. The larger he grew, the more I felt him. Once he was born, he seemed to immediately know I was his mom. As I nursed and cared for him, our bond grew stronger and stronger.

Reflect on God and His involvement with the miracle of birth. Connect your thoughts with your own new birth and with

God being born in your life. The larger He grows in you, the more you will feel Him, the closer your bond will be, and the more intimate your relationship with Him will be. God starts this process too, but expects our participation. As we reflect, may we turn to God as Eve did and may we be moved to exclaim, "I have acquired life from the Lord!"

#5
January 5: Compassion Trumps Pain

I distinctly remember the first time my oldest son deliberately disobeyed me. He was barely five months old and enjoyed scooting himself around in his walker. He waddled himself over to the water cooler and reached out his hand to push the lever. Water would have splashed all over the floor so I caught his eye and said, "No, Matthew." He stared at me for a moment, and then with defiant determination, without breaking our gaze, he slowly reached for the lever again. His facial expression clearly communicated what his infant tongue could not, "Who are you to stop me, and what are you going to do about it?"

It pained me to realize this child was actually defying me. Me, the woman who had labored to bring him into the world. Me, the woman who lost hours and hours of sleep each night because he was up. Me, whose existence and health was required for his existence and health. I had to act, or I'd be punked by this child the rest of my life, and for the rest of his life, he'd think he could do whatever brought him pleasure, no matter what any authority figure might say. He needed to learn that he owed respect and obedience to those who were responsible for supplying him his sustenance, be they his parents, his teachers, his pastor, or his employers.

Not very long after God created the universe, the wickedness of man challenged God's authority in much the same way. People were doing what they wanted to do, refusing to acknowledge or obey God. Genesis 6:5-8 relates, "Then the Lord saw that the wickedness of man was great in the earth, and that every intent of the thoughts of his heart was only evil continually. And the Lord was sorry that He had made man on the earth, and He was grieved in His heart. So the Lord said, 'I will destroy man whom I have created from the face of the earth, both man and beast, creeping thing and birds of the air, for I am sorry that I have made them.' But Noah found grace in the eyes of the Lord" (NKJ).

I added a swat on the thigh to the "no" I had given Matthew to convince him to remove his hand from the water cooler. God wiped everybody off the planet—except Noah. Even as I spanked Matthew, I had compassion on him, a compassion that trumped the pain of realizing that as cute as he was, I was raising a little sinner. Even as God planned His punishment, He had compassion on Noah who had found grace in His eyes. Even though I would have to correct him, I knew Matthew's heart was right and he'd grow to be more and more obedient; and he did. Even though God had to punish mankind, He knew there was a remnant that would be obedient to Him; and there was.

Matthew found grace in my eyes just as Noah—and we—find grace in God's. His compassion for us trumps the pain we cause Him. Let's do our best to cause Him less pain and more joy. We'll end up getting less spankings too!

#6
January 6: Remember as God Remembers

After God flooded the wickedness off of the earth, He was ready to start all over again with Noah, his wife, their three sons, and their wives. (I know those girls were glad they married into *that* family!) God made a promise never to flood the whole earth like that again. He told Noah, "Whenever I bring clouds over the earth and the rainbow appears in the clouds, I will remember my covenant between me and you and all living creatures of every kind. Never again will the waters become a flood to destroy all life. Whenever the rainbow appears in the clouds, I will see it and remember the everlasting covenant between God and all living creatures of every kind on the earth" Genesis 9:14-16 (NIV).

It rained for quite a few days the other week. Toward the end of the storm, I saw three gorgeous rainbows; one of them was even doubled. How awesome to realize I wasn't the only one seeing that rainbow. God was looking at that rainbow too, and He was remembering His promise to me. (Didn't He say the covenant was between Himself and "all living creatures"?)

What's good enough for God to do should be good enough for us to do too. How often do we remind ourselves of the promises we've made to God? In some cases, we do this already. For example, our engagement and wedding rings remind us of our marriage vows and our commitment to our spouses. The children of Israel (and some orthodox Jews today) wore phylacteries, a small case or box fastened to the forehead or left hand or arm containing a parchment inscribed with passages from Exodus 13 and Deuteronomy 6. As they moved around, these boxes bumped into their skin and they would be reminded of God and His word.

God sees the rainbow and He doesn't forget His promises to us. Why not begin setting a few tokens in front of our faces to make us remember the things God would want us to remember? Here are some ideas:

- Place a sticky note that says "Pray" on your computer screen every night. Don't check e-mail the next morning until you check in with God.
- Keep your devotional book in the bathroom and read your morning devotion right after you brush your teeth.
- Place your Bible on top of your work files and appointment book. Read it before you read them.
- Listen to some of the Bible on CD or on your iPod as you drive before you listen to news radio or other music.
- Carry a tithe envelope with you at all times. Whenever you earn or find money, immediately put 10% of it in that envelope for the work of the ministry. Drop that envelope in the offering at church each week. (I also immediately match that 10% in a savings account for myself.)

Remember as God remembers and watch how God continues to pour out blessings.

#7
January 7: God, the One Who Blesses

God's promise to Abraham, known as the Abrahamic covenant in Genesis 12:1-3, details God's unconditional guarantee to separate out a special people for Himself through which He could reveal Himself to the world. The covenant states:

- "Now the LORD had said to Abram: 'Get out of your country, from your family and from your father's house, to a land that I will show you. I will make you a great nation; I will bless you and make your name great; and you shall be a blessing. I will bless those who bless you, and I will curse him who curses you; and in you all the families of the earth shall be blessed" Gen 12:1-3 (NKJ).

This covenant is not conditional upon Abraham's actions. God alone is responsible for it. Five times in the covenant, God uses the word "bless." Four of those times, the Hebrew word "barak" (baw-rak') is used.

1. I will bless you – (vs. 2)
2. I will bless those... – (vs. 3)
3. ...who bless you – (vs. 3)
4. In you all the families of the earth shall be blessed – (vs.3)

When spoken to man in this context, "barak" means "to bestow a benefit." God is taking the responsibility to heap benefits on Abraham, on those who bless Abraham, and on all the families of the earth because of Abraham. Not a bad promise!

There is, however, one thing God says that Abraham will do; God says to Abraham "you shall be blessing." The Hebrew word for blessing used here is "berakah" which means "benediction, liberal pool, a present, and prosperity." But notice, God does not make this a condition of the covenant, but rather a natural outpouring because of it. God says, "You shall be..." The Hebrew word translated for that phrase is "hayah" which means "to exist." Literally, God is saying to Abraham, "I'm setting you up as a great nation and giving you a great name and great influence so that My greatness can flow through you to all the people of the world. You exist in Me to pour out blessing to others."

God remains today the God who blesses. His covenanted purpose remains the same too. We receive "barak" so that we can "berakah." We are blessed by God so His blessings can flow through us to others. Psalm 25:12-13 says, "Who, then, is the man that fears the LORD? He will instruct him in the way chosen for him. He will spend his days in prosperity, and his descendants will inherit the land" (NIV). God is the One who blesses, so live as the blessed of the Lord. Pass the blessings on.

#8
January 8: The Call of God

Oswald Chambers said, "To be brought into the zone of the call of God is to be profoundly altered" (My Utmost for His Highest, 1935). Abram received such a call and entered such a zone.

In Genesis 12:1-3, we listen in as God outlines Abram's call to him:

- Now the LORD had said to Abram: "Get out of your country, from your family and from your father's house, to a land that I will show you. I will make you a great nation; I will bless you and make your name great; and you shall be a blessing. I will bless those who bless you, and I will curse him who curses you; and in you all the families of the earth shall be blessed" (NKJ).

What a word! This seven-fold blessing shows us at least three characteristics of God's calls to us. First, the call is personal. God spoke directly to Abram. God is perfectly able to get our attention and speak directly to us so that we know it's Him and we are absolutely sure of what He's saying. God personalizes His calls to us, designing them specifically for the person He made us to be.

Second, God's call is pointed. Abram knew exactly what he had to do when he heard God's call. "Get out of your country, from your family and from your father's house, to a land that I will show you." Abram instantly obeyed in three of these four categories. He left his country, left his father's house, and went to the land God showed him, but he didn't leave all his family. He took Lot with him, and later Lot became a lot of trouble. When God calls, He expects us to follow the specific instructions He gives. Although we may not know why at the time, He has His reasons for telling us to do things a particular way, and we can gum up the whole works if we decide to get creative.

Third, God's call is productive. God called Abram in order to see things happen. God had much bigger things in store for Abram than the comfortable life he had in Ur. And what God had in store for Him would further the cause of the Kingdom. In the process of following God's call, Abram himself would also be abundantly blessed. So is it, when God announces His call to us. By hearing and obeying His call, we'll see things happen, the Kingdom will be expanded, He will be glorified, and we will be blessed.

Proverbs 1:33 says, "But whoever listens to me will live in safety and be at ease, without fear of harm" (NIV). Indeed, once we hear God's call, we are profoundly altered and immediately thrust into a decision: do we ignore it or do we obey it? We're never the same no matter which choice we make. To ignore God's call is to possibly have some immediate relief from the pressure of hearing the call in the first place, but we ultimately doom ourselves to a life that never reaches its full potential of joy or satisfaction. To obey God's call is to open ourselves to endless wonder and glory both in this life and the life to come.

#9
January 9: Been Waiting Long?

Waiting is one of the hardest things to do for many of us. Although it's annoying to arrive at the bank and find a long line, we know we will get up to the teller sometime that day. But waiting is especially difficult when it doesn't seem like the wait will ever end.

In Genesis chapter 15, God shows us He knows what that's like for us. Abraham was approaching the end of his patience as he had been waiting and waiting for many years for a child. Even before he could voice his frustration over this to God, his compassionate Heavenly Father spoke to him in a vision, "After these things the word of the LORD came to Abram in a vision, saying, 'Do not be afraid, Abram. I am your shield, your exceedingly great reward'" Genesis 15:1 (NKJ).

No need to fear; complete, impenetrable protection; and an abundant reward should have been assurance enough to bolster Abraham's patience. But no. Even after this strong assurance, Abraham still came up with two alternative plans to get a child. He first suggested that his servant Eliezer become his heir (Genesis 15:2-3), and then he went with Sarah's plan to have a son by her handmaid Hagar (Genesis 16:3-4). Neither plan was necessary nor acceptable to God, and choosing plan number two has had devastating implications that have lasted until today. (The Middle East crisis is the direct result of conflict between the descendants of Ishmael, Hagar's son, and the descendants of Isaac, Sarah's son.)

God's word and will, as revealed in the Bible, are promises to us we can stand on just as surely as Abraham could have stood on God's promise of a child. God's promises are sure, perfect, and best for us, no matter how long they take to manifest in our lives. So no matter how long you've been waiting, hear God saying to you, "Don't be afraid. I am your shield, your exceedingly great reward."

#10
January 10: The God Who Sees

In Genesis 16, we read about how Hagar, Sarah's maid, was served up a raw deal. What started out to be a dream job – the personal assistant of a prominent woman – turned into a nightmare when she was thrust into the middle of her employers' marital issues. It was a generally accepted custom in that time that anything belonging to the master's servant could technically be called the master's property, so a child born to Hagar would be considered Sarah's. God had promised Abraham that he would produce a natural heir, but when Sarah got impatient about not producing a child, she relied on to the worldly custom rather than the heavenly promise, and gave Hagar to her husband for her to have a child.

Well, as it always happens when we take God's matters into our own hands, the plan backfired. When Hagar got pregnant, the two women began to be at odds with each other, so Sarah "dealt harshly with her, (and) she (Hagar) fled from her presence" Genesis 6:6 (NKJ).

What happened next for Hagar was nothing short of amazing. "Now the Angel of the LORD found her..." Genesis 16:7a (NKJ). Bible scholars tell us that whenever we see the Angel of the Lord in Scripture, we are witnessing pre-incarnate appearances of Jesus. Look at that: Jesus found Hagar. For that to happen, He must have been looking for her; in the case of our Lord, in actuality, He was looking *out* for her. He comforted her with His presence, directed her with His wisdom, and encouraged her with a promise (see Genesis 6:7-12).

Hagar moved from fleeing in fear, to facing the Father, to faith in His forecast. Her response is found in Genesis 16:13, "Then she called the name of the LORD who spoke to her, You-Are-the-God-Who-Sees; for she said, 'Have I also here seen Him who sees me?' (NKJ)

When we find ourselves in fear, we have but to turn our face to the Father. He is ever looking out for us and will be for us as He was for Hagar: the God Who Sees. If we listen, we will hear a word of forecast from His word for our future. Matthew 6:8b says, "...For your Father knows the things you have need of before you ask Him" (NKJ). Once we recognize our Lord as the God Who Sees, our hearts will open in amazement; it truly dawns on us it dawned on Hagar: I also have seen Him who sees me!

#11
January 11: Nothing Too Hard for God

Abraham and Sarah were well over 80 years old and well past the age of being able to have a baby by natural means. God challenged their disbelief about their ability to conceive late in life by asking them a simple question, "Is anything too hard for the LORD?" Genesis 18:14 (NKJ). The obvious answer is, "No."

Abraham and Sarah were dealing with God without the benefit we have of the entire Old and New Testament. We can see God's track record of doing impossible stuff.

- Creating something from nothing
- Fashioning Eve from Adam's rib
- Taking Enoch to Heaven without Enoch facing death
- Flooding out the whole world and starting all over again
- Wiping out Sodom and Gomorrah by raining fire on them.
- Parting the Red Sea so the children of Israel could cross on dry ground
- Supplying manna in the wilderness to the Israelites for 40 years
- Helping little David kill the giant Goliath
- Taking the heat out of the fiery furnace into which Shadrach, Meshech, and Abednego were thrown
- Closing the lions' mouths when Daniel was in their den
- Causing a virgin to conceive
- Turning water into wine
- Casting demons from the possessed
- Restoring sight to the blind
- Causing the lame to walk
- Opening deaf ears
- Healing all manner of diseases
- Raising the dead

God did everything on the list above without even breaking a sweat. No problem exists bigger than anything mentioned, so we can be assured that none of our problems are outside the scope of God's manageability. All we need to do is trust those problems into His hands—the One who can do anything but fail.

#12
January 12: God as Judge

Some people carry with them a concept of God as a mighty kill-joy. They see Him up in Heaven looking down with a hammer in His hand, just waiting to clonk them in the head as soon as they do something wrong. That's an erroneous picture, but God does hold a hammer of sorts; He holds a gavel because He is "the Judge of all the earth" Genesis 18:25 (NKJ).

Justice is one of God's attributes. According to Nelson's Illustrated Bible Dictionary, the justice of God is explained as:

> God's fair and impartial treatment of all people. As a God of justice, He is interested in fairness as well as in what makes for right relationships. His actions and decisions are true and right. His demands on individuals and nations to look after victims of oppression are just demands.

> As Lord and Judge, God brings justice to nations and "sets things right" in behalf of the poor, the oppressed, and the victims of injustice. For the wicked, the unjust, and the oppressor, God as supreme Judge of the earth is a dreaded force. But for all who are unjustly treated, God's just action is reason for hope.

We see a wonderful picture of God's justice in the story of Sodom and Gomorrah. The wickedness of those cities had become so great, that God decided to destroy them. But first, God revealed to Abraham what He was about to do because Abraham's nephew Lot and his family lived in Sodom. Because Abraham had a balanced perception of God's justice, he said to the Lord, "Would You also destroy the righteous with the wicked? Far be it from You to do such a thing as this, to slay the righteous with the wicked, so that the righteous should be as the wicked; far be it from You! Shall not the Judge of all the earth do right?" (Genesis 18:23 and 25)

How did the story play out? "So when God destroyed the cities of the plain, he remembered Abraham, and he brought Lot out of the catastrophe that overthrew the cities where Lot had lived" Genesis 19:29 (NIV). We see God's justice at work as He carries out His judgment on the cities, but he saves Lot.

God, the righteous Judge, must punish sin, but He's not

any less His other attributes when He acts as Judge. He's still Love, and Mercy, and Grace, etc. As Judge, He hates our sin; as Mercy, He takes the punishment for those sins upon Himself, freeing us from the penalty we deserve. A respect for God as Judge is healthy to keep us living right. A heart of thankfulness to God should be our response as we realize all the times when His justice due to us was tempered by His mercy.

#13
January 13: God the Promise Keeper

One day, my youngest son Mark asked if we could go to the park. I responded, "We'll see." He hung his head and as he turned to walk away he mumbled, "We'll see means no." A teachable moment had just presented itself.

"What do you mean?" I asked.

He was quick to answer. "Every time you say, 'We'll see,' we never get to do the things we ask."

"But what about the times I say, 'Yes?'" I countered.

Without hesitation he replied, "Oh, we always do stuff then."

"You see," I explained, "My word is important. When I say yes to something, I've given you my word—my promise. I am then going to do everything in my power to be sure that thing happens. I want you to grow to understand the significance of every word you say, and I never want you to remember a time when I gave you my word and had to break it. That's why, when I'm not sure we can get something done, I'll say, "We'll see." If it happens, great. If it can't happen, I haven't broken my promise.

I was setting Mark up to understand something about God. From the time God promised Noah He would never flood the earth again, to the time He gave Sarah a son in her old age ("…and the LORD did for Sarah what he had promised" Genesis 21:1, NIV), all the way until today, God's Word is gold; He always keeps His promises. And like I did with my children, sometimes God has to say 'no,' to us; sometimes He says, "Wait;" and sometimes He says, "We'll see," usually when we have something we have to obey or accomplish first. Ah, but when God says 'yes,' that's a promise we can take to the bank.

#14
January 14: God Hears Our Children's Cries

When my boys were toddlers, I remember being able to detect their voices above the din of every other child's voice in a crowd. We could be at a park or attending some other social gathering where they were playing with lots of other children all making lots of noise, but if my boys cried out, I knew it was them. All other concentration and conversation would fly out the window as I moved to attend to the needs of my kids.

At times when my innocent little ones were crying over legitimate hurts or needs, the worst thing in the world would be if I was powerless to comfort them and make the problem go away. This instinct is even built into our bodies. We grow into our motherhood role from the moment of our child's conception within us, inseparably tied to the awesome responsibility of holding the power of life itself in our hands. Then immediately after birthing that baby, our bodies are again able to meet our infant's most necessary need and satisfy his hunger directly from our breasts. The strong urge to protect and provide for that child is primal and deep-seated.

We can well understand Hagar's distress after being tossed with her 14-year-old son Ishmael from Abraham and Sarah's home and running out of water in the wilderness. Her son was dying and crying, and she couldn't do a thing to help him. The story takes up in Genesis chapter 21:

- So Abraham rose early in the morning, and took bread and a skin of water; and putting it on her shoulder, he gave it and the boy to Hagar, and sent her away. Then she departed and wandered in the Wilderness of Beersheba. And the water in the skin was used up, and she placed the boy under one of the shrubs. Then she went and sat down across from him at a distance of about a bowshot; for she said to herself, "Let me not see the death of the boy." So she sat opposite him, and lifted her voice and wept. And God heard the voice of the lad. Then the angel of God called to Hagar out of heaven, and said to her, "What ails you, Hagar? Fear not, for God has heard the voice of the lad where he is. "Arise, lift up the lad and hold him with your hand, for I will make him a great nation." And God opened her eyes, and she saw a well of water. And she went and filled the skin with water, and gave the lad a drink. Genesis 21:14-19 (NKJ)

God hears the cries of our children even more acutely than we do, for He loves them (if we can imagine this) even more deeply. We rush to their aid with bandages to meet their immediate needs, but God rushes in with living water that quenches both in the present and the future. Just as God heard Ishmael's cries, He hears the cries of our children too. He'll come to their aid, take care of their immediate needs, and take them into an incredible future. In the process, He'll open our eyes so we can point them to the wells of water He's supplied in the wilderness.

#15
January 15: Take Your G.O.D.'s

You've probably heard of the SAT, a standardized test used in the United States to assess a student's readiness for college. It takes three hours and forty-five minutes, costs about $47, and possible scores range from 600 to 2400." High school students the world over stress out over whether or not they'll receive scores impressive enough to gain them a spot in the prestigious universities of their choice.

Are we ready to take our G.O.D.'s? What? You've never heard of a G.O.D?" According to the Elliottopedia, the G.O.D. is a God Obedience Drill. We hear about the first one in Genesis, chapter 22. "Now it came to pass after these things that God tested Abraham, and said to him... 'Take now your son, your only son Isaac, whom you love, and go to the land of Moriah, and offer him there as a burnt offering on one of the mountains of which I shall tell you'" Genesis 22:1-2 (NKJ).

The Hebrew word translated "tested" is "nacah," which here means to prove or try something to assess its strength or faithfulness. When God saw Abraham was really going to go through with the sacrifice, he stopped the test. " But the Angel of the LORD called to him from heaven and said, 'Abraham... do not lay your hand on the lad, or do anything to him; for now I know that you fear God, since you have not withheld your son, your only son, from Me'" Genesis 22:11-12 (NKJ). God had tested or "proved" Abraham's faith and Abraham passed his G.O.D.

We read of another G.O.D. in the book of Job. Satan, our

wicked enemy, challenged Job's love for God, saying, "So do you think Job does all that out of the sheer goodness of his heart? Why, no one ever had it so good! You pamper him like a pet, make sure nothing bad ever happens to him or his family or his possessions, bless everything he does—he can't lose! But what do you think would happen if you reached down and took away everything that is his? He'd curse you right to your face, that's what" Job 1:9-11 (The Message). Time for Job's G.O.D. "God replied, 'We'll see. Go ahead—do what you want with all that is his. Just don't hurt him'" Job 1:12 (The Message).

Job then faced unimaginable horrors at the hand of Satan, horrors designed to break Job's loyalty to God. But not once did Job curse God or think wrongly about Him (see Job 1:22 and 2:10). Unlike in Abraham's case, God never spoke to Job about the test. God already knew Job's strength; He was proving something to Satan. Job passed his G.O.D. "The LORD blessed the latter part of Job's life more than the first... After this (Job's G.O.D.), Job lived a hundred and forty years; he saw his children and their children to the fourth generation, and so he died, old and full of years" Job 42:12, 16-17 (NIV).

We never know when God is going to enroll us to take a G.O.D. You could be in one right now. Like with Abraham's, maybe our test will be about our personal faithfulness. Or like with Job, perhaps our test won't have anything at all to do with us, but it's a witness for others so they can see what faith looks like.

Don't worry about how long the test will take, how much it will cost, or your particular score. Just take the test to the end. Know that God will be there as the Proctor who says, "Pencils down, time's up," and as the Scorer pulling for you so He can say, "You passed your G.O.D."

#16
January 16: God of Extended Blessings

Everyone likes a winner. We love being the family of the valedictorian, holding the position as the best friend of a lottery winner, and rooting for the championship team. That graduate will go into an impressive career and make us proud, and that friend will most likely break us off a nice chunk of change. Attendees at Lakers' games all get tacos when the team scores 100 points. You see, a big reason why we love winners is not so much for the sake of the winners, but for the fact that we benefit just by being somehow associated. Things work that way in God's economy too. For example:

- God told Abraham, "In your seed all the nations of the earth shall be blessed, because you have obeyed My voice" Genesis 22:18 (NKJ).
- Jacob told his conniving father-in-law Laban, "For what you had before I *came was* little, and it has increased to a great amount; the Lord has blessed you since my coming..." Genesis 30:30 (NKJ).
- When Joseph's brothers sold him into slavery in Egypt, "His master [Potiphar] saw that the Lord was with him and that the Lord made all he did to prosper in his hand. Joseph found favor in his sight, and served him. Then he made him overseer of his house, and all *that* he had he put under his authority. So it was, from the time *that* he had made him overseer of his house and all that he had, that the Lord blessed the Egyptian's house for Joseph's sake; and the blessing of the Lord was on all that he had in the house and in the field. Thus he left all that he had in Joseph's hand..." (Genesis 39:3-6a).

When His children are obediently following Him, God has no problem pouring out blessings. Since no blessing of an infinite God can be small, what He pours on us will naturally overflow to anyone in the vicinity.

We can learn two things today from this truth. First, it makes sense to hang around those whom God is blessing so we can get some of that overflow. But also, it's great to be the obedient one through whom God shows Himself as the God of Extended Blessing.

Who is blessed because you obey God?

#17
January 17: Nothing Left Undone

At the end of Abraham's life, three translations of Genesis 24:1 combined say of him, "Now Abraham was old, well advanced in age; and the Lord had blessed Abraham in all things (NKJ), had blessed him in every way (NLT), and the LORD had made him rich, and he was successful in everything he did" (CEV). Whichever translation we read, the same idea is clear; God left nothing undone when it came to blessing Abraham.

God doesn't leave anything undone when He blesses us either. The benefits we receive from God will not be the same as those others receive, but they are always complete and perfect for us. "Beware lest anyone cheat you through philosophy and empty deceit, according to the tradition of men, according to the basic principles of the world, and not according to Christ. For in Him dwells all the fullness of the Godhead bodily; and you are complete in Him, who is the head of all principality and power" Colossians 2:8-10a (NKJ).

Nothing is left undone or incomplete in the life of the believer. If ever we are feeling empty places, God will fill them with Himself. Indeed we too will find ourselves to be "blessed in all things."

#18
January 18: Commander of the Angels

As a little child, I remember singing in the Cherub Choir at church. We sang many old standards that still make me smile when I think about them today like Yes, Jesus Loves Me and This Little Light of Mine. One of my all time favorites was Angels Watching Over Me. The chorus proclaimed, "All night, all day, angels watching over me, my Lord. All night, all day, angels watching over me." I recall singing that song to myself whenever I felt afraid or just wanted to be reminded of that comforting reality.

Perhaps it was from that song that some people began to believe they could tell the angels what to do. Maybe they figured, Since the angels are watching over me, I can talk directly to them when I feel like I need them. Noting all the violence and corruption in the world today, it would be great to pull out the benefit of commanding the angels to do stuff, but it is doctrinal error to believe this to be true. Let's look at several Scriptural examples of angels being dispatched:
- When Abraham sent his servant to find a wife for his son Isaac, Abraham told the man that God "will send His angels before you" Genesis 24:7 (NKJ).

- When God was telling the children of Israel about the feasts they should keep, He told them, "Behold, I send an Angel before you to keep you in the way and to bring you into the place which I have prepared" Exodus 23:20 (NKJ).
- As the children of Israel traveled through the wilderness, God sent angelic protection. "And I will send an angel before thee; and I will drive out [your enemies]" Exodus 33:2 (KJV).
- The Psalmist tells us what the angels do and to whom they are responsible, "Bless the LORD, ye his angels, that excel in strength, that do his commandments, hearkening unto the voice of his word" Psalm 103:20 (KJV).

The New Testament speaks of angels as well and continues to confirm the fact that God alone commands them and sends them.

- When speaking of the difference between Jesus and the angels, the writer of Hebrews says, "But to which of the angels has He ever said: 'Sit at My right hand, till I make Your enemies Your footstool'? Are they not all ministering spirits sent forth to minister for those who will inherit salvation?" Hebrews 1:13-14 (NKJ). The obvious implication here is that God is the One who gave Jesus His position, and God is also the One who sends forth the angels to minister to the saints.
- And even Jesus asked the Father God is send angels to help Him. On His way to Calvary, He said, "Or do you think that I cannot now pray to My Father, and He will provide Me with more than twelve legions of angels?" Matthew 26:53 (NKJ).

We are wasting our time on prayer lines, in church services, and in our private devotion when we command the angels to do this or that. The angels don't listen to us. They are not our servants and messengers; they are God's. *He* dispatches them to do *His* will. Yes, He can and does send them to do things for us, but that's at His authority, not at ours. This fact does not make us appreciate the angels any less, but requests for assistance are to be directed not to them, but to God, their Commander.

#19
January 19: God Thought of it First

Author Joan N. Keener wrote a delightful children's book entitled *God Thought of it First.* In the book, Keener shows some of man's helpful inventions and compares them to characteristics that certain animals have had all along. For example, she writes, "Night vision goggles use the light from the stars and moon to allow police officers to see better at night. But God is the One who thought of it first. He made the cat. Cats can see well at night because shiny layers at the back of their eyes reflect light."[2]

Of the many inventions I've seen come into existence in my lifetime, one that's extremely remarkable to me is the ultrasound. Each time I was pregnant, the most exciting doctor's visit was that first ultrasound appointment. Twenty-four years ago, the picture reflected on the screen was a grainy silhouette, but was clearly a living, human form with a beating heart. Today's ultrasounds almost give us a portrait.

But God thought of it first. As Rebekah was having a rough first pregnancy, we see God performing the very first ultrasound. "The babies jostled each other within her, and she said, 'Why is this happening to me?' So she went to inquire of the LORD. The LORD said to her, 'Two nations are in your womb, and two peoples from within you will be separated; one people will be stronger than the other, and the older will serve the younger.' When the time came for her to give birth, there were twin boys in her womb" Genesis 25:22-24 (NIV).

God looked inside Rebekah's womb and saw not only two babies, but two nations, and two futures. He knew those children and exactly what they'd be like. Nothing has changed. God saw and knew us too. Psalm 139:13-17 says, "For you created my inmost being; you knit me together in my mother's womb. I praise you because I am fearfully and wonderfully made; your works are wonderful, I know that full well. My frame was not hidden from you when I was made in the secret place. When I was woven together in the depths of the earth, your eyes saw my unformed body. All the days ordained for me were written in your book before one of them came to be. How precious to me are your thoughts, O God! How vast is the sum of them! (NIV)

---

[2] Keener, Joan N. God Thought of it First. Standard Publishing, Cincinnati, OH. 2003.

Yet another great thing about God is knowing that watching out for us, even inside of the womb, is one of His favorite pastimes. How grateful we can be that He thought of *that* first.

#20
January 20: It's a Generational Thing with God

God is all about the family. How do we know that? Not only do physical traits pass to us from our ancestors' DNA, but God has also designed the family as a channel through which His blessings will flow from generation to generation. This all started with the Abrahamic Covenant when God told the patriarch, "...and in you all the families of the earth shall be blessed" Genesis 12:3 (NKJ). In Genesis chapter 26, God reiterates this covenant to Abraham's son, Isaac, and then reminds Isaac of where his blessings are based by saying, "I will bless you and multiply your descendants *for My servant Abraham's sake*" Genesis 26:24 (NKJ, italics added). The blessing was repeated again in Genesis chapter 28 to Isaac's son, Jacob. You see, the blessings are rolling from generation to generation.

Be aware, though, that a channel is a channel. If blessings can flow from generation to generation, so can cursing. When we read the Commandments, we see how this works. Exodus 20:5-6 says, "You shall not bow down to [idols] or worship them; for I, the LORD your God, am a jealous God, punishing the children for the sin of the fathers to the third and fourth generation of those who hate me, but showing love to a thousand [generations] of those who love me and keep my commandments" (NIV).

So we see why having a healthy, spiritually-attuned family is so important. God designed family as a conduit to get His blessings to us, but that same conduit can carry junk if we let it. Picture a river flowing through lush, mountain greenery. From time to time, the water cascades from one level to the next in a beautiful waterfall. Each level is a generation, spilling the goodness from the heights in the continuous flow. However, if we pollute that river, the harmful elements will accumulate and wash downstream. Let us not be the source of the pollution, but may God's "clear water" blessings overflow from parent to child, down through the generations, and multiply as fresher and fresher wonders.

We can take encouragement in our God for whom

blessings are a generational thing. Our prayers, faithfulness, and life example before our children will not go unrewarded. "So let's not allow ourselves to get fatigued doing good." (In other words, let's not pollute the channel.) "At the right time we will harvest a good crop if we don't give up, or quit" (if we keep our conduit clean so the blessings can flow unhindered to the next generation) Galatians 6:9 (The Message, extra parenthetical notes added for emphasis).

#21
January 21: God the Ultimate Publicist

The job of the publicist is to make sure his/her client is recognized by the media. According to WiseGeek.com, "Essentially, the job of a publicist is to increase public interest in his client... While some publicists work a traditional schedule, most find that regular weekend and evening work is necessary. Publicists are often expected to travel to attend meetings or deliver presentations about a client's activities. Depending upon the industry, a publicist may essentially be on call around the clock."

In my business as an author, it's essential to have a great team of professionals, one of whom must be a fabulous publicist. Mine is amazing; her job is to get me "seen." She keeps her eye out for opportunities for my message to get to the audience. In many ways, she's the door-opener and I have to be ready to walk through those she finds ajar. I'm sure she sleeps, but judging by the time stamps on my e-mail messages and texts, she's awake and thinking about me a lot.

As I read of Abimelech's reaction to Isaac, I thought of how God functions as the ultimate Publicist. Abimelech and his advisors had watched how Isaac had prospered and figured they should be allied with him. When Isaac questioned why they had come even after they were hostile and had sent him away, they replied, "We saw clearly that the LORD was with you; so we said, 'There ought to be a sworn agreement between us'-- between us and you. Let us make a treaty with you" Genesis 26:28 (NIV). You see, God allowed Abimelech and his people to see how God was blessing Isaac, so they came asking for an agreement. Sounds like the work of a publicist to me.

Let's not get it twisted; God is not *our* publicist. The neat thing about God as a Publicist is the fact that He's His own client. We're allowed to work on His team to promote His message, and He's thinking about us a lot. He never sleeps, keeping His eyes ever open to how He can employ us to give Him glory. He opens doors for us to be "seen" so that we can in turn show Him to the world. And if we do it right, all the praises—all the publicity—will go back to Him and the world will be able to say like Abimelech, "We saw clearly that the Lord was with you."

#22
January 22: God Makes His Presence Known

When Jacob was on his way to Haran, he fell asleep and had a dream. Genesis 28:12-15 tells us that in his dream "...he saw a stairway resting on the earth, with its top reaching to heaven, and the angels of God were ascending and descending on it. There above it stood the LORD, and he said: 'I am the LORD, the God of your father Abraham and the God of Isaac... I am with you and will watch over you wherever you go, and I will bring you back to this land. I will not leave you until I have done what I have promised you.'"
(NIV).

Jacob had just been through the harrowing situation of deceiving his father and having his life threatened by his brother. Now urged on by his mother, he was running for his life. As far as we know, Jacob was striking out into new territory to him, having never traveled through that land before. He probably had no atlas, nothing but his mother's directions and the road. Perhaps he had gone as far as his day's strength would carry him, so he finally just stopped exhausted and fell asleep. That's where and when God revealed Himself to Jacob.

No matter the situation in which we find ourselves— escaping a harrowing situation, obeying the urging of a parent, or striking out into new territory—God will make His presence known to us too. Hopefully, we'll be located where we want to be found and involved in what we ought to be doing. But even if we're where we are because we've somehow blown it, God is still about the business of making Himself known. Just stop long enough for God to get your attention.

Stay aware. Look around. Be ever ready for God's revelation of Himself.

#23
January 23: God the Wrestler

I had a decision to make the other day and I wasn't sure what God wanted me to do. Most of the factors lined up but one didn't. Was that one item the test directing me to say no, or was it the spoiler trying to keep me from my blessing? I didn't know and it didn't seem like God was answering. The night before I had to make my choice, I struggled, sleeping only fitfully and awakening often. I had to face the choice early the next day and morning seemed to come all too soon. All through the night, I held to God and prayed.

I believe this experience helped me to understand a little something about the time when Jacob had a wrestling match with God. Just before he was to be reunited with his brother Esau, the Bible tells us:

> So Jacob was left alone, and a man wrestled with him till daybreak. When the man saw that he could not overpower him, he touched the socket of Jacob's hip so that his hip was wrenched as he wrestled with the man. Then the man said, "Let me go, for it is daybreak." But Jacob replied, "I will not let you go unless you bless me." The man asked him, "What is your name?" "Jacob," he answered. Then the man said, "Your name will no longer be Jacob, but Israel, because you have struggled with God and with men and have overcome." Genesis 32:24-28 (NIV)

Jacob didn't know until the end of the match that he had been wrestling with God. Jacob's spiritual antennae, though, sensed that this Man could bless him, so he held on and even proclaimed, "I will not let you go unless you bless me." Because of his tenacity, God did indeed bless him and left him different in two ways. First, from then on, Jacob walked with a limp. Second, from then on, his name was changed to Israel which literally means in the Hebrew "he will rule as God."

From time to time, like Jacob, we will have times when we too must wrestle with God. When we come away from the match, three things will have taken place.

- First, our walk will be different. There will be an inner change. Our understanding of God will have deepened enabling us to operate (walk) more circumspectly.

- Second, our name will be different. There will be an outer change. Others will recognize there's been a change and begin to call us by the new identity God has given us.
- Third, we indeed will go away from the experienced blessed.

The day after my latest wrestling match, I said yes to the decision I had to make. The inner change in my walk has been a deeper understanding of God's ability to lead me through circumstances, my own private thoughts, and the counsel of others. The outer change resulted in my gaining a new position and thus a new name. I have come away from the experience blessed.

Don't be afraid of God the wrestler. Get in the ring. It will be a match you can't lose.

#24
January 24: I'm Here for You

When we are going through difficult times, it's nice to hear someone say, "I'm here for you." That's a friend's way of saying, "You're not alone as you go through this." Even if the trial is such that it has kept you from seeing that person often, there's comfort in knowing that you can get to him or her if you have to.

Jacob learned that God is a friend who can always say, "I'm here for you." After Jacob's daughter had been raped and his sons took revenge by killing all the men of the offender's town, he realized his small band was outnumbered and therefore in trouble. God directed him to go to Bethel, settle there, and build an altar. God also caused terror to fall on all the people of all the surrounding towns so no one pursued them. When Jacob told his household of their upcoming move, he identified God as the One "who answered me in the day of my distress and who has been with me wherever I have gone" Genesis 35:3 (NIV).

God answers and accompanies us when we're going through difficult trials as well. Even if the trial is severe or we've seriously blown it, we're not alone. The anguish may be such that it's hard to see God. Look up anyway. We can still turn toward God, run to our Abba Father, and hear Him say, "Relax, I'm here for you."

#25
January 25: God's Wrath

We generally don't like to think about God's wrath. We feel more comfortable basking in God's love and grace and forgiveness. And well we should; God's wrath is nothing to play around with.

There's a clear picture of God's wrath in Genesis chapter 38 in the account of two of Judah's sons:

- Judah got a wife for Er, his firstborn, and her name was Tamar. But Er, Judah's firstborn, was wicked in the LORD's sight; so the LORD put him to death. Then Judah said to Onan, 'Lie with your brother's wife and fulfill your duty to her as a brother-in-law to produce offspring for your brother.' But Onan knew that the offspring would not be his; so whenever he lay with his brother's wife, he spilled his semen on the ground to keep from producing offspring for his brother. What he did was wicked in the LORD's sight; so he put him to death also" Genesis 38:6-10 (NIV).

The Hebrew word used for "wicked" here is "ra" which means "bad or evil." This word also comes from another root meaning "good for nothing." Vine's Expository Dictionary of Biblical Words places its definition of "ra" under the word "sin" and says, "Ra' refers to that which is "bad" or "evil," in a wide variety of applications. A greater number of the word's occurrences signify something morally evil or hurtful." Er and Onan had done an abominable thing and God simply wouldn't stand for it. He put them to death on the spot for their wickedness.

The New Testament counterpart Greek verb for "ra" (sin) is "hamartano" which literally means "to miss the mark." Perhaps that's why we don't regard the wrath of God so seriously. We don't consider ourselves to be wicked when we sin; we just see ourselves to have missed the mark. That doesn't sound quite as bad. To us, missing the mark means we're just off by a little.

Oh, but let's get this straight. The New Testament clearly states, "For the wages of sin is death..." Romans 6:23a (NIV). The Greek word for "sin" used here is—you guessed it—"harmartia." Sure, we're mighty grateful for the second part of this verse which says, "...but the gift of God is eternal life in Christ Jesus our Lord" Romans 6:23b (NIV), but don't skip over the fact that sin is still wickedness, God still hates it, and it will still lead to our demise. It's healthy for us spiritually to remember God's attribute of wrath from time to time and all He did for us through His Son so that we wouldn't have to face it. That remembrance alone should be enough incentive to keep us walking in obedience.

#26
January 26: God Can Bless Anywhere

Gen 39:20b-21 says, " But while Joseph was there in the prison, the LORD was with him; he showed him kindness and granted him favor in the eyes of the prison warden" (NIV).

Even if we've never been in prison, from time to time we may have found ourselves in some pretty precarious predicaments. Today's verse is a refreshing reminder that God is able to bless us no matter where we are. Three things pop out about God in this passage.

#1: God was with Joseph. We can be comforted, empowered, and even emboldened realizing that God is actually with us. In fact, over and over again He asserts His continual presence:
* For the LORD will not forsake His people, for His great name's sake, because it has pleased the LORD to make you His people. First Samuel 12:22 (NKJ)
* I was young and now I am old, yet I have never seen the righteous forsaken or their children begging bread. Psalm 37:25 (NIV)
* For the LORD loves justice, and does not forsake His saints; they are preserved forever, but the descendants of the wicked shall be cut off. Psalm 37:28 (NKJ)
* Fear not, for I am with you; be not dismayed, for I am your God. I will strengthen you, yes, I will help you, I will uphold you with My righteous right hand.' Isaiah 41:10 (NKJ)
* The poor and needy search for water, but there is none; their tongues are parched with thirst. But I the LORD will answer them; I, the God of Israel, will not forsake them. Isaiah 41:17 (NIV)
* Let your conduct be without covetousness; be content with such things as you have. For He Himself has said, "I will never leave you nor forsake you." Hebrews 13:5 (NKJ)

#2: God showed Joseph kindness. The Hebrew word for "kindness" used here is "checed" which the King James Version translates as "mercy." Although we never hear anything bad about

Joseph in the Bible, we know he was a human born in sin just like us. He too needed God's mercy. Mercy is **not** getting what we deserve, God's generous pardon of our sin. No matter where we find ourselves, God's mercy is extended toward us too.

#3: God granted Joseph favor in the eyes of the prison warden. The Hebrew word for "favor" used here is "chen" which means graciousness. Grace is the receipt of God's riches at Christ's expense. In other words, grace is operating when we get what we don't deserve. Why should the prison warden have treated Joseph any differently than all the other prisoners? Only one reason—God's favor, God's grace. Isn't it good to know that God's grace and favor rests on us as well?

So we can be calmed today and every day knowing that God is with us, His mercy is extended to us, and His grace and favor surround us. Hallelujah! What a God!

#27
January 27: God Gives and Interprets Dreams

We know Joseph as a dreamer. His dreams got him in trouble with his family when he told them he had dreamt that they would one day bow down to him. (See Genesis 37:6-11.) Later, we come to find that Joseph is also an interpreter of dreams. He tells his fellow prisoners the meanings of their dreams, and is eventually taken to Pharaoh to interpret disturbing dreams he was having. However, Joseph never took credit for being able to interpret the dreams; he always directed the credit to God. He told the prisoners, "Do not interpretations belong to God?" Genesis 40:8 (NIV). Joseph even told Pharaoh, "God has revealed to Pharaoh what he is about to do" Genesis 41:25 (NIV).

God is still able to give us dreams and let us know what they mean. Psalm 25:14 says, "The LORD confides in those who fear him; he makes his covenant known to them" (NIV). We can dream without being dreamers. Let's pay attention to the dreams God gives us and then live humbly as we work and watch the dreams come true in their time.

#28
January 28: The God of Replacement Blessings

Things go bad sometimes. We may find ourselves praying and praying for reprieve or vindication, or for some other sort of relief, and the help seems as though it will never come. Two wise sayings come to mind when thinking about times like that. One is "seasons change;" the other is "tough times don't last, tough people do."

Joseph could relate to both of these sayings. He'd had a rough go of it having been sold into slavery, falsely accused of attempted rape by his master's wife, and forgotten in a foreign prison. Yet, Joseph remained tough by continuing to serve and honor his God, and the season eventually changed for him. He was released from prison only to interpret Pharaoh's dream and end up as Vice Pharaoh of Egypt, in charge of saving the entire population from starvation during the coming devastating famine.

One of the rewards of Joseph's freedom was a wife, and before the famine came, the couple was blessed with two sons. The Bible tells us, "Joseph called the name of the firstborn Manasseh: 'For God has made me forget all my toil and all my father's house.' And the name of the second he called Ephraim: 'For God has caused me to be fruitful in the land of my affliction'" Genesis 41:51-52 (NKJ). Joseph could not un-ring the bell of his troubles, but God replaced those beat-downs with blessings. The bitterness of his slave labor and prison time were replaced by the joy of welcoming his first son; and all his loss was replaced by the exhilaration of having his second son.

Don't worry about what you've lost. Look at Joseph's example. Just keep living an honorable life before God. At just the right time—in His time—God will show Himself as the God of replacement blessings. When you are in need of His mercy and His assistance, He will bring His replacement power to bear on your situation. Psalm 30:10-12 bears this out, "Hear, O LORD, and be merciful to me; O LORD, be my help. You turned my wailing into dancing; you removed my sackcloth and clothed me with joy, that my heart may sing to you and not be silent. O LORD my God, I will give you thanks forever." (NIV).

God's new blessings supersede our old troubles. He's just good like that!

#29
January 29: God Supplies What We Need

In Genesis chapter 43, Joseph's brothers found themselves in a bind. The land was still experiencing a grave famine and they had run out of the food they'd bought from Egypt on their first trip. When their father told them to go back to buy more, they reminded him that they couldn't go without taking Benjamin, their youngest brother, with them. Although Jacob protested, there was no other option.

With Judah solemnly making himself the pledge for the boy, Jacob sent all the sons away, but not without a little something extra. "And their father Israel said to them, 'If *it must be* so, then do this: Take some of the best fruits of the land in your vessels and carry down a present for the man—a little balm and a little honey, spices and myrrh, pistachio nuts and almonds'" Genesis 43:11 (NKJ).

Wait a minute. I thought there was a severe famine in the land. How is it that Jacob and his family had balm, honey, spices, myrrh, pistachio nuts, and almonds? I don't know the answer to that, but what I do know is what they had is not what they needed. Regardless of the value of the stuff they had, without what they needed – bread, one of the basic necessities of life – they still would have died. So despite Jacob's reluctance to send Benjamin to Egypt with his brothers, he had no other choice if he wanted to live.

Is what we have, what we need? What precious thing or person are we holding onto today that could very well be keeping us from what we need? Are we keeping our hands so full of what's good that we fail the ability to grasp what's best? "Some trust in chariots, and some in horses; but we will remember the name of the LORD our God" Psalm 20:6-8 (NKJ). "Take heed and beware of covetousness, for one's life does not consist in the abundance of the things he possesses" Luke 12:15 (NKJ).

Today, let's choose to live not merely surviving with what we have, but thriving because we allow God to give us what we need.

#30
January 30: God is Up to Something

Joseph's scandalous brothers had sent him through hell, but the tables turned when they appeared before him needing food for their families during the famine. Joseph could have exacted harsh revenge, but instead he communicates to them God's perspective on their situation. In Genesis 45:4 - 8 we read:

> Then Joseph said to his brothers, "Come close to me." When they had done so, he said, "I am your brother Joseph, the one you sold into Egypt! And now, do not be distressed and do not be angry with yourselves for selling me here, because it was to save lives that God sent me ahead of you. For two years now there has been famine in the land, and for the next five years there will not be plowing and reaping. But God sent me ahead of you to preserve for you a remnant on earth and to save your lives by a great deliverance. So then, it was not you who sent me here, but God. He made me father to Pharaoh, lord of his entire household and ruler of all Egypt" (NIV).

No matter what we're facing, we too must realize that God is up to something in our lives. Psalm 37:23 says, "The steps of a good man are ordered ("koon" in Hebrew meaning "rendered sure, confirmed, made prosperous) by the LORD, and He delights in his way" (NKJ). We may not know why God is having us hike the paths we're trodding, but our job is to just keep walking. As long as we're following Him, we can't go wrong. When troubles threaten to drown us, no worries; He can help us walk on our fitful seas. If difficulties get heated, no problem; He can walk with us in our fiery furnaces. We won't know until we grow through what we go through that God had us on that path because He had a plan all along.

Even though He's leading through unfamiliar and possibly treacherous territory, trust God enough to keep following Him. "And we know that all things work together for good to those who love God, to those who are the called according to His purpose" Romans 8:28 (NKJ). God is up to something.

#31
January 31: God Reassures

Sometimes we get excited and without praying about it first, we step out in confidence to do things that seem okay. Then, when the excitement wanes, we start second-guessing ourselves. We say things like, "Wait a minute; what am I doing," or "I think I may be in over my head," or "What have I gotten myself into now?"

It seemed okay to Jacob at first to pack up everyone in the family and head down to Egypt when his sons returned to tell him that Joseph was still alive. But as he journeyed, he began to have second thoughts and let fear creep in. That's when God stepped in. "Then God spoke to Israel in the visions of the night and said, 'Jacob, Jacob! And he said, 'Here I am.' So He said, 'I *am* God, the God of your father; do not fear to go down to Egypt, for I will make of you a great nation there. I will go down with you to Egypt, and I will also surely bring you up *again;* and Joseph will put his hand on your eyes." Genesis 46:2-4 (NKJ).

Jacob didn't pray about this move until he was already on his way to Egypt. He set out in excitement to be reunited with his long-lost and most-beloved son, but then it seems as though he thought, "Oh wait, I haven't prayed. Maybe God doesn't want us to leave this land He had promised to us." That's when Jacob started to doubt and fear that perhaps he had jumped out of God's will. But as we see, God reassured Jacob. The move to Egypt was fine; in fact, it was in God's plan all along.

With the Holy Spirit living within us, we can relax when excitement boosts our confidence and we step out. Jesus Christ has made us free. Sure, we should pray about decisions, but if we don't immediately, God is there. His check and balance system have yet to fail. He's able either to halt our progress, or reassure us that we're on the right track. He delights in giving us "at-a-boys."

As we grow in our faith, and keep a constant connection to our God, we will find ourselves realizing that even our minutest decisions—change in route while driving from work, or choosing the long grocery store line—can lead to blessed, everlasting consequences when we find ourselves witnessing to the people we just "happened" to run into. When we do stop to pray, nothing feels better than to hear with our heart's ear, the reassurance God give.

Walk in newness of life. Check in with God often and ask God how He feels about what we're doing. When we set God's will as the default, our everyday decisions, and even our excite-induced reactions will be of Him. If we start second-guessing or being fearful, God is there to supply the reassurance we need to go on into our blessings.

#32
February 1: God Is With Us When Our Parents Die

My parents have passed away and I miss them. In both cases, we had time to adjust to the idea that we were losing them. Daddy experienced Alzheimer's disease for some time before he had several strokes, so we had lost him mentally although he was physically still with us for his last few years. Momma battled stomach cancer that eventually took her life after all her years of relatively perfect health. Even though our family journeyed through their illnesses with them, we came away from their loss not with bitterness about the end, but with lasting memories of pride and happiness about the wonderful lives we were privileged to have known.

The best thing about my parents was their lives, not their deaths. More than the unshakable self-assurance they built into us, they left us with an unwavering faith. We knew without a shadow of a doubt that they had simply relocated from earth to heaven. They had not left us alone; we knew, loved, and followed the same God they knew, loved, and followed. At the moment of their deaths, as they were beholding Him face-to-face, He was holding us heart-to-heart. Such wonderful assurance even helped to dry our tears. How can grief gain a permanent foothold when the grand truth of God and heaven exists?

As Israel (Jacob) lay dying, he gathered his sons around him to express to them this very veracity. Genesis 48:21 reads, "Then Israel said to Joseph, 'Behold, I am dying, but God will be with you...'" (NKJ). The sustaining comfort we can grasp at our parent's death is found in the arms of God; the supporting calm we can give our children as they face our death is found in being sure they have a relationship with Him.

#33
February 2: God is to be Feared

Sometimes we are a little too chummy with God. We smile, stand, and clap our way through feel-good praise choruses that announce "I am a friend of God" and others that focus primarily on what He's done for us. But how often are we concentrating on the holiness of God that rightly ought to be fearfully respected? It is this attribute of our Heavenly Father that moves us most assuredly toward obedience.

Take the story of the Hebrew midwives during the Egyptian captivity. The ruling Pharaoh, king of Egypt, had noticed that the Israelite people had multiplied to numbers that could do him harm if allied with his enemies. After enslaving them didn't quell their population growth, he came up with a new, devious plan. Exodus 1:15-17 (NKJ) tells us the story:

- Then the king of Egypt spoke to the Hebrew midwives, of whom the name of one was Shiphrah and the name of the other Puah; and he said, "When you do the duties of a midwife for the Hebrew women, and see them on the birth stools, if it is a son, then you shall kill him; but if it is a daughter, then she shall live." But the midwives feared God, and did not do as the king of Egypt commanded them, but saved the male children alive."

The fear of God caused Shiphrah and Puah to disobey the most powerful man on the earth. They exemplified the fact that a healthy fear of God causes us to defy anything that would even suggest disobedience to Him.

Naturally, we'd rather be moved by God's love, but our penchant toward sin can lead us to presume upon it. "Oh God," we reason, "since You know my weaknesses, let your love manifest your mercy and give me a pass." It's almost as if we think we can charm God like a 2-year-old weasels her way out of her daddy's punishment by cuddling up close and batting her eyes. But when her Daddy shows his obvious wrath, her demeanor changes into a respect that moves her to immediately obey. In the same way, the wrath of God is not to be presumed upon.

When the Hebrew midwives obeyed due to their fear of God, He showered them with His kindness. Exodus 1:20-21 says, "Therefore God dealt well with the midwives, and the people multiplied and grew very mighty. And so it was, because the midwives feared God, that He provided households for them"

(NKJ). Recognize the reverential fear due to God and refuse to fear any lesser power. The outcome will be an outpouring of God's kindness.

#34
February 3: When God Sees the Blood

I've always wanted to participate in a Passover celebration. I know from Scripture the reason for the celebration is to remember God's astounding deliverance of the Hebrew people from their Egyptian bondage. I also understand that many parts of the meal—the Seder—point to Jesus Christ. Messianic Jews, those who have recognized Jesus Christ as the Messiah, would probably best be able to explain the melding of the Old and New Testament messages as we ate.

However, there's one part of the story of the exodus I completely comprehend. That night so long ago, as the Hebrews ate this special meal in their homes, something both terrible and terrific was happening outside. The death angel was visiting each Egyptian household killing every firstborn therein, but in the homes of the Hebrews, everyone lived. Why? Because that same death angel saw something at the Hebrews' doors. The blood of the lamb they were eating was painted on the door frame. The Lord told Moses, "On that same night I will pass through Egypt and strike down every firstborn-- both men and animals-- and I will bring judgment on all the gods of Egypt. I am the LORD. The blood will be a sign for you on the houses where you are; and when I see the blood, I will pass over you. No destructive plague will touch you when I strike Egypt" Exodus 12:12-13 (NIV). (See also Exodus 12:21-28.)

Oh hallelujah! The Passover message is the same for you and me today. The blood of the Lamb has been painted on the door frames of our hearts. The blood of Jesus is a sign on the house that is our body. The real you and me live inside these bodies and as long as the blood has been applied, God still says to us of His eternal wrath, "When I see the blood, I will pass over you."

The death that could eternally separate us from God has passed over us never to return. Our salvation is secure. Thank God for the blood!

#35
February 4: God Can Flip the Script

The Egyptian people living under the Pharaoh who had enslaved the Israelites probably figured they had it pretty good. The great construction project for the new cities was rolling along. They would be able to enjoy and brag about their beautifully built cities and they hadn't been put upon to lift a finger to do the work. Undoubtedly, the Egyptians probably looked down on the slave laborers, esteeming them with the disgust and prejudice often still exhibited today from those who have judged themselves better simply because of job status.

But God has His ways of proving to us humans that we're all equally important no matter what job we do. Upon suffering the final and most devastating plague—when every Egyptian household experienced the death of the firstborn—the ruling class was forced to come to this understanding. They figured out that it had been a bad idea to despise the God of the Israelites. "Maybe those people were really people," the Egyptians may have thought, "and we should have been nicer. If we keep ignoring their God and treating them badly, we just may all be dead soon."

Reasoning such as this moved the Egyptians toward change. Exodus 12:33-36 says, "The Egyptians urged the people to hurry and leave the country. 'For otherwise,' they said, 'we will all die!'... The Israelites did as Moses instructed and asked the Egyptians for articles of silver and gold and for clothing. The LORD had made the Egyptians favorably disposed toward the people, and they gave them what they asked for; so they plundered the Egyptians."

God can flip the script and move our enemies to be "favorably disposed" toward us as well. We must just be sure we are doing our part in letting the Lord do His part on our behalf.

#36
February 5: Praying to our Triune God

Whenever we try to explain anything about God, all we have to use is earthly examples and the limits of language. An infinite God can hardly be adequately explained by the finite, but that's all we have to work with and the best we can do. So when I was recently asked a question about prayer and the Trinity, I found myself in this infinite-God-finite-language dilemma. The question was: to whom are we praying: God the Father, God the Son Jesus, or God the Holy Spirit?

First of all, we needed to establish a clear understanding of the Trinity. How is God one yet three? The best explanation I have ever heard was from Dr. Fred Campbell. Think of the sun in the sky.

- The sun has mass; it is a thing that exists. The mass represents God the Father. God told Moses, "I AM WHO I AM... Thus you shall say to the children of Israel, 'I AM has sent me to you'" Exodus 3:14 (NKJ).
- The sun gives off light. The light represents God the Son, Jesus Christ. Light shows us the way to God. Jesus Himself says, "I am the way, the truth, and the life. No one comes to the Father except through Me" John 14:6 (NKJ). And again He says, "I am the light of the world. He who follows Me shall not walk in darkness, but have the light of life" John 8:12 (NKJ)
- The sun radiates heat. Ever heard of solar energy? Heat represents the Holy Spirit who is our power. John 6:63 says, "It is the Spirit who gives life..." and Acts 1:8 says, "But you shall receive power when the Holy Spirit has come upon you..."

With that understood, now we can answer the question. When we pray, we are praying to the Godhead. If we must have a breakdown, we pray *to* God the Father, *through* (in) the name of Jesus Christ, and *by* the leading of the Holy Spirit. God is Creator of all and overall and it's before Him we will stand. Jesus is our passage to God ("no man comes to the Father except through me"). The Holy Spirit empowers us and directs our hearts and minds as we submit to God in prayer. The Holy Spirit "will guide you into all truth" (John 16:13), and "helps in our weaknesses. For we do not know what we should pray for as we ought, but the Spirit Himself makes intercession for us with groanings which cannot be uttered" Romans 8:26 (NKJ). However, in the same way in which we cannot separate the mass of the sun from its light and its heat, we cannot separate God the Father, from the Son, and the Holy Spirit.

The bottom line is: God's got it covered when we pray. Frankly, I really don't think God is so concerned with semantics. I don't think He minds if we call Him Father, Jesus, or the Holy Spirit – just as long as we call.

#37
February 6: Not Just Any Old Water

When things are not going so well, it seems to be a part of our human nature to get discouraged. The longer the tough times draw out, the more disheartened we can become. God understands that, but if we turn to Him, we'll find that He's able to interject Himself into our distressing moments and turn everything around.

The Israelites experienced this truth about God early in their deliverance journey. They were fresh out of Egypt, just three days past watching God drown Pharaoh's entire army, and already their triumph was being overcome by their thirst. Then wouldn't you know it, when they finally did get to some water, it was bitter and undrinkable. When the people complained to Moses, Exodus 15:25 tells us, "Then Moses cried out to the LORD, and the LORD showed him a piece of wood. He threw it into the water, and the water became sweet. There the LORD made a decree and a law for them, and there he tested them" (NIV).

God went on to comfort and supply for His people, not only with sweet water, but also with sweet manna and with meat. "Then the LORD said to Moses, 'I will rain down bread from heaven for you. The people are to go out each day and gather enough for that day. In this way I will test them and see whether they will follow my instructions'... That evening quail came and covered the camp, and in the morning there was a layer of dew around the camp. When the dew was gone, thin flakes like frost on the ground appeared on the desert floor" Exodus 16:4 and 13-14 (NIV).

Be careful about letting physical problems cloud your trust in God's ability to turn your situation around. He is still in the business of doing the miraculous. He didn't give the Israelites just any old water, He gave them sweet water, sweet manna, and meat. We too can continue to rely on God when our waters are bitter. He'll supply for us with not just any old relief, but with sweet relief that will carry us all the way to the end of our journey.

#38
February 7: God's Care in the Desert

When the children of Israel were on their way to the Promised Land, they had to walk through the desert. Not coincidentally, one of the arid places through which they traveled was called the Desert of Sin (Exodus 17:1). Naturally, it was hot and dry. It didn't take long before the people were complaining about not having water to drink. When the tumult got so bad that the people were about ready to stone Moses, God told him, "Walk on ahead of the people. Take with you some of the elders of Israel and take in your hand the staff with which you struck the Nile, and go. I will stand there before you by the rock at Horeb. Strike the rock, and water will come out of it for the people to drink" Exodus 17:5-6 (NIV).

We can learn several things for ourselves from this small segment of Scripture.

- Sometimes, when we set out to where we know God's called us, we'll need to walk through some desert places or situations.
- Sin is ever-present, even as we are following hard after God. We must watch out for it.
- Expect some hot and dry times. As we journey to where God wants us, heated contentions with others may rise, and we may feel like the anointing has dried up and God is not with us. We must, however, no matter what, stay the course. Until He changes our direction, we can trust the voice we know we heard at the beginning.
- God will always go before us.
- Remember God's track record. Notice that Moses was specifically directed to use the same "staff with which [he] struck the Nile." When times get rough, bring back to your remembrance the miracles God's done before. He hasn't changed.
- Expect the nourishment you'll need. God is not a sadist; He does not derive pleasure from inflicting pain on us. He loves to nourish us and is well able to nourish us, even when all around us is bleak and dry.

By all natural laws, water does not come from rocks. But we're not dependent upon natural laws. We're dealing with the One who created natural laws. Since He created them, He is perfectly free to break them, and He often does so on our account.

Don't second-guess yourself when you find yourself walking through desert places after you thought you had clearly heard God's voice and had begun to follow Him. You heard right. God is just carrying you into situations where He can show you just how much He's able to care for you. He wants you to understand that if He can provide water for you in the desert, He can take care of you anywhere else He may lead.

#39
February 8: Little by Little Blessings from God

We'd all like to come into a sudden fortune. It would be nice to have all those student loans paid off, the mortgage paid, or no rent charged. How about owing nothing more on the car, credit cards, insurances, or taxes? Wouldn't it also be wonderful if that budding business were in full swing, that managerial position was yours, or that top spot in the industry of your dreams was secure?

We think it would be great to arrive today at where we're going, but God knows better. Consider His explanation to the Israelites as they began to conquer the Promised Land. "But I will not drive them out in a single year, because the land would become desolate and the wild animals too numerous for you. Little by little I will drive them out before you, until you have increased enough to take possession of the land" Exodus 23:29-30 (NIV).

God knows we can only handle success a little at a time. To be good with money, we need to grow by paying off bills consistently and wisely planning a budget that balances tithing, saving, charitable giving, and personal spending. To be successful business owners, we need to learn business basics by starting small and growing gradually. How can we effectively manage 1,000 employees when we can't handle two? And fame has knocked many an aspirant right off the front pages because they got too big too fast.

Wild animals lurk in every field of endeavor. Allow God to increase you bit by bit as He drives them from your territory. Success isn't going anywhere. It will be waiting for you when it's your time to have it. Your time to completely possess your land may not be in just one year, or three, or five. Just keep working at what God is building in you. He is also at work driving the beasts out of your territory little by little "until you have increased enough to take possession of the land."

#40
February 9: Cloud or Fire?

When Moses went up onto Mount Sinai to meet with God to get the Law, the Israelite people were instructed to stay away. They were only allowed to go to the foot of the mountain and not try to run up to see God for themselves. For once, they obeyed, but God did allow them to see that something was going on up at the top. Exodus 24:12-17 tells us the whole encounter:

- Then the Lord said to Moses, "Come up to Me on the mountain and be there; and I will give you tablets of stone, and the law and commandments which I have written, that you may teach them." So Moses arose with his assistant Joshua, and Moses went up to the mountain of God.

And he said to the elders, "Wait here for us until we come back to you... Then Moses went up into the mountain, and a cloud covered the mountain.

Now the glory of the Lord rested on Mount Sinai, and the cloud covered it six days. And on the seventh day He called to Moses out of the midst of the cloud. The sight of the glory of the Lord was like a consuming fire on the top of the mountain in the eyes of the children of Israel. (NKJ)

The passage clearly says that Moses went into "the midst of the cloud." How is it then that the people saw the glory of the Lord "like a consuming fire on the top of the mountain"? One obvious answer is that God can show Himself to us in whatever way He would like. I also see here, though, the fact that a difference in relationship is affecting each entity's vision. Moses relates to God up close and personal. Moses and God have a close relationship that allows Moses to see God as a comforting cloud. God's presence is a happy, welcoming place. By contrast, the people are not talking directly to God; in fact, they are usually complaining about one thing or another. Their relationship with God is distant, and when they relate to Him, they can see Him as harsh—"like a consuming fire."

What is our relationship with God like today? Is the presence of God our happy place, or do we dread the thought of being in God's company? Is He a cloud to us that can envelop us so completely that we don't even think about eating? (Moses fasted for the 40 days and nights that He was on the mountain with God. Being that close to God even makes food the farthest thing from one's mind.) Or have we been living in such a distant location that God seems only like a far-off consuming fire whose anger over our sin will kill us if we come too close?

Thanks to Jesus Christ, no matter what we've done, we can now approach God. Jesus' work on the cross has delivered us from the wrath of God's consuming fire. Our times in His presence can be our happy place, our comforting cloud. James 4:8-10 tells us, "Come close to God, and God will come close to you. Wash your hands, you sinners; purify your hearts, for your loyalty is divided between God and the world. Let there be tears for what you have done. Let there be sorrow and deep grief. Let there be sadness instead of laughter, and gloom instead of joy. Humble yourselves before the Lord, and he will lift you up in honor" James 4:8 -10 (NLT).

#41
February 10: God in Person

Exodus 24:12 says, "Then the LORD said to Moses, 'Come up to Me on the mountain and be there; and I will give you tablets of stone, and the law and commandments which I have written, that you may teach them'" (NKJ). How awesome of God to meet with Moses in person and give him the law and commandments.

Guess what. God will still meet with us in person to communicate to us His law and commandments. All we have to do is exactly what Moses did—respond to God's invitation, "Come up to Me."

That invitation to come to God and meet with Him in person was echoed through Jesus too. John 6:37 quotes Jesus as saying, "All that the Father gives Me will come to Me, and the one who comes to Me I will by no means cast out" (NKJ). What a wonderful assurance! The Spirit of God is heard making the call as well. Revelation 22:17 "And the Spirit and the bride say, 'Come!' And let him who hears say, 'Come!' And let him who thirsts come. Whoever desires, let him take the water of life freely" (NKJ).

The cool part to this "coming" is that we're not just showing up to hang around. We are being invited to meet with God in person for a purpose—that purpose being to receive something from Him. So what do we get?

- We get His law. God desires that we know and understand His will and His ways.
- We get His commandments. God intends for us to know and understand how we are to conduct ourselves as His children.
- We get the water of life. Vine's Expository Dictionary of Biblical Words explains that the water of life is "emblematic of the maintenance of spiritual life in perpetuity." In other words, we get the power of the Holy Spirit to energize us.

The paraphrase of Matthew 11:28-30 as found in the Message Bible gives us a vivid picture of what happens when we accept the invitation to meet God in person. "Are you tired? Worn out? Burned out on religion? Come to me. Get away with me and you'll recover your life. I'll show you how to take a real rest. Walk with me and work with me—watch how I do it. Learn the unforced rhythms of grace. I won't lay anything heavy or ill-fitting on you. Keep company with me and you'll learn to live freely and lightly."

So what are you waiting for? His hands are outstretched as He says to you today, "Come up to Me."

#42
February 11: Our Times with God

The book of Leviticus is full of instructions concerning how to offer the sacrifices to God. He is very specific and particular about how every kind of offering is to be done. It's easy to get bogged down and even have our eyes start to cross as we are reading through such details as what kind of animal to bring, which side of the tabernacle to take it to, exactly how to kill it, which parts to lay on the altar, etc. But keep reading to the end of each paragraph. Over and over again, we read, "...It is a burnt offering, an offering made by fire, an aroma pleasing to the LORD" Lev 1:9, 13, and 17 (NIV).

The whole point was not the sacrifices to God, but the meeting times with God. Today (thankfully), we no longer have to take animal, grain, and drink offerings to God to secure our forgiveness or His favor. Jesus' substitutionary sacrifice ended the need for that system (see Hebrews 10:10-12). Still, however, God wants us to approach Him. The sacrifices stood as a reminder of how holy the God was to whom we were trying to gain access. The end of the sacrificial system by no means meant we were no longer supposed to go to Him. Jesus' sacrifice was like opening a fancy, 20-lane interstate highway to the Father where before there had only been a narrow, treacherous dirt road winding along the edge of a precipice with no guard rail.

Our times with God are pleasing to Him, and nowadays, we can't use the excuse of all the trouble of procuring the right animal, traveling to the temple, etc. Thanks to the cross of Calvary, we can approach God with what He really wants—ourselves. Paul begs us to do just that in Romans 12:1 when he says, "Therefore, I urge you, brothers, in view of God's mercy, to offer your bodies as living sacrifices, holy and pleasing to God-- this is your spiritual act of worship" (NIV). Every time we come to God offering ourselves, this indeed is a sweet and pleasing aroma to Him.

#43
February 12: On Approaching God

Using my computer or my smart phone, I can call my sons and see them as I talk with them as long as they have some kind of compatible device. With just a few clicks, I visited with Mark one day who was thousands of miles away at college, saw his room, and "met" his roommates. Then I visited with Matthew while he ate his bowtie pasta meal. All of us had the same thing in mind: let's call each other and talk. Those devices erased the miles and allowed us to just be together for a few moments and it felt good. Since we all had the same program, we could be together.

Prayer is like that computer program. Prayer is the program that erases the miles between Heaven and earth and ushers us into the presence of God. Through prayer, we meet Him face-to-face and have conversation. We talk and He listens; He talks and we listen. We respond back and forth. When we have the program—connection to God through Jesus Christ—we can approach God.

However, I wouldn't want make or receive a visual call and

have my boys see me if I looked bad. Each time I visit with them using this program, I want to be presentable. As with a visual call, so with prayer. I'm not saying we only pray when we're in great shape and nothing's wrong; I'm saying we ought to approach God regarding Him with respect. Aaron's sons didn't do this and were severely punished. Leviticus 10:1-2 says, "Then Nadab and Abihu, the sons of Aaron, each took his censer and put fire in it, put incense on it, and offered profane fire before the LORD, which He had not commanded them. So fire went out from the LORD and devoured them, and they died before the LORD" (NKJ).

God explained His actions. "By those who come near Me I must be regarded as holy; and before all the people I must be glorified" Leviticus 1:3. We are not to just treat God any kind of way. We are welcome to approach Him, but we must remember to do so with the proper respect for who He is. God lays forth two requirements here for approaching Him. He says, "I must be regarded as holy," and "I must be glorified." Matthew Henry's commentary explains this much better than I can.

- Note, First, whenever we worship God, we come nigh unto him, as spiritual priests. This consideration ought to make us very reverent and serious.
- Secondly, [we are] to give him the praise of his holiness, [for He is] a God of spotless purity and transcendent perfection, <Isa. 8:13>.
- Thirdly, when we sanctify God… we glorify him before all the people, confessing our own belief of his glory and desiring that others also may be affected with it.
- Fourthly, if God be not sanctified and glorified by us, he will be sanctified and glorified upon us. He will take vengeance on those that profane his sacred name by trifling with him.

Bottom line: As the gospel song says, "Call Him up and tell Him what you want." Approach God often, but approach God right.

#44
February 13: That's Just His Way

Whenever my mother would try to explain someone's strange behavior, she'd say, "Oh, that's just his way." When we heard that, we understood that person was somewhat peculiar, somewhat out of the norm. We were to deal with that person respectfully but not emulate his speech or actions. It was clear that our "ways" needed to be different from his "ways."

God expects us to recognize when people are doing ungodly things just like my mother wanted us to recognize when people were doing strange things. In the same way He warned the children of Israel to avoid mimicking the actions of the Egyptians and the Canaanites, He expects us to act differently from the practices of the perverse society that surrounds us. However, recognition of the wrong went hand-in-hand with acknowledgement of the opposite being right. Listen as He instructs His people in Leviticus 18:2-5:

> "...I am the LORD your God. According to the doings of the land of Egypt, where you dwelt, you shall not do; and according to the doings of the land of Canaan, where I am bringing you, you shall not do; nor shall you walk in their ordinances. You shall observe My judgments and keep My ordinances, to walk in them: I am the LORD your God. You shall therefore keep My statutes and My judgments, which if a man does, he shall live by them: I am the LORD" (NKJ).

The Old Testament admonition has a New Testament counterpart in Ephesians 4:17-24: "...you should no longer walk as the rest of the Gentiles walk... who, being past feeling, have given themselves over to lewdness, to work all uncleanness with greediness. But you have not so learned Christ... you put off, concerning your former conduct, the old man which grows corrupt according to the deceitful lusts, and be renewed in the spirit of your mind, and... put on the new man which was created according to God, in true righteousness and holiness" (NKJ).

Because of the pervasiveness of our sin nature, it will take some practice for us to start feeling comfortable doing things God's way. As we grow closer and closer to Him, we should start more and more readily recognizing and avoiding what's wrong as we acknowledge and adhere to what's right. At first, it will seem odd and peculiar, but pretty soon, we'll mature.

We'll become more like Christ and less like the world. We'll understand how to function as the new creature we've become (see First Corinthians 5:17). The manner in which God does things won't seem so peculiar to us anymore. Then when others question our righteous behavior that seems odd to them, we'll be able to point to the Savior, flip the negative connotation on its head, and confidently reply, "Oh, that's just His way."

#45
February 14: God's Prescription

We usually hear Numbers 6:24-26 in connection with the end of a church service or Christian program. It says, "The LORD bless you and keep you; the LORD make His face shine upon you, and be gracious to you; the LORD lift up His countenance upon you, and give you peace" (NKJ). These words are a great benediction, but I find them to be a comforting prescription for every day.

- The Lord bless you. This means God will bestow benefits upon us.
- The Lord keep you. The Hebrew word for "keep" is "shamar" which means to hedge about as with thorns. In other words, God is standing guard around us to protect us.
- The Lord make His face to shine upon you, and be gracious to you. God's face, the part that turns (paniym), will illuminate us—that is, His attention will shine upon us wherever we move as if we were in a spotlight—as He showers His favor our way.
- The Lord lift up His countenance upon you. God will lift us to a new place in Him, conforming us into the image of His dear Son.
- The Lord give you peace. "Shalowm" means safety, happiness, welfare, health, and prosperity. When we have God's peace, we have all if this and more.

Try speaking these verses to God personally. Say, "Lord, thank you for blessing me and keeping me. Thank you for making

Your face shine upon me, and for being gracious to me. I look forward today to how You will lift up Your countenance upon me, and give me peace."

These five points will nourish our souls better than any one-a-day tablet could ever nourish our bodies. What a great prescription! Let's take one Numbers 6 multi-Godamin every morning. (Gives a new meaning to "Have a nice day," doesn't it?)

#46
February 15: Where God Speaks

Numbers 7:89 tells us, "Now when Moses went into the tabernacle of meeting to speak with Him, he heard the voice of One speaking to him from above the mercy seat that was on the ark of the Testimony, from between the two cherubim; thus He spoke to him" (NKJ).

That had to be awesome for Moses to have this special place to go to so He could hear God speak. And it was awesome—for Moses. But what about the million or so other children of Israel? If they wanted to hear what God had said, they had to hang around outside the tabernacle and wait for Moses to come out and tell them. Now that's a bummer, especially if one of them wanted to talk to God, or needed to hear from God personally.

We're fortunate. Thanks to Jesus' sacrifice on the cross, the way to God has been opened. When Christ died, the curtain was split in two that used to separate the regular guy from the mercy seat. The tearing symbolized the opening of God's arms to us, bidding us to come directly to Him. (See Matthew 27:51.)

Thanks to the indwelling Holy Spirit, our tabernacle is anywhere we are. For example, since I have to be to work so early, my morning prayer time happens while I'm driving to my job. I know it's unconventional but don't worry; I don't bow my head and close my eyes. Nonetheless, I talk with God during my commute. The sunrise is a perfect altar. I begin by adoring God via His many names: Jehovah Jirah, Jehovah Rapha, Jehovah Nissi, etc. Then I go through my same rotation of concentration I used at home: Monday I pray for my husband and myself, Tuesday for the kids, Wednesday for ministries, and so on. It's cool to realize that my Toyota Highlander can be a sanctuary even when it's moving at 65 miles per hour (or there abouts)!

And God speaks to my heart as I drive along. I arrive to work at peace and ready for the day knowing I've spent quality time alone at the mercy seat of God.

God will speak to you too wherever you are. Your heart is His home and His sanctuary. Spend time today and every day consciously communing (even if you're commuting) with Him.

#47
February 16: God of Celebration

"What comes into our minds when we think about God is the most important thing about us. Man's spiritual history will positively demonstrate that no religion has ever been greater than its idea of God. Worship is pure or base as the worshipper entertains high or low thoughts of God." I agree with this quote from A.W. Tozer's classic book on the attributes of God, *The Knowledge of the Holy*. Tozer and other learned theologians have listed God's attributes and have done extensive studying on them to help us get to know God better. The main attributes we can find from these men's studies include infinitude, sovereignty, holiness, trinity, omniscience, faithfulness, love, omnipotence, self-existence, self-sufficiency, justice, immutability, mercy, eternal, gracious, and omnipresence. However, in my studies about God so far, I have not come across the attribute we're looking at today—the attribute of celebration.

Before God busted the Israelites out of their Egyptian bondage, He was already planning the celebration party. He set up the Passover and then instructed them to commemorate it annually when they got free. In Numbers 9:2, God actually commands it, "Have the Israelites celebrate the Passover at the appointed time" (NIV). In fact, throughout the Jewish year, God instituted seven feasts: Passover, Unleavened Bread, First Fruits, Weeks, Trumpets, Day of Atonement, and Tabernacles.

God is not against memorial and festive remembrances. Scripture does not denounce our Christmas and Resurrection holidays, or our birthday and anniversary observances. There's nothing wrong with getting together to happily honor someone at a rite of passage like a bar mitzvah, quinceañera, sweet sixteen party, or wedding. God means for us to rejoice with those who rejoice. We get into trouble when we let the revelry get out of hand

and accompany the occasion with a license to sin by overspending just for show, overindulgence in alcohol and/or drugs, and going overboard in other various forms of debauchery.

Perhaps we can't see God's celebration attribute because we don't understand His purposes for celebration. If you notice, each celebration God instituted for those Old Testament saints pointed back to something He'd brought them through. We'll see more of the God of celebration when we start concentrating on what He desires to bring us through rather than dwelling on what we desire for Him to do.

#48
February 17: Move When God Says Move

When my children were young, I expected them to respond immediately when I called them. They didn't have the choice or the leisure to hear my voice calling them and not move. As the adult, it was my job to keep an ever-watchful eye out for their well-being, so my voice could carry a life or death direction. If they were not in the habit of responding immediately, something terrible could befall them. Since they never knew what I wanted until they moved to answer, they needed to always move without delay.

As with Mom, even more so with God. When God was leading the children of Israel through the desert on their way to the Promised Land, He directed them with the cloud. When the cloud stopped, they were to stop and set up camp. The cloud would then rest over the tabernacle. When God wanted them to move, the cloud would move. They'd pack up camp and follow the cloud until it stopped again. "Whether the cloud stayed over the tabernacle for two days or a month or a year, the Israelites would remain in camp and not set out; but when it lifted, they would set out. At the LORD's command they encamped, and at the LORD's command they set out." Numbers 9:22-23 (NIV).

Whether we hear God's voice (in prayer, while reading the Word, through a sermon, etc.) or see His hand moving today, our conditioning should be the same as that of the children of Israel in the desert and my children in my home. With no question or debate, we need to move when God says move. From the God who loves and cares for us and only has an ever-watchful eye out for our well-being, there can be nothing but good on the other side of His commands.

#49
February 18: Forgiveness and Consequences

Somehow we've gotten it in our minds that forgiveness means everything will be fine now. We figure we can commit a transgression, ask for forgiveness, and go on our merry way like nothing ever happened.

We've got that twisted.

Forgiveness does not negate the fact that "the wages of sin is death" Romans 6:23 (NIV). Sure, the rest of that verse says, "...the gift of God is eternal life through Christ Jesus our Lord," but those gravesites haven't disappeared. If you participate in rampant infidelity or abusive behavior, you can change your ways and be forgiven, but your marriage died and the divorce grave still exists. If you smoke cigarettes your whole life and decide to quit at age 60, God forgives you for polluting your temple, but the irreversible damage you've done to your lungs is still likely to cut your life short, sending you to an earlier grave than you should have experienced. Sexual promiscuity will likely lead to STD's from which there may be no physical cure. You can convert and God forgives, but the grave of that shameful past still mars the ground.

The Israelites learned that forgiveness and consequences from God operate this way. Numbers 14:17-23 says, "Now may the Lord's strength be displayed, just as you have declared: The LORD is slow to anger, abounding in love and forgiving sin and rebellion. Yet he does not leave the guilty unpunished... The LORD replied, 'I have forgiven them, as you asked. Nevertheless, as surely as I live and as surely as the glory of the LORD fills the whole earth, not one of the men who saw my glory and the miraculous signs I performed in Egypt and in the desert but who disobeyed me and tested me ten times—not one of them will ever see the land I promised on oath to their forefathers. No one who has treated me with contempt will ever see it'" (NIV).

We treat God with contempt when we keep on sinning and keep on presuming upon His forgiveness, thinking there will be no consequences to suffer. God is not fine with our sin and we shouldn't be either. Beware the dire consequences – the graves our sins dig – and let's allow that to be enough to move us to obedience.

#50
February 19: God's Chosen Priest

In Numbers chapter 16, a group of "250 Israelite men, well-known community leaders who had been appointed members of the council" (verse 2) challenged the leadership of Moses and Aaron. God punished the rebels with extinction (read 16:31-35), then He put a period behind His leadership choice in an unusual way.

Numbers 17:1-8 reads: "The LORD said to Moses, 'Speak to the Israelites and get twelve staffs from them, one from the leader of each of their ancestral tribes. Write the name of each man on his staff... The staff belonging to the man I choose will sprout, and I will rid myself of this constant grumbling against you by the Israelites.' ...The next day Moses entered the Tent of the Testimony and saw that Aaron's staff, which represented the house of Levi, had not only sprouted but had budded, blossomed and produced almonds"
(NIV).

God's choice for high priest was evident. He still knows how to choose His leaders and how to make those choices evident to us. Aaron's staff "had not only sprouted but had budded, blossomed and produced almonds." The meaning of this can be double-edged.

The first message is to recognize and respectfully follow and honor the pastor God has placed over us. God selects pastors to lead churches. When we join a church, we are to submit to the pastor whom God has placed over that house.

The second message is to realize that the New Testament describes us as "a royal priesthood" (see First Peter 2:9), so it is incumbent upon us to pay attention to the call God has placed on each of us individually. We must consider the "staff" that is our spiritual life and calling.

- Sprout: A sprout is new growth. Your staff sprouts when it becomes alive in you. You will know you've been called and what you've been called to.

- Bud: A bud is a plant that may develop into a flower; something not yet mature or at full development. As your staff buds, your passion will move you to actively develop your gifts.
- Blossom: The blossom is the flower of a seed plant. The flower blossom holds that which is able to spread to produce more blossoms. At the blossoming stage, your ministry begins to take wing and others are the recipients of the giftedness God's placed within you.
- Produce Almonds: This is the part of your ministry when you begin to see the fruit. Your ministry is serving and benefiting others, and those so touched are sprouting, budding, and blossoming themselves.

What of your staff? Is it sprouting, budding, blossoming, and producing almonds? No matter the stage, how exciting to realize you are God's chosen.

#51
February 20: Only What God Says

When the children of Israel neared the land of the Moabites, Balak the king of Moab started to get worried. He saw this sea of people approaching and had heard the stories of how they had defeated two other powerful kings: Sihon, king of the Amorites, and Og, king of Bashan. Balak decided to get some divine help, so he called on Balaam, a local prophet who he knew had a hook-up with God. You get a sense from reading the story that begins in Numbers chapter 22, that Balak felt if he paid Balaam enough, he could sway the prophet's words and buy himself a curse over these troublesome invaders.

Balaam may or may not have been crooked, but he knew what to say to Balak's appeal. When messengers came from Balak with the first request to curse the children of Israel, Balaam answered, "Even if Balak gave me his palace filled with silver and gold, I could not do anything great or small to go beyond the command of the LORD my God" Numbers 22:18 (NIV). Then when Balaam arrived in Balak's presence, he responded face-to-face to the king, "Well, I have come to you now... But can I say just anything? I must speak only what God puts in my mouth" Numbers 22:38 (NIV).

I like Balaam's answers. What more is there to talk about? When faced with a troubling situation, a daunting problem, or even a relatively minor everyday type of decision, Balaam's words teach us something about the right attitude to have. Whatever we face, we'll be okay as we go through it if we determine not to "do anything great or small to go beyond the command of the LORD" and if we decide to "speak only what God puts in [our] mouth."

Practice the discipline of listening today. Place God's promptings before reactions. Surrender your automatic responses to the possibility that God might want you to do or say something different. He might even move you to stillness or silence: having you to do or say nothing at all. If you don't know what to do, don't improvise. Patiently wait until He gives you an assured answer, and then confidently move on that. God is well able to lead and guide; He just needs you to follow.

#52
February 21: The Assignment with the Gift

God told Moses to give the following instructions to the children of Israel:

Speak to the children of Israel, and say to them: "When you have crossed the Jordan into the land of Canaan, then you shall **drive out all the inhabitants** of the land from before you, **destroy** all their engraved stones, **destroy** all their molded images, and **demolish** all their high places; you shall **dispossess** the inhabitants of the land and dwell in it, for I have given you the land to possess. And you shall **divide the land** by lot as an inheritance among your families; to the larger you shall give a larger inheritance, and to the smaller you shall give a smaller inheritance; there everyone's inheritance shall be whatever falls to him by lot. You shall inherit according to the tribes of your fathers. But if you do not drive out the inhabitants of the land from before you, then it shall be that those whom you let remain shall be irritants in your eyes and thorns in your sides, and they shall harass you in the land where you dwell" Numbers 33:51-55 (NKJ). [Emphasis added.]

Although God was giving the land to His people, he also gave them an assignment. In other words, the gift came with responsibility. This is an example of how God continues to operate with us today. His gifts are ours free and clear; however, we are still responsible for their maintenance. If someone gives us a car and the pink slip, we own the car, but in order to continue to enjoy it, we have to buy the gas, insurance, and annual license tags; and take it in for scheduled oil changes, etc.

Let's keep our relationship with God in good repair. Enjoy the gift of salvation by living a life of holy maintenance.

#53
February 22: God Has Plans

We naturally realize that we do not start at the top. Our universe is designed in such a way as to teach us that reality:

- Plants grow by first sending roots down. Once we plant a seed in the ground, action begins, but we aren't witnesses to it. We don't see the development of the system that will sustain the vegetation because all we care about is the final product—that flower we can enjoy or that food we can eat.

- Each of us starts out as an infant, totally dependent upon another human being for survival. All things being equal, we grow and mature little by little every day until we reach adulthood.

- We go through school by starting at pre-school or kindergarten with the basics. Five and six-year-olds aren't reading C.S. Lewis's works; they start out simply reading the "C" and the "S".

- In business, we enter a company as a trainee. Even if we start our own company and name ourselves as CEO, we start out small, with what we can handle, and then build the business over time.

We need to carry that same understanding into our spiritual lives when we realize that God has plans to prosper us. He will not start us off at the top of where He wants to take us. There are wonderful parallels on this point in Deuteronomy chapters 7 and 8 with how God dealt with the children of Israel.

When God is up to something:

- **He will awaken our memory.** Moses told the children of Israel, "...you shall remember well what the LORD your God did..." Deuteronomy 7:18 (NKJ). We must never forget where God has brought us from. That is the firm foundation of faith on which He is building us now.
- **He will advance us little by little.** Moses told the people, "And the LORD your God will drive out those nations before you little by little; you will be unable to destroy them at once, lest the beasts of the field become too numerous for you" Deuteronomy 7:22 (NKJ). God knows we have to learn how to handle success so He'll give it to us bit by bit. In whatever field we're in, there are beasts out there ready to devour us, so God orchestrates our climb to build our awareness and make us wise to the dangers around us as He elevates us.
- **He will attract our attention.** Remember the manna the children of Israel had to eat? God had more in mind than simply feeding them when He supplied it. Deuteronomy 8:3 tells us, "So He humbled you, allowed you to hunger, and fed you with manna which you did not know nor did your fathers know, that He might make you know that man shall not live by bread alone; but man lives by every word that proceeds from the mouth of the LORD" (NKJ). God does not intend for us to get it twisted: we are on our way somewhere because He is making it possible. We can never allow ourselves to forget that even our success is all about Him.

Get ready for your success, but keep focused on God's advancement program. God has plans.

#54
February 23: Did God Really Mean That?

The Old Testament laws were rough. God didn't mess around. He expected sin to be exposed as quickly as possible and wiped out. If someone suggested, "Let's go and serve other gods of the people around us," that person had to be put to death (see

Deuteronomy 13). If someone testified falsely against his brother, whatever he wanted done to his brother would be turned on him (see Deuteronomy 19). And both the man and the woman were put to death who participated in sex outside of marriage (see Deuteronomy 22).

Parents were not exempt from God's directions about handling their wayward, grown children either. Deuteronomy 21:18-21 says, "If a man has a stubborn and rebellious son who will not obey the voice of his father or the voice of his mother, and who, when they have chastened him, will not heed them, then his father and his mother shall take hold of him and bring him out to the elders of his city, to the gate of his city. And they shall say to the elders of his city, 'This son of ours is stubborn and rebellious; he will not obey our voice; he is a glutton and a drunkard.' Then all the men of his city shall stone him to death with stones; so you shall put away the evil from among you, and all Israel shall hear and fear."

Has God changed since the Old Testament? Has he gotten softer on sin? Not at all. God still detests following other gods, lying, fornication, and dishonoring parents. We graciously now have the forgiveness of the Cross to look to and God holds back His immediate wrath. However, He's just as dishonored and we are just as guilty. Consequences of our sinful actions will also catch up with us just as surely if we don't change our ways.

Still, don't utterly ignore the point behind the discipline plans of the Old Testament. We are still responsible for training our children in the way they should go and disciplining them when they are wrong. As in Deuteronomy 21, we need to admit the faults of our wayward children, and if they refuse to accept our rebuke and correction, we need to let go and allow the authorities – the teacher, principal, boss, or police – to do their job in disciplining them. (It's tight; but it's right.)

Let's allow the rules of the Old Testament to remind us of God's holiness and of His determination to form holiness in us. God has not changed. Let the grace of the New Testament and the reverential fear of the Old drive us to want to live holy before Him.

#55
February 24: Positive Verbs from God

The English teacher in me gets very excited about the meanings of words and my choleric temperament finds joy in action. Put those two together and it's easy to understand why verbs are my favorite part of speech. There are three categories of verbs: action, linking, and state of being. I love them all. The state of being verbs (is, am, are, etc.) simply show that something exists as in the sentence, "God <u>is</u>." Linking verbs (seems, appears, etc.) show a particular connection between the subject and the predicate as in, "James <u>seems</u> interested in basketball." And the action verbs tell us what the subject is doing as in, "Jack <u>jumps</u>." Yes, verbs establish existence, light a fire under us, get us moving, and get things accomplished.

How exciting it is, then, to read of the verbs God speaks over His people. Read the entire passage found in Deuteronomy 28:1-14 (NKJ) to catch the flavor of the context. When God blesses, wow, He goes all out. Pay particular attention to the verbs God uses; here are some snippets:

- "And all these blessings shall come upon you and ***overtake*** you..." verse 2
- "The LORD ***will command*** the blessing on you..." verse 8
- "The LORD ***will establish*** you as a holy people to Himself..." verse 9
- "And the LORD ***will grant*** you plenty of goods..." verse 11
- "The LORD ***will open*** to you His good treasure..." verse 12
- "And the LORD ***will make*** you the head and not the tail; you shall be above only, and not be beneath..." verse 13

Of course, there is a caveat to all these great blessings, some verbs that apply to us.

- "...because you ***obey*** the voice of the LORD your God..." verse 2
- "...if you ***keep*** the commandments of the LORD your God and ***walk*** in His ways" verse 9
- "...if you ***heed*** the commandments of the LORD your God, which I command you today, and are careful to observe them. So you ***shall not turn aside*** from any of the words

which I command you this day, to the right hand or to the left, to go after other gods to serve them." verses 13-14

So let's understand this grammar lesson. All I have to do is obey God's voice, keep His commandments, and be careful not to turn from them. He promises to <u>command</u> blessings that will <u>overtake</u> me (Heb. nasag = reach out and grab me), to <u>establish</u> me as His own, to <u>grant</u> me plenty of goods, to <u>open</u> to me His good treasure, and <u>make</u> me to be above only. I obey, and He commands, establishes, grants, opens, and makes. Easy choice. Such a deal!

#56
February 25: What's in a Name?

In Judges chapter 13, the Angel of the Lord appears to Manoah and his wife to tell them they will be the parents of Samson, the next judge of Israel. Twice, the Angel identifies Himself by name; once in verse 11, He says, "I am," and once in verse 18, He says His name is "Wonderful."

As New Testament believers, we recognize the above names and realize that Manoah and his wife were talking to Jesus. Jesus is God and God identified Himself to Moses as "I am." Then in Isaiah 9:6, the famous passage that heralds the coming of Jesus says. "...and his name shall be called Wonderful, Counsellor, The mighty God, The everlasting Father, The Prince of Peace" (KJV). The Hebrew word here used for "Wonderful" comes from the same root as the identification used by the Angel of the Lord to Manoah and his wife in Judges 13:18.

I'm so grateful for the name of Jesus. It's a strong tower into which I can run for safety (Prov. 18:10), and there is no other name by which I can be saved (Acts 4:12). A name is personal, and I'm grateful for my personal, God—the true Mr.Wonderful.

#57
February 26: Removing His Hand

God is immensely serious about His work and His workers. When He has a job for us to do, He expects for us to do it. When we don't, there will be a cost.

Take Samson for example. Chapters 13 – 16 of Judges tell us his whole story. Here he was, a judge in Israel, expected to relieve God's people from the oppression of the Philistines. Despite his weakness for the wrong women, God had allowed Samson to have some successes against the enemy. His downfall came when he shared with Delilah the secret of his great strength. This woman had tried to destroy him three previous times. By not jealously protecting the vow he had made to God, he set up the circumstance for his own ruin.

We never want to find ourselves in Samson's position. When God removes His hand of favor and blessing, we could end up like this sad judge. Consider the digression outlined in Judges 16:20-21.

1. "And she [Delilah] said, 'The Philistines are upon you, Samson!' So he awoke from his sleep, and said, 'I will go out as before, at other times, and shake myself free!' But he did not know that the LORD had departed from him" (verse 20). God will lift His hand when we despise the vows we've made to Him. Ecclesiastes 5:4-5 says, "When you make a vow to God, do not delay in fulfilling it... It is better not to vow than to make a vow and not fulfill it" (NIV)

2. "Then the Philistines took him and put out his eyes..." (verse 21). Of all my senses, I think I value my sight the most. It's pretty depressing to always be in darkness, especially if that darkness goes beyond the physical. When God removes His hand, we can no longer see what we actually should be seeing.

3. "...and brought him down to Gaza..." (verse 21). The most uncomfortable place to be is in the midst of a bunch of people who despise everything you stand for. When God removes His hand, we will find ourselves in places we hate and have no business being.

4. "...They bound him with bronze fetters..." (verse 21). The enemy has a way of tying us up in our sin. Proverbs 5:22-23 says, "The evil deeds of a wicked man ensnare him; the

71

cords of his sin hold him fast. He will die for lack of discipline, led astray by his own great folly" (NIV). When God removes His hand, we'll find ourselves entrapped.

5. "...and he became a grinder in the prison" (verse 21). What a waste when we are no longer operating in the wonderful calling God had intended for us. When God removes His hand, we'll end up spinning our wheels, working begrudgingly at that which God never called us to do.

Weak, blind, in the wrong place, bound, and grinding out life. What a pathetic end. As his hair grew back, he was reminded of who God had intended for him to be. He gained enough renewed strength to kill a bunch of the Philistines as he died by collapsing their own temple onto them all. But Samson never regained his physical sight nor did he ever return to work as Israel's judge.

Samson's story is a tragic one. Let's be determined today to stay the course. Be diligent about that which God has called us to do and guard that calling carefully.

#58
February 27: God's Word is Enough

In First Samuel chapter one, Hannah prays to have a son. She is so distraught over her distress that she is not even able to eat, so she goes to God with a very specific prayer. She is so serious about it that she adds a vow to her request. She says first, look on my affliction; then, remember me; then, give me a male child. Finally she vows to give him back to the Lord and that no razor would come upon his head. (I Sam. 1:11)

Eli the priest saw Hannah praying and when he recognized her sincerity, he blessed her and prophesied that God would grant her petition. Right then, Hannah stopped crying, changed her whole attitude, and acted as if her prayer had been answered.

That's what has caught my eye. Hannah didn't have her baby; in fact, she wasn't even pregnant yet, but look at her attitude. Once she received the word from God, her faith in His word took over and she moved as if the manifestation was already there. May we learn to live by faith in God's word even before we see results. "For we walk by faith, not by sight" First Corinthians 5:7 ((KJV).

#59
February 28: God's Standards

Standards of behavior exist in every relationship and institution. In kindergarten, we learned to sit on the mat for story time and lie on our blankies for naps. In elementary school, we were expected to sit in our seats at the appropriate times, line up for recess, and share the playground equipment. The standards got more complicated in middle and high school because not only the teachers, but other kids were imposing standards of behavior on us, and if we wanted to be cool, sometimes those standards clashed. Then there were the standards regarding relationships. We worried about doing things right with friends, best friends, boy/girlfriends, teachers, counselors, etc. Later there came employers and the stresses associated with the standards of the workplace.

First and foremost though, were the standards we learned at home. Dad and Mom expected us to act a certain way in their presence and show forth the standards we learned when in public. Common phrases may have been, "We don't act that way in this family," or "Do not embarrass us."

God has set standards too. When Saul was chosen as the first king of Israel, Samuel "explained to the people the behavior of royalty, and wrote it in a book..." First Samuel 10:25 (NKJ). Kingship was new to everyone and explanation was needed. First Peter 2:9 says of us, "But you are a chosen generation, a royal priesthood, a holy nation, His own special people, that you may proclaim the praises of Him who called you out of darkness into His marvelous light" (NKJ).

There is a standard set for the behavior of royalty and that's who we are as the people of God. There are certain ways we do and don't act in this family. Let's please not embarrass ourselves.

#60
February 29: The Heart Seer

When Saul needed to be replaced as king of Israel, God sent Samuel in search of the replacement with very strict instructions. "Now the LORD said to Samuel, 'How long will you mourn for Saul, seeing I have rejected him from reigning over Israel? Fill your horn with oil, and go; I am sending you to Jesse the Bethlehemite. For I have provided Myself a king among his sons... Do not look at his appearance or at the height of his stature... For the LORD does not see as man sees; for man looks at the outward appearance, but the LORD looks at the heart'" 1 Sam 16:1 and 7 (NKJ).

People who appear to be perfect for the job, groomed for the position, or just right as a future spouse, may not be. Take a clue from God, the heart seer, and look deeper. We may not be able to see the person's heart, but we can read character. Old adages have stuck around because of the kernels of truth they possess, and two apply here: You can't judge a book by its cover, and things (nor people) are not always what they seem. Pray about the people we're about to let into our lives.

As God could see the future king's heart, so He can see the true character and intentions of the hearts of those around us. Instead of falling for the pretty or handsome face, being bedazzled by an impressive resume, or choosing the first applicant, ask God, the Heart Seer, to reveal to you the qualifying or disqualifying truths about that person. His guidance will keep us from entangling ourselves with toxic people. Instead, His voice will direct us to engage in mutually beneficial relationships.

#61
March 1: Trust God and Let Go

I never saw my mother drink alcohol and I asked her once why she didn't drink. She said she had tasted wine and she liked it, so that's exactly why she didn't drink. I was a kid at the time and really didn't understand. She went on to explain that she realized how detrimental it was to be an alcoholic, so since she liked the taste of wine, she saw that if she gave in to what she liked, she could end up in a situation that would definitely dishonor God, destroy her life and health, and disjoint her family.

Don't we face similar temptations? We greedily hold on to what we want—what we have a taste for—whether we should embrace it or not. We get comfortable with anger, unforgiveness, jealousy, revenge, and pride. It's even tougher to get us to let go of that shady side of our character or that secret sin we think no one knows about.

In our hearts, though, and sometimes even with friends, we divulge the negative and sinful issues we're carrying. Owning up to our leanings is good and positive, but then it's time to do something about them. Giving in to drinking alcohol to the extent she liked would have led my mother down a path away from God's best. Giving into our leanings will do the same thing.

Be like my mom: refuse to allow what you like to define a destructive course for your life. Momma—like all the rest of us who really want God to use us—had to let go of what she liked and what she wanted in deference to the possibility of that thing sending deep roots into her life that would later be too hard to pull out.

At first, letting go is really painful. Our hands cramp around what we want to keep hold onto. We'll have to trust God when we let go. I'm telling you from a person who has made it to the other side of some things, there are Godly wonders in store once we let go of what we want and trust Him to give us what He wants us to have.

The prophet Samuel says, "*As for* God, His way *is* perfect; the word of the Lord is proven; He *is* a shield to all who trust in Him" Second Samuel 22:31 (NKJ). The Psalmist expands on that thought in the 18th division. "The Lord is my rock and my fortress and my deliverer; My God, my strength, in whom I will trust... I will call upon the Lord, *who is worthy* to be praised; so shall I be saved from my enemies... And the floods of ungodliness made me afraid... [but] In my distress I called upon the Lord, and cried out to my God. He heard my voice from His temple, and my cry came before Him, *even* to His ears" Psalm 18:2-6 (NKJ).

God is trustworthy. Put your hope and confidence in Him and let go.

#62
March 2: Except

"And Solomon loved the LORD, walking in the statutes of his father David, except that he sacrificed and burned incense at the high places" First Kings 3:3 (NKJ).

It was certain that Solomon loved the Lord. It was also certain that Solomon lived by (walked in) the same statutes by which his father, the great King David, lived. However, the foreshadowing of a problem began early in Solomon's reign. When he was still a young man, he was doing most things well, but in First Kings 3:3, we read the word "except." When Solomon decided to leave the high places and use them, he allowed an opening for corruption to creep in.

For a while there in his early reign, things were flowing along well. Solomon was rewarded by God for asking for wisdom (chapter 3), everyone in the kingdom had peace and prosperity (chapter 4), he planned and built the temple of God (chapters 5 – 6), he constructed an amazing house of his own (chapter 7), and dedicated the temple (chapter 8). In chapter 9, we read of zero unemployment, and by chapter 10, his fame had so spread that the Queen of Sheba felt compelled to visit to see for herself if the rumors of the great wisdom and wealth of this king and his empire were true. They were.

Oh, but that exception of the high places which was but a tiny crack eight chapters earlier became a gaping chasm by chapter eleven. Solomon's love for many foreign women caused him to allow them to build temples to their gods on those high places, and then he joined his wives as they worshipped those gods (see First Kings 11:1-8). The outcome? "So the LORD became angry with Solomon because his heart had turned from the LORD God of Israel, who had appeared to him twice, and had commanded him concerning this thing, that he should not go after other gods; but he did not keep what the LORD had commanded. Therefore the LORD said to Solomon, 'Because you have done this, and have not kept My covenant and My statutes, which I have commanded you, I will surely tear the kingdom away from you and give it to your servant'" First Kings 11:9-11 (NKJ).

Indulged exceptions to God's word always make God angry and lead to loss. Can it be said of you, "She's got it together, except..." or "In the main he's pretty solid, except..."? What are those little exceptions with which you refuse to deal?

Beware. Indulging those exceptions can one day turn into problems larger than you ever expected, and you'll lose more than you thought you were gaining by making those exceptions in the first place. It is God's will that we get rid of our exceptions; that is, tear down our high places.

#63
March 3: Just Do God

At the end of each school year, the final chapel service we had at our school was conducted by the outgoing senior class. After they gave the message, they each spoke from their hearts to the remaining students. Every year, it was the same admonition: don't procrastinate, you'll be sorry; listen to the teachers, we found out they really did know what they were talking about; etc. One year, however, one student told the student body something different. Brittney said, "Just do you. You're probably going to keep on being lazy and waiting until the last minute anyway just like I did. And you'll probably end up working hard to make things up just like I'm doing. I hope I graduate and I hope you graduate, but since you're not going to listen anyway, just do you."

Brittney's sarcastic advice was given to let the upcoming classes see that it would actually be an ignorant move to continue doing things their way. Hopefully, her listeners would be astute enough to figure, "Wow, if I "just do me," I will end up struggling and possibly missing graduation. I need to change and do things some other way."

I thought of Brittney's advice as I read of the widow of Zarephath this morning in First Kings 17:8-24. She was going about "just doing her." There was a severe famine in the land and Elijah requested that she bring him some water and a little bread. Knowing she was down to her last little bit of flour and oil, she told him she was gathering sticks to cook that last meal for herself and her son and then they'd have no more and would die. Elijah said to her, "Do not fear; go and do as you have said, but make me a small cake from it first, and bring it to me; and afterward make some for yourself and your son. For thus says the LORD God of Israel: 'The bin of flour shall not be used up, nor shall the jar of oil run dry, until the day the LORD sends rain on the earth'" I King 17:13-14 (NKJ).

In essence, Elijah told the widow, "Don't do you right now. Do God. By doing for me, God will do for you." The amazing thing is that she actually changed her plan. The provisions she had did not line up with the directive she was being given, but her attitude was, "No matter what the circumstances, I'll do God before I'll do me."

Today, no matter what the provisions look like, listen to the Spirit, change your plan, and just do God.

#64
March 4: Lip Service vs. Body Service

During the divided kingdom era in the Old Testament, Ahab was an extremely wicked king of Israel. In fact, the Bible says, "Ahab... did evil in the sight of the LORD, more than all who were before him. And it came to pass, as though it had been a trivial thing... he took as wife Jezebel the daughter of Ethbaal, king of the Sidonians; and he went and served Baal and worshiped him. Then he set up an altar for Baal in the temple of Baal, which he had built in Samaria. And Ahab made a wooden image. Ahab did more to provoke the LORD God of Israel to anger than all the kings of Israel who were before him" I King 16:30-33 (NKJ).

God got sick of Ahab, Jezebel, and all their shenanigans, especially after Jezebel massacred the prophets of God she could find (see First Kings 18:4). Moreover, He was disgusted that the populace – the children of Israel – went right along with their wicked royal leaders, giving lip service to loving God, but giving body service to Baal, the false god, through their worship of the images. So God sent the prophet Elijah to Ahab for a contest up on Mount Carmel to settle the question, "Who really is God?" Once everyone was gathered, Elijah spoke these words, "How long will you falter between two opinions? If the LORD is God, follow Him; but if Baal, follow him" I King 18:21 (NKJ).

The Hebrew word (pacach) translated "falter" in this verse is translated as "waver" in the NIV and NLT, "hesitate" in the NASB, "not decide" in the NCV, and "sit on the fence" in The Message. Pacach literally means "to hop, to limp, and to dance." The picture is drawn of a person indecisively jumping back and forth so as not to fully commit to either side.

Well, what happened after Elijah asked his question? The rest of First Kings 18 details one of the most exciting incidents in the Bible as God humiliated the prophets of Baal and left no shadow of a doubt about who He is – the true and living God.

My question for you is this: what is it going to take to get you to stop straddling between two opinions? What has God said that you just won't believe and obey? In what areas of your life are you faltering, wavering, hesitating, not deciding, sitting on the fence, and hopping back and forth? Make up your mind. Stop giving lip service to loving God while your body service is attached to your Baal. As the prophet said, "If the LORD is God, follow Him; but if Baal, follow him." Just remember, to keep hopping is to have made a choice – you've chosen Baal, and by doing so, you've chosen the corresponding consequences. Think it through.

#65
March 5: God's Ideas Trump Ours

My brother and his Marine Corps buddies taught me how to play Bid Whist. In most hands of this card game, players are required to choose a trump suit. Wikipedia explains that the cards thus designated as trump cards for that hand of play outrank all cards of plain or non-trump suits. In other contexts, the term "trump card" can refer to any sort of action, authority, or policy which automatically prevails over all others. We never played the card game to win anything but bragging rights, but those Marines would play that game as though they were taking the next important hill. What fun it was to strategize with your partner, depend upon the support of the cards he held, and toss down a trump card to wipe out what the opposing team thought would be a sure winner.

God's ideas operate much like trump cards. We have our thoughts about how things should play out, and then He comes along and tosses a trump on the table. This happened to a guy in Second Kings chapter five.

Naaman, the commander of the army of the king of Syria, had unfortunately contracted leprosy. His wife's servant girl, a young lady from the land of Israel, told her mistress, "If only my master were with the prophet who is in Samaria! For he would heal him of his leprosy" First Kings 5:3 (NKJ). Word of this got to

Naaman and so he went to Elisha to be healed. Elisha didn't even come out of his house, but sent word to Naaman saying, "Go and wash in the Jordan seven times, and your flesh shall be restored to you, and you shall be clean" First Kings 5:10.

Washing seven times seems like a simple enough direction, but Naaman didn't see it that way at first. The story continues, "But Naaman became furious, and went away and said, 'Indeed, I said to myself, 'He will surely come out to me, and stand and call on the name of the LORD his God, and wave his hand over the place, and heal the leprosy. Are not the Abanah and the Pharpar, the rivers of Damascus, better than all the waters of Israel? Could I not wash in them and be clean?' So he turned and went away in a rage" First Kings 5:11-12. Naaman's servants then had to talk some sense into him saying, "My father, if the prophet had told you to do something great, would you not have done it? How much more then, when he says to you, 'Wash, and be clean'?" First Kings 5:13. I guess Naaman must have looked at his white, diseased, leprosy skin and realized how stupid he was sounding. So he got himself down to the Jordan, dipped seven times, and sure enough, "his flesh was restored like the flesh of a little child, and he was clean" First Kings 5:14.

God's idea for Naaman's healing trumped Naaman's idea for how his healing should happen. That's always the way. God's ideas trump ours. There's nothing wrong with having ideas, but we must be careful never to let them interfere with the manner in which God decides to handle our situation. As in Bid Whist, we just have to be good-natured about the fact that sometimes, our best play will be trumped by a better play. God's got all the trump cards. I'm glad He's at the table.

#66
March 6: Surprise!

We know the classic surprise party routine. The guest of honor enters a room (sometimes blindfolded, sometimes in the dark) and suddenly lots of his or her closest friends and acquaintances jump from their hiding places to yell, "Surprise!" Smiles and hugs ensue and a good time is had by all.

Elisha's servant must have felt something like a blindfolded birthday boy when he was suddenly allowed to see the army of the Lord that had come to the rescue. After running panic-stricken to Elisha with news of being surrounded by a great army, the servant announced, "Alas, my master! What shall we do?" First Kings 6:15 (NKJ)

The Scripture goes on to tell us of Elisha's response. "So he answered, 'Do not fear, for those who are with us are more than those who are with them.' And Elisha prayed, and said, 'LORD, I pray, open his eyes that he may see.' Then the LORD opened the eyes of the young man, and he saw. And behold, the mountain was full of horses and chariots of fire all around Elisha" First Kings 6:16-17 (NKJ).

Surprise!

When fear strikes, God has a habit of opening eyes and saying, "Surprise!" When the children of Israel left Egypt, they feared they were surrounded by the sea, the mountains, and the approaching Egyptian army. But surprise! Moses told them, "Do not be afraid. Stand still, and see the salvation of the LORD, which He will accomplish for you today...
The LORD will fight for you, and you shall hold your peace" Exodus 14:13-14 (NKJ). Their open eyes then beheld their escape route through the miraculously divided sea. When Martha's brother Lazarus had died because Jesus had taken too long to get to her home, she feared all hope was gone. Jesus reassured her that He Himself was the resurrection that her brother needed and then he headed for the tomb. However, when He told the people to roll the stone away, Martha protested. Jesus told her, "Did I not say to you that if you would believe you would see the glory of God?" John 11:40 (NKJ) Surprise! When Jesus called his name, Martha's eyes beheld Lazarus living again.

What's your fear today: illness, loneliness, financial reversal, trouble with children, etc? Stand still, look up, and allow God to open your eyes to His ability to calm those fears. He is no respecter of persons. He loves you just as much as He loved Elisha's servant, the children of Israel, and Martha. Be ready to smile when He says of your situation, "Surprise!"

#67
March 7: God of the Desperate Cry

The Merriam-Webster dictionary defines "desperate" as "having lost hope, giving no ground for hope, involving or employing extreme measures in an attempt to escape defeat or frustration, suffering extreme need or anxiety, and involving extreme danger or possible disaster of extreme intensity." The word comes from the Latin "desperatus:" "de" meaning "away," and "sperare" meaning "hope." So when we are desperate we are away from hope.

King Hezekiah knew what desperation felt like. Second Kings chapter 20 reveals that he faced one of the major sources of the feeling of desperation for many people—facing his death for which he was not ready. We know he wasn't ready because God sent Isaiah the prophet to him to tell him to set his house in order because he was about to die (see verse 1). Hezekiah then wept bitterly and sent up a desperate cry to the Lord saying, "Remember now, O LORD, I pray, how I have walked before You in truth and with a loyal heart, and have done what was good in Your sight" Second Kings 20:3 (NKJ).

God heard Hezekiah's desperate cry and told Isaiah to go back to him and say, "Thus says the LORD, the God of David your father: 'I have heard your prayer, I have seen your tears; surely I will heal you. On the third day you shall go up to the house of the LORD. And I will add to your days fifteen years. I will deliver you and this city from the hand of the king of Assyria; and I will defend this city for My own sake, and for the sake of My servant David'" Second Kings 20:5-6 (NKJ).

Have you ever been desperate? Perhaps you are feeling desperation right now. Do what Hezekiah did; cry out to God. God will give you exactly what you need because, as with Hezekiah, He is still the God who hears your prayers and sees your tears. Remember how the word "desperate" means "having no hope?" That's not you. Read Romans 5:1-5:

- Therefore, having been justified by faith, we have peace with God through our Lord Jesus Christ, through whom also we have access by faith into this grace in which we stand, and *rejoice in hope* of the glory of God. And not only that, but we also glory in tribulations, knowing that tribulation produces perseverance; and perseverance, character; and character, **hope**. Now **hope** does not disappoint, because the love of God has been poured out in our hearts by the Holy Spirit who was given to us. (NKJ, emphasis added)

Three times in this passage, Paul mentions hope. Hope is the opposite of desperation. When you are at the end of yourself, you've just reached the start of what God can do. Cry out to God. Place your hope in Him. He will come through for you.

#68 March 8:
Prayers God Always Answers with "Yes"

I was speaking with a discouraged friend this week who felt it was a long time since her prayers had received a "yes" answer from God. She's been in a winter season of her life for some time and the stress is wearing on her spirit. She had even begun to feel as though her personal sins were so huge that God had just said, "I'm finished with you."

Have you ever been there? I have, so I knew exactly how she was feeling. Sometimes, when those winter seasons of life last more than the usual 3-month stretch, we get antsy about what could be causing the drought. It's at times like these when we must rely on the only thing left standing—the truth.

1. God loves you. Regardless of the situation or the surrounding and pressing circumstances, God has not stopped loving you.
2. Those sins you think are so insurmountable: pish-tosh! There is not one sin that wasn't washed away at Calvary. If your particular sin could keep you from God, Jesus' death and resurrection were ineffective.
3. Seasons of life don't have the same time restrictions as calendar seasons. The major similarity between the two is that seasons do change.
4. God does answer your prayers. "Yes" is the answer we usually want; however, "no" and "wait" are also answers. The question is, can we trust Him to be doing the right thing when His answers are other than "yes"?

God always answers with a "yes" when our prayers center

on His glory. Jabez had everything going against him: his brothers were dishonorable, and his mother even saddled him with a name that meant "to grieve and be sorrowful." Yet, Jabez's prayers had nothing to do with bewailing his family situation and his pitiful lot in life. He called on God saying, "Oh, that You would bless me indeed, and enlarge my territory, that Your hand would be with me, and that You would keep me from evil, that I may not cause pain!" First Chronicles 4:10 (NKJ). We have no idea how long it took, but this verse ends with the wonderful declaration that "God granted him what he requested."

The prayer of Jabez did not ignore the fact that he wanted to be blessed ("bless me indeed, and enlarge my territory"), but the focus was not so much on him as it was on the end result, to bring God glory. You see, Jabez was looking to use his blessing and enlarged territory to show others that God's hand was with him. By being kept from evil and not causing pain, others would look at Jabez and see his God. When Jabez expressed the focus of his requests, God knew his heart was right and granted them.

I am not suggesting that my friend's heart is not right. In fact, knowing her as I do, I believe her heart is one of the purest toward God that I know. I am suggesting that we all need to take a closer look at our prayers and their ultimate purpose. Are we more concerned with our comfort or God's glory? Can we turn the corner in our prayer lives and focus more on God and what He wants and less on ourselves and what we want? Can we trust that even in winter seasons of life, God still has us in the palm of His hand and He knows exactly what He's doing? Once the results of our prayers are completely about His glory, "this is the confidence that we have in Him, that if we ask anything according to His will, He hears us. And if we know that He hears us, whatever we ask, we know that we have the petitions that we have asked of Him" First John 5:14-15 (NKJ).

#69
March 9: The Battle-Winning
Strategy and Helper

Do you want to know how to win battles? Take a clue from some of the Israelites. First Chronicles chapter five gives us a glimpse of some battle-winning strategy.

- The sons of Reuben, the Gadites, and half the tribe of Manasseh *had* forty-four thousand seven hundred and sixty valiant men, men able to bear shield and sword, to shoot with the bow, and skillful in war, who went to war. They made war with the Hagrites, Jetur, Naphish, and Nodab. (First Chronicles 5:18-19, NKJ)

The sons of Reuben, the Gadites, and half the tribe of Manasseh went into the battle prepared.
- They had 44,760 valiant, skilled soldiers
- They were strong enough to carry all their armor and swords
- They were expert marksmen
- They were capable, competent, and proficient in the ways of war
- They were engaged in the battle—no one was slothful or holding back

These guys were the Green Beret of their day, the SWAT officers, the special unit. Yet there was one more piece to their victory strategy. Even though they used every ounce of training and their own ability, they did not forget to carry with them their biggest gun of all—reliance upon God. "And they were helped against [their enemies], and the Hagrites were delivered into their hand, and all who *were* with them, *for they cried out to God in the battle. He heeded their prayer, because they put their trust in Him*" First Chronicles 5:20, NKJ (emphasis added).

When we face our enemies—especially the hellish horde, our spiritual foes—it's a good battle plan to start by rallying the troops. Pull together those stalwart saints who we know will engage in the battle on their knees with us. Then wear and carry the armor; don't get caught without the belt of truth, the breastplate of righteousness, the good news shoes, the shield of faith, the helmet of salvation, and the sword of the Spirit, which is the Word of God. Keep practiced up in proper sword use by "rightly dividing the Word" (see Second Timothy 2:15), and be strong and courageous, standing firm against all the methodology of the adversary.

Then, let's not forget to pull God into the mix. It is His power that will ultimately help us to win. Notice that the Israelites cried out to God "in the battle." *As* they fought, God "helped them against...all who were with [the enemy]." My mom used to say,

"Work like everything depends on you; pray like everything depends on God." The winning strategy is to fight and pray. It works every time.

#70
March 10: God's Choices; Our Choices

Here in America, we choose our Presidents via the democratic process of voting. The citizens of this country size up many candidates, listen to debates, read newspaper articles, and watch the pundits as they argue back and forth. Some of us pray about our decision. In the end, according to our system, the majority rules. In the last election, Barack Obama was voted to become our 44th President of the United States.

Around the same time, Iran chose a leader. The citizens of that country voted too, but the country was in an uproar because it was questionable as to whether or not those votes were counted accurately. According to the masses of people demonstrating in the streets, the guy who was re-elected as their leader, Mahmoud Ahmadinejad, was not the guy most of the people voted for.

The democratic process works when it is not corrupted and when the minority honors the choice of the majority. However, God's system of putting people in leadership positions is not a democracy. God rules by theocracy. According to Wikipedia:

> **Theocracy** is a form of government in which a god or deity is recognized as the state's supreme civil ruler... In Biblical Greek, "theocracy" means a rule by God. For believers, theocracy is a form of government in which divine power governs an earthly human state, either in a personal incarnation or, more often, via religious institutional representatives (i.e., a church), replacing or dominating civil government.

When it came time for David to take over as king in place of Saul, God told Samuel the prophet. Samuel, in turn, anointed David to be king. The only problem was that Saul had not yet given up the throne. First Chronicles chapters 11 and 12 detail how thousands and thousands of men began to switch their allegiance from Saul to David. "For at that time they came to

David day by day to help him, until it was a great army, like the army of God... and (they) came to David at Hebron to turn over the kingdom of Saul to him, according to the word of the LORD" First Chronicles 12:22-23 (NKJ).

We'd like theocracy to apply to our country, but even if it can't, we can allow it to apply in our personal lives. Are we choosing to faithfully follow those whom God has set up for us to follow? Women, are we choosing our mates wisely, according to divine leading rather than devilish lust? Men are you choosing your earthly spiritual leaders (pastors and mentors) by God's direction? Children, are you being obedient to the righteous parents God has placed over you?

God is still well able to choose our leaders. The question is, will we wisely choose to follow those who God has chosen?

#71
March 11: It's Inevitable

Certain outcomes are just the natural byproduct of certain actions. If we plant a rose bush, water and prune it correctly, we'll end up with roses. If we study our school work, attend classes, and pay attention to the professors, we'll end up with a degree. If we save money—even a little bit each month—we'll end up with the finances we'll need for a rainy day and for some things we can enjoy. Roses, a degree, discretionary income: all the inevitable outcome of dedicated, determined action on our part.

When we determine to allow the presence of God to reign in our lives, there is an inevitable outcome associated with that determination. First Chronicles 13:14 reads, "The ark of God remained with the family of Obed-Edom in his house three months. And the LORD blessed the house of Obed-Edom and all that he had" (NKJ). Simply by allowing the ark—the presence of God—to remain in his house, Obed-Edom's house was blessed. The Hebrew word for "blessed" is "barak" and is used here to mean "abundantly benefited."

Could you use an abundant benefit today? Determine to allow the presence of God to take up residence in your home and in your life. Blessing is inevitable.

#72
March 12: Our Great Big God

When Solomon was about to ascend to the throne, his father, King David, charged him with the job of building a temple for the name of the Lord. This would be a daunting task. David had stored up an abundant supply of materials and treasures for him to use for that purpose, but when he got ready to start the work, he began to amass even more. While securing the help of Hiram, king of Tyre, Solomon said, "And the temple which I build will be great, for our God is greater than all gods. But who is able to build Him a temple, since heaven and the heaven of heavens cannot contain Him?" Second Chronicles 2:5-6a (NKJ).

Solomon realized that all the cedar, silver, gold, and precious stones he could use still would never really be enough to build an earthly structure large enough or great enough to house our heavenly Father. That didn't mean he should give up on his effort. Solomon still gave it his very best shot. He built an amazingly grand temple using the best architects and artisans, and all the best components.

The point of Solomon's temple was not to contain God, but to glorify Him. Our best efforts are to be put forth to do the same thing. We don't bring God down to our level, we raise our praise to Him and do our best for him to lift Him up. Jesus Himself said, "And I, if I am lifted up from the earth, will draw all peoples to Myself" John 12:32 (NKJ). Our job is to do the lifting. Like Solomon, we want others to see and understand that "our God is greater than all gods." Nothing shabby or shoddy coming from our hands will make that declaration.

#73
March 13: Indoor Cloud

We're used to seeing clouds outside, up in the heavens. Wouldn't you be surprised to see a cloud inside a building? Well, that's exactly what the people of God saw at the dedication of Solomon's temple. Second Chronicles 5:13-14 says, "Indeed it came to pass, when the trumpeters and singers were as one, to make one sound to be heard in praising and thanking the LORD, and when they lifted up their voice with the trumpets and cymbals and instruments of music, and praised the LORD, saying: 'For He is good, for His mercy endures forever,' that the house, the house of the LORD, was filled with a cloud, so that the priests could not continue ministering because of the cloud; for the glory of the LORD filled the house of God" (NKJ).

Notice here that God's glory manifested itself when His people praised and thanked Him in unity. The one sound heard was "in praising and thanking the Lord." The people weren't thinking of themselves, the musicians weren't performing for the accolades of the people, and the singers weren't trying to garner votes from the judges. Everyone present had only one thought in mind, "For He is good, and His mercy endures forever!" It's as if God sighed in appreciation and His sweet breath filled the room as that cloud. The priests even had to stop ministering; God's presence was simply overwhelming.

God still desires such praise and thanks from us. He doesn't want performance and a talent show while we're in church; He simply wants our sincere praise and thanks. One day, if we can ever all get on one accord in church at the same time, God could manifest an indoor cloud for us as well. God's presence would be so overwhelming that the preacher couldn't preach, the deacons couldn't deac, and the ushers couldn't ush. To welcome God's presence to that degree, be a committee of one during your church service and spend that time in concentrated praise and thanks to our God who is so good that His mercy endures forever.

#74
March 14: God Welcomes You Back

When the work on the temple of God was finished in Second Chronicles chapter 6, Solomon brought all the people together for a dedication service. In front of them all, the king knelt down, spread out his hands toward heaven, and began to pray. He acknowledged two things: the greatness of God, and the people's penchant to sin. He then went through a list of situations about which he asked God to forgive the people.

- Verse 22: "If anyone sins against his neighbor..."
- Verse 24: "Or if Your people Israel are defeated before an enemy because they have sinned against You..."

- Verse 26: "When the heavens are shut up and there is no rain because they have sinned against You..."
- Verse 28: "When there is famine in the land, pestilence, or blight...whatever plague or whatever sickness there is..."

By the time King Solomon gets toward the end of the prayer, he's realizing that the people could continue to sin until God would get so fed up with them that He'd put them out of their wonderful Promised Land. To cover even this possibility, Solomon prays,

"When they sin against You (for there is no one who does not sin), and You become angry with them and deliver them to the enemy, and they take them captive to a land far or near; yet when they come to themselves in the land where they were carried captive, and repent, and make supplication to You in the land of their captivity, saying, 'We have sinned, we have done wrong, and have committed wickedness'; and when they return to You with all their heart and with all their soul in the land of their captivity, where they have been carried captive, and pray toward their land which You gave to their fathers, the city which You have chosen, and toward the temple which I have built for Your name: then hear from heaven Your dwelling place their prayer and their supplications, and maintain their cause, and forgive Your people who have sinned against You"
Second Chronicles 6:36-39 (NKJ).

This is a prayer that God is still ready to answer today for Israel. It's also a prayer that can be applied to us. No matter what we've done, God stands ready to embrace us if we would just come back. Yes, He is angry about our sin. He hates sin, and He went to the ultimate length to provide a way out of sin's trap for us by sending Jesus to take our sin away. Now even though we insult such a great provision by willfully sinning, He still welcomes back the confessing culprit.

No matter what you're in or where you are right now, come back to God. Your sins may have taken you captive to "a land far or near." Perhaps that's a land of alcohol or drug addiction, a land of illicit sexual affairs, a land of white collar crime, or a land of violence upon others. Perhaps it's an inner land of bitterness, envy, strife, gossip, unforgiveness, or malice. From whatever land has taken you captive, the call is still the same: come back. Confess and return with your whole heart. It's still true that "whoever calls on the name of the Lord shall be saved" Romans 10:13 (NKJ).

#75
March 15: God's Conditions

Second Chronicles 7:14 "If My people who are called by My name will humble themselves, and pray and seek My face, and turn from their wicked ways, then I will hear from heaven, and will forgive their sin and heal their land" (NKJ).

One of the absolutely most difficult things to do is to humble ourselves. We don't like to be wrong, but sometimes-- considering the fact that we are not perfect (another thing we don't like to admit)--we are wrong. We usually go kicking and screaming into concession only because some more powerful source forces us to admit the very human shortcoming of being wrong. In fact, we'll sometimes (more often than not, I'm afraid) remain in the power struggle long past our full realization that we are in the wrong, just to keep from having to admit it.

Humbling ourselves only comes about when we realize that the other party will let us down graciously. Although fully justified to make fun of us, mock us, or show us up for the dummies we are, we need the party in the right to offer us a gentle out. In other words, we'll more easily humble ourselves when we know there's grace coming back at us from the one in the right.

We're in a power struggle with God every day. We don't want to bend over to lay down before Him our sinful ways, our time, our talent, or our treasure. It's a humbling experience to give up that to which we have become accustomed, that which we have come to cherish. By humbly giving those things to God, we're saying, "These no longer belong to me. You take them, God. Repair them, revive them, bless them, or even destroy them if that's what You deem best. I let them go."

Once we meet God's conditions, the blessing process can begin! What's the process?
1. Humble yourself
2. Pray
3. Seek God's face

4. Turn from your wicked ways (That's a tough one to admit.)
THEN
1. God will hear you from Heaven
2. God will forgive your sins
3. God will heal your land

Meet God's conditions. Start out by humbling yourself. Then get ready to experience some of that "land healing."

#76
March 16: When God Says No

God always answers our prayers; we just have to remember that sometimes, His answer is either "no" or "wait."

Consider the incident in Second Chronicles 11:1-17 with Rehoboam who assembled "180,000 chosen men who were warriors, to fight against Israel, that he might restore the kingdom" back to himself in Judah (vs. 1). You see, he planned to deal harshly with Israel, His neighbor and brethren, but they and their king Jeroboam rebelled. Rehoboam then felt perfectly justified in attacking because, as Solomon's son, he was the rightful next king. However, through one of God's spokesmen, God told Rehoboam, "You shall not go up or fight against your brethren" (vs. 4). The end of verse four says, "Therefore they obeyed the words of the LORD, and turned back from attacking Jeroboam."

Watch what Rehoboam did next. He didn't whine and complain about not being able to do what he wanted to do. Verses 5 – 15 go on to tell us of his activities:
* Rehoboam dwelt in Jerusalem.
* He built cities for defense in Judah.
* He fortified the strongholds.
* He put captains in the strongholds.
* He placed stores of food, oil, and wine in the strongholds.
* In every city he put shields and spears, and made them very strong, having Judah and Benjamin on his side.
* He accepted the priests and the Levites who were in all Israel. These holy men left their common-lands and their possessions, came to Judah and Jerusalem, and took their stand with Rehoboam because Jeroboam and his sons had rejected them from serving as priests to the LORD.

* He appointed for himself priests for the high places, for the demons, and the calf idols which he had made.

What was the result of all of this? All who "set their heart to seek the LORD God of Israel, came to Jerusalem to sacrifice to the LORD God of their fathers. So they strengthened the kingdom of Judah, and made Rehoboam the son of Solomon strong for three years, because they walked in the way of David and Solomon for three years" (vss. 16 – 17).

What's the point? When God says "no" or "wait," let's not just sit idly by. We must continue to live fully in the place where God has us. Fortify ourselves, our families, and our homes. Put necessary things in place. Accept assistance and prayer covering from other holy people, and get mentored by spiritually-grounded saints who can tell us about our high places, help us ward off the demons, and warn us about the idols we are in danger of making. We mustn't cry and complain, but putting hand to plow, we can be productive right where we are. We'll see a fruitful product and still have good success.

#77
March 17: God's Game Plan

In Second Chronicles chapter 14, King Asa was doing really well. He had a heart for God and we read about a miraculous deliverance:

- "And Asa had an army of three hundred thousand from Judah... Then Zerah the Ethiopian came out against them with an army of a million men and three hundred chariots... So Asa went out against him... And Asa cried out to the LORD his God, and said, "LORD, it is nothing for You to help, whether with many or with those who have no power; help us, O LORD our God, for we rest on You, and in Your name we go against this multitude. O LORD, You are our God; do not let man prevail against You!" So the LORD struck the Ethiopians before Asa and Judah, and the Ethiopians fled... So the Ethiopians were overthrown, and they could not recover..." Second Chronicles 14:8-13 (NKJ).

For 35 years, King Asa ruled honorably and Judah was so obviously blessed by God that the people from Israel defected to him "when they saw that the Lord was with him" (vs. 9). He even removed his own mother from the position of Queen Mother when she "made an obscene image of Asherah" (vs. 16). But in the 36th year, when Baasha king of Israel came against Judah, Asa made a treaty with Syria to join him in stopping Baasha's advance. The alliance worked and Baasha's advancement was halted, but King Asa's actions did not please the Lord. Here's the message that came to Asa:

- "...Because you have relied on the king of Syria, and have not relied on the LORD your God, therefore the army of the king of Syria has escaped from your hand. Were the Ethiopians and the Lubim not a huge army with very many chariots and horsemen? Yet, because you relied on the LORD, He delivered them into your hand. For the eyes of the LORD run to and fro throughout the whole earth, to show Himself strong on behalf of those whose heart is loyal to Him. In this you have done foolishly..." Second Chronicles 16:7-9 (NKJ).

What happens to us after an amount of time of living under God's blessings? Like Asa, we must start thinking we're smart enough and strong enough to handle enemy attacks with our own ingenuity. You see, when we were baby Christians – new in the faith – we knew we had no strength and were helpless in the face of challenges unless God came in to show Himself strong. We asked and we saw God move! At the beginning, Asa gathered the troops and then he prayed and God worked. Nothing has changed in God's game plan. Hebrews 13:8 says it plainly, "Jesus Christ is the same yesterday, today, and forever." God intends for us to depend on Him in every new challenge the same way we depended upon Him when we didn't know any better.

James 5:15-16 says, "And the prayer offered in faith will make the sick person well; the Lord will raise him up. If he has sinned, he will be forgiven. Therefore confess your sins to each other and pray for each other so that you may be healed. The prayer of a righteous man is powerful and effective" (NIV). What are you trying to handle on your own today? Gather the troops, pray, and watch God work.

#78
March 18: Huge Problems? No Sweat for God

When Asa, Solomon's grandson, became king, there was no turmoil going on in the land. For the first ten years of his reign, "the land was quiet" (First Chronicles 14:1, NKJ). The passage is quick to point out, though, that "Asa did what was good and right in the eyes of the Lord his God" (verse 2). In other words, don't get it twisted, Asa's submission to God was resulting in blessing. Asa then used the peace wisely. Verse 7 tells us, "Therefore he said to Judah, 'Let us build these cities and make walls around them, and towers, gates, and bars, while the land is yet before us, because we have sought the LORD our God; we have sought Him, and He has given us rest on every side.' So they built and prospered" (NKJ). Asa also had an army of 300,000 mighty men of valor. There may have been peace, but Asa was no dummy. He knew other kings were always on the lookout for someone to overthrow.

And soon enough it happened. "Zerah the Ethiopian came out against them with an army of a million men and three hundred chariots" (verse 9). What's 300,000 against a million? Asa's army was outnumbered more than 3 to 1. So Asa did what he'd always done; he relied on God. "LORD, [Asa cried], "it is nothing for You to help, whether with many or with those who have no power; help us, O LORD our God, for we rest on You, and in Your name we go against this multitude. O LORD, You are our God; do not let man prevail against You!" (verse 11)

Asa knew his good fortune had been riding on his relationship with God, and he had continually given God thanks and glory for it. Now that a problem arose, it was not time to switch gears and think God had changed. God could still be relied upon to take care of him and his people. In fact, Asa realized that Zerah was not attacking him; Zerah was attacking God. Read again the last line of Asa's prayer, "You are our God; do not let man prevail against You!"

What was the outcome for Asa? "The LORD struck the Ethiopians and [they] fled. And Asa and the people who were with him pursued them... so the Ethiopians were overthrown, and they could not recover, for they were broken before the LORD and His army. And they carried away very much spoil" (verses 12-13).

Asa understood a very important principle. When we live our lives to glorify God, He is on display. Therefore, when someone comes against us, in reality, they are coming against God who is in us. And God cannot be outdone or defeated. Keep prayed up and keep practiced up living for God in the good times. When your "Zerah" attacks, no sweat. Turn him and his army over to God and make Asa's prayer your own. Say, "Help me, O LORD my God, for I rest on You, and in Your name I go against this multitude. O LORD, You are my God; do not let man prevail against You!"

#79
March 19: Available to be Found

Do you remember playing Hide and Go Seek when you were a child? Someone would be the seeker. She'd close her eyes, face the base, and begin to count by fives. When she reached one hundred, she'd shout, "Ready of not, here I come!" She couldn't see the other kids in the game, but they usually could see her from their hiding places. It would then be her job to find the hiders.

Somewhat like the childhood game, we may come upon times when our eyes are tightly closed as we count off the troubles bombarding us. Once we open our eyes, it may seem as though we're all alone, but we're not. God is not only within earshot, His eyes are watching our every move. When we seek for Him, He is easy to find because He's always close to the base with us.

Second Chronicles 15:2 says, "...The LORD is with you while you are with Him. If you seek Him, He will be found by you..." (NKJ). Just call out. God really does want us to know Him and He makes Himself available to be found.

Ready or not, God's right there.

#80
March 20: Watching in a Good Way

When I was little, one thing I understood about God was that He was always watching me. He was able to watch everything everybody did anywhere in the whole world. I didn't have a problem with this concept; I simply believed it. After all, if God was as big and as powerful as Sunday School teachers and the pastor said He was, why couldn't He see everything everywhere at the same time?

I also had no problem with this concept as long as I was doing the right thing. I actually felt comforted to know of God's perpetual presence. This understanding about God became somewhat bothersome, however, when I wanted to willingly misbehave. I'd push it far into the back of my mind when I strayed off the straight and narrow, but I never could quite shake the knowledge that God was with me, watching everything I was doing. Although this healthy wariness didn't always keep me from committing every sin, it did succeed at producing a healthy amount of guilt—just enough to cause me to repent, turn, and be thankful when at times God revealed the precarious situations from which I escaped thanks to His eyes being on me.

As Christians, we have to come to terms with God's omnipresence. It's necessary for us to reconcile our violations with His vigilance, our crooked actions with His constant attentiveness. Rather than dread God's surveillance, let's remember the blessing of this attribute of God as expressed in Second Chronicles 16:9a. "For the eyes of the LORD run to and fro throughout the whole earth, to show Himself strong on behalf of those whose heart is loyal (completely, fully committed) to Him" (NKJ; additional words from NIV and NAS).

God is not watching us to hit us over the head with a hammer every time we mess up. He's watching us because He loves us. He excitedly waits for us to give Him the opportunity to show Himself strong on our behalf. Now that's watching in a really good way!

#81
March 21: The Deception of Other Gods

The first Commandment says, "You shall have no other gods before Me" Exodus 20:3 (NKJ). Does this mean that there are other gods that exist that we can put before the almighty God? If so, then God would have to have created other gods who were lower than Himself. Those created gods would then have the ability to rise up and tempt us to worship and obey them. Is that how it is?

Not really. All that God created was good until iniquity was found in Lucifer (see Ezekiel 28:13-15). When Lucifer (now known as Satan) led the insurrection in Heaven, God threw him out, along with the third of the angels that followed him. (Talk about a bad business partnership decision!) Since that time, human-kind has been in a war "against principalities, against powers, against the rulers of the darkness of this world, against spiritual wickedness in high places" Ephesians 6:12 (KJV). These enemies of our God tempt us to worship gods we create in our minds and with our hands.

Whole nations have revolved around the worship of such made-up gods, and Satan and his cohorts work diligently to help us believe in them. The devil and his minions actually have some ability to cause things to happen, moving us to trust in the veracity of the gods we've set up for ourselves. But there's a razor blade in the apple.

Take into consideration the example we see of King Ahaz. Second Chronicles 28:22-23 tells us: "Now in the time of his distress King Ahaz became increasingly unfaithful to the LORD. This is that King Ahaz. For he sacrificed to the gods of Damascus which had defeated him, saying, 'Because the gods of the kings of Syria help them, I will sacrifice to them that they may help me.' But they were the ruin of him and of all Israel" (NKJ).

Do not be deceived. God is still the only power in all the universe able to guide us, direct us, and do what we need done in our lives. When we wander away from Him and decide to trust in some other god, we are deciding to take matters out of His hands and put them into Satan's. Remember the bad business partnership those angels made? Do you really want to be like them?

#82
March 22: Face Time

If you have an iMac® computer, an iPhone®, or an iPad®, the Apple company provides an "app" (a service) called Face Time. Using Face Time, you can make or receive video phone calls. Now granted, sometimes you may not want the person calling to be able to see you, but let's not quibble over such details. Lately, while visiting Atlanta, GA, I had lunch with a friend I hadn't seen in person in 20 years. We had kept up with each other through letters, emails, and occasionally by phone, but it was certainly good to see Jenny face to face. We've determined not to let another 20 years go by before we're together again, but in the meantime, we can possibly at least see each other using Face Time. It's also comforting to see the faces of my sons as we talk since they no longer live at home.

God wants face time with us too. Second Chronicles 30:9 says, "…for the LORD your God is gracious and merciful, and will not turn His face from you if you return to Him" (NKJ). Notice that the verse says if we return to God, He will not turn His face from us. If we're not seeing Him, we are the ones who have turned away. All we have to do is turn toward God and we'll find He has always been looking in our direction.

We turn rightly to God when we face Him with every intention of living right before Him. The sins of the past are just that: in the past. Since God can forgive you, go ahead and forgive yourself. Turn toward God. The most comprehensive of all the Beatitudes says, "Blessed are the pure in heart, for they shall see God" Matthew 5:8 (NKJ). And isn't that our ultimate aim: to see our God face to face?

Don't you want some face time with God? He's looking your way, waiting to have face time with you.

#83
March 23: God's Got Your Back

My brother Nick is the oldest in our family and I'm the youngest; there are 14 years between us. When I was entering kindergarten, he had already started his Marine Corps career. At 5-years-old, I didn't know much about how all the military worked, but I knew my big brother was a Marine, protecting the country, and that meant he was protecting me. I carried the notion in my mind that no bully would ever be able to intimidate me because all I needed to do was call my brother and the power of the United States Marine Corps would instantly come to my aid. Because of the relationship I had with my brother, no one could have convinced me otherwise.

When King Sennacherib of Assyria (the bully) decided to attack Judah, he presented a pretty convincing argument to King Hezekiah's folks questioning God's ability to defend them against him. He brought up the fact that he and his father before him had conquered many strong nations who had all appealed to their gods for protection but to no avail. In his mind, why should things be any different now? He boasted, "Who was there among all the gods of those nations that my fathers utterly destroyed that could deliver his people from my hand, that your God should be able to deliver you from my hand? Now therefore, do not let Hezekiah deceive you or persuade you like this, and do not believe him; for no god of any nation or kingdom was able to deliver his people from my hand or the hand of my fathers. How much less will your God deliver you from my hand?" Second Chronicles 32:14-15 (NKJ)

Sennacherib went even farther. He developed a full-blown marketing plan to get his message out that God wasn't able to help. He dispersed his servants among the people of God to speak against God (like paid public announcements), he wrote letters to revile the Lord (like pop-ups and junk mail), and he even advertised in a loud voice in Hebrew, the people's own language.

Nevertheless, King Hezekiah reassured the people saying, "Be strong and courageous; do not be afraid nor dismayed before the king of Assyria, nor before all the multitude that is with him; for there are more with us than with him. With him is an arm of flesh; but with us is the LORD our God..." Second Chronicles 32:7-8 (NKJ). Then he and the prophet Isaiah prayed and cried out to heaven. Sure enough, God routed the Assyrians, causing Sennacherib to flee "shamefaced to his own land," (vs. 21) only to be murdered in his temple by his own sons.

Don't let anybody talk you out of trusting God. It doesn't matter what they say or how loud they say it to the contrary, God is who He says He is and will do what He says He will do. The latter part of Hebrews 11:6 makes this plain, "...he who comes to God must believe that He is, and that He is a rewarder of those who diligently seek Him" (NKJ). God has got your back.

#84
March 24: Give Our Grown Kids to God

Second Chronicles 33 tells us of King Manasseh. He was the son of Hezekiah, a very righteous king, so righteous that several chapters were dedicated to discuss his heart for the Lord and all the good he did. You might think that after his death, his son would have wanted to follow in his steps and receive the same abundance of blessings. But oh no, Manasseh did evil. Not only did he rebuild the altars to foreign gods, but also "he caused his sons to pass through the fire, practiced soothsaying, used witchcraft and sorcery, and consulted mediums and spiritists. He did much evil in the sight of the Lord, to provoke Him to anger. He even set up a carved image, the idol which he had made, in the house of God..." First Chronicles 33:6-7 (NKJ).

As I read, my heart was broken for this family's legacy. We're not told that Hezekiah neglected his son. Everyone knew of his love and dedication to the Lord. In fact, the nation had returned to the correct worship of God under his rule. Now here was this renegade son, seducing Judah "to do more evil than the nations whom the Lord had destroyed before the children of Israel" First Chronicles 33:9.

Of course, God would not stand for such sin and He punished Manasseh by allowing the king of Assyria to take him away to Babylon with hooks and bound with fetters of iron. That got Manasseh's attention. "Now when he was in affliction, he implored the Lord his God, and humbled himself greatly before the God of his fathers, and prayed to Him; and He received his entreaty, heard his supplication, and brought him back to Jerusalem into his kingdom. Then Manasseh knew that the Lord was God" First Chronicles 33:12-13.

Manasseh made a complete turn-around. He built the wall, took away the foreign gods and the idol in the house of the Lord, and cast out all the altars he had built. At the end of his life, all his sin was remembered, but it was recalled in contrast to his prayer, how God received his prayer, and how he humbled himself (see verse 19).

The best we parents can do is obey Proverbs 22:6, "Train up a child in the way he should go," and trust God to bring the rest to pass, "and when he is old, he shall not depart from it." If our kids act a fool after they leave our homes, they will have to answer to God for that for themselves. We certainly don't want our children to have to suffer, but if they have to do so, it's best that they do at the hands of our loving God who knows best how to get our grown children's attention.

#85
March 25: Turning the Heart of the King

God can cause our staunchest enemies to flip and suddenly assist us. They may not even be aware of why they are doing it, but they do it anyway. Take the example of the story of the rebuilding of the temple.

The book of Ezra chapters 1 – 6 tells us that God stirred the heart of King Cyrus of Persia to decree that the descendents of the Jews who had formerly been removed from Jerusalem be allowed to return and rebuild the temple. King Cyrus would even pay for the construction project out of his people's taxes. As the years went by, Darius then became king, and a "delegation from beyond the river" came upon the construction site and decided to challenge the workers as to their right to build. When the elders over the job answered that they had been given permission by the former king, the delegation sent a letter to King Darius asking for proof. King Darius had the matter researched and indeed found King Cyrus's original proclamation. King Darius then reaffirmed that decree and those who had questioned the Jews "diligently did according to what King Darius had sent" (6:13).

Once everything was cleared up, we're told:

> So the elders of the Jews built, and they prospered through the prophesying of Haggai the prophet and Zechariah the son of Iddo. And they built and finished it, according to the commandment of the God of Israel, and according to the command of Cyrus, Darius, and Artaxerxes king of Persia. Ezra 6:14 (NKJ)
> Then the children of Israel who had returned from the captivity... kept the Feast of Unleavened Bread seven days with joy; for the LORD made them joyful, and turned the heart of the king of Assyria toward them, to strengthen their hands in the work of the house of God, the God of Israel. Ezra 6:21-22 (NKJ)

Cyrus, Darius, and Artaxerxes were heathen kings, but God turned their hearts to show favor to His people. Even today, no king, ruler, president, or dictator can resist when God decides to turn their hearts. Fear no man. Our only requirement is to be sure our hearts are turned toward God; He can handle the hearts of those who oppose us. Proverbs 16:7 says it best: "When a man's ways please the LORD, he makes even his enemies to be at peace with him" (NKJ).

#86
March 26: The Good Hand of God

Both Ezra and Nehemiah used the same phrase when referring to God's hand.

Ezra 7:9 "On the first day of the first month he began his journey from Babylon, and on the first day of the fifth month he came to Jerusalem, according to the good hand of his God upon him" (NKJ).

Ezra 8:18 (When asking for servants for the house of God) "Then, by the good hand of our God upon us, they brought us a man of understanding... namely Sherebiah..." (NKJ).

Nehemiah 2:8 (When requesting timber for the temple building) "And the king granted them to me according to the good hand of my God upon me" (NKJ).

The Hebrew word for "good" is "towb" and it means "good" in the same way we would understand it in English. Anything that is beautiful, best, better, bountiful, cheerful, pleasant, precious, prosperous, sweet, wealthy, and/or well-favored would be considered to be good. The Hebrew word for "hand" is "yad" and it refers to the open hand indicating power, means, and direction. Ezra and Nehemiah realized that they were where they were, they had what they had, and were surrounded by those who they needed because of God's powerful, open-handed provision.

"The good hand of God" is a phrase we can use when we notice all that God has done—when we count our blessings. The power, means, and direction of God's good hand both supplies for us and also slaps away that which would attack us. That good hand sometimes reaches out to us with gifts of provision, but it also reaches out to us as a shield of protection, and source of direction. It can hedge us in and harm our enemies at the same time.

Ezra and Nehemiah were onto something when they spoke of the good hand of God. Let's remember on a consistent basis all the good hand of God does for us each and every day.

#87
March 27: God Raised No Fools

Sometimes people try to put things over on you. Almost every time I took my car to get my oil changed, the auto mechanic would try to sell me a new air filter. Once I reminded him that I had a husband who would look into that for me, he stopped pushing the filter and simply changed the oil like I requested. It seems like he was willing to dupe a woman, but knew better than to try to trick a man. In that and other cases when someone is trying to pull the wool over my eyes, I think back to common sense lessons my mother taught me and remind myself, "My momma didn't raise no fool."

Nehemiah must have thought the same kind of thing referring to God while he and the returned remnant were rebuilding the walls of Jerusalem. Nehemiah tells us, "Now it happened, when Sanballat, Tobiah, the Arabs, the Ammonites, and the Ashdodites heard that the walls of Jerusalem were being restored and the gaps were beginning to be closed, that they became very angry, and all of them conspired together to come and attack Jerusalem and create confusion. Nevertheless we made our prayer to our God, and because of them we set a watch against them day and night" Nehemiah 4:7-9 (NKJ).

You see, Nehemiah and those working with him didn't just stand around bemoaning the fact that their enemies were dead set on coming against them. That would have been foolish. Instead, they prepared themselves to defend themselves. Nehemiah encouraged the people by telling them, "Do not be afraid of them. Remember the Lord, great and awesome, and fight for your brethren, your sons, your daughters, your wives, and your houses" (verse 14).

What happened next was a move any parent would have been proud to see his child make. "And it happened, when our enemies heard that it was known to us, and that God had brought their plot to nothing, that all of us returned to the wall, everyone to his work. So it was, from that time on, that half of my servants worked at construction, while the other half held the spears, the shields, the bows, and wore armor; and the leaders were behind all the house of Judah. Those who built on the wall, and those who carried burdens, loaded themselves so that with one hand they worked at construction, and with the other held a weapon. Every one of the builders had his sword girded at his side as he built. And the one who sounded the trumpet was beside me" (verses 15-18).

Yes, God is "great and awesome," but His power is not diminished in the least when we stand our ground. In fact, He's the One who gives us the backbone to be able to do just that. So the next time someone is threatening you or trying to pull a fast one on you, hearken back to the story of Nehemiah and the workers on the wall. Say to yourself, "God didn't raise no fool." Call out the plot, prepare to defend yourself if necessary, and keep on working for the kingdom—building your wall.

#88
March 28: The Reaction To Understandable Words

In Nehemiah chapter 8 (NKJ) during the time when the destroyed walls of the city were being rebuilt, "the Book of the Law of Moses, which the Lord had commanded Israel" (verse 1) was discovered and brought out before the whole assembly. Then Ezra the priest "read from it in the open square... from morning until midday, before the men and women and those who could understand; and the ears of all the people were attentive to the Book of the Law" (verse 3). Other teachers and Levites then "read distinctly from the book, in the Law of God; and they gave the sense, and helped them [the people] to understand the reading" (verses 7-8).

When the people heard God's word, they responded with three reactions. First, "all the people answered, 'Amen, Amen!' while lifting up their hands. And they bowed their heads and worshiped the LORD with their faces to the ground" (verse 6). Second, "All the people wept when they heard the words of the Law" (verse 9). Third, after being told not to be sorrowful because the day was holy to their Lord, "all the people went their way to eat and drink, to send portions and rejoice greatly, because they understood the words that were declared to them" (verse 12).

God intends for us to understand His word. When we do, any of the above three reactions to it is appropriate. Sometimes, the word of God causes us to worship Him, either with shouts of "Amen," or with bowed heads and faces to the ground. At other times, our comprehension of what God has said will make us weep. And still there are other times when the word of God elicits great celebration.

In the midst of the telling of this story in Nehemiah lays a popular verse of Scripture. It's in verse 10 that we read, "the joy of the LORD is your strength." The context of these words connects our strength to the joy of the Lord by one strong tie: the understanding of the word of God. In other words, understanding the word of God produces joy in our lives because we know that that Word makes us strong enough to face whatever life may throw our way.

So the next time you're feeling weak in faith, pick up God's word. Use a modern translation if necessary—like the New Living Translation (NLT), the New International Version (NIV), or the New American Standard Bible (NASB)—because God intends for us to comprehend what He has written. You'll find that the understandable words from His heart to yours will produce such strength that your joy will be full.

#89
March 29: His World; His Rules

I've entered friends' houses where I have to take off my shoes before I can walk on their carpet. I've been the main speaker in some churches where, before I was a licensed minister, I couldn't deliver my message from the pulpit. In department stores, I've passed by doors marked "Employees Only." And I understand when you meet the Queen of England, you aren't allowed to touch her.

Everywhere we go, there are rules that may seem silly to us. I could debunk all of the above examples with the excuses that I wiped the bottoms of my shoes, my message will be coming from God's word no matter where I stand, it's a shorter distance to walk if I use the employees' door, and the Queen looks like she needs a hug. Nevertheless, I abide by the rules because it's not my house, my church, my store, or my country. We all do it. Their house; their rules. And we know that if we break those rules, we can expect the corresponding consequences.

Why then is it so difficult to see the world this way? God made it; heck, He made *us*. Whether we understand them or not, whether we agree with them or not, He's made the rules for us and for His world. The cool thing is that God's rules are not arbitrary. There is a rhyme and reason to them that are about His glory and from His love for us. So when we disagree and disobey, the consequences are our own fault. In explaining this to the people in the book of Nehemiah, the Levites put it this way, "However You are just in all that has befallen us; for You have dealt faithfully, but we have done wickedly" Nehemiah 9:33 (NKJ).

The last stanza of one of Frank Sinatra's most famous songs sums up the view of many of us. We don't want to kneel to anybody and we shout pridefully, "I did it my way." There's one huge problem with this sentiment: we are not our own. If all man has is himself, he is truly a pathetic soul. We are responsible to the God of the universe, and sooner or later, we indeed will kneel. Look at the record in both the Old and New Testaments:

- Isaiah 45:22-24 – Look to Me, and be saved, all you ends of the earth! For I am God, and there is no other. I have sworn by Myself; the word has gone out of My mouth in righteousness, and shall not return, that to Me every knee shall bow, every tongue shall take an oath. He shall say, 'Surely in the LORD I have righteousness and strength. To Him men shall come, and all shall be ashamed who are incensed against Him.' (NKJ)

- Philippians 2:9-11 – Therefore God also has highly exalted Him and given Him the name which is above every name, that at the name of Jesus every knee should bow, of those in heaven, and of those on earth, and of those under the earth, and that every tongue should confess that Jesus Christ is Lord, to the glory of God the Father. (NKJ)

So take your shoes off, speak from the small lecturn, use the public door, don't touch the Queen, and obey God. You'll avoid both hassle and hell. Not a bad deal.

#90
March 30: More Than Coincidence

One Friday morning, I drove to another city to speak at a women's retreat. After teaching my two workshops, I lingered in the conference room packing up all the things I had used in my presentation. The ladies had departed to have lunch just outside

SHARON NORRIS ELLIOTT

the room in a beautiful atrium. Not wanting to barge in once their lunch had begun, I just packed my car and headed back home. However, I was close to the school at which I taught. Although it was the end of summer, I knew the offices would be open and I could check my box for any early messages before the start of the new semester.

Of course, one of my buddies was in her office so I stopped in to chat. As we exchanged summer stories, another couple of co-workers peeked their heads in. One lady began to talk about a man who was very depressed because his cancer did not seem to be responding to treatment. Not knowing her personally, as I listened, I was able to decipher that she was speaking of her husband. I asked if it would be okay if we prayed together about it. She said sure, so we grabbed hands and I prayed for God's healing and comfort for this man, this wife, and their family.

After we prayed and we all got ready to leave my friend's office, my co-worker said, "You know, I thought I just stopped by here today to look for a lost key. Now I know I stopped by to receive that prayer." That's funny; I hadn't planned to stop in at the school either. In fact, I didn't even know the site of that women's retreat was so conveniently close to the school. Coincidence? I don't think so.

When Esther (a beautiful Jewish woman) became King Ahasuerus' queen, she had no idea that the anti-Semitic Haman would stir up a plot to kill all the Jews in the kingdom. (Read Esther chapter 3 for the story and reason for the plot.) Esther's cousin, Mordecai, figured that as queen, maybe she could speak to the king on the Jews' behalf to save them. He sent her a message saying, "Do not think in your heart that you will escape in the king's palace any more than all the other Jews... Yet who knows whether you have come to the kingdom for such a time as this?" Esther 4:13-14 (NKJ)

God has a wonderful way of placing us just where He needs for us to be. All we have to do is keep our eyes and ears open to His nudges. We never know when we have arrived at a place at God's bidding "for such a time as this."

108

Part 2

Glimpses of God

In the

Books of Poetry

(100 Devotions)

#91

March 31: God Takes Note

My parents showed up at every important event in which I participated. If I was playing in a piano recital, singing in a choir concert, or directing a play, I could look out into the audience and see my mom and dad, sitting side-by-side, rooting me on. One of my favorite pictures of them was taken at my college graduation. There they were again, side-by-side in the bleachers of the Biola gymnasium, ready to take note with pride and cheer me on in the culmination of my accomplishment.

God takes note with pride of our accomplishments in spiritual pursuits. Listen to how He brags about Job. "⁸Then the Lord said to Satan, 'Have you considered My servant Job, that *there is* none like him on the earth, a blameless and upright man, one who fears God and shuns evil?'" Job 1:8 (NKJ). After Satan destroyed Job's possessions and killed his children, Job still remained upright, so Satan went back to God. This time, God reiterated His previous remark with an added comment. "Then the Lord said to Satan, 'Have you considered My servant Job, that *there is* none like him on the earth, a blameless and upright man, one who fears God and shuns evil? And still he holds fast to his integrity, although you incited Me against him, to destroy him without cause'" Job 2:3 (NKJ).

Sometimes we may feel as though we are doing all we should, we're taking all kinds of flack in the name of our faith, and there are no kudos coming our way. It seems like the more we do right, the more hassle we invite. Has God turned His back to look elsewhere for a while? Does it even concern Him that we're suffering?

Rest assured: God has a prime seat "in the bleachers," watching with pride and cheering us on in our spiritual accomplishments. He is actually 100% in control of every single thing that comes our way. He may never explain to us why He has allowed us to face whatever we're going through. Our correct response is just to hold on to what we know of our loving Heavenly Father. Nothing gets past Him. He's at every event—taking note.

#92
April 1: The Gardener

Beautiful landscaping is a wonder to behold. I love to walk through a lovely garden or sit in a gazebo surrounded by lush greenery and lovely flowers. Some gardeners actually sculpt the hedges and manipulate them to look like animals and form archways.

Our God is the greatest Gardener of all. Besides creating all the beauty of nature, He continues to design special hedges. Note what even Satan says about God's landscaping exploits: "Does Job fear God for nothing? Have You not made a hedge around him, around his household, and around all that he has on every side? You have blessed the work of his hands, and his possessions have increased in the land" Job 1:9-10.

More than a decorative accessory for a beautiful garden, God sculpts hedges of protection around His saints. Unless He says so, nothing can break through those barriers. If allowed in, intruders are carefully scrutinized on 24-hour surveillance and held to the strictest parameters as to what they are permitted to do while in our territory. As long as we stay within our designated hedge, God is there with us so we're good.

Enjoy the garden hedges designed specifically to protect you today.

#93
April 2: God is Fair

Don't ever think God is unfair. If anyone knows who should get his or her "come-uppins," it's God. Nothing is hidden from Him.

Job and his friends wrestled with this idea. Job couldn't understand why he was being singled out for attack, and his friends tried to help him understand it. Although his friends came up with theories and ideas that were true, none of them were true of Job's particular case. In the end, they all just had to accept the fact that God had done what God wanted to do with Job, no fault of Job's. And God is fair in doing whatever He wants to do.

Job's friend Bildad got this point right. He says, "Behold, God will not cast away the blameless, nor will He uphold the evildoers" Job 8:20 (NKJ). In simpler terms, God will bless those who do what is right, and punish those who do wrong. God has His eye on both the blameless and the blame-worthy. Another verse of Scripture puts it this way:

"Neither is there any creature that is not manifest in his sight: but all things are naked and opened unto the eyes of him with whom we have to do" Hebrews 4:13 (KJV).

There is no need for us to worry about good being rewarded and evil being punished. We can let God handle that. Let's just be concerned with making sure we keep our personal lifestyle right before Him.

#94
April 3: Route Guidance

When using my GPS (Global Positioning System) device, once I've input the address of the location I want to reach, the voice comes through saying, "Proceed to the highlighted road; route guidance will begin." The lady in the satellite (that's what I call her) knows where I am, knows where I want to go, and knows a variety of routes I can take to get there. If I make a wrong turn or have to take a detour, she says, "Recalculating route," and gets me back on the right road toward my destination.

God is our ultimate Route Guidance. Job says of Him, "But He knows the way that I take; when He has tested me, I shall come forth as gold" Job 23:10 (NKJ). The Hebrew word for "way" used here is "derek (deh'-rek) which literally means "road (as trodden)," but figuratively also means "a course of life or mode of action." So God not only literally knows where we are physically, He also knows where we are in our life; that is, He is aware of our dreams, our hopes, and our desires, as well as our current situation, circumstances, foibles, and failures. He knows the detours we're facing and how frustrated we are when yet another roadblock slows our progress.

But better than the lady in the satellite, God's route guidance is always engaged. Proceed to the highlighted road found in the Scriptures—read His word daily—because route guidance has begun.

#95
April 4: Never Wicked

If you haven't ever read Shakespeare's *Macbeth*, or if you haven't read it in a long time, a good afternoon's activity would be to curl up with a good translation and do so. Besides the intrigue and suspense, a very interesting feature is the writer's inclusion of the three witches. These other-worldly creatures suggest that Macbeth will be the king. Even though they also tell him, "Fair is foul, and foul is fair," (Act 1, Scene 1), that hint of becoming sovereign (along with a strong push from his scandalous wife) begins the course of events that will reveal the depths of the man's true, depraved inner motives. Although all seemed to be coming about just the way the wicked sisters had said, the tables turn on Macbeth in the end. He interpreted their words one way, but there was another way to look at things that made certain his downfall.

We never have to worry about this kind of thing happening to us when we hear God's word or when we see Him move. There's never any double-entendre and God is never wicked. Job 34:10-12 says, "Therefore listen to me, you men of understanding: far be it from God to do wickedness, and from the Almighty to commit iniquity. For He repays man according to his work, and makes man to find a reward according to his way. Surely God will never do wickedly, nor will the Almighty pervert justice" (NKJ).

Never worry that God's word has some kind of trick attached. And know that whatever He does is right and just. He does not say one thing and do another. He is never wicked.

#96
April 5: God's Eyes

Anthropomorphisms are descriptions of God using human characteristics. We know that "God is Spirit, and those who worship Him must worship in spirit and truth" John 4:24 (NKJ). We also know that we were made in His image. In Genesis 1:26, we hear God saying, "Let Us make man in Our image, according to Our likeness" (NKJ). As Spirit, God does not literally have eyes and hands and feet. However, the only way God could relate to us and break through to our understanding is through the use of terminology familiar to our humanity. So, He had the Scripture writers use these recognizable terms when describing Himself to us. Take a look at some verses about God's eyes:

For His eyes are on the ways of man, and He sees all his steps. Job 34:21 (NKJ)

For the eyes of the LORD run to and fro throughout the whole earth, to show Himself strong on behalf of those whose heart is loyal to Him. In this you have done foolishly; therefore from now on you shall have wars." Second Chronicles 16:9 (NKJ)

The eyes of the LORD are on the righteous, and His ears are open to their cry. Psalm 34:15 (NKJ)

For the ways of man are before the eyes of the LORD, and He ponders all his paths. Proverbs 5:21 (NKJ)

The eyes of the LORD are in every place, keeping watch on the evil and the good. Proverbs 15:3 (NKJ)

For My eyes are on all their ways; they are not hidden from My face, nor is their iniquity hidden from My eyes. Jeremiah 16:17 (NKJ)

You are great in counsel and mighty in work, for your eyes are open to all the ways of the sons of men, to give everyone according to his ways and according to the fruit of his doings. Jeremiah 32:19 (NKJ)

"Behold, the eyes of the Lord GOD are on the sinful kingdom, and I will destroy it from the face of the earth; yet I will not utterly destroy the house of Jacob," says the LORD. Amos 9:8 (NKJ)

And there is no creature hidden from His sight, but all things are naked and open to the eyes of Him to whom we must give account. Hebrews 4:13 (NKJ)

God's eyes see our steps, watch so He can show Himself strong, and keep track of when we, His righteous ones, are hurting. Nothing we do is hidden from His all-seeing eyes, and don't get it twisted, He doesn't miss what the evil are doing either.

May God's eyes—the fact that He sees all, all the time—be both a deterrent and a comfort to you today.

#97
April 6: God Has His Reasons

We don't know why God does the things He does. All we need to know is God's attributes and then we can confidently flow with whatever He decides to do. In other words, once we learn to trust God for who He is, we'll be okay with whatever He does because we'll know that whatever He does is always in line with His character. We can accept what God does even if we don't quite understand everything about why He is doing it. For example, if we know God is love, we can rightly judge the imitations of human love that come our way. If we recognize that God is almighty and has all power, we can securely rest in His protection of us, and so on.

Job's young friend Elihu gave some counsel to Job along these same lines. He said, "God thunders marvelously with His voice; he does great things which we cannot comprehend... Also with moisture He saturates the thick clouds; he scatters His bright clouds. And they swirl about, being turned by His guidance, that they may do whatever He commands them on the face of the whole earth. He causes it to come, whether for correction, or for His land, or for mercy" Job 37:5, 11-13 (NKJ).

Elihu says that we don't even know what God is doing when it comes to the rain. He points out that God has three reasons for sending the rain: it comes "for correction, or for His land, or for mercy." This insight can help us to relax and flow with God's purpose when trouble comes our way. Perhaps the problem exists because we need correction.

Hebrews 12:7-8 says, "If you endure chastening, God deals with you as with sons; for what son is there whom a father does not chasten? But if you are without chastening, of which all have become partakers, then you are illegitimate and not sons" (NKJ).

We may be facing our trial because God wants to tend His land. We learn from our trials and if we're attentive, we grow stronger from them and can look back and realize that God was teaching us something we needed to know. James 1:3-4 says, "Knowing that the testing of your faith produces patience. But let patience have its perfect work, that you may be perfect and complete, lacking nothing" (NKJ).

Finally, God may be sending the rain as a soothing salve because we are in need of mercy. When we've been in a dry spot, rain symbolizes refreshment and cleansing. For example, God uses this metaphor of pouring out blessings when we faithfully tithe.

"Bring all the tithes into the storehouse, that there may be food in My house, and try Me now in this," says the LORD of hosts, "If I will not open for you the windows of heaven and pour out for you such blessing that there will not be room enough to receive it." Malachi 3:10 (NKJ).

So the next time we are singing the "why-me-God" blues, remember that God has His reasons. All we need to do is hang on and continue to trust in who He is. Nothing He brings or allows in our lives is out of His control, and nothing He ushers to us is contrary to His character.

#98
April 7: He's Totally Fair

God gets blamed for lots of things He has had absolutely nothing to do with. Along with assigning fault, we often add insult to injury by taking His own word out of context as we apply it to the situation. When a serious illness won't go away, we blame God *(I thought I was healed by Jesus' stripes, but I prayed for healing, and God ignored me)*. When a loved one dies, we blame God *(The Lord giveth and the Lord taketh away)*. When we're struggling against giving up immoral feelings or a negative habit, we blame God *(God knows how He made me)*.

Illness, death, struggles, and all the other stuff with which we deal are tough. We tend to cope with the stress of the situation by injecting the word into it. However, when we do so, we are handling things backwards. If we're going to successfully navigate the tough stuff, we need a completely opposite modus operandi. When life smacks us in the face, we need to start with the Word of God and then inject the stress of the situation into it. In other words, don't judge the Word by the situation; judge the situation by the truth of the Word. Illness and death are the result of the fall of man. God is able to heal us physically, but He doesn't always, and unless Jesus returns first, "it is appointed unto man once to die" (Hebrews 9:27). As for immoral feelings and negative habits, God does not "tempt us toward evil" (James 1:13-14), so these must be seen as the outgrowth of temptation and/or deception.

The Message Bible translates Job 37:23 as follows:

"Mighty God! Far beyond our reach! Unsurpassable in power and justice! It's unthinkable that he'd treat anyone unfairly." God loves us, He's almighty, and He's totally fair. He allows nothing that will destroy us, nor does He cause us to desire that which would not please Him. To the contrary; He empowers and encourages us. It's absolutely "unthinkable that He'd treat anyone unfairly."

#99
April 8: Feeling Froggy?

Sometimes, maybe even most of the time, we can feel pretty good about ourselves. Yes, we're thankful when we're not facing discomfort, debilitating illness, crippling debt, and tough decisions. And when things are going well, it's very easy to start patting ourselves on the back a bit too much. We may pray less, read the Bible not as often, and find little excuses to skip church. After all, since God is orchestrating such great circumstances, why not take advantage of the energy we feel and spend time on some new and varied activities? In other words, we're feeling "froggy," (that is, unjustifiably too sure of ourselves).

At times like these good times, we run the risk of sounding like Job toward the end of his book in the Bible. After hearing all his first three friends had to say about the reasons for his misfortunes, Job gave a rundown of all the good things he had been doing right in his life. Job was feeling "froggy" in his attitude toward himself. Listen to some of God's own words to Job:

Then the LORD answered Job out of the whirlwind, and said: "Who is this who darkens counsel by words without knowledge? Now prepare yourself like a man; I will question you, and you shall answer Me. Where were you when I laid the foundations of the earth? Tell Me, if you have understanding. Who determined its measurements? Surely you know! Or who stretched the line upon it? To what were its foundations fastened? Or who laid its cornerstone, when the morning stars sang together, and all the sons of God shouted for joy? Or who shut in the sea with doors, when it burst forth and issued from the womb; when I made the clouds its garment, and thick darkness its swaddling band; when I fixed My limit for it, and set bars and doors; when I said, 'This far you may come, but no farther, and here your proud waves must stop!'

"Have you commanded the morning since your days began, and caused the dawn to know its place, that it might take hold of the ends of the earth, and the wicked be shaken out of it?...

"Have you comprehended the breadth of the earth? Tell Me, if you know all this. Where is the way to the dwelling of light? And darkness, where is its place, that you may take it to its territory, that you may know the paths to its home? Do you know it, because you were born then, or because the number of your days is great?...

"Who has divided a channel for the overflowing water, or a path for the thunderbolt, to cause it to rain on a land where there is no one, a wilderness in which there is no man; to satisfy the desolate waste, and cause to spring forth the growth of tender grass? Has the rain a father? Or who has begotten the drops of dew? From whose womb comes the ice? And the frost of heaven, who gives it birth? The waters harden like stone, and the surface of the deep is frozen...

"Can you lift up your voice to the clouds, that an abundance of water may cover you? Can you send out lightings, that they may go, and say to you, 'Here we are!'? Who has put wisdom in the mind? Or who has given understanding to the heart?...

"Who provides food for the raven, when its young ones cry to God, and wander about for lack of food?" Job 38:1-41 (NKJ)

Sometimes, we need to read all the way through Job chapters 38 – 40 just to keep the "frogginess" at bay in our own attitudes. If we don't do it ourselves, God is perfectly able to send reminders our way, and I don't think we want that, do we?

#100
April 9: God's Ownership

Job and his friends went around and around about the reasons for Job's problems. Their speeches posed many conjectures including the possibility that Job had sinned. In the final analysis, though, God never explained to Job why he had had all the troubles. At the end of the book of Job, God spends several chapters merely proving to Job that He could do whatever He wanted because He was God. This was not said as a bully would say it; the comment was simply a matter of fact. One short sentence summed it all up for me. God said, "Everything under heaven is Mine" Job 41:11b.

If we, who say we trust in God, ever grasp the enormity of that statement, we'd stop worrying, we'd stop complaining, we'd stop wondering, and we'd stop entering into hassles. Since everything under heaven is His, that means our worries, problems, questions, and hassles are His. That issue with the co-worker? It's His. That anxiety about that child? It's His. That hassle over the grade? It's His. That question about the future? That's His too.

Ownership means control. Since everything under heaven is God's, that means everything under heaven is under His control. We need to adopt the stance that approaches each ripple and wave in the tide of life by saying, "God, this problem is yours." Then if any question remains, it should then be worded, "What do you plan to do about it?"

#101
April 10: One Thing I Know For Sure

A popular talk show host coined the phrase, "One thing I know for sure." Following this statement, she would utter her observations about the world, humanity, or just life in general. Her audiences would listen and nod approvingly, then show their agreement with thunderous applause.

Although many of the pronouncements of that talk show host were observable truths of common sense and knowledge, they don't compare to the certainty we have in our God. All through Scripture, the inspired writers tell us of things we can know for sure. The things they write are precious and valuable truths that can lift us when we're down, warn us when we're in danger, help us when we're in trouble, and sustain us when we're at the end of our rope.

One of these "for sure observations" is made by Job. After all his struggles and God's reprimand, he comes to a realization and states, "I know that You can do everything, and that no purpose of Yours can be withheld from You" Job 42:2 (NKJ).

Have we yet realized that God can do everything and no purpose of His can be withheld from Him? In other words, when God wants a thing to happen, it will happen. We can't stop Him from doing whatever He wants to do, or from allowing whatever He desires to allow. We're fine with this concept as long as things are happening in our favor. However, we recoil at this truth when adversity strikes. We start sentences either aloud or in our thoughts with, "How could a loving God...?"

The fact is, we must come to the simple realization that Job reached. As The Message Bible interprets this verse, no matter what's happening in our lives, we must affirm, "I'm convinced: You can do anything and everything. Nothing and no one can upset your plans." The repetition of this truth—especially when we don't understand how it can be so—will begin to cement into our spirits a deeper understanding of God and His ways that will sustain us through the trial.

Nothing about God's love, grace, and mercy is diminished by rough seas. Know for sure that even in turmoil, God can do everything; no purpose of His can ever be withheld from Him.

#102
April 11: God's Excellence

When it comes to the works of my hands, I consider myself a perfectionist. I strive to have whatever issues forth from me to be the best it can possibly be. Handouts that are stapled together must be straight, none of the pages cockeyed, and none of the staples too low or high. The Power Point presentations must be clear, interesting, and easy to follow. And heaven forbid I would ever knowingly allow a spelling or grammatical error to slip through on any of my written work, postcards, or brochures. Mind you, I'm not going to flip out if any of these things ever takes place, but I would feel embarrassed and be apologetic.

Why would I apologize for little, unintentional errors? Because I believe excellence is an attribute of God that He expects us to emulate. God is excellent. Psalm 8:1 says, "O LORD, our Lord, how excellent is Your name in all the earth, who set Your glory above the heavens!" (NKJ). The word "excellent" comes from an Aramaic word "'addiyr" (ad-deer') which means "wide, large, powerful, famous, gallant, glorious, noble, principal, and worthy." And what is excellent about God? His name. "Shem" (shame) – the word for "name" used in this verse – is "an appellation, as a mark or memorial of individuality; honor, authority, character, renown, and report." In other words, God is large and worthy based upon His honorable individuality. He is above everything and everyone else in character, authority, and glory. He is excellent.

So how does all this about God's excellence tie in with my perfectionist demands? An excellent God does things excellently. As I said above, I believe excellence is an attribute of God that He expects us to emulate. While here on Earth, living before us in the person of Jesus Christ, God taught us how to be excellent by looking at how He did things. People of that day even remarked of Him saying, "He has done all things well," Mark 7:37 (NKJ).

The Old Testament's Daniel is a role model for living a life of excellence that God will abundantly bless. At every turn, Daniel gave testimony of His God. He gave God the glory whenever he was called upon to use His gifts. There was never any doubt in anyone's mind, no matter whether you were a king or commoner, who it was that Daniel was serving. The great King Nebuchadnezzar knew it, Neb's son and successor, Belshazzar knew it, and the overthrowing king Darius knew it. And when Darius promoted Daniel, the Bible says, "Then this Daniel distinguished himself above the governors and satraps, because an excellent spirit was in him; and the king gave thought to setting him over the whole realm" Daniel 6:3 (NKJ).

If excellence was good enough for Daniel and Jesus, it's good enough for me. Let's take everything we do not just to the next level, but to the excellent level as we honor God with the works of our hands.

#103
April 12: Purpose Fulfiller

There is a lot of talk today about purpose. Many of us are searching to spend our time doing more than just work to earn enough to live. We are on a quest to find that for which we were born – to find our destiny.

The Psalmist prays, "May He grant you according to your heart's desire, and fulfill all your purpose" Psalm 20:4 (NKJ). Only God, the One who made us and knew us before we knew ourselves, can reveal to us the purpose for which we were created. And living in that purpose will be the joy of our existence.

One of my sons called to excitedly report about a fabulous job he just secured. In this job, he is experiencing a blossoming of his strengths, so he's beginning to tap into what it's like to live in his purpose. My mother's heart swelled with joy and pride for him. No one could erase the broad smile on my face.

God looks upon us with a smile too. He's a proud parent when his children are living their dreams. But God goes further than we can go as parents of our kids. I didn't supply my son with his dream job, God did. God can make happen for us what we can't make happen for ourselves. And when God puts us in positions, those are positions of purpose.

James 1:17 says, "Every good and perfect gift is from above, coming down from the Father of the heavenly lights, who does not change like shifting shadows" (NIV).

Journey with God toward your purpose. Allow Him to reveal it, then walk joyously in what He's laid out for your life.

#104
April 13: Why Serve Any Other but God?

Every now and then we hear on the news of some rich person's child who has run amuck. He's raced his $200,000 car recklessly; she's spent an enormous amount of money frivolously; he's caught with women he ought not be with; she's scandalized by racy photos she shouldn't have posed for. I always think, *don't they realize who they are? They have everything they need; there's no reason for them to act that way. Their parents must be embarrassed and devastated.*

Others should think those thoughts of us when we, Christians, act contrary to who we profess to be. We claim to be intimately related to the God of the universe, the Lord of life, and the empowering Spirit of the Almighty. Why are we bowing to fear, our fantasies, our ancient foe, and our flesh? From time to time, we need a reminder of Who it is we serve and what our relationship with Him affords us. Let's revisit the 23rd Psalm.

"The LORD is my shepherd; I shall not want." The King of kings and Lord of lords is the One with whom we have relationship. He is caring for us. Knowing who our Shepherd is and being close with Him means there is no need for us to have a care in the world. Why are we trippin'?

"He makes me to lie down in green pastures; he leads me beside the still waters." Green pastures indicate our sustenance. We're supplied by abundance all around us. Still waters indicate peace. As we follow His lead, we will be at peace in the decisions He directs us to make.

"He restores my soul; he leads me in the paths of righteousness for His name's sake." Sometimes we get out of whack, probably because we've taken our gaze from Him. When refreshment and relief are necessary, He gives that to us by refocusing our eyes on the paths we should be walking.

"Yea, though I walk through the valley of the shadow of death, I will fear no evil; for You are with me; Your rod and Your staff, they comfort me." Even when times are tough, we must remember that He's with us as we *walk* (not climb or run or struggle) *through* (meaning there is an end to be obtained) the valleys of our lives which are mere *shadows* (meaning there is no destroying substance). We are comforted in those valleys by His use of the rod and staff, employed by the Shepherd only as tools to correct and protect His sheep which He prizes and highly values.

"You prepare a table before me in the presence of my enemies; you anoint my head with oil; my cup runs over." Even in the face of the haters, God's blessings to us are not blocked; in fact, that's where and when they shine brightest. We're humbled to realize His precious anointing rests on us, so much so, that there's enough to flow over to anyone who comes in contact with us.

"Surely goodness and mercy shall follow me all the days of my life; and I will dwell in the house of the LORD forever." As we pass through this life, we are leaving a legacy. Goodness and mercy are *following* us. We're already in the Lord's house as our bodies are temples of the Holy Spirit, and it's not over when we leave this life; we get to dwell in the house of the Lord forever.

So I ask you, why serve any other besides our God?

#105
April 14: On the Voice of God

We read about the voice of the Lord seven times in the 29th Psalm. "The voice of the LORD is over the waters; the God of glory thunders; the LORD is over many waters. The voice of the LORD is powerful; the voice of the LORD is full of majesty. The voice of the LORD breaks the cedars, yes, the LORD splinters the cedars of Lebanon… The voice of the LORD divides the flames of fire. The voice of the LORD shakes the wilderness; the LORD shakes the Wilderness of Kadesh. The voice of the LORD makes the deer give birth, and strips the forests bare; and in His temple everyone says, 'Glory!'" Ps 29:3-5, 7-9 (NKJ). All told, the phrase "the voice of the Lord" is repeated 47 times in the Old Testament.

It would probably be an awesome study to look up all of those 47 mentions of God's voice and see exactly what His voice was saying or doing each time. For the purposes of our devotional thought for today, it's enough for us to know three things:

#1.   God has a voice. If God's voice is mentioned 47 times, it's pretty obvious that God indeed has a voice. (We realize we are using an anthropomorphism to explain something about God, but if it's fine with God to explain Himself to us in human terms, we can glean understanding from the image.) It's great to know that God has the capacity to communicate with His creation.

#2.   God uses His voice. Beings possessing voices use them unless something is wrong. There is no lack in God, so the voice He has, He uses. He is not silent. He wants us to know Him and to know His ways, so He expresses Himself using His voice.

#3.   God's voice makes a difference. God not only possesses a voice and has the capacity to use His voice, but God's voice also makes things happen. Years ago, a television commercial advertised the importance of the knowledge of a financial institution. The ad showed people going about their normal, everyday activities and then the camera zoomed in on a couple having what seemed to be a random conversation. One person mentioned, "E.F. Hutton said…" At those words, everyone on the sidewalk immediately stopped and tuned in to the couple's conversation. The voice-over then announced, "When E.F. Hutton talks, people listen."

Remember today that God has a voice and He's using His voice—through His Word, the Bible, through sermons, etc.—to communicate with us. Are we allowing His voice to make a measurable, meaningful difference in our lives? As with E.F. Hutton, when God talks, do we listen?

#106
April 15: God is Extol-able

We don't use the word "extol" much. In fact, apart from when church used King James English, I don't think I've ever heard it used. But this is a great word. It comes from the Latin *extollere* which means "to lift up." The Hebrew word *ruwm* carries the same meaning with a twist: to rise or raise, to be high actively. In our culture, "to be high" has a negative connotation, but when speaking of lifting God, not only are we to be high, but we are to be actively high in our response to Him. Synonyms of the word extol are bless, carol, celebrate, exalt, praise, glorify, laud, magnify, and resound. None of these are quiet, timid, shy, and whispering types of words.

Psalm 30:1-4 says, "I will extol You, O LORD, for You have lifted me up, and have not let my foes rejoice over me. O LORD my God, I cried out to You, and You healed me. O LORD, You brought my soul up from the grave; you have kept me alive, that I should not go down to the pit. Sing praise to the LORD, You saints of His, and give thanks at the remembrance of His holy name" (NKJ).

I write for and speak to people from all walks of life and from many different church traditions. Lots of these people sincerely love the same God I love. But for the life of me, I can't figure out how the quieter traditions manage to remain so staid when they worship a God like ours; a God like the one described in Psalm 30. The same people who will stand up, clap their hands, raise banners and victory signs, and scream at the tops of their lungs for their favorite sports teams, will sit silent and stone-faced in a worship gathering as songs and sermons recall the acts of our wondrous Lord. How is that even possible?

I submit to you today that just as the Psalmist says, our Lord is extol-able. He has done and continues to do so much that just one thought of His goodness should be enough to put a smile on our faces, clapping in our hands, a spring in our steps, and shouts for joy (dare we say with raised arms) from our lips.

Here's the challenge: The next time you're in a worship gathering and you hear of the goodness of God, be actively high in lifting up our Lord. Let the reality of His awesome nature flood your soul. Lift your hands, stand to your feet, say "Amen," sing a little louder. Don't let your favorite sports team get more glory than you are willing to give to God.

#107
April 16: Momentary Anger

I received few spankings that I can remember (trust me, the ones I received were memorable), but my mother was good at doling out punishments. The minute the transgression was discovered, she'd slap a week of being grounded, or worse yet, of restriction from using the telephone. I would much rather have received the lecture and then the spanking so I could be finished with the whole sordid situation and get on with living life. But no, those punishments always lasted the full length of the sentence—there was no whining, plea bargaining, or best behavior ploy that could get me out of it any sooner.

The strange thing was that Mom didn't stay mad at me. More than anything else, I had hurt her heart. Even so, throughout the lockdown or lock out, Mom continued being her regular self. She wasn't rolling her eyes at me every time she looked my way or our paths crossed in the house. She didn't even continue to remind me of my sin. We even laughed and joked and basically responded to each other normally although I was under lock and key. I didn't enjoy the restrictions, but I accepted them because I knew I was guilty, and because I knew my mother and her rules deserved more respect than I had given them. When the disciplinary period ended, my privileges were reinstated. I was happy because of the receipt of my freedom, but the true joy came because of the full restoration of our relationship.

Psalm 30:5 says, "For His anger is but for a moment, his favor is for life; weeping may endure for a night, but joy comes in the morning" (NKJ). The Hebrew word for "anger" used in this verse ('aph) contains the idea of forbearance or long-suffering, and carries the picture of a person breathing rapidly through the nose as one who would be doing his best to hold back from striking out. God can snuff us out because of our sin, but His anger is "but for a moment." The disciplinary punishments will still prevail in our lives, but even as we go through them, His love for us won't change. We'll understand a little more about what our disobedience does to His heart, accept our guilt and His forgiveness, and recognize again that both He and His rules deserve more respect than we had given them. When our privileges are restored, we'll have gained our freedom, but more so, we'll experience the joy of the full restoration of our relationship with our ever-loving Heavenly Father.

#108
April 17: God in Prosperity

We aren't always bad off. There are times when things are actually pretty good in our lives. The kids bring home great report cards, the spouse does something especially thoughtful and it's not even our birthday, the bills are paid, the car is running well, and there's enough computer ink and paper to handle the project on which we're working. We're healthy, energetic, and hopeful. Basically, all is right in our world. I think we'd agree that a situation such as this would qualify under the title "Experiencing Prosperity."

We're in God's face constantly when times are tough, but let's not forget that God is entitled to His props when we find ourselves experiencing prosperity as well. The Psalmist recognized this as he proclaimed, "Now in my prosperity I said, 'I shall never be moved.' LORD, by Your favor You have made my mountain stand strong..." Psalm 30:6-7a (NKJ). I believe the writer of this Psalm may have been reflecting upon his reading of the area of the Pentateuch scroll which says, "And you shall remember the LORD your God, for it is He who gives you power to get wealth, that He may establish His covenant which He swore to your fathers, as it is this day" Deuteronomy 8:18 (NKJ).

Yes, the next time we sit down to pay bills, or pat our kids on the back for a job well done, or pick up the keys to the things we own, let's give God a thankful thought, acknowledging that it is by His favor that we have what we have.

#109
April 18: God's Great Goodness

An old hymn by R.C. Ward says:

Verse One:
When waves of affliction sweep over the soul,
And sunlight is hidden from view,
If ever you're tempted to fret or complain,
Just think of His goodness to you.

Chorus:
Just think of His goodness to you;
Yes, think of His goodness to you.
Tho' storms o'er thee sweep,
He is able to keep;
O think of His goodness to you.

Verse Two:
The world may forsake you, and those whom you trust
May prove to be false and untrue;
There's One you can trust even unto the end;
Just think of His goodness to you.

Verse Three:
Misfortune's dark cloud may hang over the way,
Despite your best efforts to do;
The Savior is guarding your treasures up there,
Just think of His goodness to you.

I wonder if the hymn writer penned these words after reading Psalm 31:19. "Oh, how great is Your goodness, which You have laid up for those who fear You, which You have prepared for those who trust in You in the presence of the sons of men!" (NKJ)

Sometimes, instead of asking of God to explain stuff to us, complaining to Him about stuff that's happening around us, and begging Him for stuff to bless us, we just need to sit back and marvel at His goodness to us. That's what both R.C. Ward and the psalmist were doing. Let's join them, shall we?

#110
April 19: Not Holding It Over Me

I think something most of us passionately hate is to be in a position where someone has something they hold over our heads. Like the friend who volunteered to pay a bill for you one time when your money was tight, then "reminds" you of it a year later when you want to go out for lunch. Or like the co-worker who swapped some sick time with you when your mom was ill, but never forgets to brag about her generosity in doing so. Or like the parents who say they are doing a favor out of the goodness of their hearts, but bring that favor up later to say how much it cost them. You were grateful for each gift and never acted like you weren't. Each act of kindness was a wonderful blessing, but now each time you hear about it, the gift feels less and less sweet because it's actually being held over your head. Somehow the gift has turned into a wound that you inflicted.

Thankfully, God doesn't treat us that way with His gifts. It cost Him everything to save and forgive us, but He never makes us feel bad about His sacrifice. To the contrary, He wants us to rejoice about all He's done. In fact, He tells us, "Blessed is he whose transgression is forgiven, whose sin is covered. Blessed is the man to whom the LORD does not impute iniquity, and in whose spirit there is no deceit" Psalm 32:1-2 (NKJ).

When someone needs us, and we're in the position to help, we're wrong if we don't help, but we're just as wrong if we help and hold it over their heads later. In fact, Luke 6:38 which tells us, "Give, and it will be given to you: good measure, pressed down, shaken together, and running over...," is embedded in a passage about how to express love to one another. The Greek word "give" (didomi) can be translated as bestow, commit, deliver, grant, and minister; all words which point to the attitude of expecting nothing in return. We do indeed get a return, but it's not because we gave to get. We get something in return because God blesses others to give to us in exactly the same way we gave. The giving and receiving happens in an infinite line, not in a circle just going back and forth.

God doesn't hold our sins or our neediness over us. As we grow to be more and more like Christ, let's be sure we don't do that to others either. If Jesus can forgive our sins and never count it again against us, surely we can extend that much love to those we're fortunate enough to help.

#111
April 20: The Life Coach

Advertisements abound for life coaches. This whole field is relatively new. Not long ago, any coach was associated with a sport. For many young people, their football, basketball, swim, track, or tennis coach gave them not only instruction about the game, but also lessons on life. We get wise words and metaphors from the sports world. Sayings like "it's not over until it's over," "go the last mile," "get your second wind," "teamwork doesn't have an 'I' in it," and "no pain no gain," come to us as a result of great coaches using sports to teach about living well.

Perhaps society has wised up to the fact that we all need someone who can encourage us, set a spark under us, and be the wind beneath our wings. So folks who never graced a field or court are now employing life coaches who can do for them as sports coaches have done for years for their players.

It's nice, and probably even profitable, to have someone we can turn to who can bolster us when we're down or in need of a little push. Never forget, though, that we can get that uplift for free (no offense meant to the life coaches out there). God says, "I will instruct you and teach you in the way you should go; I will guide you with My eye" Psalm 32:8 (NKJ).

Second Peter 1:3 says, "His divine power has given to us all things that pertain to life and godliness, through the knowledge of Him who called us by glory and virtue" (NKJ). Getting to know God is like hiring a life coach. His number is Jeremiah 33:3 ("Call to Me, and I will answer you, and show you great and mighty things, which you do not know" NKJ.) Make an appointment.

#112
April 21: God and Beautiful Music

I studied classical piano for eleven years. Each time I turned the page in John Thompson's instructional books, there was a new song and a new musical element to learn. Once I finished that series, my teacher, Mrs. Dolly Perry, moved me through an encyclopedia of the classics. All the while, I also repeatedly practiced scales and assorted drills in *Hanon: The*

Virtuoso Pianist study book. Even in that volume, every time I turned a page, there was a different musical challenge.

The funny thing about all that variety, newness, and diversity, is that never once did we add new tones to the piano. Every piece of music was made with a different combination of the same 12 tones found in a normal octave. Embedded in those limited dozen tones are infinite possibilities for melodies that God expects us to use to praise Him. Psalm 33:1-3 tells us, "Rejoice in the Lord, O you righteous! For praise from the upright is beautiful. Praise the Lord with the harp; make melody to Him with an instrument of ten strings. Sing to Him a new song; play skillfully with a shout of joy."

God calls praise "beautiful" when it comes from the righteous and the upright. We musicians are further obligated to play skillfully so we can praise Him with excellence as we lift to Him our new, melodious songs. Rehearsals should take on a renewed dynamic of excitement over getting it just right, knowing music stands as an offering up of our praise. Let's no longer take junk to the throne room. Whether we're singing or playing a musical instrument, let's give those 12 tones back to God so we can hear Him say, "Beautiful!"

#113
April 22: International Politician

Admittedly, most of us know very little about international politics. It's about all we can do to keep up with the political happenings that affect us in our own city, let alone in the state, the country, neighboring countries, and nations half-a-world away. Not only is the political landscape different, but the mindset of the general populace differs from ours as well. What folks in other places accept as normal actions of their government, we may view as abhorrent and intolerable. Even with the obvious differences between democratic, socialist, and totalitarian human forms of government, God still operates outside of, above, and despite them all.

And whatever form of government we think is best, wherever we live, we'd best be about the business of praying that our leaders get in line with God. Psalm 33:10 – 19 tells us God's role in international politics and it's quite sobering.

- "The Lord brings the counsel of the nations to nothing; He makes the plans of the peoples of no effect. The counsel of the Lord stands forever, the plans of His heart to all generations. Blessed *is* the nation whose God *is* the Lord, the people He has chosen as His own inheritance.
- "The Lord looks from heaven; He sees all the sons of men. From the place of His dwelling He looks on all the inhabitants of the earth; He fashions their hearts individually; He considers all their works.
- "No king *is* saved by the multitude of an army; a mighty man is not delivered by great strength. A horse *is* a vain hope for safety; neither shall it deliver *any* by its great strength.
- "Behold, the eye of the Lord is on those who fear Him, on those who hope in His mercy, to deliver their soul from death, and to keep them alive in famine." (NKJ)

Even if the nation in which we live ultimately refuses to follow God, He looks past the government and sees about His people. Those who fear (respect) Him and hope in His mercy can know with certainty that He will deliver their souls from death and keep them alive in famine.

Still, it would be more wonderful if the whole nation—heads of state as well as citizens—would honor God. It would be great if God didn't have to pick around the unbelievers to bless His children. How much more joyous and safe and relaxed life would be if as a nation we honored God as our Head. He's the best international politician there will ever be. Pray today that your nation is one that is blessed because its God is the Lord.

#114
April 23: When God Hears, Results Follow

When I was a little girl, my mother took me to an audiologist for a hearing test. The doctor fitted me with the headphones and told me to raise my right hand when I heard a beep in my right ear, and raise my left hand when I heard a beep in my left ear. Pretty simple. Always concerned about my grades, this was a test I knew I could pass.

Thankfully, I did pass; my hearing was sharp. That long-ago appointment came to mind as I read Psalm 34. Verses 4 and 6 say, "I sought the Lord, and He heard me, and delivered me from all my fears... This poor man cried out, and the Lord heard *him,* and saved him out of all his troubles." (NKJ)

Just as hearing those beeps caused me to raise my hands, hearing our calls causes God to act. When we seek Him because of our fears, He hears and delivers. When we cry to Him because of our troubles, He hears and saves. God never just passively hears; He actively listens with a view to move on our behalf. Like most husbands who want to take action when we tell them of our problems, God puts things in motion to fix our brokenness when we share our pain with Him.

Seek God and cry out when fears and troubles assail. Expect God to come through. Let's be particularly grateful today that when God hears, results follow.

#115
April 24: God's Hearing Is Listening

There's a difference between the questions, "Did you hear me?" and "Are you listening to me?" We can hear something yet not really be listening to it. Most of us have learned to tune out many of the sounds that bombard our ears daily so that we can concentrate on that which is most important. As I work at my desk at home, planes and helicopters occasionally fly overhead, birds chirp outside, the computer gives off a low hum, and the wind gently blows through my lemon tree. Although my ears hear those sounds, I don't react to them because I'm not *listening* to them. However, when I'm listening, I may react with annoyance because of the planes, helicopters, and hum of the computer; but may be moved to relaxation by the birds' songs and the calming sound of the breeze.

God's hearing is always the listening kind that produces action on His part. Psalm 34:4 and 6 say, "I sought the LORD, and He heard me, and delivered me from all my fears... This poor man cried out, and the LORD heard him, and saved him out of all his troubles (NKJ). When God heard the Psalmist, he was delivered from his fears and saved out of all his troubles.

God is not simply a hearer, but a listener. When we seek and cry out to Him, we have His undivided attention, and He's ready to move on our behalf. This fact is not, however, a blank check we can cash in heaven's bank to get everything for which we ask. God listens not only to our words, but also to our intentions. God does not supply our greed, our lust, or our misguided purposes. Consider these verses:

- I, the LORD, search the heart, I test the mind, even to give every man according to his ways, according to the fruit of his doings. Jeremiah 17:10 (NKJ)
- You know when I sit and when I rise; you perceive my thoughts from afar. Psalm 139:2 (NIV)
- For the word of God is living and active… and able to judge the thoughts and intentions of the heart. Hebrews 4:12 (NAS)

God is listening and He acts in our best interest every time we speak to Him.

#116
April 25: God Likes Us

We hear all the time that God loves us. John 3:16 is probably the most popular verse in the Bible and it talks about God's love. In fact, in First John 4:8, we even find out that God Himself *is* love. "He who does not love does not know God, for God is love."

But I cannot recall ever being told that God likes us. How could He? After all, we're wretched sinners. It's God's grace that allows Him to love us, and grace is necessary because we do not and cannot deserve His love. The very definition of grace is "undeserved favor," so we kinda carry around the idea that love is detached from who we are personally. God is working on us, bringing us to perfection, so He'll only be totally okay with us when we reach Glory.

Today's passage for concentration changed this view for me. Psalm 37:23-24 says, "The steps of a good man are ordered by the Lord, and He delights in his way. Though he fall, he shall not be utterly cast down; for the Lord upholds him with His hand." Wow, God delights in us even if we flub up from time to time. God likes us!

Rejoice that God not only loves you, but He actually likes you too. Show Him that you like Him too. Spend some extra time just hanging out with your Friend today.

#117
April 26: God Knows

Perhaps you had a mom like I had: one from whom nothing could be hidden. Momma just seemed to know when I needed a hug, when something was wrong, and especially when I had done something I had no business doing. It's a Mommy-Sense that just seems to come with the territory of becoming a mom. And it's a vitally essential intuition that helps develop our children's all-important conscience – that inner voice by which they will self-regulate when they are away from us. I acquired it too once I had my sons, but I fortified my intuition by praying, "Lord, please let them get caught the first time," so that no particular sin would become a habit in their lives.

Psalm 44:20-21 says, "If we had forgotten the name of our God, or stretched out our hands to a foreign god, would not God search this out? For He knows the secrets of the heart" (NKJ). In His omniscience, God knows everything we think, plan, and do. Not only does He know it, but He searches it out. He's able to penetrate to the core of our real intent and expose it. He's acutely aware when we forget His name by turning from Him to follow the foreign gods of our own lusts, our own greed, our own passions, and our own whims. He knows the secrets of the heart.

So we have two choices. We can continue to do our own thing at our own peril ("It is a fearful thing to fall into the hands of the living God" Hebrews 10:31, NKJ), or we can turn to God in true repentance and clean up our act. Try starting with really meaning each phrase of the prayer model Jesus taught to His disciples in Luke 11:2-4:

- "Our Father in heaven, hallowed be Your name." Is God's name holy in your sight? Do you honor Him for the awesome God that He is?

- "Your kingdom come." While Jesus was on earth, He frequently told the people, "The kingdom of Heaven is at hand." He was referring to Himself. So is it truly your desire to see God's kingdom come in your life? In other words, what are you doing about obeying Jesus, living for Jesus, and letting Jesus transform you?
- "Your will be done on earth as it is in heaven." Are you seeking God's will or your own?
- "Give us day by day our daily bread." Are you satisfied with God's provision? Are you caring for that which God has given you (time, talent, and treasure) as you should?
- "And forgive us our sins, for we also forgive everyone who is indebted to us." Are you harboring unforgiveness and bitterness toward anyone? If so, are you allowing that unforgiveness and bitterness to drive your thoughts and actions?
- "And do not lead us into temptation, but deliver us from the evil one." Are you even trying to avoid sin and stand against Satan?

God knows the secrets of our hearts. Let's admit what He already knows, turn from our sinful ways, and begin to flourish in newness of life.

#118
April 27: Present Help

When I was a young girl, our family lived two blocks from a firehouse. As I walked my dog or went to the library, I would pass the building. Sometimes the big door was open and I could see the big red fire engine parked beside the paramedic's van. The firemen would usually be busily doing whatever firemen do. As I passed, they'd always give a friendly wave. They'd participate in community projects too, and on my 18th birthday, they supplied me with the voter registration application I needed so I could perform my civic duty in upcoming elections.

That firehouse comforted me being so close. I had no idea just how comforting when we experienced a fire at our home one Fourth of July weekend caused by kids shooting off fireworks toward our roof. Those friendly neighborhood firemen were at our home in no time. Thanks to their quick response and expertise, the damage was contained to just two areas of the roof and ceiling and somehow, there was nothing in our house that sustained water damage.

Psalm 46:1 reminded me of those firemen. It says, "God is our refuge and strength, a very present help in trouble." Like those firemen, in both calm and crisis, God is close at hand. He's good to us when things are well, participating in our lives, and supplying us with our needs. But aren't we glad about His proximity when we face a catastrophe! Notice that the verse says He's not only a help, He's a "very present help." God's nearness when we need Him is something like the insurance commercial in which the folks in a predicament sing the company jingle and their agent pops onto the scene.

Faster then the insurance agent or the fire department, if you're feeling as though God is far from you today, be comforted by Psalm 46:1. Sing the company jingle, "God, I need you," and you'll find that there's nothing better than the "very present help" of our loving, powerful, awesome Heavenly Father.

#119
April 28: Still on the Throne

Throughout time, when one country wants to completely overthrow another, the invading army will go after the enemy's king. No matter what they have called themselves, history records the rise and fall of dictators, emperors, pharaohs, czars, magistrates, potentates, sovereigns, monarchs, and extreme commanders. The strength of the nation ultimately rests in the power of the ruler. Capture the king; conquer the people.

It's good news today to read the words of Psalm 47. "For the Lord Most High is awesome... For God is the King of all the earth... God reigns over the nations; God sits on His holy throne" Psalm 47:2, 7, and 8 (NKJ).

Ever since the insurrection of Satan, the demonic forces led by that arch foe have besieged God's kingdom. It's not a battle fought with guns and bombs; it's a culture war waged in the hearts and minds of the people. Will our mindset and will turn toward or away from God's manifesto as revealed in the Bible, or will we be moved to reject the Christian worldview and defect to the enemy's camp?

Choose your side. Just realize that no matter how hard the culture tries to contest God's laws, combat God's people, or counter God's will, it will never conquer God's kingdom. Exalt today knowing that God is still on His very secure throne and we're citizens of His nation. Hallelujah!

#120
April 29: Creator and Renovator

Whenever I think of God as the Creator, I think of the first few chapters of Genesis. There we follow the amazing "bara" creation which speaks of how God made something out of nothing. That same Hebrew word is used in Psalm 51:10 when the Psalmist implores God, "Create in me a clean heart, O God, and renew a steadfast spirit within me" (NKJ). God didn't stop creating something from nothing when He was finished with the universe. He continues the work of creation with our good-for-nothing hearts.

Since our hearts are deceitfully wicked (see Jeremiah 17:9), polluted beyond recognition, God doesn't waste time on trying to clean them out. He simply creates new ones for us. It's then our job to also allow Him to "chadash" (renew, repair, and rebuild) or spirit which involves our will to want to follow the direction of our newly created heart.

It's all like the new window treatments we're getting. The old frame is outdated and one of the pulleys doesn't even work any longer. The workman is totally replacing the track and will be covering it with a beautiful mahogany valance. That new track and valance represents the heart. It's totally new like nothing that's been up there before. However, the design of the blinds, although different, is somewhat like the old ones that were already there. My choice is now a renewed design, one that will only work beautifully as it is attached to the new track under the lovely new valance. Those blinds are like my spirit.

When we ask God to create in us a clean heart and renew in us a steadfast spirit, we're asking for a total transformation. Let's participate in the change and enjoy the renovated outcome as our loves project the glory of God.

#121
April 30: Wanted Alive, Not Dead

I grew up watching westerns on TV. Some of the favorite shows in our home were *Bonanza* and *Gunsmoke*. Even now, my husband enjoys a good shoot-em-up movie. In just about every episode or flick, the bad guy would be "wanted dead or alive." Of course, he'd put up a good fight, there'd be a dramatic chase scene, and some damsel in distress would have to be rescued in the process. Ultimately, the meanie would be caught and duly punished, and the good guy would ride away victorious into the sunset having his wounds tended to by that same damsel who would now become his wife. (I know, I should write screenplays!)

Our sin makes us the bad guys in life's drama, but the Good Guy (God) wants to catch us not to punish us, but to transform us. In fact, our punishment was already meted out on Jesus on the cross of Calvary. We're running around hiding and putting up a fight for nothing. In fact, God is searching for us to reward us with mercy, grace, favor, and blessings. The posters for our capture read: Wanted Alive, Not Dead.

Consider Psalm 51:15-17 which says, "Unseal my lips, O Lord, that my mouth may praise you. You do not desire a sacrifice, or I would offer one. You do not want a burnt offering. The sacrifice you desire is a broken spirit. You will not reject a broken and repentant heart, O God" (NLT). And how about Romans 12:1 that reads, "Therefore, I urge you, brothers, in view of God's mercy, to offer your bodies as living sacrifices, holy and pleasing to God—this is your spiritual act of worship" (NIV).

No more running; no more hiding; no more fighting against Heaven's will. God's not interested in our dying for Him; He wants us to live for Him. And as we do, He expects us to open our mouths and praise Him. It's the least we can do.

#122
May 1: My Box and God's Bottle

I have a lot of people to pray for and things to do. In order to get everyone on my prayer list prayed for and everything on my to-do list done, I had to figure out a system. I amaze my friends by how much I can get done in the same 24-hour period they have, and I do so by dividing my chores into bite-sized pieces. Piece by piece, lots of things can be accomplished. So, I divided my prayer list the same way.

Years ago, I started using my prayer box. My box holds 3-by-5 index cards and 7 dividers. The dividers are labeled as follows: Me, James, Children, Ministries, Single Christians, Christian Marriages, The Unsaved. Behind each divider are cards on which I write specific prayer needs. Each of our children and grandchildren has his/her own card, and it's the same for each ministry, single friend, and family. The unsaved are merely listed by name because the only thing I pray for them is that they receive salvation. On Monday, I pray for myself and my husband James, Tuesday is dedicated to the children, and so on through the week. This way, I cover everyone within the week, spend quality time in prayer, and still get other things done throughout the day.

Now don't get me wrong; I also pray for people throughout the day and even on days that are not specifically set aside for them. For example, whenever I'm driving and I see cars like the ones driven by our children, I pray for them. So when I see a Chrysler 300, I pray for Lori; or when a Dodge Charger whizzes by, prayers go up for Mark, and so on. My box helps me remember all the important issues. It also serves as a praise reminder, because I can look back over the years and see how God has always faithfully answered.

Unlike me, God needs no special reminders to keep our concerns before Him. He knows and cares about everything we go through. Psalm 56:8 says, "You number my wanderings; Put my tears into Your bottle; *Are they* not in Your book?" (NKJ) What a blessing and comfort to know that God is looking over us, looking out for us, looking to be right there with us when we hurt – close enough to catch our tears. His deep care for us should move us to care deeply for others. Maybe we can't catch each other's tears in bottles, but we can catch each other's concerns in a box. May we care for others as God cares for us.

#123
May 2: Hiding Place

If you haven't read Corrie Ten Boom's book, *The Hiding Place*, you have missed one of the Christian classics of all time. She and her family helped to hide Jews in their home during the Nazi occupation of Holland. Although their hiding place was never discovered, the family was betrayed on February 28, 1944, arrested, and sent to the prison camps. Only Corrie lived through the experience, but she did so with her faith in tact. According to www.corrietenboom.com/history:

- Corrie and Betsie (her sister) spent 10 months in three different prisons, the last was the infamous Ravensbruck Concentration Camp located near Berlin, Germany. Life in the camp was almost unbearable, but Corrie and Betsie spent their time sharing Jesus' love with their fellow prisoners. Many women became Christians in that terrible place because of Corrie and Betsie's witness to them.

Due to what was later found to be a clerical error, Corrie was released. The history goes on to note:

- Four Ten Booms gave their lives for this family's commitment, but Corrie came home from the death camp. She realized her life was a gift from God, and she needed to share what she and Betsie had learned in Ravensbruck: "There is no pit so deep that God's love is not deeper still" and "God will give us the love to be able to forgive our enemies." At age 53, Corrie began a world-wide ministry which took her into more than 60 countries. She died on her 91st birthday, April 15, 1983.

Thankfully, at least in America for now, we do not have to hide from those who want to kill us because of our race or faith. However, racism and religious hatred exist and is outwardly demonstrated to the point of murder in other parts of the world. Like Corrie, though, we must remember that we always have a hiding place. Psalm 57:1 states, "Be merciful to me, O God, be merciful to me! For my soul trusts in You; and in the shadow of Your wings I will make my refuge, until these calamities have passed by" (NKJ).

Take refuge today in God, the best hiding place ever.

#124
May 3: De-fense!

As basketball fans, we find ourselves often yelling the hopeful chant, "De-fense! (clap, clap) De-fense!" What we mean is that we want our team to stop the other team from gaining an advantage. You see, when our team is on defense, the other team has the ball. Without our team's intervention, the opponent could score.

Psalm 62:5-6 says, "My soul, wait silently for God alone, for my expectation is from Him. He only is my rock and my salvation; *he is my defense*; I shall not be moved" (NKJ, emphasis added). When challenges and life's negative circumstances seem to be getting the upper hand, we can yell out to God, "De-fense! (clap, clap) De-fense!" He is our center, towering over the height of every problem. He is our guard, effectively blocking every charge of the opposition. And He is our power forward, rejecting the shots of disappointment and defeat designed to score points against our advancement and success.

Psalm 94:22-23 echoes the same sentiment. "But *the LORD has been my defense*, and my God the rock of my refuge. He has brought on them their own iniquity, and shall cut them off in their own wickedness; the LORD our God shall cut them off" (NKJ, emphasis added).

Get your shout on! De-fense! (clap, clap) De-fense!

#125
May 4: See God in the Sanctuary

A home is wonderful. It's the location where all the "stuff" of our life has a place. Our homes, and the stuff in our homes, usually reflect our personalities too and what's important to us. For example, my friend Annvernette and her husband's home in New Orleans is warm and inviting as well as knock down, gorgeously appointed. Their home not only says, "Welcome," but you know you're special to them because they took the time to share with you and surround you with so much beauty. If you come to our home, you would see lots of pictures of family and you'd see lots of books. These items reflect our devotion to our loved ones and our thirst for knowledge.

142

I believe it is especially true of a woman that her home is an extension of who she is. We "see" her in her home. The same is true of God. We see Him (or we ought to) in His home. Psalm 63:2 says, "I have looked for You in the sanctuary, to see Your power and Your glory" (NKJ). Did we look for God in His house the last time we attended church? Did His house reflect His power and glory? Deeper still, now that we realize that our hearts are God's home, do we see His power and glory there? "Or do you not know that your body is a temple of the Holy Spirit who is in you, whom you have from God, and that you are not your own?" First Corinthians 6:19 (NAS).

Perhaps it's time to do some interior and exterior renovation to the temple of God – the sanctuary that is you – so that it looks more like God's house. When folks "visit," when they come in contact with us, may they look for God in the sanctuary that is our lives, and see His power and glory.

#126
May 5: Like Momma

For some of us it was Momma; for some, it was Grandma, Big Mama, or Granny; for others it was that favorite aunt. Whoever that mother figure happened to be, no matter how old we get, we enjoy remembering snuggling with and being hugged by her. I loved leaning against my mother's soft shoulder and having her pull me close. She could say, "Don't worry about it," and kiss bumps and bruises, and actually make everything feel better. It was magic.

We grow up, we move away, and sometimes long distances separate us from our mothers. In my case, my mother has moved on to Glory and, all things being equal, I probably won't see her again for a while yet. Although I have the sweet memories of her care and tender hugs, I miss her actual voice and touch.

If you are far from your mom or in the same situation I'm in, at times when we're in need of a mother's love, we can rely on our God. "As one whom his mother comforts, so I will comfort you," says Isaiah 66:13 (NKJ). The word "comfort" here is the Hebrew word "nacham" which means "to sigh, to be sorry, [and] in a favorable sense, to pity and console." God pulls us close, tells us not to worry about it, sighs along with our pain, kisses our bumps and bruises, pities, and consoles us.

Just like Momma.

#127
May 6: When God Rises Up

Has it ever happened that you were acting up either at school or at home, and just when you were at the height of your foolishness, the teacher or your parent walked in? You were caught red-handed in your misbehavior. Your heart started beating faster and your mind started racing for any excuse to make the scene look not so bad. You knew the hammer was about to fall.

Now think of a time when you were doing exactly what you were supposed to be doing when the teacher or your parent walked in. The arrival of authority didn't faze you at all. In fact, you met authority's entrance with a welcome smile or nod. It actually felt good to be "caught" doing the right thing.

Psalm 68:1and 3 is a picture of this idea. "Let God arise, let His enemies be scattered; let those also who hate Him flee before Him… But let the righteous be glad; let them rejoice before God; yes, let them rejoice exceedingly" (NKJ). The Message Bible states these verses this way, "Up with God! Down with his enemies! Adversaries run for the hills!… When the righteous see God in action they'll laugh, they'll sing, they'll laugh and sing for joy" (MSG). The Hebrew word for "arise" used here is "quwm" and it means "to accomplish, be clearer, and establish." You see, when God shows up, He has a point to accomplish, something He wants to make clear, and a position He intends to establish.

Which side of the equation are we on when God shows up? When God rises up ready to accomplish something in our lives, are we found ducking for cover, trying to dodge His hand, and back-peddling out of our mess? Or are we smiling, laughing, and singing for joy at His arrival?

God only wants to make clear His wants, establish us in His ways, and accomplish His will through us. Up with God; let God arise in our lives today!

#128
May 7: Only Wondrous Things

While waiting in the doctor's chair for my optometrist to come in and examine my eyes, my attention was drawn to a large poster on the wall labeling all the components of the eye. Once I got past structures like the optic nerve, the retina, the iris, and the cornea, lots of those other pieces, and their reasons for existence, were lost on me, much less the pronunciation of their names. I'm sure glad my doctor knows what the sclera, conjunctiva, fovea centralis, vitreous chamber, hyaloid canal, and ora serrata are.

I couldn't help but think of Psalm 72:18 as I marveled at that poster. "Blessed be the LORD God, the God of Israel, who only does wondrous things!" (NKJ) All of that and more went into the creation and formation of the human eye. Go into your computer and Google any part of the body—the ear, the nose, the stomach, the heart, even the tongue—and you'll find tons of labels pointing out the various components of each.

The human body is a wondrous thing, as is everything God made. In fact, God is not able to do anything that is *not* wondrous. Other Biblical authors proclaimed God's wonders as well. Job 9:10 says, "Who does great things, unfathomable, and wondrous works without number" (NAS). Psalm 86:10 declares, "For You are great, and do wondrous things; you alone are God" (NKJ). And Daniel remarked, "It is my pleasure to tell you about the miraculous signs and wonders that the Most High God has performed for me. How great are his signs, how mighty his wonders! His kingdom is an eternal kingdom; his dominion endures from generation to generation" Daniel 4:2-3 (NIV).

Take some time today to look at the world around you in a new way. Consider things you would otherwise ignore and meditate on their wonders. A blade of grass, a bird in flight, a piece of fruit, a strand of hair, the starry sky: pick anything. All are the work of the Master Craftsman, our God who only does wondrous things.

#129
May 8: Thanks Due to God

"We give thanks to You, O God, we give thanks! For Your wondrous works declare that Your name is near" Psalm 75:1 (NKJ).

For years, my family and I would attend the beautiful and famous Rose Parade every New Years Day. We were die-hard parade fans who'd spend the night to get the best possible spot right at the blue line painted on Colorado Blvd. there in Pasadena, CA. On parade morning, it seemed like forever before the event began. We'd peer up the street, eagerly awaiting any sign or sound. Then one year, an amazing sight greeted our eyes. The stealth bomber flew over head announcing the start of the parade. What an amazing display! Every year since that fly-over, the stealth has heralded the coming of the spectacle that was about to issue down the street.

From this we learn it's always better to look up to God than to look up at people, up at promises, or even up the street in expectation of what's coming. Just as the crowd in Pasadena had to look up to see the sleek stealth bomber announcing the coming of the parade, if we but look up toward God, we'll see His wonderful works announcing His nearness to us.

- Behold a towering tree with its branches reaching up toward their Creator and give thanks for that same Creator who is close enough for us to touch.
- Behold a bird in flight remembering how its Creator feeds it daily and give thanks for that same Creator's care to feed and clothe us.
- Behold the seashore and notice how the waves crash just that far and no farther and give thanks that God keeps plenty of catastrophes away from us.
- Behold a sunrise or a sunset and think of the movement of the planets, the gravitational balance, and how we are hurtling through space. Give thanks that God's hand is close enough to steady us.

God's wonderful works continuously declare His nearness. We give thanks.

#130
May 9: God is Known

Psalm 76:1a caught my eye. "In Judah God is known..." (NKJ). The Psalmist continues by telling us how it is that God is known in this region. He tells us God's name is considered to be great, His tabernacle is known to be in the area, and everyone knows God's dwelling place is in Zion. The writer also lets us know how God has protected them by breaking the arrows, shields, and swords that have come against them in battle.

I jokingly refer to our humble home as "Elliott Manor." So, can it be said "In Elliott Manor God is known"? Is there evidence in our lives to point to the greatness of God's name? Is there any indication on our property of God "tabernacling" with us? In other words, is the manor a place of prayer and peace – a place where God's glory rests? Can folks come to our home and hear memories related of God's protection and deliverance when hardships have struck?

What about your life and home? Insert the name of your household. Would this be a true statement? In _____ household, God is known.

#131
May 10: God Responds to Our Voice

When my boys were toddlers, I taught them to respond immediately when they heard my voice. I didn't want them to yell, "What?" from another room, and I certainly did not tolerate being ignored and having to call to them several times before they made a move. I explained to them that they may not be aware that responding to my voice immediately could be a matter of grave importance; their welfare could be at stake. They were obedient to that teaching, they knew my voice, and they responded to it appropriately.

However, even before they learned that lesson for themselves, I had modeled it for them. Ever since their birth, I had responded to their voices. Like most mothers, I discovered that uncanny ability to discern a distressful cry from a sleepy one, an angry cry from a hungry one, and an uncomfortable cry from an I-want-my-way-now one. No matter what kind of cry, I responded appropriately. And I knew the voices of my children as distinctly different from all the other babies and toddlers in a nursery, the park, or at any play date.

God knows our voices and responds to our cries. Psalm 77:1 says, "I cried out to God with my voice-- to God with my voice; and He gave ear to me" (NKJ). Notice that the phrase "to God" appears twice and "to me" appears once. In the King James version, that preposition "to" is translated "unto" which is the Hebrew word "'el (ale)" denoting "motion toward." In other words, when we cry out to God using our voices, we are moving toward Him, and when He hears us, He moves toward us. Our voiced cries to our loving heavenly Father set in motion a divine head-on collision, a meeting that will produce results.

It's fine to pray silently in our hearts and minds, but this verse makes it clear that God responds to our voices as well. In fact, if you read the entire 77th Psalm, you'll see that the writer was in deep distress and desperately in need of God's response. When we are in dire straits, seldom do we passively, quietly just sit around. We voice our issue. We need to be heard because the situation is urgent.

Don't be afraid to speak up in prayer. Your compassionate Father knows your voice, loves to hear it, and is eager to respond to your needs.

#132
May 11: When Life Deals a Bad Hand

When playing the card game Bid Whist, it's important to be dealt a hand full of either high cards or low cards. Each player must look at the hand she's been dealt and project how many books she can win. Then each player bids or announces her projection. If she has lots of aces, kings, queens, and maybe a joker, she'll project that she can win 4 or 5 books of high cards. If she has aces, twos, threes, and maybe a joker, she'll guess that she can win 4 or 5 books of the lowest cards. The worse hand to be dealt is a bunch of sevens, eights, and nines.

Sometimes it feels like life has dealt us a bunch of middle cards. No matter which way the bid goes, our cards are going to lose. But wait, that's unless our sevens, eights, and nines are trump cards. If clubs have been called as trump, our middle numbers can beat an ace of some other suit.

In Psalm 77:1-15, the psalmist was feeling like he'd been dealt middle cards and his life situation was causing him to question whether or not God was his partner. Look at verses 1 – 9:

> I cried out to God with my voice-- to God with my voice; and He gave ear to me. In the day of my trouble I sought the Lord; my hand was stretched out in the night without ceasing; my soul refused to be comforted. I remembered God, and was troubled; I complained, and my spirit was overwhelmed. Selah. You hold my eyelids open; I am so troubled that I cannot speak. I have considered the days of old, the years of ancient times. I call to remembrance my song in the night; I meditate within my heart, and my spirit makes diligent search. Will the Lord cast off forever? And will He be favorable no more? Has His mercy ceased forever? Has His promise failed forevermore? Has God forgotten to be gracious? Has He in anger shut up His tender mercies? Selah. (NKJ)

Wow, that's a bad hand: the soul refusing to be comforted, the spirit being overwhelmed, can't sleep, so troubled you can't speak. This person had so little faith that he asked, "Has God forgotten me?"

But when we look again at our hand, we have trump cards. Our trump cards are listed in verses 10 – 15:

> And I said, "This is my anguish; but I will remember the years of the right hand of the Most High." I will remember the works of the LORD; surely I will remember Your wonders of old. I will also meditate on all Your work, and talk of Your deeds. Your way, O God, is in the sanctuary; who is so great a God as our God? You are the God who does wonders; you have declared Your strength among the peoples. You have with Your arm redeemed Your people, the sons of Jacob and Joseph. Selah. (NKJ)

We play our trump cards when we remember what God has already done. When we can't find reason to rejoice in our current situation, our recourse is to play these six trump cards:
- Remember the works of God and His wonders that He has performed in the past.
- Meditate on all His works.
- Talk of His wonderful works.

- Stand on who we know Him to be (He's in the sanctuary, He is great, and He does wonders).
- Declare His strength to people.
- Realize that regardless of what's going on, we have been redeemed.

And don't despair; you have a Partner who has already played the winning cards at Calvary on your behalf. And He continues to play them at God's right hand as He makes continual intercession for you (see Romans 8:34 NKJ). God's love and mercy are not shut down. You just play your trump cards and watch how you and your Partner will win every time.

#133
May 12: Pain Relief

A very touching song that's often sung at funerals is *I Won't Complain* penned by Clay Evans. In wrapping up speaking about how good God's been throughout life, the final lines of the chorus say, "All of my good days, outweigh my bad days, so I won't complain." This sentiment is indeed comforting when we're looking back after the illness that ravished a body has now been "healed" by death, or after the war has ended and the soldier has given his or her all, or even after a long life well-lived in health and prosperity is now transitioning into Glory. However, during the suffering, it's hard to recall the good days. But that's exactly what this hymn and Psalm 77 encourages us to do.

After speaking of trouble so bad that he can't sleep; after his diligent search for God who seems to have cast him off; after feeling as though mercy has ceased, the promises have failed, and God has utterly forgotten about him, the Psalmist says, "This is my anguish; but I will remember the years of the right hand of the Most High. I will remember the works of the LORD; surely I will remember Your wonders of old. I will also meditate on all Your work, and talk of Your deeds" Psalm 77:10-12 (NKJ).

The reality of who God is and what He's done is the power that holds us up when we're in anguish. No matter how bad we feel and how dark our days, it's worth remembering that God has not changed nor will He ever change. He is still the peace that passes all understanding, our shelter in the time of storm, our rock, our fortress, and the One who can be trusted. God is still the light and in Him is no darkness at all. God is still love.

All of Psalm 77 gives us the perfect pattern for pain relief. God's shoulders are broad enough to handle it when we must pour out our grieving heart to Him (verses 1-10a). However, we mustn't stop there. Even before our tears have completely dried, say with the Psalmist, "But I will remember..." Then start recalling in the same way the Psalmist did from verses 10b – 12.
* "I will remember the years of the right hand of the Most High."
* "I will remember the works of the LORD."
* "Surely I will remember Your wonders of old."
* "I will also meditate on all Your work"
* "[I will] talk of Your deeds.

The truth is indeed the light. As we remember the years of God's right hand – the years in which we've see His power; as we remember His works and wonders; as we meditate and deliberately focus on all His work; we'll find that our hearts will begin to heal and our talk will reflect His awesome nature.

#134
May 13: God is at Church

In the Amplified Bible, Psalm 77:13a says, "Your way, O God, is in the sanctuary [in holiness, away from sin and guilt]."

For the children of Israel, the sanctuary was the place where they would meet with God. God manifested, revealed, or showed Himself at the tabernacle. While journeying through the wilderness, God's people could literally see the glory of God hovering over it in the form of a cloud by day and fire by night. They came to view the tabernacle, and later Solomon's temple, as the place where God lived. I guess that's why when I was growing up, we viewed the church building as God's house.

Since the resurrection of Jesus, God has done some renovation on His house. He's added rooms, so to speak. What rooms has He added? He's added the Sharon room and the James room (that's me and my husband). And He's added the room with your name on it if you are a believer in Jesus Christ. "Or do you not know," says Paul, "that **your body is the temple** of the Holy Spirit who is in you, whom you have from God, and you are not your own?" First Corinthians 6:19 (NKJ, emphasis added).

Does this excuse us from going to church? No. The New Testament does not negate the Old Testament; rather, the New confirms the Old. The fellowship of believers is the entire building. We wouldn't live in a house that was only a bathroom or only a den. Even a bachelor pad has sections specified for various needs. So it is with the church and the body of Christ. Your room only functions to its full capacity and potential as it is connected with the rest of the house. The New Testament confirms this as well in Hebrews 10:25 when it says, "Let us not give up meeting together, as some are in the habit of doing, but let us encourage one another—and all the more as you see the Day approaching" (NIV).

So get up and go to church. There we learn His ways, are reminded of His desires, find rest from our worries, and obtain encouragement for our journeys. We discover how to live in holiness, away from sin and guilt. God is in the sanctuary.

#135
May 14: For His Name's Sake

God loves us, that's for sure. However, His actions on our behalf are not so much because of His love for us, but because of His own glory. Throughout the Old Testament, the patriarchs, priests, and prophets always deferred to God's glory as the reason for God's actions. A striking example comes when God was seemingly totally exasperated with the complaining of the children of Israel in the wilderness. During a conversation with Moses, God revealed that He had decided to wipe them out and start over with Moses to raise up a people who would respect and glorify Him. Moses's reasoning with God against God's own plan appealed to the showing of His glory. Moses told God that if He killed all the people, the Egyptians would hear about it and say, "Because the LORD was not able to bring this people to the land which He swore to give them, therefore He killed them in the wilderness" Numbers 14:16 (NKJ). In other words, the bottom line of Moses's argument was, "Lord, if you kill them, You'll look bad."

God's answer to Moses went right to the heart of the matter. "I have pardoned, according to your word; but truly, as I live, all the earth shall be filled with the glory of the LORD" Numbers 14:20-21 (NKJ). In other words, God was saying that even though He was going to let those stiff-necked people live, He was not going to allow them to punk Him or pimp Him. His glory would have the final say. In the case of the children of Israel at this juncture, all the complainers died in the next 40-year interval of their wilderness trek, and the next generation went into the Promised Land.

God's glory has the final say when the unrepentant sinner suffers the consequences of His wrath, and the repentant sinner enjoys the relief awarded by His mercy. As with the God/Moses conversation, God moves on our behalf ultimately for His glory— for His name's sake. The Psalmist put it this way:

- Oh, do not remember former iniquities against us! Let Your tender mercies come speedily to meet us, for we have been brought very low. Help us, O God of our salvation, for the glory of Your name; and deliver us, and provide atonement for our sins, for Your name's sake! Psalm 79:8-9 (NKJ)

May we live a repentant people, ever ready to appeal to the mercies of God so that ultimately, God's glory will be on display.

#136
May 15: Is It Really Smart to Tie God's Hands?

When people say, "My hands are tied," they are usually talking to you about some reason why they can't help you. More often than not, that reason stems from something you did or didn't do. For example, my students come to me at the end of the year wanting to better their grade in my class. By that time, I have to tell them that my hands are tied. I can't help them because they didn't help themselves by studying as they should have studied over the course of the whole class. Or perhaps someone sought to take out a loan for that great house and the banker says, "I'm sorry, my hands are tied because you have just too much credit card debt." The hopeful borrower simply spent too much money on little things and now that big thing she really wants is out of reach.

Yes, in both examples above, the person in need tied the

hands of the person who could have helped. If only they could go back, retrace their steps, and rethink their decisions, the outcome now would be far different and definitely to their advantage. But alas, the student must settle for the lower grade, and the borrower must stay in that apartment a bit longer.

We put ourselves in the same kinds of situations with God by not listening to His voice. Psalm 81:11-12 says, "But My people would not heed My voice, and Israel would have none of Me. So I gave them over to their own stubborn heart, to walk in their own counsels" (NKJ). This sounds a lot like Romans 1:18-28 which reads in part:

> The wrath of God is being revealed from heaven against all the godlessness and wickedness of men... since what may be known about God is plain to them, because God has made it plain to them... For although they knew God, they neither glorified him as God nor gave thanks to him... they became fools and exchanged the glory of the immortal God for images made to look like mortal man and birds and animals and reptiles. Therefore God gave them over in the sinful desires of their hearts..., to shameful lusts... [and] to a depraved mind, to do what ought not to be done. (NIV)

So my question stands: is it really smart to tie God's hands? By not listening to God, by not heeding His voice, we open ourselves up to God simply taking His hands off of us. He cannot bless our mess, and if we simply decide to live in it, He'll let us. He'll cry over us and shake His head as He watches us drown in our waywardness, but He'll allow what we insist upon.

No, it's not smart to tie God's hands. Listen, heed, and let God bless you.

#137
May 16: The Cry of God's Heart

"Oh, that My people would listen to Me, that Israel would walk in My ways! I would soon subdue their enemies, and turn My hand against their adversaries. The haters of the LORD would pretend submission to Him, but their fate would endure forever. He would have fed them also with the finest of wheat; and with honey from the rock I would have satisfied you" Psalm 81:13-16 (NKJ).

Yes, this Psalm was originally written to reveal the disappointing cry of God's heart over Israel's disobedience. Be quick to remember, though, that the Church of God includes all who name the name of Christ as Savior, Redeemer, and Lord. We, Gentiles, have been grafted in and so are as much God's children as is Israel. This cry then from God's disappointed heart could very well be directed at us.

God desires that we walk in His ways. Look at all He will do when we simply obey:

- God will subdue our enemies.
- God will turn His hand against our adversaries.
- Haters of the Lord who are around us will get what's coming to them.
- God will feed us the necessities of life from the finest He has.
- God will provide "honey from the rock," those things which are over and above the necessities, to satisfy us.

And all we have to do is listen (hear intelligently) and walk (continually follow) in His ways (the road He's marked out for us)? Sounds like a no-brainer to me!

#138
May 17: No Good Thing Withheld

The story is told of a man who gets to heaven and is given a tour. The tour guide angel shows the man such glories as the streets of gold, the mansions Jesus has been preparing for each of His saints, and God's throne room. As they are walking down one particular celestial pathway, they pass a room to which the door is partially ajar. Inside the room, for as far as the eye could see, were all sorts of beautifully wrapped presents.

The new arrival asks, "What's that room all about?"

The angel answers, "Oh, that's the room holding answers to prayer."

The puzzled man inquired further, "Well, what are they all doing still here?"

The angel replied, "God answered as soon as His saints made their request, but when we showed up with the delivery, the requester had moved on, having not been patient enough to wait to receive what God had for them."

Psalm 84:11 says, "… no good thing will He withhold from those who walk uprightly" (NKJ). The NIV renders that verse this way: "… no good thing does he withhold from those whose walk is blameless," and The Message Bible says, "He doesn't scrimp with his traveling companions." We conduct ourselves rightly and honorably, not just to get things, but because we love God. However, know that God's unfailing love for us will be manifested to those of us whose hearts are determined to walk in His ways.

Patiently wait for God's wonderful answers to your prayers. Answered prayer and good things are just as natural an outcome of an obedient life as a bountiful harvest is of good seed planted in good soil.

#139
May 18: God Will Speak

My sister and I often teased our mother about speaking for Daddy and then complaining about how he wouldn't talk. You see, although Daddy was a pastor, at home, he was very quiet. We hardly ever heard him say a word. He wasn't disconnected or distant; he just conducted his life quietly. There was never any question as to whether he loved us. We knew what was expected of us because we followed his example. He was highly educated, read lots of books, and anchored his life on God and family. What more in life is there really to do?

When Daddy did speak, his words carried weight. We knew he had something important to say if he took the time to say it. We listened, took note, and treasured the meaning of his words. If we were upset or confused, Daddy could speak to the situation and no matter what had seemed wrong, everything became all right. Even if we had done something stupid, Daddy could speak into our stupidity and restore us. The laughter and joy would return to our home and our hearts.

I miss my daddy's quiet presence and healing words; but I

know where Daddy got those traits. Psalm 85:8-9 says, "I will hear what God the LORD will speak, for He will speak peace to His people and to His saints; but let them not turn back to folly. Surely His salvation is near to those who fear Him, that glory may dwell in our land" (NKJ). God will speak what we need to hear. No matter what our circumstance might be – even when we've descended into folly (stupidity) – He is near enough to speak words of rescue and peace, making everything all right once again. The glory that had vanished is able to return to our lives, causing us to be able to keep on going on our kingdom journey.

Won't you listen to God speaking today? He will speak peace to you, especially as you turn back from your folly. Sure, your heart will beat a little faster as you talk with Him about where you've been and what you've been doing, but His words will show you just how near salvation is. Just listen and watch the glory return to your life. Indeed, God will speak.

#140
May 19: Ready to Forgive

One of the best facts about God (if there can be a "best" about all that He is) is His mercy. He is such a dad when it comes to this attribute. No matter how much we miserably blow it, and no matter how much He has to discipline us, He keeps on loving us and being a Father to us. In fact, Psalm 86:5 says, "For You, Lord, are good, and ready to forgive, and abundant in mercy to all those who call upon You" (NKJ).

The fact that He's "ready to forgive" (callach [saw-lawkh'] in Hebrew) means He is able to be placated, appeased, or stopped from being angry. And what stops Him from being angry? Confession. Admit it; agree with God when you've been wrong, turn from that thing, that person, that place, or that action, and start living the way He would want.

With a good, merciful Father who is always ready to forgive us, can't our love for Him and thankfulness toward Him help us do a little better at not miserably blowing it so much.

#141
May 20: Just Wait and See

When I know I'm right about something, there's no need for me to argue my point. No amount of persuasive logic from anyone will be able to turn me from what I know to be true. I can quickly end the conversation by saying (politely, of course), "Just wait and see."

We can take that same confident stand when any questions arise about whether or not our faith is real. We can side with the Psalmist who said, "Among the gods there is none like You, O Lord; nor are there any works like Your works. All nations whom You have made shall come and worship before You, O Lord, and shall glorify Your name. For You are great, and do wondrous things; you alone are God" Psalm 86:8-10 (NKJ).

A great example of God's influence over anybody is found in the opening chapter of the book of Ezra. The Israelites had spent years in captivity, subjugated by other nations. Suddenly, in the first year of his reign, "the LORD stirred up the spirit of Cyrus king of Persia, so that he made a proclamation throughout all his kingdom, and also put it in writing, saying, 'Thus says Cyrus king of Persia: All the kingdoms of the earth the LORD God of heaven has given me. And He has commanded me to build Him a house at Jerusalem which is in Judah'" Ezra 1:1-2 (NKJ). Here was a heathen king being moved by God to build Him a house!

A famous New Testament example of the same thing is the conversion of Saul, the former persecutor of the early Church, who became Paul and penned many of the letters we have today as holy Scripture (see Acts 9:1-31 and 13:9).

Neither Cyrus nor Saul initially believed in God, but that didn't matter to God. Their unbelief didn't affect the truth of who He was one bit. Neither does the unbelief of our friends, coworkers, or anybody else on the planet. One thing's for sure, one day all nations will worship Him because He is God alone. Just wait and see.

#142
May 21: What's on Your List?

If you were asked to list important things about God, what would be on your list? A Psalmist has made his list in Psalm 86:15. "But You, O Lord, are a God full of compassion, and gracious, longsuffering and abundant in mercy and truth" (NKJ). What does each of these attributes mean?

- Compassion: God has pity for us so He acts to spare us of what would be our terrible fate apart from Him.
- Gracious: Favor or kindness shown without regard to the worth or merit of the one who receives it and in spite of what that same person deserves. (from Nelson's Illustrated Bible Dictionary)
- Longsuffering: Long patience; God is slow to anger.
- Mercy: Kindness. God is just nice to us.
- Truth: This word carries with it the reality of God's stability, trustworthiness, and faithfulness.

Now here are two assignments. First, read Psalm 86:15 by putting in the explanation of each of the words the psalmist used. Second, here's your challenge. Be a psalmist yourself and write your own verse about God; however, don't use any of the attributes this psalmist used. Fill in the blanks:

But You, O Lord, are a God full of _____, and _____, _____, and abundant in _____ and _____.

Have a wonderful day basking in the wonder of our God.

#143
May 22: God is Faithful

Psalm 89:8 says, "O LORD God of hosts, who is mighty like You, O LORD? Your faithfulness also surrounds You" (NKJ). The Hebrew word for faithfulness is "'emuwnah" (em-oo-naw'). Vine's Expository Dictionary of Biblical Words explains, "The basic meaning of 'emunah is certainty and faithfulness. The Lord has manifested His faithfulness to His people: 'He is the Rock, his works are perfect, and all his ways are just. A faithful God who does no wrong, upright and just is he' Deuteronomy 32:4. All his works reveal his faithfulness (Psalm 33:4), and His commandments are an expression of his faithfulness (Psalm 119:86)." In short, God is stable, steady, true, and as firm as a rock solid. He possesses the attributes of total security and moral fidelity.

As the Psalmist reflects on God's might, God's faithfulness becomes the subject of Psalm 89:8. What kind of God would He be to possess all the strength of the universe, but yet be unwilling or unable to use it for good? If He used that strength to overpower us, He'd be a tyrant. If He used it to coddle us, He'd be a wimp existing for us to boss Him around. No, God uses His might to show us how much He loves us. He forgives and picks us up over and over again, not because He's weak, but because He's strong. He's there no matter where we are when we fall, how hard and how far we fall, nor what we were doing to cause us to fall.

So like the Psalmist, when we think of God's strength—His might—we realize that His use of that strength on our behalf is a reflection of nothing more than His great faithfulness.

Thank You, God, for Your incredible faithfulness to us.

#144
May 23: Punished but not Forsaken

Think back on how many times we disobeyed our parents and got caught. In most homes, when that happened, there were consequences. Maybe we got a spanking, perhaps we were sent to our room for a "time out," or it could have been that we were given some extra chores. Whatever the case, if our wrong was discovered, we were punished.

The wonderful thing about being punished by loving parents, though, came after the punishment ended. When the tension of the disobedience passed, our parents eventually forgave us, and the relationship was restored. We could smile upon seeing one another and enjoy being in the same room. Even though our parents had to discipline us, they never gave up on us. We were chastised but never forsaken. Even if we were rebuked just before dinner, we were still allowed to eat (even if we had to eat alone in our room or at a separate table). Our disobedience never made us un-children of theirs.

Psalm 89:30-34 says, "If his sons forsake My law and do not walk in My judgments, if they break My statutes and do not keep My commandments, then I will punish their transgression with the rod, and their iniquity with stripes. Nevertheless My lovingkindness I will not utterly take from him, nor allow My faithfulness to fail. My covenant I will not break, nor alter the word that has gone out of My lips" (NKJ).

Just like with our earthly parents, our disobedience will bring about punishment from our loving God because He cares enough to stop us from acting a fool. Still, even if He has to rebuke us harshly, He will faithfully remain our Father. He will never break His covenant with us to sovereignly and divinely parent us through this life.

#145
May 24: Our Days are Numbered

Way back in the beginning, people lived a long, long time. Adam lived to be 930 years old and his son, Seth, lived to be 912. Methuselah lived longest, dying at the age of 969, probably in the year of the great Flood. By Genesis, chapter 6, man was beginning to walk away from God, so He voiced a new decision. "Then the LORD said, 'My Spirit will not contend with man forever, for he is mortal; his days will be a hundred and twenty years'" Genesis 6:3 (NIV).

After years and years of more and more sin, man's lifespan shortened yet again; however, man's experiences with God had taught him a thing or two. By the time of the writing of the Psalms, the spiritually-attuned psalmist was able to put his finger on some truths about life and about God's involvement with us. In Psalm 90:10-12 we read, "The days of our lives are seventy years; and if by reason of strength they are eighty years, yet their boast is only labor and sorrow; for it is soon cut off, and we fly away. Who knows the power of Your anger? For as the fear of You, so is Your wrath. So teach us to number our days, that we may gain a heart of wisdom" (NKJ).

Although the current world life expectancy averages at 67.2 years, according to the U.S. Census Bureau, Statistical

Abstract of the United States: 2011, the average life expectancy in the United States of America is 78.3 years, right within the range stated in Psalm 90. Notice what the Psalmist says. Our days are full of "labor and sorrow," and they are "soon cut off and we fly away." Why is that? It's the same reason why God originally cut the multi-century lifespan down the first time to 120—sin. God's anger over sin reached to our world, touches our bodies, and we suffer the consequences. We get older and our bodies don't respond like they used to. We start to break down and wear out.

There's great news, though, for the believer. The Psalmist gives us a big hint about how to live out these fleeting days to their fullest. We can request that God would "teach us to number our days, that we may gain a heart of wisdom." If we form the habit of living wisely and following God's commands, we will live a full and satisfying life. No matter how many days God allows us to see, they will be days full of wonder at His presence, and excitement in our participation in kingdom work. Every hour will be bathed in thankfulness for His glory and power.

Our days may be numbered, but they are numbered by our loving God who, from age to age, does all things well.

#146
May 25: In Him I Will Trust

In our marriage, it is our created tradition for my husband to plan our anniversary trip each year. He not only plans it, though, but he plans it secretly. My only job is to be sure to clear my calendar for the number of days necessary. Then he usually tells me of our upcoming destination about a week or so ahead, just so I'll know how to pack. We've been to exotic locations like Hawaii and Jamaica, but he's getting more and more creative as the years pass. Last year, he kept the destination secret until we actually arrived near the place. I hadn't even known which direction we were turning out of the driveway! That year, we spent three days at a resort in San Diego, and then returned home for just one night, only to take off again for 3 more days in Las Vegas. Again, the second half of the trip was a complete surprise. This year, we're driving up the California coast to San Francisco, stopping as we see fit along the way. It will be a vacation/adventure – something new once again.

Undoubtedly, I must trust my husband quite a bit to submit to being taken who-knows-where. I got to thinking: *The faith I have in putting myself in God's care should at least equal the faith I have in putting myself in James's care.* Am I as trusting of my heavenly Father as I am of this earthly man? Can God take me wherever He wants without my questioning Him? Do I give God a smiling okay when He says, "Let's turn off here," or "Explore this canyon with Me," or "Let's walk through this wilderness"?

Psalm 91 should reflect my daily attitude of trust toward God. Verses 1 – 2 say, "He who dwells in the secret place of the Most High shall abide under the shadow of the Almighty. I will say of the Lord, "He is my refuge and my fortress; My God, in Him I will trust."

I know I'm fortunate to have a husband I can so completely trust with my well-being. I'm amazingly blessed to know the God of the universe in whom I can trust even more fully. How about you?

#147
May 26: The Ever-Present Friend

It's easy to feel alone when we're facing crisis points in our lives. Intellectually, we know that others have struggled with the same types of issues, but it's different when it's you. It doesn't even help too much when people who have been there say, "I know just how you feel." Right then, you just want to shout, "No you don't! This was *my* best friend who betrayed me," or "It's *my* credit rating that's ruined since I can't pay my bills due to this extensive unemployment time," or "We're not talking about your loved one who passed on; that was *my* momma or *my* daddy or *my* child or *my* spouse who died!"

The best thing good friends can do when we're hurting is to just be within reach. The knowledge that we can get to them if we need them is amazingly comforting. And when we're ready and we do finally call on friends like that, they know what to say and do.

God is just such a friend and more. He is ever-present (omnipresent), being there whenever and wherever we need Him. But more than that, He says of each one of us, "Because he has set his love upon Me, therefore I will deliver him; I will set him on high, because he has known My name. He shall call upon Me, and

I will answer him; I will be with him in trouble; I will deliver him and honor him. With long life I will satisfy him, and show him My salvation" Psalm 91:14-16 (NKJ).

What a friend we have in God!

#148
May 27: That's My God at Work

On our recent vacation, my husband and I decided to wing it with only a map and a full tank of gas. We were in the San Francisco area, and since I had never crossed the Golden Gate Bridge, we took off to make that happen. Traffic was horrendous, but we finally made it to the famous site. We drove across under a heavy fog that made it impossible to even see the tops of the towers.

With that mission accomplished and more than half a day of sunlight left, we decided to drive through Sausalito, another place I hadn't seen. We did so and then saw a sign pointing us temptingly toward Stinson Beach. *Why not?* We reasoned. Well, that two-way road to Stinson Beach wound us around mountains and through valleys; it was much more of a drive than we had bargained for. Two hours later, we finally zig-zagged our way back through San Rafael and got ourselves back onto Highway 101 headed back across the Golden Gate Bridge ($6 toll and all). What a ride!

Even though we had taken an unplanned turn, that drive was devastatingly beautiful. Around every bend was yet another amazing vista; visible only to eyes that took that out-of-the-way road. I kept thinking, *Wow, God did all this work for us to enjoy today.*

Psalm 92:4 perfectly sums up my feelings, "For You, Lord, have made me glad through Your work; I will triumph in the works of Your hands" (NKJ). At first read, I wondered how I could be the one triumphing in the works of God's hands. Then I got it. In the same way I used to yell, "That's my kid," when Mark scored a basket on the basketball court, I can triumph in the works of my God's hands when I see them. I guess I'm yelling, "That's my God at work!"

So the next time you see a gorgeous sunset, the waves rolling in, a mountain vista, or a starry night sky, be glad through

God's work, and triumph in the works of His hands. You may even want to shout out, "That's my God at work!"

#149
May 28: Listen to Your Monitor

Eight of us had a fabulous girls' night out last week when we attended jazz pianist Keiko Matsui's last West Coast concert of her season. I'd never heard her music before. She's incredible! She blends a surprising mixture of classical, jazz, and rhythm and blues that's easily and pleasingly palatable.

At the beginning of the concert, Keiko had a problem with her monitor. During the first song, she tried to signal the sound technicians to adjust the volume. That didn't happen, so after her second song, when she addressed the audience, she also took a moment to tell the sound guys that she was hearing distortion whenever she played loudly. Even when they changed the monitor for her, the distortion seemed to continue. Eventually, either the crew got the monitor to work or Keiko just gave up and finished the evening's amazing performance. We in the audience never heard any distortion; all we heard was classical-jazz brilliance.

I began to wonder how often during the performances of our lives do we stop and make necessary adjustments when we sense distortion. Even if nobody else hears, sees, or senses that something is wrong, are we so intimately tuned in to God's heart that we insist on getting things right before we move on?

Psalm 95:7-8a says, "For he is our God and we are the people of his pasture, the flock under his care. Today, if you hear his voice, do not harden your hearts…"(NIV). Incorporate times of determined quietness before God so you can listen for any distortion that may be keeping clarity away from your life. If there is some, once you discover its source, change the monitor, adjust the volume, do whatever you have to do to get your hearing clear. When you can clearly hear what you're playing, you can play your song beautifully.

By the way, I'm buying Keiko Matsui's new CD, entitled Mojo. Have a great day (and start making it a regular habit) listening to your monitor.

#150
May 29: The Lord, *He* is God

Psalm 100 is a favorite of many people. In fact, many of us have it memorized. Once someone starts it off with the beginning words, "Make a joyful noise unto the Lord all ye lands..." lots of us can continue and finish it. We can rattle it off, nodding our heads in agreement and smiling because the message is a joyous one that rings in our hearts.

However, when I read that Psalm this morning, the first words of verse 3 popped out at me in a particularly special way. It says, "Know ye that the Lord, He is God." Further breaking down that portion, I found a spotlight shining on the word "He." Read that sentence out loud and emphasize the word "He:" Know ye that the Lord, *He* is God.

This may sound silly, but I'm really thankful that God is God. If the universe were different, I could have been created by some evil being, void of attributes such as love, grace, mercy, and patience – all of which I need from my Creator on a daily basis. I'm glad today that God—the loving, gracious, merciful, and patient God—is the God who created me and is the God I am privileged to serve.

It is my prayer for you today that you rejoice to know that the Lord, *He* is God.

#151
May 30: To Infinity and Beyond

One of my favorite children's movies is *Toy Story*. The main characters are Andy's toys, and the plot revolves around them. A new toy, Buzz Lightyear, is added to the mix. Buzz believes he can fly, his light is an actual laser, and he's on earth to protect the planet. Woody, Andy's favorite plaything, tries to convince the high tech robot that he's only a toy, but Buzz is determined to stick to his mission. Even though later in the movie Buzz realizes he's a toy, the special gadgets with which he was made, help all the other toys in the end. Buzz never stops shouting his battle cry, "To infinity and beyond!"

Sadly for Buzz, some of you reading this devotion either

may never have heard of him or you may have forgotten all about him. His battle cry is mute without a remembrance of him. There is One, however, who can assertively proclaim that cry. Psalm 102:12 says, "But You, O LORD, shall endure forever, and the remembrance of Your name to all generations" (NKJ). No matter how pagan our society seems to be becoming, the Bible is clear that God's name will be remembered by our offspring, and by theirs, and by theirs, and on and on eternally.

Just as it happened in *Toy Story* when Buzz Lightyear was added to the collection of toys, new Christians will be continually added to the family of God. Just as Woody told Buzz he was now one of Andy's toys, it's our job to let our children and new believers know they are a part of an elite collection. They are God's. All they have brought with them, although just gadgets in their own hands, are gifts that can be used for the Master's service. "His mercy is on those who fear Him," says Luke 1:50 (NKJ), "from generation to generation"—to infinity and beyond.

#152
May 31: All His Benefits

If you've been following the devotions this year, you know the focus each day is on something the Bible tells us about God. Most days, something that I've read in the Scriptures has stirred my soul and caused my eyebrows to rise in wonder. Usually I add some personal memory the verses have resurrected, or relate some deeper meaning God has revealed. Today, there's nothing I can add to the passage to make it any clearer than it already is. The writer of Psalm 103 simply lists the wonderful things God has done for us, and reflects on the marvelous way God treats us. Enjoy being reminded.

- Bless the LORD, O my soul; and all that is within me, bless His holy name! Bless the LORD, O my soul, and forget not all His benefits: who forgives all your iniquities, who heals all your diseases, who redeems your life from destruction, who crowns you with lovingkindness and tender mercies, who satisfies your mouth with good things, so that your youth is renewed like the eagle's.

- The LORD executes righteousness and justice for all who are oppressed. He made known His ways to Moses, his acts to the children of Israel.
- The LORD is merciful and gracious, slow to anger, and abounding in mercy. He will not always strive with us, nor will He keep His anger forever. He has not dealt with us according to our sins, nor punished us according to our iniquities. For as the heavens are high above the earth, so great is His mercy toward those who fear Him; as far as the east is from the west, so far has He removed our transgressions from us.
- As a father pities his children, so the LORD pities those who fear Him. For He knows our frame; he remembers that we are dust. As for man, his days are like grass; as a flower of the field, so he flourishes. For the wind passes over it, and it is gone, and its place remembers it no more. But the mercy of the LORD is from everlasting to everlasting on those who fear Him, and His righteousness to children's children, to such as keep His covenant, and to those who remember His commandments to do them.
- The LORD has established His throne in heaven, and His kingdom rules over all. Psalm 103:1-19, (NKJ)

#153
June 1: God, The Beach Dude

In the United States of America, the first Monday of September is celebrated as a holiday called Labor Day. Established in 1882, Labor Day is "a workingman's holiday; a creation of the labor movement... dedicated to the social and economic achievements of American workers." (United States Department of Labor, www.dol.gov)

Labor Day officially marks the end of summer. Children return to school, workers settle in to fall routines, and the fashion conscious put away their white clothes and shoes. Many coastal dwellers love to spend the holiday at the beach, soaking up summer's last warm, carefree day.

Well, for all you sand babies out there, be it known that God Himself is a beach dude. When speaking of God's plans for the water He created, the Psalmist remarked, "You [God] have set a boundary that they [the waters] may not pass over, that they may not return to cover the earth" Psalm 104:9 (NKJ).

Yes, the beach was God's idea. While you're out there next Labor Day weekend, watch how the waves deliberately back pedal once they reach the shore. It's as if each beautifully cascading white top reminds itself, "God said go this far and no farther."

From time-to-time, however, nature seems to get out of control. We've both witnessed and experienced hurricanes, for example, whose winds whip the waves into a frenzy, carrying the waters out of their boundaries to the destructive dismay of thousands. It's not a far stretch to see these storms as earthly examples of what God's primary enemy will do in our lives if given an opportunity. If allowed, Satan will take the best God has given us and stir it into something destructive.

With all that in mind, let's keep our talents and gifts focused for God's use and disciplined by His guidelines and limits. And whether we're physically on the sand this holiday or mentally picturing the incoming tide, worship God today for His awesome creative genius and His ultimate control in regard to the beauty and power of nature—especially the wonder of the boundary of ocean's waves.

#154
June 2: Enduring Mercy

We live in a disposable society. No matter how hard we try to conserve and recycle, the throw-away nature of many conveniences seems to be firmly entrenched. Young mothers appreciate the convenience of disposable diapers over the labor-intensive use of cloth ones. We opt for pre-moistened wipes rather than reusable washcloths, and we wash our cars with disposable clothes instead of reusable towels. We even opt for paper plates for our home-cooked meals rather than using our stoneware of china. Environmentalists tell us our planet will pay a dear price for these decisions, but since few of us live near a landfill, we just continue dropping our trash into the nearest bin and keep moving.

Thankfully, nothing about God is disposable. Psalm 107:1 tells of one of the vital things about Him that is lasting. "Oh, give thanks to the LORD, for He is good! For His mercy endures forever" (NKJ). Mercy—Gods' forbearance that keeps us from getting what we truly deserve—is always available. Not only is mercy not disposable, but it is also not recyclable. Like the weekday manna, enough mercy is supplied for one day and then we find that "through the LORD'S mercies we are not consumed, because His compassions fail not. They are new every morning; great is Your faithfulness" Lamentations 3:22-23 (NKJ).

Thank God for His enduring mercy.

#155
June 3: God Satisfies

A popular candy bar was featured in a widespread advertising campaign which boasted "Snickers® satisfies." Commercials depicted frazzled people frantically making their way to office vending machines to get their candy "fix." They'd hungrily tear the wrapper and bite into the rich, sweet chocolate. With a deep sigh, their facial expressions softened, they began to smile, and they headed back to their desks satisfied enough to get back to business.

Psalm 107:8-9 declares, "Oh, that men would give thanks to the LORD for His goodness, and for His wonderful works to the children of men! For He satisfies the longing soul, and fills the hungry soul with goodness" (NKJ). Make your way to a window, a park, a family photo album, or a calm corner of your mind. Tear off the wrapper of life's current struggles and bite into thoughts of the multitudinous goodness of God. Now take a deep sigh, relax the muscles in your face, smile, and return to the work at hand realizing your hungry soul is filled with His goodness, and your longing soul is contented by Him.

In truth, God satisfies.

#156
June 4: Mercy Suits Our Case

A minister friend of mine, Sister Burden, has a favorite saying: Mercy suits our case. Almost every time I've heard her pray, I've heard her say this. She is a sweet, gentle mother of the church and an evangelist whose life journey has taught her many things. I take to heart the gentle things she says so I pondered over the meaning of this phrase.

It takes an awareness of our sinfulness to understand that mercy suits our case. Nelson's Illustrated Bible Dictionary tells us that mercy is "the aspect of God's love that causes Him to help the miserable... either because of breaking God's law or because of circumstances beyond their control... God's mercy on the miserable extends beyond punishment that is withheld... (and) because God is merciful, He expects His children to be merciful." Only when we grasp the enormity of our wretchedness can we begin to grasp the enormity of His mercy. We were born as lost sinners, disconnected from God. Our state was sin; the remedy was out of our control. His mercy reached down through Jesus to pay the penalty for our sin and reconnect us to God, giving us hope for Eternity.

A full recognition of who we are and who God is should cause us to see ourselves in the Psalmist's words: "Then they cried out to the LORD in their trouble, and He saved them out of their distresses. He sent His word and healed them, and delivered them from their destructions" Psalm 107:19-20 (NKJ).

The gavel has come down on our case before the Judge of all. Guilty. But thanks be to God that we can cry out to the Judge Himself who has looked compassionately on us. Even though we are red-handedly guilty, mercy suits our case. Through the blood of Jesus, He has saved us out of our distresses, sent His word and healed us, and delivered us from that which would destroy us. Mercy has opened the prison doors of everything that seeks to enslave us. All we need to do is walk out from among whatever those strongholds have been.

#157
June 5: A Reason to Chill

If I get nervous or frightened, I experience the same physical reaction now as an adult as I used to experience when I was a little girl. My heart starts pounding, my stomach ties in knots, and my mind begins searching for an escape. I can manage those feelings pretty well now, and I've become wise enough not to linger in them; still, the initial fight or flight response automatically sets in.

Christ followers have additional protection against rising blood pressure when anxiety and/or fear try to take up residence. Psalm 107:19-20 says, "Then they cried out to the LORD in their trouble, and He saved them out of their distresses. He sent His word and healed them, and delivered them from their destructions" (NKJ). When our minds begin to hunt for a way out of trouble, all we need is to remember to open (or pull up on your iPad) the emergency escape route map. There are 66 escape routes, all clearly marked for every possible God-ordained path away from or safely through distress. God has "sent His word" (the 66 books of the Bible) for healing and deliverance.

Our bodies will naturally respond to tension; however, we have every reason to chill when faced with stressful circumstances. God's word is readily available for relief and release.

#158
June 6: On Calming Storms

Scott Krippayne's amazing song entitled *Sometimes He Calms The Storm* alerts us to the proper perspective we need to have about the troubles that pass through our lives. The bottom line explains that sometimes God calms the storm around us, but sometimes, He lets the storm rage while He calms us.

When Peter walked on water, he wasn't walking on the smooth surface of a calm sea. He strode to Jesus on boisterous waves. Wind was whipping around, wreaking havoc with his hair and threatening to blow the tunic right off of his back. Yet, Peter walked on, staying on top of the waves as long as his eyes were on Jesus.

It's the nature of a storm to cause devastation. We can expect a certain amount of fallout; it just doesn't have to be us that falls out. Jesus eventually did calm the storm Peter was experiencing, but not until He had calmed Peter. And what calmed Peter? The simple knowledge that Jesus was there on the waves.

Psalm 107:29-30 says, "He calms the storm, so that its waves are still. Then they are glad because they are quiet; so He guides them to their desired haven" (NKJ). Our inner storms matter most to our Lord because we matter so much to Him. External circumstances run a distant second to His concern about the condition of our hearts.

Turn your attention today away from the storm raging around you. Focus on Jesus and Jesus alone. He will direct you as to how to walk on the waves. Before you know it, either the waves won't matter to you anymore, or the storm will have passed. Either way, you will still be afloat.

#159
June 7: Want a Miracle?

My niece and her husband, Cheryl and Erick Bell, bought a fixer-upper and have spent their years in that house lovingly and painstakingly refurbishing it. Much of the work they've done on their own. I once asked Cheryl if she ever considered calling the folks from that home makeover TV show to see if they'd come out and redo their house. Cheryl laughed as she responded, "Oh no, those people whose homes are rebuilt by that show have all gone through devastating traumas and I don't want to have that kind of story."

I agreed with Cheryl. As much as I love to see God come to my rescue, I don't look forward to being in the position of needing to be rescued. Miracles are for people at the utter end of their own strength. They realize, many times in tears, that there's absolutely nothing more that they can do about the situation. They've come to the place in which they have literally given up; they've thrown up their hands in surrender. Ahhh, now they are finally in the position where God wants them: hands raised, hearts humbled. Now it's miracle time!

Psalm 109:26-27 says, "Help me, O LORD my God! Oh, save me according to Your mercy, That they may know that this is Your hand-- that You, LORD, have done it!" (NKJ) God shows Himself through the miraculous; His hand is clearly seen when there could have been no other possible explanation for the amazing outcome. Do we really want to see God work? Do we really want to see God use us? Then we need to get ready to be placed in hard situations, under painful circumstances, and in insecure conditions, because it's when we can't do anything else that God shows off what He alone can do.

#160
June 8: At the Right Hand of the Poor

I suspect that whenever there has been an extended time of recession or economic depression, people adapt and learn new ways to survive with less money. I also suspect that during such times, people rethink their dependencies and turn to God. A wise saying proclaims, "We don't learn that God is all we need until God is all we have."

Could it be possible that God is using our financial struggles to get our attention? Maybe we were running so fast after money, being so greedy of gain, and being so addicted to the better-latest-upgrade that we were forgetting our Source of supply. When God allows all of that to be taken or jeopardized and we consider ourselves poor, we can then look around and see Him. Why? Psalm 109:31 says, "For He shall stand at the right hand of the poor, to save him from those who condemn him" (NKJ).

No, we are not going to be released from the debts we've incurred just because we decide to notice God's right beside us. But God will, like with every other tough problem, guide us through. And maybe, just maybe, when we come out on the other side of the storm, we won't so easily forget the One who is always right beside us, whether we're poor or not.

#161
June 9: God Overwhelms

We can find ourselves taken aback, even somewhat awestruck, in the presence of celebrities. Years ago, I sang in a concert choir led by the director of Aretha Franklin's orchestra. When her tour came to town the year she debuted "Pink Cadillac," my connection with the conductor and her road crew scored me special tickets to her concert, including an exclusive back stage pass. Following the performance, a few of us sat on benches in the back stage hallway waiting for her entourage to ready itself to leave the theater. The star's dressing room door suddenly opened right in front of us and Ms. Franklin poked her head out. She smiled at us and asked, "Did you like the show?" We were completely dumbfounded and just sat there, stupidly staring, in awe that the Queen of Soul was actually speaking to us. Trying not to embarrass us further, she simply asked the question again even more sweetly. That shocked us out of our awe. We gladly answered that the show was amazing (and it had been). She gave us all autographed copies of the new album.

I'd like to think I've matured enough not to be tongue-tied if I'm ever in the presence of a famous person again. But that memory came to mind as I read Psalm 114:7-8. "Tremble, O earth, at the presence of the Lord, at the presence of the God of Jacob, who turned the rock into a pool of water, the flint into a fountain of waters" (NKJ). We talk about having a relationship with the Lord and being on a first-name basis with God, but what will we do the day we actually stand before Him? When He looks at us and says, "Well done, my good and faithful servant," will we just stand there like I did in Aretha's presence, staring in disbelief that we're really there and He's really talking to us? Will we charge into His arms and bury ourselves in His welcoming hug? Will we fall to our knees in reverent awe? Will we tremble in His presence, get quiet, cry, laugh, shout, faint, or hyper-ventilate?

I have no idea what I'm going to do. I believe, though, that experiencing the reality of Heaven and God's presence will be completely overwhelming. No wonder we'll need new resurrection bodies—our earthly ones couldn't handle the overpowering greatness of being that close to God.

We get all excited with the idea of knowing that we know God the Father thanks to God the Son through the power of God the Holy Spirit. Take time today—even right now if possible—to actually think on the greatness and grandeur of God. We're in touch with the God who can bring water from rocks, change the course of history, heal the sick, and raise the dead. "'Do you not fear Me?' says the LORD," in Jeremiah 5:22. "Will you not tremble at My presence, who have placed the sand as the bound of the sea, by a perpetual decree, that it cannot pass beyond it? And though its waves toss to and fro, yet they cannot prevail; though they roar, yet they cannot pass over it" (NKJ). I know God loves us and will hold us close as a dear father does with his dear children; however, let's not always be so cavalier about God. Occasionally, maybe even pretty regularly, it will do us good to remember who God really is and worship before Him in awe.

#162
June 10: What's on God's Mind?

We've all heard the phrase, "I've got a lot on my mind." When people say that, they usually mean something is troubling them or the gauge in their life is nearing the overwhelming point. We might even have to get right in their face and snap our fingers just to get their attention. Folks with a lot on their minds don't need another thing to have to think about.

Not so with our God. Psalm 115:12-13 reads, "The LORD has been mindful of us; he will bless us... He will bless those who fear the LORD, both small and great" (NKJ). The word "mindful" used here is translated from the Hebrew word "zakar (zaw-kar')" which means "to mark so as to be recognized, to remember, to mention." It is the same word used in Genesis 8:1 at the end of the great flood when "God remembered Noah." The rain stopped and the waters began to dry up. It's the same word used in Genesis 19:29 when God destroyed Sodom and Gomorrah but "remembered Abraham, and sent Lot out of the midst of the overthrow." Zakar is also the word used in Genesis 30:22 and First Samuel 1:19-20 when God remembered Rachel and Hannah and opened their wombs so they could conceive.

No matter what we're facing, a flood of unexpected circumstances, a firestorm of other people's issues, or a personal emptiness, we're on God's mind and He remembers us. It's not overwhelming to Him to keep us on His mind and then to bless us.

Keep it on your mind today that you are on God's mind. To be zakar-ed by God means we are recognized, remembered, and mentioned. (You do know that Jesus is constantly praying for you. See Romans 8:34.) And His remembrance is always accompanied by blessing. Thank God that you are on His mind; look for the blessing.

#163
June 11: The Listener

It's one thing to be heard, but yet another to be listened to. Listening shows we care; listening demonstrates love. When someone has listened to us, we feel a sense of satisfaction and worth. We know that the listener esteems as important our opinions and/or feelings. To be listened to is to be valued and respected. But that's not all; when someone has truly listened, we expect that their corresponding actions would adjust to reflect their understanding of what we have said. When a person hears but doesn't listen, there's no change in behavior. Our talking has been in vain. If a person doesn't truly listen to us, we find ourselves less and less willing to open up. Then eventually, we stop communicating altogether because we know our words and feelings just aren't valued. And when our words and feelings are not esteemed, the relationship itself loses its significance as well.

God listens. Psalm 116:1-2 says, "I love the LORD, because He has heard my voice and my supplications. Because He has inclined His ear to me, therefore I will call upon Him as long as I live" (NKJ). There are three important words related to listening in these verses. The word "heard" in verse one comes from the Hebrew word "shama'" which means "to hear intelligently, with implication of attention [and] obedience." The word "inclined" in verse two is "natah" which means "to stretch or bow down." This is the idea of leaning in close to hear what's being said. Finally, the word "ear," also in verse two, is "'ozen" which means "broadness." The idea here is to broaden out the ear with the hand, like when we put our hand to our ear as if to catch more of the sound.

When these three words—heard, inclined, and ear—are understood, Psalm 116:1-2 has extra-special impact. These verses are letting us know that God listens attentively and closely, blocking out all distractions as we talk to Him, with the intention of doing something about what we have said. As we watch God operate in response to our prayers, the relationship is strengthened. We grow more and more in love with the God who hears and cares enough to move on our behalf.

Knowing that God listens this attentively to us causes us to feel valued and therefore loved by Him. We, in turn, respond by loving Him. It's a precious cycle. Let's continue that cycle by becoming more like God when we extend an attentive, listening ear to others.

#164
June 12: Precious in His Sight

Having grown up going to Sunday School, I learned lots of Christian songs. You could always find me with all the rest of the

little kids my age singing loud and strong one of my favorites:
Jesus loves the little children, all the children of the world.
Red and yellow, black and white
They are precious in His sight.
Jesus loves the little children of the world.

Even as a little kid, I relished in the fact that Jesus loved me. That knowledge gave me comfort and confidence. More still, I knew I was special because I was "precious in His sight."

As I matured, my parents reinforced the concept that I had high value by the way they loved and cared for me. My parents' nurturing and the constant assurance of God's love for me combined to be some amazing soil in which to grow. I never felt I wouldn't be able to accomplish anything to which I put my hands, mind, and heart. If I did falter (and sometimes I did), the foundation on which I had been raised was both sturdy enough and cushioned enough to make the fall one from which I could always rise again.

The lessons and love of my parents are nestled in my heart now that they have moved on to Glory, but I still go to Sunday School. Now that there may be more years behind me than there are ahead of me, I'm comforted by another mention of being precious in God's sight. Psalm 116:15 says, "Precious in the sight of the LORD is the death of His saints" (NKJ). Don't get me wrong; I'm hoping my death is still quite far into my future. In fact, I pray that God plans for me what He said to Job, "You shall come to the grave at a full age, as a sheaf of grain ripens in its season" Job 5:26 (NKJ). Nevertheless, just as I did with that childhood song, I find comfort and confidence knowing there is still something to come about me that will be "precious in His sight."

Don't trip out when thinking about your own death. As long as you know the Lord; better yet, as long as the Lord knows you, everything—even death—is going to be fine.

#165
June 13: The Answer Key

Whenever I devise a test or quiz for my students, I always make an answer key. After the kids have completed the exercises, I will use the answer key to see if what they have written matches with what I've said the answers should be. If the students have listened to the words of my lessons in class and have read the appropriate books, when it's time to give the answers to the test, they will be well aware of the correct things to write. Their answers will match the answer key and they will be happy with their high grade.

Psalm 119:41-42 says, "Let Your mercies come also to me, O LORD—your salvation according to Your word. So shall I have an answer for him who reproaches me, for I trust in Your word" (NKJ). God's mercies—checed (Hebrew)—refer to His kindness, His favor, His pity, and His good deeds toward us. God's salvation—teshuw'ah (Heb.)—refers to His rescue (either literal or figurative), deliverance, help, and safety. If we internalize this verse as our own, we come to understand that God's kindness and good deeds flow to us resulting in our deliverance, rescue, and assistance. When others want to defame our name or sully our character—when who we are in God is tested—we'll have an answer because we have come to trust in God's word.

We learn of God's mercies and His salvation through His word. By taking advantage of both, we'll have the answers we need when we face life's challenges. God's word then, is the answer key to the tests we face in this life. The neat thing about this answer key is that God allows us to see it in order to match our lives to it daily. He actually prefers for us to copy the answers. Like with my students, as we continue to listen to His lessons and read the right book (the Bible), when it's time for the tests, we can confidently take them, knowing that our answers line up with God's.

#166
June 14: This is Going to Hurt Me...

If you were disciplined as a child by being spanked, just before the corrective action, your mother might have said, "This is going to hurt me more than it's going to hurt you." You rolled your eyes (in your imagination, not for real or else that would have made matters even worse) and thought, *How in the world could that be true when she's about to beat the living daylights out of me?* Your tears and pleading didn't stop the lashing, and your sore backside helped you to remember to mend your ways, at least for a little while. Still, Mom didn't look like she was hurting as much as you were.

Hopefully, you grew up to understand that there's more than one way to hurt. Our mothers were indeed hurting because they were looking into the future and seeing our undisciplined ways leading us into difficulties as adults if we didn't get turned around. It pained them to think about our growing up controlled by out-of-control whims, unmanageable desires, and unruly actions. They could see down the road and realized their charge to teach us, train us, and point us in the right direction. But our heads were hard, and getting our attention made the adage true: A hard head makes a soft behind.

We can thank our mothers for their efforts and for not giving up on us. We deserved those spankings and probably should have gotten more.

In the same way in which we can be grateful for our mother's loving discipline, we can be grateful for God's. Psalm 119:75 says, "I know, O LORD, that Your judgments are right, and that in faithfulness You have afflicted me" (NKJ).

I am thankful both to God and to my mother for faithfully afflicting me. Their judgments were right. My mother punished me because I was her child and she loved me. God does the same thing for the same reason. Consider Hebrews 12:5-8, "...My son, do not despise the chastening of the Lord, nor be discouraged when you are rebuked by Him; For whom the Lord loves He chastens, and scourges every son whom He receives. If you endure chastening, God deals with you as with sons; for what son is there whom a father does not chasten? But if you are without chastening, of which all have become partakers, then you are illegitimate and not sons" (NKJ).

When you have a spanking coming, you know you're in even more trouble when you run. It hurts God's heart to have to spank us. Let's take our discipline remembering it's given out of love to keep us straight.

#167
June 15: God's Law to Love

The Law in the Old Testament gets a bad rap. Many people, even Christians, complain about the restrictiveness of the Old Testament laws. Don't do this, don't do that. Be careful to carry things out a specific way, or else. We feel much more comfortable with what we consider to be the New Testament message of grace through Jesus Christ. "Whew!" we sigh, "How nice to dodge the hammer of the Law thanks to the relief of G.R.A.C.E.—God's Riches At Christ's Expense."

What do we do, then, with Christ's own words "Do not think that I came to destroy the Law or the Prophets. I did not come to destroy but to fulfill" Matthew 5:17 (NKJ)? Jesus didn't have a negative view of the Law; in fact, as the Word made flesh, He *was* the Law.

The writer of Psalm 119 held the proper attitude toward the Law. He expressed, "Oh, how I love Your law! It *is* my meditation all the day. You, through Your commandments, make me wiser than my enemies; for they *are* ever with me" Psalm 119:97-98 (NKJ). God's Law makes me wise by showing me that of which God approves. The Law reveals God's holiness, thus showing me what God is like. The better I know God, the closer I can grow to Him.

Grace is fabulous and we ought to be thankful for it; however, let's not pit grace against the Law. They both are now and always have been from God, and both are to be loved.

#168
June 16: God is Right

What is our attitude toward the word of God? Most of us would say we believe it. We may even say we love it. If either or both of those statements are true, then we ought to be acting in agreement with it. That which I believe and love, I hang my life upon.

Psalm 119:128 says, "Therefore all Your precepts concerning all things I consider to be right; I hate every false way" (NKJ). You see, the psalmist took his belief, formed an opinion, and acted upon it. Essentially he says, "I accept your precepts as true (belief), and I consider them to be right (opinion); therefore, I hate every false way (action).

Let's approach the word of God as the psalmist did. In every one of life's situations – good, bad, or indifferent – read and accept God's precepts as true, form a strong opinion that Gods' word is right, and then act in obedience to that word. We'll win every time.

#169
June 17: Our Help

It certainly is nice to have help. As much as we proudly depend upon ourselves to take care of our own business, we can all still appreciate it when someone comes alongside to help. God is not opposed to our having help either. In fact, the first thing God did after giving Adam a job was to supply him with help. God Himself said, "It is not good that man should be alone; I will make him a helper comparable to him" Genesis 2:18 (NKJ).

That phrase "a helper comparable to him" comes from 3 Hebrew words. Helper is `ezer (ay'-zer) which means "aid;" comparable is neged (neh'-ghed) which means "part opposite, a counterpart or mate;" and for him is le- (le) which has many applications but in this case means "belonging to." In other words, God supplied specifically for Adam a personal assistant who had gifts and talents opposite from his own that were necessary for the adequate and excellent completion of the task God had set before him.

The relationship between a husband and a wife continues today as the perfect example of the relationship between Christ and the Church which is His bride and His body. Among so many other things He does for the Church, He helps her. This is the same relationship God has directly with us as His people. He helps us by supplying specifically for us a personal assistant (the Holy Spirit) who has all we need to adequately and excellently complete the tasks God has set before us.

Psalm 121 gives us amazing reassurance knowing God is our help.

> "I will lift up my eyes to the hills-- from whence comes my help? My help comes from the LORD, who made heaven and earth. He will not allow your foot to be moved; he who keeps you will not slumber. Behold, He who keeps Israel shall neither slumber nor sleep. The LORD is your keeper; the LORD is your shade at your right hand. The sun shall not strike you by day, nor the moon by night. The LORD shall preserve you from all evil; he shall preserve your soul. The LORD shall preserve your going out and your coming in from this time forth, and even forevermore" (NKJ).

Make yourself keenly aware today of all the ways in which God has been and is being your help. And realize as I said, it's nice to have help.

#170
June 18: He Knows Me

Sometimes we feel like no one really knows us. We can be misunderstood on the job, misrepresented in a social setting, mistreated by acquaintances, and mishandled by family members. We can have our best intentions insulted and our bodies injured. We want to shout, "What is this, Disrespect Me Day? Doesn't anybody really know and understand me?"

Especially on days like that, turn to Psalm 139 and read verses 1 – 6:

- O LORD, You have searched me and known me. You know my sitting down and my rising up; you understand my thought afar off. You comprehend my path and my lying down, and are acquainted with all my ways. For there is not a word on my tongue, but behold, O LORD, You know it altogether. You have hedged me behind and before, and laid Your hand upon me. Such knowledge is too wonderful for me; it is high, I cannot attain it. (NKJ)

Some people may see these verses as ominous. *Oh no, God is hanging over my shoulder just waiting for a chance to club me when I slip up.* However, the tone of this Psalm is one of trust in an approachable God, a God who knows absolutely everything about us and loves us anyway. These opening verses of this 24 verse piece ends with the Psalmist exclaiming that the very idea of such a wonderful, unconditional love sets his mind on tilt.

What a wonderful revelation it is to know that even though God knows everything about us, He loves us, and there's absolutely nothing we can do to make Him stop.

#171
June 19: Tripping Up the Haters

Peggy hated me. From 1st grade through 5th grade, I was

184

bullied almost daily by her. Finally, the day came when a face-off loomed. I had just crossed the street on my way home after school. Since Peggy was restricted from crossing that street, she yelled to me from her side the most unbelievable threat I had ever heard. She said, "Come over here so I can kick your butt!"

Even though all the kids around expected to see a fight, something clicked in my 11-year-old brain. "Why would I do that?" I thought. I simply looked at her and said, "No." I then proceeded to triumphantly continue my walk home. That day I realized I was in charge of both my actions and reactions. Threats couldn't make me act out of character or against my better judgment. That refusal may not have stopped the taunts, but I honestly don't remember being bothered by Peggy any more. Once I took control of my trepidation, I guess the thrill of hassling me was gone. I had tripped up the hater.

To this day, I still don't know why Peggy's hatred of me existed. If I had known Psalm 140:4 back in those days, I could have prayed like the Psalmist, "Keep me, O Lord, from the hands of the wicked; preserve me from violent men (or violent Peggy's), who have purposed to make my steps stumble" (NKJ, parenthesis added, of course). Who knows, maybe I only would have suffered until the 3rd grade.

Aren't we glad that God is in the business of helping us trip up the haters? Satan, the enemy of our souls, is intent on making us stumble as we walk through our Christian journey. If we know of people who have "purposed to make (our) steps stumble," we can pray Psalm 140, verse 4. If we aren't aware of any particular "Peggy's," praise God, but we can still pray this verse to thwart the intentions of those who may be scheming against us in the background. Together with God, we'll trip up the haters!

#172
June 20: God—The Complaint Department

We usually don't think of complaining as a positive thing. When little kids complain, we're quick to tell them, "Quit your whining." When adults complain, we tend to squint, roll our eyes, and let out a heavy sign of disdain. Inside we're probably thinking, *Why don't they just get over it and move on*?

While it may be true that no human within earshot is

interested in hearing our complaints, God doesn't seem to have a problem with them. In Psalm 142:1-3, the writer tells us how he handled his complaints. "I cry out to the LORD with my voice; with my voice to the LORD I make my supplication. I pour out my complaint before Him; I declare before Him my trouble. When my spirit was overwhelmed within me, then You knew my path..." (NKJ).

The Hebrew word for "complaint" – siyach (see'-akh) – simply means "a contemplation, an utterance: communication, complaint, meditation, prayer, or talk." And the word translated "trouble" is "tsarah" (tsaw-raw') which means "tightness, adversary, adversity, affliction, anguish, distress, and tribulation." Since God does not rebuke the Psalmist for his words, we can understand that it really is okay to complain to Him about our problems. As the passage so aptly says, God is the One who is already aware of what I'm going through. (Notice that the word "knew" is in the past tense.)

So go right ahead: kick and scream your complaints to God, the complaint department. Your overwhelmed spirit doesn't surprise or overwhelm Him. Once you get it all out, you'll have clearer vision and you'll be better able to focus on the One who not only knew the path you had been walking, but also knows the path of your escape. First Corinthians 10:13 promises, "No test or temptation that comes your way is beyond the course of what others have had to face. All you need to remember is that God will never let you down; he'll never let you be pushed past your limit; he'll always be there to help you come through it" (The Message).

#173
June 21: God's Long Life Formula

I bought a book some years ago entitled "Real Age." The author suggests that our calendar age is really of no consequence. What actually determines our age is how we treat our bodies. The book takes the reader through his theory and then asks all kinds of evaluation questions through which to calculate your "real age." For example, starting with your actual calendar age, you would add a certain number of years if you smoke and eat a high salt diet, but you would subtract a certain number of years if you get regular exercise and know how to reduce your stress. In the end, the reader is supposed to come out with not only the "real age" number, but also a behavior modification plan to start ticking the time backwards in an effort to lengthen the years of life.

I should have saved the $25 dollars.

Proverbs 10:27 is God's "real age" formula. "The fear of the LORD prolongs days, but the years of the wicked will be shortened" (NKJ). Also look at Proverbs 9:10-11, "The fear of the LORD is the beginning of wisdom, and the knowledge of the Holy One is insight. For by me your days will be multiplied, and years will be added to your life" (ESV).

It's very simple, when we respect God, we will obey. Obedience to God makes us wise, gives us knowledge, and allows us to operate by the insight He gives. God's wisdom includes the good sense to stop smoking, drinking alcohol, and doing drugs because our bodies are His temples. We'll be mindful of the places we go and the company we keep, steering clear of obvious dangerous and unsavory situations and acquaintances. We'll read the Bible and pray so as to receive continued and up-to-the-minute direction and deliverance straight from the heart of God. When we conduct our lives this way, we live longer.

We already own the book that teaches us the real age/long life formula. Let's apply it.

#174
June 22: Strength with God

Decisions. Sometimes they are not easy. There is, however, a way we can always know we are making the right decision. It's simple: lay all our choices side-by-side and then choose the one that is God's way.

"The way of the LORD is strength for the upright, but destruction will come to the workers of iniquity" Proverbs 10:29 (NKJ). The difficulty we face really isn't in choosing to do things God's way. A choice is simply a choice: nothing difficult about that. The complexity arises when we start looking into the future to predict the consequences of the choices we have before us.

- If I tell Teddy I want to remain a virgin until I get married, he'll leave me for some other girl and I'll be alone without the love of my life for the rest of my life.

- If I refuse to take this job because they require me to work every Sunday and expect me to lie for the management every once in a while, I'll never get another job in the industry.
- If I just don't mention the under-the-table funds I've received, I'll get away with paying less taxes.

Granted, when the alternatives we predict seem either extremely daunting or extremely advantageous, it takes guts to choose to do things God's way. However, today's verse gives us some fabulous courage: the way of the Lord is *strength for the upright*. Just choosing to go His way supplies strength. Besides, we can't see into the future; God is already there. You might lose Teddy. Good. Now he's out of the way of the guy you really need. So you don't get that job. Now you're available for God to place you where He wants you. So your income is larger and you pay more taxes. Your income is larger – duh.

We can look into the future and be certain of one thing for sure: if we do things God's way, we'll be strong enough to handle whatever happens. To choose iniquity is to choose destruction. Choose God's way and be strong.

#175
June 23: Approaching Our Holy God

Universities want to know what kinds of people are being let into their schools, so from time to time, I am called upon to write recommendation letters for my students. Those who have towed the line for four years – having kept their grades up, participated in clubs, and exhibited positive character – are excited and confident about asking for my recommendations because they know I'll really make them look good. However, those who are barely scraping by, have a poor attitude, and exhibit less-than-honorable character are not so enthused about seeking a letter from me. I may not tear them down, but I won't lie either.

So it is when we approach God with our needs. Sooner or later, some situation will arise in our lives beyond our control and above our means. How we've handled ourselves before God up to that point now becomes an issue. Have we been walking according to His precepts? Have we been obedient to His commandments? Have we been spending time with Him? Have we been actively loving Him with all our heart, soul, mind, and strength, and loving our neighbor as ourselves? If so, the words of Proverbs 14:26-27 apply to us. "In the fear of the LORD there is strong confidence, and His children will have a place of refuge. The fear of the LORD is a fountain of life, to turn one away from the snares of death" (NKJ).

The Hebrew phrase "fear of the Lord" used in these verses (yirah) means "to morally reverence." In other words, when we live right before God – that is, respecting and honoring Him by our right living – we can approach Him in our times of need with "strong confidence." We then have bold assurance and security; we know where to turn for safety and for life, for relief from the stresses, strains, and problems that beset us.

God is not a punk. We are wrong to expect we can act any kind of way that suits our desires when everything is going okay, and then when we get in a jam, run to God and He'll bail us out. If that's our attitude, we shouldn't be surprised if we find ourselves sitting in the "jail cells" we've created for ourselves.

God is holy, righteous, and just, and He still hates our sin. Let's exercise the fear of the Lord; be morally reverent. Then when the tough times arise, we can approach our Abba Father with strong confidence, knowing we'll find a welcome place of refuge and fountain of life.

#176
June 24: Big Brother is Watching You

At one point in my teaching career, I taught the junior English class and we studied George Orwell's classic novel, *1984*. Written in 1949, Orwell envisioned a future in which "Big Brother is Watching You" constantly; Big Brother being the ruling, dictatorial political party which has robbed the culture of all personal freedoms and is seeking to control each person's very thoughts. Telescreens monitor every movement as the Thought Police scrutinize every word and facial expression looking for any hint of a rebellious attitude.

Our classroom discussions turned to the security cameras all around us today. They are mounted on almost every business and inside every store. Traffic control cameras are along the streets and highways, and the red light cameras are ready to catch us running the signal at intersections. We also talked about the GPS tracking devices in our cell phones and the amazing accuracy and clarity of satellite imagery. It took a little longer than Orwell projected, but Big Brother certainly does seem to be watching and we're not so sure how we feel about that. On the one hand, we feel protected; on the other, our privacy feels violated.

An old hymn says, "I sing because I'm happy. I sing because I'm free. God's eye is on the sparrow, so I know He watches me." Rather than the fear inspired by the telescreens and the Thought Police from *1984*, that song gives me the comfort of knowing I am watched over by God Himself. Even more reassurance comes from Proverbs 14:3 which says, "The eyes of the Lord are in every place, keeping watch on the evil and the good."

I'm glad to know Someone who cares about me is watching over me. It's even more comforting to know that He's got His eye on the evil that could befall me. I'll take Jesus as my big brother, and God as my security camera any day!

#177
June 25: How to Make God Happy

It's always a good idea to make the person in charge happy. When the boss is happy, the office runs well. When the teacher is happy, students may get a pass on homework. When the pastor is happy, the sermons are more exciting. When the President is happy, the country is rolling along well. And everyone knows when Momma is happy, the home is happy.

It stands to reason then, that if you can make God happy, your world will run much more smoothly. Here's the secret. Proverbs 15:8 says, "The prayer of the upright is His delight."

Yep, that's it. God is happy when we pray, when we simply talk with Him. Now be clear: prayer is a conversation, not a monologue. Prayer requires open and honest discussion between us and God. We talk, God listens. God talks, we listen.

Make God happy today and every day. Nothing is better than a good old-fashioned heart-to-heart with someone we love. That's what prayer is supposed to be.

#178
June 26: In the Director's Chair

It's pretty amazing to watch your children's talents sprouting. When our son Matthew was about seven-years-old, he "produced" a play in his bedroom. He draped a blanket from the top to bottom bunk as the curtain; employed his little brother, Mark, as the cast; and directed the scene he had written. From there, as he grew, he participated in church plays, acting now and then, but settling mainly behind the scenes and mostly behind the camera producing and directing films.

We, his parents, got behind this budding talent, purchasing him a video camera, sending him to the summer film program at USC, and ultimately beaming from the Biola University gymnasium bleachers as he received his bachelor's degree in Cinema and Media Arts. So far, he's produced and directed several of his own award-winning films and has directed others for colleagues.

There's something very special about that director's chair. The person sitting there is the go-to guy. No matter what their individual expertise, everyone in the scene and on the set defers to him. The actors have learned their lines, the costume designers have chosen the clothing, the lighting people have picked their filters, and the sound effects folks have gathered all their wares; but still the director puts it all together.

As with movie-making, so with us. As I think of Matthew's responsibilities as a film director, I'm reminded of Proverbs 16:9, "A man's heart plans his way, but the LORD directs his steps" (NKJ). God sits in the director's chair—a very capable controller of the scenes of our lives. As the actors and crew on set wouldn't dream of contradicting the director of the film, so it is that we shouldn't think of ever contradicting our God's direction. Just play the scenes His way. Watch how moment after moment will be Academy Award winning performances of His incredible power and favor in our lives.

#179
June 27: Run, Forrest, Run

Forrest Gump was one of the most creative and poignant films ever made. In it, Tom Hanks played the mentally challenged

SHARON NORRIS ELLIOTT

title character who not only witnessed, but in some cases, actually influenced key events of the later part of the 20th century. The film won a slew of Academy Awards in 1994 including Best Picture. Despite being mentally challenged, as a child, Forrest was physically challenged as well, and had to wear leg braces so he could walk. However, his strong mother, played brilliantly by Sally Field, and his best friend, Jenny, encouraged him to push past his disabilities. In an early pivotal scene, Forrest is being bullied and Jenny yells to him, "Run, Forrest, run." Forrest does so, and as he builds up steam, the leg braces break away, and the foreshadowing is cast showing the audience that Forrest will run successfully through the rest of his life.

Forrest Gump knew only that he should run, but he never knew in advance what he would be running into. No so with us. Proverbs 18:10 says, "The name of the LORD is a strong tower; the righteous run to it and are safe" (NKJ). Other Bible translations substitute "strong tower" for strong fortress, a fortified tower, and a place of protection. Psalm 56:3-4 further assures us that we have a place of safety into which we can run. It says, "Whenever I am afraid, I will trust in You. In God (I will praise His word), in God I have put my trust; I will not fear. What can flesh do to me?" (NKJ)

So the next time you are feeling bullied by the cares of this life, and the discouragement has built up around your spiritual legs like restrictive braces, hear the Holy Spirit shouting, "Run, Saint, run!" Run into the protective name of the Lord. Turn toward your fear, stick your thumbs in your ears, wiggle the rest of your fingers at it, and proclaim, "Nah, nah, nah, nah, nah. I'm safe in trusting my God." Then run, Saint, run through the rest of your life, not only witnessing of God's great love and power, but successfully influencing others to turn to Him as well.

#180
June 28: How We Know Anything

Our five senses are marvelous. Without sight, how would we know color; without touch, how would we know texture? Without taste, how would we know sweetness; without hearing, how would we know musical tones; and without smell, how would we know the perfume of the flowers? Through all these senses, we gain our information about the world around us; however, the

192

two senses upon which we seem to lean the most are our hearing and our sight. In fact, it's common for us to combine the two. When we want to let people know we truly understand what we have heard them say, we will often respond with the phrase, "I see what you're saying.

The Hebrew word for "hear" is "shama" which means "to hear intelligently, often with implication of attention and obedience." The Hebrew word for "see" is "ra'ah," which means "to see literally or figuratively, to have experience, gaze, and take heed." When we truly hear and see, we fully perceive and understand.

As with all else wonderful, we have God to thank for discernment, sensitivity, and insight. Proverbs 20:12 simply states, "The hearing ear and the seeing eye, the LORD has made them both" (NKJ). Today, as we hear and see anything physically, and as we comprehend anything intellectually and emotionally, let's be careful to thank God for such spectacular ways to experience His world.

#181
June 29: The One Who Repays

Poignant and/or funny lines from movies often make their way into the vocabulary of our culture. For example, when we want to explain life's ups and downs, we quote Forest Gump's mother and expound, "Life is like a box of chocolates; you never know what you're going to get." If we know a person has a low threshold for accepting reality, we tell her, "You can't handle the truth." And when we are itching for a reason to retaliate, we can be heard luring the offender into our clutches with the invitation, "Go ahead, make my day."

But no matter how tempting it may seem to want to taste the victory over our foes, God adamantly identifies Himself as the One who repays. In no uncertain terms, Proverbs 20:22 clearly tells us, "Do not say, 'I'll pay you back for this wrong!' Wait for the LORD, and he will deliver you" (NIV). Romans 12:19-21 makes this same admonition clear in New Testament language. "Do not take revenge, my friends, but leave room for God's wrath, for it is written: 'It is mine to avenge; I will repay,' says the Lord. On the contrary: 'If your enemy is hungry, feed him; if he is thirsty, give him something to drink. In doing this, you will heap burning coals on his head.' Do not be overcome by evil, but overcome evil with good." (NIV).

So as Christians, no more threatening that "I'm gonna get you, sucker." Instead wait, treat your enemy well, and crush evil with good. Depend on God to do that paying back in His own manner and time. Trust that He can and will do a far better repayment job than you ever could.

#182
June 30: God Made the Rich and the Poor

Sometimes, because of their money, it seems as though rich people think they're better than poor people. On the other hand, poor people could be seen to react to rich people's perceived put-downs by believing that, in the main, being poor makes them actually better. The poverty-stricken may not think they are looking down their noses at the rich, when in actuality, that's exactly what's happening. Each side hates the other because of possessions or lack thereof. Both are wrong.

Proverbs 22:2 says, "The rich and the poor have this in common, the LORD is the maker of them all" (NKJ). The Hebrew word for "maker" is "`asah (aw-saw')" meaning "to do or make" and it has a wide application. Depending upon how it is used, it could allude not only to accomplishing something, but also to appointing it. So does God simply create the people who are rich and poor, or does He also appoint them their lot? The Matthew Henry Commentary provides a good explanation:

> Among the children of men, divine Providence has so ordered it that some are rich and others poor, and these are intermixed in societies: The Lord is the Maker of both, both the author of their being and the disposer of their lot. The greatest man in the world must acknowledge God to be his Maker, and is under the same obligations to be subject to him that the meanest is; and the poorest has the honor to be the work of God's hands as much as the greatest... Notwithstanding the distance that is in many respects between rich and poor, yet in most things they meet together, especially before the Lord, who is the

Maker of them all, and regards not the rich more than the poor. (See Job 34:19). Rich and poor meet together at the bar of God's justice, all guilty before God, concluded under sin, and shapen in iniquity, the rich as much as the poor; and they meet at the throne of God's grace; the poor are as welcome there as the rich. There is the same Christ, the same scripture, the same Spirit, the same covenant of promises, for them both. There is the same heaven for poor saints that there is for rich… And there is the same hell for rich sinners that there is for poor. All stand upon the same level before God, as they do also in the grave. The small and great are there.

Whatever your evaluation of your station—either rich or poor—remain humble before God; for Paul admonished "to everyone who is among you, not to think of himself more highly than he ought to think, but to think soberly, as God has dealt to each one a measure of faith" Romans 12:3 (NKJ).

#183
July 1: Make It Make Sense

The high school students I teach have a knack for attempting to give me bogus excuses for why their homework is not done. Having taught for nearly 30 years, I can pretty much smell a ruse when it walks in the classroom door. *Just take your zero like a man*, I want to say, *please stop trying to play me for a fool*. Whenever these long explanations start, there's always a point at which I need to tell the student, "Just make this make sense to me." Of course, when the story is deceit, it will never make sense.

I take my cue from God as relates to my view about truth (knowledge) verses a lie (deception). Proverbs 22:12 says, "The Lord guards knowledge, but he destroys false words" (NCV). The Message renders this same verse like this, "God guards knowledge with a passion, but he'll have nothing to do with deception."

We may as well stop trying because we will never be able to make our lies make sense to God. We just need to man-up (or woman-up as the case may be), confess the truth to Him, and stop playing Him for a fool. He will have nothing to do with deception. The truth will set us free.

#184
July 2: The Task God has Given

"And I set my heart to seek and search out by wisdom concerning all that is done under heaven; this burdensome task God has given to the sons of man, by which they may be exercised" Ecclesiastes 1:13 (NKJ).

When I think of exercise, I think of strenuous workouts including running, sit-ups, push-ups, jumping jacks, and strength training. My mind sees images of stair-steppers, treadmills, bicycles, and free weights. I envision sweating, sore muscles, and a rapidly beating heart. However, as I look past all of this, I see myself in better health, with more energy, moving about in a toned body, and living longer.

Solomon was the wisest man ever to live on the planet because God gave him the wisdom he asked for. However, God didn't just plunk into Solomon's heart all the wisdom he would ever need. Solomon obtained it progressively as he continually turned his heart toward God in the search. So when Solomon began to ponder about the task God has given to us humans while on this earth, I think he was onto something as he realized that God was "exercising" us.

It may be a hassle to think about always having to work for a living, but our toil is God's way of building our muscles, both physically and spiritually. As we work, we may sweat and strain, but we should also be relying on God to get us through it. Our work and our reliance together build spiritual muscle. Our hearts toward God get stronger; our vision of Him more clear.

Let's look at work a little differently today. Let's see it as a God-ordained workout that is leading to a healthier spiritual life.

#185
July 3: Wisdom, Knowledge, and Joy

My husband is enjoying his retirement. I often hear him say, "I worked all my life to be able to go whenever I want and do whatever I want." King Solomon echoed that same sentiment in

Ecclesiastes 2:24 when he said, "Nothing is better for a man than that he should eat and drink, and that his soul should enjoy good in his labor. This also, I saw, was from the hand of God." But in order to have complete satisfaction and continue to honor God in these golden years, he (and all the rest of us) must understand what Solomon goes on to say is the reason why this man can enjoy good. "For God gives wisdom and knowledge and joy to a man who is good in His sight..." verse 26a.

There's the holy catch. The man who is first "good in His sight" exercises three characteristics from God that are required in order to fully enjoy good: wisdom, knowledge, and joy.

- Wisdom is the ability to judge correctly and to follow the best course of action, based on knowledge and understanding. The first principle of biblical wisdom is that man should humble himself before God in reverence and worship, obedient to His commands.
- Knowledge is the truth or facts of life that a person acquires either through experience or thought. The greatest truth that a person can possess with the mind or learn through experience is truth about God, acquired only as God shows Himself to man. Moral knowledge affects a person's will. It is knowledge of the heart, not the mind alone.
- Joy is a positive attitude or pleasant emotion; delight. The joy which the people of God should have is holy and pure. This joy rises above circumstances and focuses on the very character of God. The joy required of the righteous person is produced by the Spirit of God and looks beyond the present to our future salvation and to our sovereign God, who works out all things for our ultimate good, which is Christlikeness.

Bottom line: in order to enjoy good, we must live humbly before God, judging correctly, following the best course of action once we know all the true facts, and exhibiting a holy and pure joy that rises from Christlikeness. Our enjoyment of life – whether we're retired like my husband, or working as a homemaker, on a job for a boss, on a job as a boss, or as an entrepreneur – hinges upon our being like Christ.

We cannot rely on our own wisdom and knowledge, nor can we trust circumstantial happiness as we live this life. Only by exercising the wisdom, knowledge, and joy God gives will we find true contentment and really be able to rest in enjoying good. Let's examine ourselves today to see if we are operating in all areas and to all people in the wisdom, knowledge, and joy God expects of us. Is Christlike character shining through?

Now that's enjoying the good life!

(Definitions of knowledge, wisdom and joy from Nelson's Illustrated Bible Dictionary, Copyright (C) 1986, Thomas Nelson Publishers)

**#186
July 4: God in the Ups and Downs

The Bible says some great things will happen in our lives. We will dance, laugh, gain, love, and embrace. We will have peace, speak up, sew, and keep things. We will build things up, plant, heal, and experience birth. We'd also all love it if the message about the happenings of our lives only consisted of these positives. Some Biblical messengers would have you think this actually was the case.

However, contrary to messages that would try to convince you that something is wrong with your faith if you experience hardships, the Bible also says some really bad things will happen. We will mourn, weep, lose, hate, and have no one to hug. We will be in war, need to keep silent, tear stuff up, and lose things. We will see stuff break down, pluck up what has been planted, kill, and experience death. (See Eccl. 3:1-22.)

A balanced faith realizes the reality of good and evil, and understands that in a fallen world, some of both will affect everyone. That same balanced faith must be in the God of the universe in order to make it through the negative experiences.

This may sound like a downer of a devotion, but no need for depression or throwing in the towel. We Christians have Romans 8:35-39 as our trump card:

> Who shall separate us from the love of Christ? Shall tribulation, or distress, or persecution, or famine, or nakedness, or peril, or sword?As it is written: "For Your sake we are killed all day long; we are accounted as sheep for the slaughter." Yet in all these things we are more than conquerors through Him who loved us. For I am persuaded that

neither death nor life, nor angels nor principalities nor powers, nor things present nor things to come, nor height nor depth, nor any other created thing, shall be able to separate us from the love of God which is in Christ Jesus our Lord. (NKJ)

No matter what your reality is today, absolutely nothing can separate us from the love of God.

#187
July 5: God Lets Life Unfold, So Work

An automobile commercial on television says, "It has been said that 'good things come to those who wait;' but we say, 'good things come to those who work.'" I still have no idea how the ad campaign people relate this to the car, but what a true statement for our lives!

I don't know if the advertising executives who wrote that commercial knew of Solomon, but they sure echoed his sentiments. This wisest king who ever lived said, "What profit has the worker from that in which he labors? I have seen the God-given task with which the sons of men are to be occupied. He has made everything beautiful in its time. Also He has put eternity in their hearts, except that no one can find out the work that God does from beginning to end. I know that nothing is better for them than to rejoice, and to do good in their lives, and also that every man should eat and drink and enjoy the good of all his labor-- it is the gift of God" Ecclesiastes 3:9-13 (NKJ).

Solomon recognized that none of us would ever know what God was doing from beginning to end. Our best bet in life is not to just sit around, waiting to find out what God is going to do next; our best course of action is to be industrious—to enjoy the good of all our labor. Work is God's gift to us. We may know *that* God has made everything beautiful in its time, but we do not know *how* God is going to reveal it all. So in the meantime, let's just work and let God unfold life for us. As the commercial says: Good things come to those who work; i.e. to those who rejoice, do good in their lives, eat, drink, and enjoy the good of all his labor, for that very labor is the gift of God.

#188
July 6: God and Forever

When studying *Beowulf*, the ancient English story of the mighty warrior and his amazing deeds, it's helpful to understand what a kenning is. A kenning is a two or three word descriptive renaming of someone or something. The words chosen should accurately depict the character of the person or thing. So for example, Grendel, the hideous monster Beowulf must defeat, had murdered 30 innocent people in one night. Grendel is known by the kenning "corpse maker." Since his warriors had traveled with him over the ocean, Beowulf's men are called "sea rovers." And the hero himself is known as the seafarer's leader, the arch-warrior, and the thane's commander.

God can be known by the kenning Forever Father. Not only is being eternal one of His personal attributes, it's also a trait ascribed to all He does. Ecclesiastes 3:14 says, "I know that whatever God does, it shall be forever. Nothing can be added to it, and nothing taken from it. God does it, that men should fear before Him" (NKJ). Once God decides a thing or starts the wheels in motion so to speak, that's it; the outcome is set forever.

What are some of the forever things pertaining to our Forever Father does?

- The counsel of the LORD stands forever, the plans of His heart to all generations. Psalm 33:11 (NKJ)
- Your faithfulness endures to all generations; you established the earth, and it abides. Psalm 119:90 (NKJ)
- Declaring the end from the beginning, and from ancient times things that are not yet done, saying, 'My counsel shall stand, and I will do all My pleasure,' Isaiah 46:10 (NKJ)
- In hope of eternal life which God, who cannot lie, promised before time began. Titus 1:2 (NKJ)
- Every good and perfect gift is from above, coming down from the Father of the heavenly lights, who does not change like shifting shadows. James 1:17 (NIV)
- Forever, O LORD, thy word is settled in heaven. Ps 119:89 (KJV)

These six verses only scratch the surface of the foreverness of God. Humans like us, trapped in a singular understanding of time where everything in our sphere has a beginning and an end, can scarcely wrap our minds around the idea of eternity. But Scripture makes it clear that our Forever Father, the un-caused Cause, indeed is eternal and operates with a limitless, everlasting mindset. It only makes sense: certainly an eternal being's works would be as He is. "Whatever God does, it shall be forever."

#189
July 7: God and Our Vows

We use our words much too loosely and thoughtlessly. I especially cringe when I hear people evoke God's name in their fits of rage. Besides the blatantly blasphemous outcry of the name of Jesus to show frustration, or attaching God's name to a curse word, I'm particularly offended when someone declares, "I swear to God," and then continues by asserting what he/she will or won't do.

The words of our mouths are important, especially when we make vows to God. Ecclesiastes 5:4c-5 says, "Pay what you have vowed--Better not to vow than to vow and not pay" (NKJ).

What vows have you made to God?

- I'm going to stop smoking, overeating, drinking in excess, fornicating, etc. since I know my body is the temple of the Holy Spirit.
- I'm going to start exercising, drinking water, eliminating salt, etc.
- I'm going to read my Bible every day.
- I'm going to pray more diligently.
- I'm going to be a better husband, wife, father, mother, son, daughter, student, employee, church member, etc.
- I'm going to tithe regularly.
- God, if you just get me out of this one I'll...

God says we are fools when we make vows to Him and then don't follow through. Why? Because He's true to His word. When we call on Him in a vow, He starts to move in our direction to assist us. He puts things in motion in the heavenly realm to bring about the blessings associated with the carrying out of those

vows. For example:
- When we seek God for help by vowing to turn away from evil, God starts the health machine working because He says, "Do not be wise in your own eyes; fear the LORD and depart from evil. It will be health to your flesh, and strength to your bones" Proverbs 3:7-8.
- When we vow to read our Bibles regularly, God starts to send stronger faith our way because "...faith comes by hearing, and hearing by the word of God" Romans 10:17.
- And when we vow to tithe, God starts binding up that which would seek to destroy us as He indicates when He says, "Bring all the tithes into the storehouse... And I will rebuke the devourer for your sakes, so that he will not destroy the fruit of your ground, nor shall the vine fail to bear fruit for you in the field..." Malachi 3:10-11 (NKJ).

You see, God's not like us. He actually takes us at our word (contrary to how we don't take Him at His). Therefore, when we renege on our vows, we throw a wrench in the works of the very machine that already started to manufacture blessings for us. Foolish!

So let's not vow unless we mean it. And the next time we feel the need to make a vow to God, let's remember the seriousness of what we are saying, and the lengths God Himself will go to in order to help us see it through. This knowledge should spur us on to successfully fulfill that vow, and engender a heart of gratefulness to God.

#190
July 8: God's Patience

The book of Second Kings in the Bible tells us about the divided kingdom era. Israel and Judah split after the reign of Solomon and each section has a king. The kings of Israel were generally evil, while the kings of Judah generally tried to lead the people to stick with God. Neither section ever seemed to be able to totally turn the people's eyes exclusively back to pure worship of God, so it was a downhill slide for both until the end of the Old Testament when God finally said He'd had enough. After 400 years of silence between the testaments, God then ushered in the

Church age through Jesus Christ and, in terms of Biblical history, that's where we are today.

Look at God's long-suffering. As evil as the kings were, He let them reign for years and years. Sometimes the kings would come up against an enemy who was oppressing them, and with a promise to change his ways, the king would cry out to God for help. God would help him – deliver him and the people from the oppressor – and then the king and the people would go right back to their evil by ignoring God and worshipping Baal. Then God would let that king die and another would reign, only to play out the same scenario.

God's patience is not a license to sin; yet, how many times do we – like the evil kings of Israel and Judah – take advantage of it? Ecclesiastes 8:11 tells us what our problem is: "When the sentence for a crime is not quickly carried out, the hearts of the people are filled with schemes to do wrong" (NIV). You see, when we think we have gotten away with something, we don't stop, count ourselves lucky, and repent promising never to do that again. To the contrary, when we are not punished immediately, we are emboldened to go a little farther next time.

Please note that Romans 6:23a has not changed, "For the wages of sin is death..." (NIV), and neither has Numbers 32:23b, "...be sure your sin will find you out" (KJV). Those evil kings got their come-uppins and we will too. God's patience gives us a chance to repent and change. Do we really want God to deal with us in our sin? Let's trust what God can do with an obedient heart.

Part 3

Glimpses of God

In the

Major and Minor Prophets

(50 Devotions)

#191
July 9: Move Closer to Daddy

My pastor tells the story of needing to discipline his children. Like me and many other parents who love their children, he believes it necessary and in order to use spanking as one of the corrective measures God placed at a parent's disposal (See Proverbs 13:24; 22:15; 23:13-14; and 29:15). As his boys faced their upcoming spanking due to a transgression of theirs, the younger one was overheard giving the older one some sage advice: If you move closer to Daddy while he spanks you, it won't hurt as much.

During the time of Isaiah, the children of Israel were being disciplined for turning against God. As God allowed other nations to rise up and punish them, the prophet writes, "For the people do not turn to Him who strikes them, nor do they seek the LORD of hosts" Isaiah 9:13 (NKJ). The only One who could help them was the One disciplining them because they continued to defy Him.

It's difficult to turn toward the one disciplining us. Teenagers are especially good at holding grudges against a parent who has placed them on punishment, or against teachers who dole out a discipline for their wrongdoing. Adults are no better. We are ready to defend ourselves when a mistake or a wrong is pointed out, rather than accept the rebuke, correct our erroneous word or deed, and make the appropriate apologies if necessary. Teens and adults alike turn away from the disciplinarian rather than toward the one who loved us enough to point out that we were wrong.

Hebrews 12:11 says, "Now no chastening seems to be joyful for the present, but painful; nevertheless, afterward it yields the peaceable fruit of righteousness to those who have been trained by it" (NKJ). And Proverbs 27:6a says, "Faithful are the wounds of a friend..." (NKJ). The NIV Bible translates that Proverb as, "Wounds from a friend can be trusted..." In the same spirit that God does it, our parents, teachers, and even caring friends discipline and correct us because they love us. They simply do not want us to continue to act a fool.

My pastor's son had the right idea. The next time you are being disciplined by someone who loves you, move closer. From up close, you'll experience the love in the chastisement, and by changing your ways, you'll experience the peace that right living (righteousness) can bring.

And especially remember the advice when God is disciplining you. Be a quick study and "move closer to Daddy."

#192
July 10: Exactly What We Need

Different problems dictate different responses. When we're cold, we need to dress in warm clothing, wrap up in a blanket, or snuggle in front of a cozy fire. When we're lonely, we need companionship. If we run out of gas, we need someone to come along with a gas can or we need a push to the gas station. If we're out in the rain, we need an umbrella or at least a hooded parka. That umbrella won't do us any good if we're out of gas, and that warm blanket doesn't double for human camaraderie.

God knows how each of our unique situations requires unique responses from Him. He's not only aware, but He's able to handle whatever we need. Isaiah 25:4 reads, "For You have been a strength to the poor, a strength to the needy in his distress, a refuge from the storm, a shade from the heat..." (NKJ). When the situation is meager (poor) and miserable (distressed), God responds as strength. When the situation is stormy, God responds as a refuge. And when the situation is hot, God responds as shade, blocking out the damaging rays of the problem.

Notice that God does not simply *supply* strength, refuge, and shade; He Himself *is* your strength, He *is* your refuge, and He *is* your shade.

- On God as strength: "The LORD is my strength and my shield; my heart trusted in Him, and I am helped..." Psalm 28:7 (NKJ)
- On God as refuge: "I will say of the LORD, "He is my refuge and my fortress; my God, in Him I will trust." Psalm 91:2 (NKJ)
- On God as shade: The LORD is your keeper; the LORD is your shade at your right hand. Psalm 121:5 (NKJ)

All of life's vicissitudes can be handled if strength, a place of refuge, or shade is introduced to the equation. Any large, looming problem is no match for God as strength. Anything threatening your sense of safety and security will find itself locked out before God as refuge. And relationship issues heat up but must cool right down when blocked by God as shade.

Let God be who He is in every area of your life and you'll be fine.

#193
July 11: Wiper

What was the first thing that came to your mind when you read the word "wiper"? I thought of windshield wipers because I need new ones for the front windshield of my car. Since I live in Southern California, I use them infrequently. When the first rain of the fall was forecast, I figured I should test them. Sure enough, I found they are not ready to do their job. The heat and sun has dried out the rubber blades; the left wiper left unsightly streaks, and the right one talked to me as 3 inches of the tip hung loose from the arm allowing it to scrap my windshield like fingernails on a chalkboard. If I didn't get them replaced, I was going to have a tough time seeing during the next rainy commute.

Good wipers can be reminders of one special thing about God. Isaiah 25:8 says, "And the Lord God will wipe away tears from all faces" (NKJ). He's never worn out by the heat of our issues, He's not out of practice from infrequent use, and He doesn't half-way do things in our lives. God is the ultimate clear-er of our rainy day vicissitudes. The Hebrew word for "wipe" used here is "machah" which can also mean "reach to, smooth, blot out, erase, destroy." When we cry, God is there reaching out to smooth our rough times, blot out our tears, and erase our heartaches. He can destroy the roots of our sorrows with His peace that "surpasses all understanding," a peace that "will guard (our) hearts and minds through Christ Jesus" Philippians 4:7 (NKJ).

Without God wiping our tears, it's tough to see clearly when we're engulfed in the rain of sadness and distress. Let God operate as the wiper of your tears today. Trust me; there will be no streaks.

#194
July 12: Judge, Lawgiver, and King

It is 100% wrong to have a judge in your back pocket. In our judicial system, that means the judge will take bribes or coercion from you to do what you want done regardless of the legality of his actions.

Some people look at God as a Judge they can have in their back pocket. They think God can be told what to do, regardless of the wisdom or worthiness of the request. God is sovereign and things work the other way around. We don't tell God what to do; He tells us. The neat thing about that, though, is that when we follow His instructions, we come out on top.

Isaiah 33:22 says, "For the LORD is our Judge, the LORD is our Lawgiver, the LORD is our King; he will save us" (NKJ). Our Judge is our Lawgiver and our King, and He is on our side. He rules in our lives as King, instructs us through our lives as Lawgiver, and evaluates our case as Judge. And even though we blow it from time to time, He throws out the evidence because He's also the One who has paid the price for our sin. When the gavel comes down, the verdict is "not guilty" by reason of the shed blood of Jesus.

The Judge, Lawgiver, and King has spoken.

#195
July 13: The Bag of Tricks

My favorite cartoon was Felix the Cat. Felix started every episode just trying to live life without trouble. He'd whistle as he walked along or as he worked. Then trouble always found him in the form of the evil Professor or Master Cylinder. Both of these adversaries wanted nothing more than to obtain Felix's magic bag of tricks which Felix was always able to use to escape from their sinister schemes.

Like Felix, most of us don't go looking for trouble, but trouble often finds us. And trouble is real. Having faith doesn't mean we ignore problems as if they didn't exist and just skip on our merry way. We shouldn't beat ourselves up because we feel hurt or frustrated or misused. Nothing is wrong with us if we experience a financial reversal, disappointment, disillusionment, or grief. No, we are not weak in faith because distress-producing tribulations come our way. We are people of faith because no matter what trouble rears its ugly head, we have the rock-solid assurance that the trouble won't consume us. We have in our possession the ultimate bag of tricks – the real and true God.

King Hezekiah turned to this very "bag of tricks" when his nation was threatened. The Assyrian king had sent his bullying messenger, the Rabshakeh, to intimidate King Hezekiah and in a letter had queried, "Have the gods of the nations delivered those whom my fathers have destroyed?" Isaiah 37:12 (NKJ). King Hezekiah took the letter, spread it before the Lord, and prayed, "O LORD of hosts, God of Israel... You are God, You alone... Incline Your ear, O LORD, and hear; open Your eyes, O LORD, and see; and hear all the words of Sennacherib, which he has sent to reproach the living God. Truly, LORD, the kings of Assyria have laid waste all the nations and their lands, and have cast their gods into the fire; for they were not gods, but the work of men's hands-- wood and stone. Therefore they have destroyed them. Now therefore, O LORD our God, save us from his hand, that all the kingdoms of the earth may know that You are the LORD, You alone" Isaiah 37:16-20 (NKJ).

Felix the Cat realized the trouble that came his way was not ever really directed at him. The problems he faced were always ultimately focused on getting to his bag of tricks. King Hezekiah saw the same ploy. If the Assyrians destroyed the children of Israel, they would essentially be destroying the assertion that Israel worshipped the true God. It's the same with us. Our evil adversary, the devil, couldn't care less about us. He is trying to besmirch the glory of God. If he can get us to give up on our "bag of tricks" – our faith in God through Jesus Christ and in the power of the Holy Spirit – we'll go down and God's honor will be tarnished.

Hold on in faith. Let God show Himself mighty as He delivers you. There will be no other answer as to how you got out and got over except to give God the glory. Troubles are big, but our God is bigger. As Corrie ten Boom said, "There is no pit so deep that our God is not deeper still."

#196
July 14: Never Tired

I don't know about you, but by the end of my busy days, I'm extremely tired. I have to rise quite early to complete my morning routine and travel time to make it before the start of 7:30am classes or 7:00am meetings. Even on alternate days when I have a later class to teach, my mornings are full before work with praying, reading my Bible, writing devotions, and then getting to work to grade papers, tweak lesson plans, and check on student progress. Once home in the evenings, I switch the educator hat for the writer/speaker hat and plunge into the business of the ministry for which I have a driving passion. Not to be last or slighted in all of this is my husband whom I adore. I relish the time we can spend just being together or watching college football, cheering on the Lakers, and figuring out who-done-it on *NCIS®*, *CSI®* (all cities), and *The Mentalist®*. Since I'm not triplets, as you can see, my wonderfully full like leaves me exhausted by day's end.

But all the busy-ness we could ever schedule into our calendars is but a drop in the bucket in comparison to God's Day-Timer. In addition to keeping the sun shining, the tides rising and falling, and the planets spinning, we expect Him to be available for our every beck and call. And even as He's holding the stars in place, directing the songs of the nightingales, and orchestrating the seasons, he's watching out of us. He's listening when we hit our knees in the morning, request His protection as we traverse the roadways, and ask Him to bless our food. He's still healing the sick, opening doors of opportunity, and holding back devastation we didn't even realize was headed our way.

And through all that, unlike me at the end of the day, God is never tired. Not only does He have to energy to do it all, He also has the wisdom concerning exactly what to do when. Isaiah 40:28 confirms, "Have you not known? Have you not heard? The everlasting God, the LORD, the Creator of the ends of the earth, neither faints nor is weary. His understanding is unsearchable" (NKJ).

#197
July 15: God says Shush

Making the long "shush" sound through your teeth as you place your index finger over your mouth means, "Be quiet." Making that same sound in a short burst while pointing your finger and sternly squinting at the verbose perpetrator means, "Shut-up!" Sometimes, God needs to shush us quiet.

God's way of saying, "Shush" is in Isaiah 41:1a (NKJ), "Keep silence before Me, O coastlands, and let the people renew their strength!" What's the connection between silence and strength? When we are quiet, God's voice can get through to us. When we act upon God's leading, it's impossible for us to be weak. So you see, silence begets strength. "But the LORD is in His holy temple," says Habakkuk 2:20. "Let all the earth keep silence before Him" (NKJ).

Allow God to say, "Shush," to you. Try going through a full 24 hours using only necessary words. At times when you usually would have been talking, listen instead. Tune in to the voice of the Spirit of God and follow His promptings before you answer, decide, or react. You will find your strength renewed in the end. "But those who wait on the LORD shall renew their strength; they shall mount up with wings like eagles, they shall run and not be weary, they shall walk and not faint" Isaiah 40:31 (NKJ).

#198
July 16: On Holding Hands

I love holding hands. There's something special about the touch of someone you love. I can recall reaching for my children's hands as we crossed a street or walked through a crowded store. It's also a fond memory for me to think about them reaching for my hand when they wanted comfort or just wanted to be sure I was within reach.

Nowadays, those children are out of the house, living on their own, and I rarely see them in person, much less get the opportunity to hold their hands. The most special hand-holding I get to do now is with my husband. I love to hold his hand. He reaches for my hand in church when we pray. My husband's hands are strong. He used them to work to provide a wonderful, comfortable home for us; He used them to fix things and discipline the children; and he uses them both to love and protect me. Whenever he holds my hand as we pray, I also realize how his hands symbolize his leadership and guidance to follow God.

All these hand-holding thoughts flood my mind and heart as I read, "I, the Lord, have called You in righteousness, and will hold Your hand," Isaiah 42:6a (NKJ). At first, I took this personally, as if God were talking to me. Then I realized that the pronoun "you" in the passage is capitalized. God is speaking here to Jesus. He goes on to tell Jesus, "...I will keep You and give You as a covenant to the people, as a light to the Gentiles, to open blind eyes, to bring out prisoners from the prison, those who sit in darkness from the prison house" Isaiah 42:6b-7 (NKJ).

After reading the context, I thought, *Shucks, this verse isn't about God holding my hand.* This verse is about the oneness of the Godhead—about how God the Father connects with God the Son. That's all well and good, but what about holding *my* hand. Then I remembered I had 65 other books in the Bible, filled with verses about God. Surely there must be something that talked about God holding my hand. Check out these verses:

- Psalm 73:23 "Nevertheless I am continually with Thee; Thou hast taken hold of my right hand." (NAS)
- Psalm 37:23-24 "If the LORD delights in a man's way, he makes his steps firm; though he stumble, he will not fall, for the LORD upholds him with his hand" (NIV).
- Psalm 63:8 "My soul clings to you; your right hand upholds me" (NIV).
- Isaiah 41:10 "So do not fear, for I am with you; do not be dismayed, for I am your God. I will strengthen you and help you; I will uphold you with my righteous right hand" (NIV).
- Isaiah 41:13 "For I, the LORD your God, will hold your right hand, saying to you, 'Fear not, I will help you" (NKJ).

As wonderful as it is for me to hold my husband's and children's hands, it's even more wonderful to know that God holds my hand. God's hand assures us of His presence, His guidance, His protection, and his provision. We're secure, stable, strengthened, and sure because God holds our hand and holds us in His. We're in good hands when we're in God's hands.

#199
July 17: No Sharing

I once heard a famous person say that she had sworn off organized religion because a pastor said that God was a jealous God. She went on to make the quizzical comment, "Jealous, of me?"

That person is way off base in her understanding of God's identification of Himself as "a jealous God." The context of God's own comment is His dictation of the Ten Commandments to Moses. He gets to the second commandment and says, "You shall not make for yourself a carved image, or any likeness of anything that is in heaven above, or that is in the earth beneath, or that is in the water under the earth; you shall not bow down to them nor serve them. For I, the LORD your God, am a jealous God..." Exodus 20:4-5 (NKJ). Vine's Expository Dictionary of Biblical Words explains the meaning of "qanna," the word used here for "jealous:"

> This adjective occurs 6 times in the Old Testament. The word refers directly to the attributes of God's justice and holiness, as He is the sole object of human worship and does not tolerate man's sin.

It's not that God is jealous of us; He's jealous or zealous for our worship. As our Creator and Sustainer, He has every right to expect and even demand our due reverence and respect. Yet, instead of forcing Himself down our throats, He functions as our loving Father, "who richly provides us with everything for our enjoyment" First Timothy 6:17 (NIV). Still in all, as that same loving Father, He's fair (just) in warning us that we won't like the outcome if we choose to ignore Him and worship other gods. He's forthright in letting us know that other gods we could choose to worship will let us down. Those gods hold neither the power, the provision, nor the prospect that He holds. God alone is all mighty. God alone has and therefore can supply us with everything we need. And God alone owns Heaven.

God is not ashamed of who He is nor of what He intends for us. He is secure in His identity—in His God-ness. So when it comes to His due, He tolerates no sharing. He communicated this idea to the prophet Isaiah saying, "I am the LORD, that is My name; and My glory I will not give to another, nor My praise to graven images" Isaiah 42:8 (NKJ).

I don't know if this devotion will ever reach the ears of that famous person who thought the preacher was saying that God was jealous of her, but if it does, I sincerely hope the misconception about God on this matter of jealousy is cleared up. I pray too that she comes to understand that fame and fortune only last for this lifetime; only what is done for God—through the acknowledgement of His power by way of Jesus Christ—will last. God is not jealous *of* her; He is jealous *for* her praise as she submits her life to Him through the blood of Jesus—the one and only door (see John 10:1-10) to the true and living God.

#200
July 18: The Eraser

A whole industry exists because of the humble pencil. Many writing instruments have tried, but none have replaced it. Even more important than the graphite writing point (contrary to the common name, pencils are not made of lead), is the other end of the pencil: the eraser. With the eraser, we can change our minds, edit our answers, and rub out our mistakes. The eraser represents the all-important do-over, and when we mess up, isn't that what all of us want?

How fortunate are we to have a God who understands that part of us. In Isaiah 43:25, He says, "I, even I, am He who blots out your transgressions for My own sake; and I will not remember your sins" (NKJ). "Blot out" translates from the Hebrew word "machah" (maw-khaw') which means (guess what) "to stroke or rub; to utterly wipe away or out, to erase." God takes His divine eraser to our sins, rubs until they are gone, and then blows the erasures away.

But just in case one verse is not enough to convince us that our sins are erased, read these cross references:

- "No more shall every man teach his neighbor, and every man his brother, saying, 'Know the LORD,' for they all shall know Me, from the least of them to the greatest of them, says the LORD. For I will forgive their iniquity, and their sin I will remember no more." Jeremiah 31:34 (NKJ)

- "For I will be merciful to their unrighteousness, and their sins and their lawless deeds I will remember no more." Hebrews 8:12 (NKJ)
- "This is the covenant that I will make with them after those days, says the Lord: I will put My laws into their hearts, and in their minds I will write them," then He adds, 'Their sins and their lawless deeds I will remember no more.'" Hebrews 10:16-17 (NKJ)
- "As far as the east is from the west, so far has He removed our transgressions from us." Psalm 103:12 (NKJ)

And exactly what is God's divine eraser? What does He use to blot our out sins? Revelation 1:5 tells us God erased our sins with "Jesus Christ, the faithful witness... who loved us and washed us from our sins in His own blood" (NKJ).

Never look at a pencil and eraser the same again!

#201
July 19: God's Earth Made on Purpose

Lots of us do our share to preserve the Earth. My husband and I recycle cans and plastic bottles. I put my trash, even the smallest candy wrappers, into trash receptacles. We don't pour used oil down storm drains and we keep our cars in good repair so as not to emit too many damaging emissions into the air.

The save-the-planet people may not realize it, but whatever religion or faith they follow, when they show concern about the Earth, they are doing something that honors the God of the Bible. Isaiah 45:18 identifies our God as the One "who created the heavens, who is God, who formed the earth and made it, who has established it, who did not create it in vain, who formed it to be inhabited," and this God goes on to finish this verse by identifying Himself with these words: "I am the LORD, and there is no other" (NKJ).

Enjoy the pleasures of the planet today. Take time to admire the splendor of the vast sky with its clouds by day and stars by night. Stand in the shade of a beautiful tree, inhale the fragrance of a lovely rose, or feel the cool grass between your toes. Go outside and take a deep breath of the free air perfectly blended with just the right mixture of oxygen and other elements essential for our survival. Reflect upon the order in which everything you see was originally created, each day's work to support the next—light; then the firmament dividing the waters, then the dry land with herbs, grasses, trees, etc.; then the lights (sun, stars, etc.); then fish and birds—until the sixth day when God produced His crowning creative jewel, the human. Realize anew, as the above verse indicates, that God "did not create [the Earth] in vain, [He] formed it to be inhabited."

God made the Earth with a purpose. All we can see in it every single day ought to remind us that God's purpose for creating the Earth was to make a place for us to live and enjoy. With all this in mind, I suppose it only makes sense that we Christians should be the most supportive save-the-planet people of all.

#202
July 20: Where to Look

If we live in a city, any one of us would be hard pressed to look in any direction without seeing some sort of advertisement. Marketing gurus have found a way to shout at us from every conceivable angle. Billboards, bus benches, license plate frames, cereal boxes, the backs of ticket stubs, the reverse side of sales receipts, ink pens, refrigerator magnets, key chains, and on, and on, and on. Everywhere our eyes turn, something screams, "Use me, try me, buy me, call me, and hit my website." If we took the advice of every prompt that popped into view, we'd quickly be headed to the poor house with a truck load of stuff we probably never needed in the first place.

How do we sort through all the madness thrown at us each day? God answers with His own advertisement:

"Look to Me, and be saved, all you ends of the earth! For I am God, and there is no other" Isaiah 45:22 (NKJ).

In a world of advertising eye candy and marketing pizzazz, God simply says for us to look to Him and be "yasha" – that's Hebrew for "to be safe, free, helped, rescued, and delivered." In other words, looking to God in every area of our lives leads to victory. The chorus of an old hymn by William Ogden and Beatrice Brown (© 1957) says it simply:

Look and live, my brother live;
Look to Jesus now and live;
It's recorded in His word, Hallelujah,
And it's only that you look and live.

#203
July 21: Written on His Hand

When I was in high school, I first heard about people claiming to be able to tell you something about yourself by reading the lines in your hands. It was called palm reading. I never went to one of those spooky places with the neon sign of a hand in the window, but I do remember looking at the palms of my hands and thinking to myself, *Those lines form an "M" in my hand and don't mean anything.* Even as I look at the palms of my hands now, I notice that the lines on my palms are the places at which my hands bend – nothing more.

I'm thankful for my hands. My fingertips are so sensitive that they are able to warn my brain of danger, and they are so unique that their prints distinguish me from everyone else on the entire planet. My opposable thumbs separate me from the animal kingdom, allowing amazing manual dexterity. I can point out directions, scratch an itch, smooth away wrinkles, wipe away crumbs, apply make-up, hug my loved ones, pat a shoulder, applaud my approval, snap to the beat, and hold someone else's hand.

But a most wonderful thing to consider is not the wonder of my own hands, but the significance of God's. Of course, we are speaking anthropomorphically when we speak of God using human characteristics because we know that as Spirit, He does not physically have hands or feet or eyes. He must, however, communicate to us in terms we can understand, so to express His tender thoughts toward us, He tells us, "See, I have inscribed you on the palms of My hands" Isaiah 49:16 (NKJ).

All we see when we look at the palms of our hands are random lines; God looks at the palms of His hands—which are with Him at all times—and sees our names. With our names in His hands, He points us in the right direction, scratches to comfort the places in our lives that are irritating us, smoothes out the wrinkly problems, and wipes away the crumbs of the past. With our names in His hands, He applies the make-up of His character, transforming us daily into His image. With our names in His hands, he hugs us close, pats our shoulder, applauds His approval of us, snaps the beat of excitement and joy into our days, and holds our hands so we know He's constantly with us.

God goes nowhere without His hands and we're inscribed on them.

#204
July 22: Wait Up

The phrase "wait up" can be used in two contexts. When I have an evening speaking engagement to which I go without my husband, it's always nice to come home because I find that James will "wait up" for me. He foregoes his comfort and stays awake so there will be someone to greet me when I get home. The second use of the phrase happens when I am walking along with my son Matthew. He is taller than I am so his legs are longer. Since his youth gives him more energy and vigor than I now possess, I often find myself lagging behind and imploring him to "wait up." With this, I mean I need him to slow down so I can catch up to where he is and we can walk together.

God shows us that His people benefit when they "wait up" for Him. "Kings shall be your foster fathers, and their queens your nursing mothers; they shall bow down to you with their faces to the earth, and lick up the dust of your feet. Then you will know that I am the LORD, **for they shall not be ashamed who wait for Me**" Isaiah 49:23 (NKJ). If we as God's children are patient, no matter what hardships we may be going through at the time, God will work everything out for our good, even if that means putting us in a position to be served by those much greater than we. We simply need to "wait up" because God is on His way. And when God shows up—as He definitely will—we will have nothing of which to be ashamed.

Why does it seem God has yet to show up in your situation? Think of the two uses of "wait up" once again. Maybe you've refused to "wait up" for God. Instead, you've given up or have gone to sleep thinking He's not going to show up. Or maybe you feel it's taking God too long, so you've rushed ahead without Him. Sooner or later, you'll realize that when you outrun God, you arrive at places where He is not. Is that really what you want? Slow down; "wait up." Once you are side-by-side with God again, match your pace with His so that when you get where you want to go, He'll be there with you.

#205
July 23: Cut from the Rock

I don't know much about mining, but my limited observation tells me it's a tough job. The treasures in the mountain – gold, iron, diamonds, etc. – don't give themselves up easily. These resources must be painstakingly dug or blasted out, at the peril of the life and limb of the miners, and at the expense of the shape of the mountain. The riches don't come easily or cheaply. However, once cut out, retrieved, and properly refined or shaped, the raw materials are transformed into precious and useful objects. They are cut out to become more than their original state. If they could see and talk, these materials could look back at the severely-bruised mountain, thankful both for the time of formation and for the time of release.

Isaiah 51:1 says, "Listen to Me, you who follow after righteousness, you who seek the LORD: look to the rock from which you were hewn, and to the hole of the pit from which you were dug" (NKJ). We too are raw materials, set securely in Christ, the Rock of our salvation. Our "mining" did not come cheap. The Rock was "…wounded for our transgressions, he was bruised for our iniquities…" Isaiah 53:5. We are now His treasures, "His workmanship, created in Christ Jesus for good works, which God prepared beforehand that we should walk in them" Ephesians 2:10. Like gold, iron, and diamonds, we are cut out to become more than our original state.

Why is it then, that like the raw materials in the mountain, we don't easily give ourselves up? Maybe it's because we are ignorant to what we can become. Are we acting like the treasures Jesus died for us to be, or are we just lazily languishing in our original, unrefined state? Gold and diamonds only shine when extracted from the place of their formation and refined and cut into useable shapes. Philippians 2:15 says, "That you may become blameless and harmless, children of God without fault in the midst of a crooked and perverse generation, among whom you shine as lights in the world" (NKJ).

Look to Jesus, the Rock from which you were hewn, and be not only thankful for the time of formation, but also for the time of refining leading to release into the world to get busy doing that for which you have been mined and shaped. You were cut out for more.

#206
July 24: God's Purpose for His Word

Years ago, a stage play and then a movie was produced entitled *Jesus Christ Superstar*. This production chronicled the last week of the earthly life of Christ through the eyes of Judas Iscariot. It was easy to tell that work was not produced by Christians because the early versions ended with the crucifixion of Jesus. Any believer would have obviously ended the story with the resurrection. Later productions added the proper ending to the story.

Still, even the first version made a significant impact on my life. The movie played a major role in causing me to totally dedicate my life to the Lord. Why? It showed the characters in this most magnificent drama as real people, just like you and me. Mary was drawn to Jesus but wasn't quite sure of how she should love Him. Except for Judas, the disciples were portrayed as dedicated, yet still not quite understanding everything. And Judas, having been raised as a "good Jew" was shocked by Jesus' declaration that He was God. He thought Jesus had lost his mind and needed to relax about all of this for His own good.

Even though the play was not done by Christians, the screenwriters used the most potent script imaginable and the power intrinsically packed in the Word of God broke through. By seeing those Bible characters as real people, I came to understand that I could be a part of God's plan too. The play wasn't intended as a witnessing tool, but God's Word always witnesses to His glory and will pull people toward Him.

Isaiah 55:10-11 says, "For as the rain comes down, and the snow from heaven, and do not return there, but water the earth, and make it bring forth and bud, that it may give seed to the sower and bread to the eater, so shall My word be that goes forth from My mouth; it shall not return to Me void, but it shall accomplish what I please, and it shall prosper in the thing for which I sent it" (NKJ).

God has a specific purpose for His Word in each of our lives. He has sent it to us and it will do what He sent it out to do. We might as well just surrender to it.

#207
July 25: Who is the Star?

It seems to have been born in me to perform before an audience. My mother loved to tell the story of one Easter when I was about three years old. I, like all the other Sunday School kids, had my Easter speech to say. Dressed in my frilly Easter dress – outfit complete with hat, gloves, lace socks, and white patent Mary Janes – I was ready for my big moment. As the pastor's daughter, I somehow knew all eyes would be especially on me to see if I could get it right.

One kid before me stumbled over his words; another could hardly be heard even with the microphone held close to his mouth. Yet another little girl just dissolved into tears and never did get her speech said. Then it was my turn. I recited my two-liner like a pro, without a mistake. The congregation applauded. "Hey," my little brain must have thought, "I like that." So I began to ad lib. I struck into a full chorus, choreography and all, of the Hokey Pokey. My mother was mortified but I was quite pleased with myself. I had stolen the show and my performance made me the star that Easter Sunday.

But I wasn't supposed to be the star of Easter Sunday.

Reading Isaiah 58:13-14 caused me to shudder to think of how many other times I had sought to allow my performance to overshadow the message I was assigned to deliver. Those verses say, "If you turn away your foot from the Sabbath, from doing your pleasure on My holy day, and call the Sabbath a delight, the holy day of the LORD honorable, and shall honor Him, not doing your own ways, nor finding your own pleasure, nor speaking your own words, then you shall delight yourself in the LORD; and I will cause you to ride on the high hills of the earth, and feed you with the heritage of Jacob your father. The mouth of the LORD has spoken" (NKJ).

This truth is applicable to all of us, whether we're up in

front of an audience, living before an unsaved husband, training up children, or working in an office. Someone is always watching. How much of His message is overshadowed by our performance of what we think others will want to see? When people walk away from an encounter with us, do they remember us, or do they remember Him? As the passage above states, we honor God by *not* doing our own ways, finding our own pleasure, nor speaking our own words.

Let Him be the star today.

#208
July 26: God's Rights

The second paragraph of the United States' Declaration of Independence states, "We hold these truths to be self-evident, that all men are created equal, that they are endowed by their Creator with certain unalienable Rights, that among these are Life, Liberty and the pursuit of Happiness." One of the keystone points of democracy is citizens' rights. Americans wave the Declaration of Independence and specifically the Bill of Rights in every possible scenario and at every hint of what's deemed by the offended party as "unfair."

However, something is seemingly built inside of all people that screams for rights and justice. We all want to be treated fairly. We believe we at least own ourselves and so we have the right to demand rights.

Well yes, in our horizontal dealings with other people, there is a case for human decency and everyone should be treated equitably. However, as believers, we must operate under a different paradigm when considering our vertical relationship with God. We are not the owners of ourselves; God owns us, and since He does, He has the right to govern us as He so chooses. God explained to the prophet Jeremiah how this works:

> Then the word of the LORD came to me [Jeremiah], saying: "O house of Israel, can I not do with you as this potter?" says the LORD. "Look, as the clay is in the potter's hand, so are you in My hand, O house of Israel! The instant I speak concerning a nation and concerning a kingdom, to pluck up, to pull down, and to destroy it, if that

nation against whom I have spoken turns from its evil, I will relent of the disaster that I thought to bring upon it. And the instant I speak concerning a nation and concerning a kingdom, to build and to plant it, if it does evil in My sight so that it does not obey My voice, then I will relent concerning the good with which I said I would benefit it. Now therefore, speak to the men of Judah and to the inhabitants of Jerusalem, saying, 'Thus says the LORD: "Behold, I am fashioning a disaster and devising a plan against you. Return now every one from his evil way, and make your ways and your doings good"'" Jeremiah 18:5-11 (NKJ).

Here's the bottom line: If we have been receiving blessings but then start to act foolish toward God and His word, God has every right to withhold those blessings and send disaster. If we've been acting foolish and turn to God for forgiveness, He has every right to block disaster and send blessing. God is not wishy-washy in this; He is acting out of His justice, His love, and His rights as the One "to whom we must give account" Hebrews 4:13 (NKJ).

#209
July 27: Like Fire

According to Wikipedia, the free encyclopedia on the internet, "nuclear fission is a nuclear reaction in which the nucleus of an atom splits into smaller parts, often producing free neutrons and photons in the form of gamma rays, and releasing a tremendous amount of energy." Think of that, a piece of matter so small that it cannot be seen by the naked eye, yet if split apart, enough energy is released to level the landscapes of cities all around. The atom, then, is a package we don't open haphazardly. We respect that energy and pay close attention to what it can do.

The prophet Jeremiah says of God's word that it was "in my heart like a burning fire shut up in my bones; I was weary of holding it back, and I could not" Jeremiah 20:9 (NKJ). There was so much power in the messages God had given the prophet, they were burning him up as he held them inside. Once released—split open like the atom—that Word went everywhere, its power enough to level the landscape of sinners' hearts.

God's Word is indeed like fire, able to change everything in its path. Those called to preach and teach must let the messages out, respecting the power of the Word so it's delivered with clarity and compassion. That delivery harnesses and directs the power so that it's received as from a nuclear power plant rather than from an atomic blast.

#210
July 28: Within Reach

My desk is set up so that all of my supplies are within easy reach. I can put my hands on my Synonym Finder when it's time for me to make a great outline for a talk. My pens, pencils, highlighters, scissors, and letter opener are in a wire mesh cup to my right next to the small matching bowl of paperclips, and the matching bin for current letters and files. On the left side of the disk are my prayer list box, pencil sharpener, phone, and a plastic bin holding note pads and stamps. Business cards, return address labels, staples, tape, and other oft-used items are in other parts of the desk. The rest of my office isn't very big, so one desk chair swivel and a few steps connect me with all my writing life needs. And when I'm working from home, my husband, with his sound advice, witty comments, and great cooking is also fortunately close at hand.

When the job where I was employed full time for 17 years went out of business, I really couldn't say that I was unemployed thanks to someone else who is within reach and who kept me busy with work for Him. Jeremiah 23:23 says, "'Am I a God near at hand,' says the LORD, 'And not a God afar off?'" (NKJ).

The answer to the question is, "Yes, God, You are near at hand; You're not a God who is afar off." The best thing I can have within reach at my desk is my God, my employer. Guess what? He's within your reach too; He's near at hand, not afar off. Whether you work behind a desk at home or from a high rise, at a school or in boardrooms, in front of a camera or behind the scenes – wherever you work, God is within reach and He's the main supply we need.

#211
July 29: For Our Own Good

Jeremiah 24:5 – 7 says:

Thus says the LORD, the God of Israel: "Like these good figs, so will I acknowledge those who are carried away captive from Judah, whom I have sent out of this place *for their own good*, into the land of the Chaldeans. For I will set My eyes on them for good, and I will bring them back to this land; I will build them and not pull them down, and I will plant them and not pluck them up. Then I will give them a heart to know Me, that I am the LORD; and they shall be My people, and I will be their God, for they shall return to Me with their whole heart. (NKJ, emphasis added)

Our children can't understand how we could allow the white-coated person to stick them with those painful needles, yet we as parents realize this small amount of pain is necessary for far more important reasons down the road. Without the pain now, there will be excruciating and possibly even deadly circumstances later. As with the Israelites, sometimes God will allow us to go through some hard times. In fact, He may even set those hard times up for us. That's tough to swallow, but our righteous, just, loving heavenly Father always has only our best in mind. The hardships are *for our own good*.

Hang in there. If you're a child of God, realize He knows what you're going through. His eyes are on you and you are never out of His hands or His care. You don't want to be in the right place at the wrong time. When everything is in place, God will bring you back, build you up, and plant you in good soil. He will give you a heart to understand Him. All the doubt will be removed once the fog lifts. You'll be able to see God clearly and love Him unconditionally with your whole heart.

#212
July 30: With You to Save You

The children of Israel went through quite a lot of ups and downs throughout the Old Testament. Unfortunately, most of the downs they brought on themselves by turning from their commitment to serve God alone. However, as exasperated as God was with them, He never utterly forsook them. God would enumerate their sins to them, tell them all the punishment and discipline they were about to face, and then let them know He'd be there for them on the other side of it. An example of God's word to the people at one of these times is found in the thirtieth chapter of Jeremiah.

"I am with you and will save you," declares the LORD. "Though I completely destroy all the nations among which I scatter you, I will not completely destroy you. I will discipline you but only with justice; I will not let you go entirely unpunished" Jeremiah 30:11 (NIV).

The children of Israel could look forward to seeing God devastate the nations who had subjected them, but they also understood that they themselves would not get off scott free. Their own sin demanded payment.

Nothing has changed. God is with us to save us too. He will handle all the adversaries that seek to tear us away from where God wants us to be. He has sent Jesus Christ as the payment for our sin and we can rely on that as having made us His children. But don't get it twisted, God will allow the consequences of our willful disobedience to play out. As with the children of Israel, we will never, not be God's children once we have Jesus, but know that disobedient children are dealt just discipline by loving fathers. God would be less than who He is as our loving Father if He did not chastise us when we mess up.

Hebrews 12:7-11 says, "If you endure chastening, God deals with you as with sons; for what son is there whom a father does not chasten? But if you are without chastening, of which all have become partakers, then you are illegitimate and not sons... Now no chastening seems to be joyful for the present, but painful; nevertheless, afterward it yields the peaceable fruit of righteousness to those who have been trained by it" (NKJ).

God is with us to save us, not just from the ultimate penalty of our sin, but from the foolishness of our own actions.

#213
July 31: The New Covenant Maker

Many preachers and Bible teachers have said, "The Old Testament is the New Testament concealed; the New Testament is the Old Testament revealed." So true. The writers of the books of the New Testament refer to Old Testament passages to make their claims. It's like the Old Testament is the advertising campaign, and the New Testament is the actual launch of the product. For you English buffs, the Old Testament is like future tense—salvation and forgiveness will come. In the New Testament, the Gospels are present tense—salvation and forgiveness is here in the earthly life of Jesus. The epistles are future perfect progressive tense, indicating the continuous action of our living this saved and forgiven life that will be completed at some point in the future. And the Revelation is future progressive tense indicating our ultimate salvation—that is the complete freedom from even the influence of sin—that will be happening or going on at some point in the future when we all get to heaven.

One example of the Old Testament jiving with the New is a comparison of a passage in Jeremiah with a passage in the Revelation. In the Old Testament book, Jeremiah is relating God's comforting words about what will happen in His relationship with His people after they return from their captivity. God says, "But this is the covenant that I will make with the house of Israel after those days...: I will put My law in their minds, and write it on their hearts; and I will be their God, and they shall be My people. No more shall every man teach his neighbor, and every man his brother, saying, 'Know the LORD,' for they all shall know Me, from the least of them to the greatest of them... For I will forgive their iniquity, and their sin I will remember no more" Jeremiah 31:33-34 (NKJ).

Now look at the New Testament words revealed to John via a loud voice from heaven. "Behold, the tabernacle of God is with men, and He will dwell with them, and they shall be His people. God Himself will be with them and be their God. And God will wipe away every tear from their eyes; there shall be no more death, nor sorrow, nor crying. There shall be no more pain, for the former things have passed away." Then God Himself told John, "Behold, I make all things new... Write, for these words are true and faithful." Revelation 21:3-5 (NKJ).

A new covenant and refreshment are not reserved only for

the children of Israel. God is in the new-covenant-making/restoration/refreshment business. As He gathered the Israelites back into His loving arms after their sin, He longs to gather us in from our sin as well. After all, "the Word [Jesus] became flesh and dwelt among us" (John 1:14, NKJ), and told us personally, "If anyone loves Me, he will keep My word; and My Father will love him, and We will come to him and make Our home with him" John 14:23 (NKJ). So now, "having been justified by faith, we have peace with God through our Lord Jesus Christ, through whom also we have access by faith into this grace in which we stand" Romans 5:1-2 (NKJ).

I'd say God's made with us a pretty good new covenant. Wouldn't you agree?

#214
August 1: Respect Planter

God sent His Son to save us and He's supplied the Holy Spirit to keep us, but still we act a fool. God wants to be good to us, but we are so hopelessly wicked in our sinful nature that God often has to get our attention in other ways.

When dealing with the children of Israel, God ran across the same thick-headedness that continues to plague us today. Through the prophet Jeremiah, God says, "And I will make an everlasting covenant with them, that I will not turn away from doing them good; but I will put My fear in their hearts so that they will not depart from Me. Yes, I will rejoice over them to do them good, and I will assuredly plant them in this land, with all My heart and with all My soul" Jeremiah 32:40-41 (NKJ).

Do you see it? Couched smack dab in the middle of God's affirming words to make an everlasting covenant, to not turn away, to do good, to rejoice over them, and to plant them in the land, God has dropped the words "but I will put My fear in their hearts." The Hebrew word "yirah" translated here as "fear" means "moral reverence." We are so lame-brained and bent toward disobedience that God knows He can't even depend upon His goodness to keep us by His side. Since it's not naturally anywhere in us already, God has had to plant in us the respect for Him we need to keep us on the right road. In other words, the desire we feel to submit to God was planted there by God. Gone is any basis for boasting in our righteousness, piety, or humility. It's just not in us apart from God placing it there.

Here is yet another reason to praise Him. God knows us so well, He has gone to every possible length to keep us close. Hallelujah. What a Savior.

#215
August 2: God Called

We get lots of phone calls, e-mails, and junk mail promising all kinds of deals. Advertisers tout that we can take advantage of a holiday sale on roofing, start a new career by attending a specific vocational school, and have younger-looking skin in 30 days by slathering on their product. All we have to do is call back, go to the website, or write in to get all the information.

The advertising efforts make sense. How else would we know about the products or businesses? I actually may need a new roof, a new career, and younger-looking skin one of these days. It's perfectly logical that someone with something he/she deems valuable to offer would try to contact as many people as possible to promote the product or service.

Well, God called and He left a simple message: "Call to Me, and I will answer you, and show you great and mighty things, which you do not know." Jeremiah 33:3 (NKJ). Even if we already have a new roof, a great career, and smooth skin, God's got something valuable to offer that we all need—great and mighty things. Until we dial Him up, we won't know what those things are. Every day we refuse to call is a day void of the great and mighty that God has for our lives.

What are you waiting for? Return His call.

#216
August 3: God Knows Our Intent

In Jeremiah chapters 41 and 42, Nebuchadnezzar, the king of Babylon, had taken over all the land of the children of Israel. He had left only the poor people in the land to continue to farm it. When some renegades hassled them, they ran to the prophet Jeremiah, asking him to pray for them. They said, "Whether it is pleasing or displeasing, we will obey the voice of the LORD our God to whom we send you, that it may be well with us when we obey the voice of the LORD our God" Jeremiah 42:6 (NKJ).

That sounds like a really good prayer, and it would have been had they been sincere. Jeremiah said he'd pray for them and went away and did so. Ten days later he returned and told them that God said to stay in the land, farm it, and don't be afraid of the king of Babylon. God would protect them. However, God knew their hearts and had told Jeremiah the real truth about them. Jeremiah revealed their true nature to them saying, "For you were hypocrites in your hearts when you sent me to the LORD your God, saying, 'Pray for us to the LORD our God, and according to all that the LORD your God says, so declare to us and we will do it'" Jeremiah 42:20 (NKJ).

No matter how good our prayers sound, if we don't mean them down in our hearts, God knows that. God is not a punk. Our surface whining, pleading, and complaining is not going to trick Him into doing our will or believing that we are genuinely sincere. Do we really intend to obey whether what He says to us is pleasing or not?

It's amazingly simple to do those things God says which we don't mind doing. It's pleasing to submit to husbands who love us and to love wives who submit to us. It's pleasing to bless people who bless us. It's pleasing to give out of an abundance. But oh what happens to us when the not-so-pleasing verses pop up? It's not pleasing to wait until marriage to have sexual pleasure when we're in our mid-thirties with no prospects in sight. It's not pleasing to deny our appetite when we know we have to look out for our health. It's not pleasing to love our enemies and do good to those who despitefully use us. It's not pleasing to forgive those who have wronged us. It's not pleasing to accept death and sickness as inevitabilities of sin in this world.

Are we hypocrites or can we sincerely say, "Whether it is pleasing or displeasing, we will obey the voice of the LORD our God"? Let's trust God enough to realize whatever He says and appoints for our lives – whether pleasing or displeasing to our flesh or psyche – comes from the hand of Him who loves us and knows best when we don't. God is good.

#217
August 4: No Pit So Deep

While imprisoned in a wretched German prison camp during the Holocaust, Corrie ten Boom held tight to her faith in God. She and her family had been incarcerated for hiding Jews in a little secret room behind a closet in their home. (Read the amazing true story in her griping book, *The Hiding Place*.) She watched her sister die in that camp and upon her own miraculous release – due to what she would later learn was a clerical error – discovered that the rest of her family had also been killed. Despite the horrors, the hardships, and yes, even times of questioning; Corrie immerged to leave us a quote that has always stuck with me: "There is no pit so deep, that God's love is not deeper still."

In Lamentations 3:55-57, the weeping prophet Jeremiah understood this same sentiment. He says, "I called on Your name, O LORD, from the lowest pit. You have heard my voice: 'Do not hide Your ear from my sighing, from my cry for help.' You drew near on the day I called on You, and said, 'Do not fear!'" (NKJ)

Whenever we are "in the pits" of life, we can remember that we are never out of earshot of God. In fact, since He promised to never fail us, leave us, nor forsake us (see Deuteronomy 31:6 and Hebrews 13:5), we can know that He is in the pit **with** us. You've heard of pit stops? Well, God stops when we're in the pits and draws near when we make pit calls. Shout yours up to Him. There's no pit so deep that He can't hear you when you're in it, preserve you while you're in it, and bring you out of it.

#218
August 5: God Can Find and Use You

Ezekiel was just another displaced soul who had been taken captive with others of the children of Israel. Like many people caught up in a bad situation, he had been keeping track of the years, months, days, and maybe even hours of his ordeal. Then something amazing happened. "Now it came to pass in the thirtieth year, in the fourth month, on the fifth day of the month, as I was among the captives... that the heavens were opened and I saw visions of God...the word of the LORD came expressly to

Ezekiel... in the land of the Chaldeans... and the hand of the LORD was upon him there" Ezekiel 1:1-3 (NKJ).

Ezekiel was in the worst possible condition imaginable. He and his people had been taken captive by an enemy army at the permission of God. God was punishing His people for their gross disobedience, so it was disciplinary action they rightly deserved. Still, in what seemed to have been a God-forsaken place, during what seemed to have been a God-forsaken time, in what seemed to have been a God-forsaken situation, God found Ezekiel. But not only did God find him, God spoke to him, revealed Himself to him, and placed His hand on him to use him.

The Psalmist knew God could find and use him too. Psalm 139:7-17 says, "Where can I go from Your Spirit? Or where can I flee from Your presence? If I ascend into heaven, You are there; if I make my bed in hell, behold, You are there. If I take the wings of the morning, and dwell in the uttermost parts of the sea, Even there Your hand shall lead me, and Your right hand shall hold me. If I say, 'Surely the darkness shall fall on me,' even the night shall be light about me; Indeed, the darkness shall not hide from You, but the night shines as the day; the darkness and the light are both alike to You... My frame was not hidden from You, when I was made in secret, and skillfully wrought in the lowest parts of the earth... How precious also are Your thoughts to me, O God! How great is the sum of them!" (NKJ)

No matter what place, time, or situation we find ourselves in today – no matter how long we've been there – let's be encouraged. God can find us, God can reveal Himself to us, God can place His hand on us, and God can use us. His thoughts toward us are precious. Praise His name!

#219
August 6: The Glory that's Due

I've heard that celebrities don't necessarily mind bad publicity as long as their name continues to circulate among the public. An inaccurate mention is better than being ignored, subsequently getting no mention at all. Everything about fame depends upon getting one's name "out there," so it's not surprising to find people going to extremes sometimes to get noticed.

When people decide to ignore God, He will go to extremes

to get noticed. Of course, He deserves to be noticed; He deserves glory. I was struck by this thought when I read eight times in just two chapters of Ezekiel (chapters 29 and 30) God saying that people "will know that I am the Lord."

God gets His name "out there" in these two chapters, but it's not in a way any one of us would like. His comment follows His declarations to:

- Leave you in the wilderness
- Bring a sword upon you
- Make land utterly waste and desolate
- Diminish them
- Take away wealth, and
- Pour out my fury.

God says He will scatter, break, and disperse so that they "will know that I am the Lord."

The nations to which God is talking in Ezekiel 29 and 30 had had their chances to acknowledge Him yet had ignored Him for years. What about us? Both Psalm 29:2 and Psalm 96:8 say, "Give unto the LORD the glory due to His name..." Have we given God the notice He deserves or is He going to have to make some extreme declarations in our lives followed by "then they will know that I am the Lord"? Will God have to do some drastic thing to get His name "out there" with us?

#220
August 7: God Gets No Pleasure

When Osama Bin Laden was killed, some people in America rejoiced in the streets. After all, this one man had accepted blame for masterminding the 9-11 terrorist attacks within our borders. Acts carried out under his direction left many loved ones with empty arms and hearts when the planes used as missiles hit their marks. Even the plan that missed its target crashed in a field killing all aboard. Wasn't the celebration of punishment for Bin Laden justified?

Not in God's sight.

Ezekiel 33:11 states, "Say to them: 'As I live,' says the Lord GOD, 'I have no pleasure in the death of the wicked, but that the wicked turn from his way and live...'" (NKJ). Bin Laden professed to devoutly follow a religion that does not believe that Jesus Christ is "the way, the truth, and the life," and there's no other way to get to God except by the acknowledgement of who Jesus is. (See John 14:6) The atrocities sanctioned by Bin Laden were indeed wicked acts, but God had no pleasure in his death. Why? Because He is longsuffering (patient) toward us, not willing that any should perish but that all should come to repentance" Second Peter 3:9 (NKJ).

We see Bin Laden's sin as so much worse than our own. The truth is: none of us deserve salvation. "For all have sinned and fall short of the glory of God" Romans 3:23 (NKJ). Any sin is enough to preclude us from Heaven. It's only thanks to God's amazing grace and mercy that our lives were not cut short before we had a chance to come into the saving knowledge of Christ, trust Him as our Savoir, and be welcomed as part of the family of God.

By all indications, Bin Laden is spending the rest of all eternity in hell's fires along with everyone else who died without the saving knowledge of Christ. That's nothing for us to celebrate. God gets no pleasure in an unsaved soul. Let's busy ourselves today and every day spreading the Gospel so the tragedy of a lost soul won't happen to anyone with whom we come in contact.

#221
August 8: The Point is: Live for God

Adherents to the radical fringe of a popular religion maintain that their god rewards them if they murder "the infidels." The definition of an infidel is anyone who does not believe in their god and their faith. Although on the surface this may seem to be a compelling witnessing technique – believe or die – it's not effective when it comes to heart change. Our bodies respond to fear, but our hearts respond to love.

The God of the Bible, the true and living God, loves us and is interested in our lives, not our deaths. "…'As I live,' says the Lord GOD, 'I have no pleasure in the death of the wicked, but that the wicked turn from his way and live. Turn, turn from your evil ways!…'" Ezekiel 33:11 (NKJ) God repeats this sentiment several times in His word.

- "For I have no pleasure in the death of one who dies," says the Lord GOD. "Therefore turn and live!" Ezekiel 18:32 (NKJ)
- The Lord is not slow in keeping his promise, as some understand slowness. He is patient with you, not wanting anyone to perish, but everyone to come to repentance. Second Peter 3:9 (NIV)
- Therefore I exhort first of all that supplications, prayers, intercessions, and giving of thanks be made for all men... that we may lead a quiet and peaceable life in all godliness and reverence. For this is good and acceptable in the sight of God our Savior, who desires all men to be saved and to come to the knowledge of the truth. 1 Timothy 2:1-4 (NKJ)

How aptly this fits with the words of James as he, through the Holy Spirit, tells us, "For as the body without the spirit is dead, so faith without works is dead also" James 2:26 (NKJ). You see, we don't just get saved in order to drift through life staying out of as much trouble as possible until we die. We get saved in order to live for God. Being a Christian and doing nothing for God is like having a university education and refusing to take a job offered in your field of study. We spent all that money but refuse to use the knowledge we gained. Ridiculous. It's just as ridiculous to be walking around as a saved individual having no Christian works to show for it. If that's the case, God's word says our faith is dead.

God intends for us to *live* for Him. What proof of your faith does your life produce? As the old question asks, "If you were on trial for being a Christian, would there be enough evidence to convict you?"

#222
August 9: Hear From God; Leave Different

Nine words spoken by my pastor Rev. Welton Pleasant profoundly impacted my life. He said, "When you open your Bible, God opens His mouth." It was not news to me that the Bible is God's message to us—His very word; however, that statement put an entire new spin on my quiet times. I sincerely expected now to hear from God every time I read the Scriptures. In fact, these daily devotions are a direct result of this quest after God's voice, and upon hearing it, what difference it can make in my life.

God intimated at this same connection between His voice and our change as He directed Ezekiel in the manner of worship. He said, "But when the people of the land come before the Lord on the appointed feast days, whoever enters by way of the north gate to worship shall go out by way of the south gate; and whoever enters by way of the south gate shall go out by way of the north gate. He shall not return by way of the gate through which he came, but shall go out through the opposite gate." More than a traffic flow issue through the sanctuary, festival, or feast day event, this instruction seems more like a life flow issue. When the people came into the presence of God, He expected them to leave a different way; He expected their lives to be changed.

How is it even possible to hear God's voice and remain unaffected by the contact? Let's take our experience with God beyond the church building and church events. Each time we read the Bible, hear a sermon based on the Bible, or rejoice to a song written from the Scriptures, know that God is opening His mouth. However you came to your quiet time or worship experience, listen closely for God's voice, and expect and determine to leave a different way.

#223
August 10: A Personal Relationship

There is some pretty exciting preaching material in Daniel chapters 1-3.

- Chapter one tells us of Daniel and his three friends being taken hostage from Jerusalem and honoring God by refusing to defile themselves by eating King Nebuchadnezzar's provisions. Upon being tested by the king, they turned out to be stronger, wiser, and ten times better than all the magicians and astrologers in his realm.
- In chapter two, the great king has a troubling dream that none of his magicians can interpret. God shows the dream and the interpretation to Daniel who reveals it to the king; thus causing the king to say, "...Truly your God is the God of gods, the Lord of kings, and a revealer of secrets, since you could reveal this secret." Then the king promoted Daniel..." Daniel 2:47-48 (NKJ).
- Chapter three relates one of the Bible's most famous stories. Here the king sets up a huge golden image and

requires everybody to bow to it. Daniel's three friends, Shadrach, Meshach, and Abed-Nego, refuse to bow when challenged by the king's haughty attitude "…if you do not worship, you shall be cast immediately into the midst of a burning fiery furnace. And who is the god who will deliver you from my hands?" (Daniel 3:15) When they are thrown into the fiery furnace and saved by God, again the king admits, "There is no other God who can deliver like this" Daniel 3:28-29 (NKJ).

Even after these three incidences, King Nebuchadnezzar had not caught on. The king only understood God as being the God of Daniel and his three buddies until we get to chapter four. Here the king has another troubling dream that Daniel interprets. God shows the king that he would be humbled for seven years, scrounging around like an animal, until he would "…come to know that Heaven rules" Daniel 4:26 (NKJ). Finally, after that prophecy was fulfilled, the king testifies, "Now I, Nebuchadnezzar, praise and extol and honor the King of heaven, all of whose works are truth, and His ways justice. And those who walk in pride He is able to put down" Daniel 4:37 (NKJ).

The exciting sermons from the first three chapters of Daniel center on the four Hebrew boys and their stalwart stand for God in front of the mighty Babylonian king; yet, their ordeals weren't really about them at all. God had them; He was aiming at the heart of the king.

God desires more than to just be acknowledged as God; He desires to be accepted as God in our hearts on a personal level. Jesus showed this same desire to us in Matthew 16:13-16. It reads:

"Jesus… asked His disciples, saying, 'Who do men say that I, the Son of Man, am?' So they said, '…John the Baptist, …Elijah, and …Jeremiah or one of the prophets.' He said to them, '*But who do you say that I am*?' Simon Peter answered and said, 'You are the Christ, the Son of the living God'" (NKJ).

Is your relationship with God based only on what you've seen in others? If so, there's a deeper walk with God awaiting you, a personal relationship that He desires to have with you. God has no step-children. Each one of us is His very own. Who is God to you?

#224
August 11: Who is the God Who Will...?

Nebuchadnezzar was the very powerful and influential king of Babylon who besieged Jerusalem and took the Hebrew people captive. Among the captives were Shadrach, Meshach, and Abed-Nego. These young men refused to take on Babylonian ways or bow to the king's gold image. Everyone else was doing it, so their refusal to worship the king's god incensed the king, leading him to order them to bow or else suffer the consequences of being thrown into a burning fiery furnace. The king's arrogant demand ended with the mocking statement, "And who is the god who will deliver you from my hands?" (Daniel 3:15, NKJ)

Over and over again as believers, we hear this same type of challenge when we stand for right in a society in which everyone else is doing what ought not to be done. If we refuse to cheat on a test or on our taxes, the world mocks us saying, "Who is the god who will blame you for doing what you have to do to get over?" If we take a Biblical stand concerning alternate lifestyles (the sin, not the people), the world challenges, "Who is the god who will punish people for wanting to live and love however they choose?" If we decline invitations to place Jesus on equal footing with the religious leaders of other faiths, society chides us with, "Who is the god who will put himself above what others believe?"

Our answer to the "who-is-the-god-who-will" questions must begin as the Hebrew boys' answer began, "...our God whom we serve is able to...". The God we serve is able to help us pass tests and earn enough to pay our taxes. The God we serve is able to show us how to live and supply us with the love He wants for us. The God we serve is King of kings, Lord of lords, Wonderful, Counselor, Mighty God, Everlasting Father, Prince of Peace, the great I AM. No matter what situation we find ourselves in, our great God is able to deliver us in such a way that brings Him ultimate glory and sets us truly free.

No matter what may be going on in our lives, we can stay encouraged with the knowledge that God will always be "the God who will." He's the God whose birth we herald, whose death we remember, and whose resurrection we celebrate. He is the God who will still enter hearts, delivering us from the clutches of sin and the enemy of our souls.

#225
August 12: The Shining Spirit Within

When King Darius the Mede took over Belshazzar's kingdom, he inherited the Hebrews who had been taken captive years before by Nebuchadnezzar, Belshazzar's dad. Darius divided the rulership of his newly possessed kingdom among 120 satraps (like mayors) and placed three men (like governors) over them. One of those three was the Hebrew Daniel. It didn't take long though for Darius to realize there was something extra-special about Daniel, and any ruler worth his salt moves to place his best people in the most influential positions. Daniel 6:3 states, "Then this Daniel distinguished himself above the governors and satraps, because an excellent spirit *was* in him; and the king gave thought to setting him over the whole realm" (NKJ).

You can imagine the uproar among the other governors and satraps. Not only were they being passed over, they would soon be answering to this former captive. Unthinkable!

"So the governors and satraps sought to find *some* charge against Daniel concerning the kingdom; but they could find no charge or fault, because he *was* faithful; nor was there any error or fault found in him. Then these men said, 'We shall not find any charge against this Daniel unless we find *it* against him concerning the law of his God'" Daniel 6:4-5 (NKJ).

Daniel was all that and a bag of chips because he lived a life consistent with His belief in the God he served. He was an excellent worker because his God was an excellent God. He was a compassionate and honest ruler because his God was a compassionate and honest ruler. People could find no fault in Daniel because there was no fault in the God his life mirrored.

The Spirit of God can shine through our lives in the same way it shone through Daniel's. We must just remember to stand up for God as Daniel did and live a life consistent with the character of who we know God to be. No fault or charge can successfully and legitimately be leveled against us unless our haters attack the law of our God. While remaining respectful of those around us who don't believe in our God (as Daniel did when speaking with Belshazzar—see Daniel 5:13-30), we don't need to back down from telling them the truth about Him. We can confidently stand up for God because God is well able through us to stand up for Himself.

#226
August 13: Loving Parental Discipline

Sometimes our parents have to get on our case. It ain't pretty. It certainly isn't comfortable. If we're honest, at least 99% of the time, they are right in their assessment of our wrong. And if we're even more honest, about that same percentage of the time, in spite of their previous teaching and warnings, we have brought their disappointment and wrath upon ourselves. They have no choice but to speak up and act because they love us enough to want to keep us on the correct and safe path. However, despite said tongue lashings, punishments, curfews, or restrictions, our parents still love us, home is still home, and the relationship that was temporarily damaged by our disobedience or stupidity will be repaired and restored.

That's how loving parental discipline works. God, our Grand Parent, uses the warning/punishment/restoration parenting technique with us. Watch how He dealt with the backslidden Israelites in Hosea, chapters 5 and 6:

- [God says], "For I will be like a lion to Ephraim, and like a young lion to the house of Judah. I, even I, will tear them and go away; I will take them away, and no one shall rescue. I will return again to My place till they acknowledge their offense. Then they will seek My face; in their affliction they will earnestly seek Me."
- [Then the prophet Hosea says], "Come, and let us return to the LORD; for He has torn, but He will heal us; he has stricken, but He will bind us up" Hosea 5:14-6:1 (NKJ).

All through the Old Testament, God had been warning His people against following other gods and copying the practices of the people of the land who didn't know or honor Him. The Israelites refused to obey, so now God is reading them the riot act and doling out the punishment. However, Hosea knows His Father. "Let us return," he says. What God has torn, He will heal and what God has stricken, he will bind up.

We parents can take a lesson on loving parental discipline from God's playbook. After we've had to lay down the law to our kids and they've seen the error of their ways, we need to provide for them a loving path back into fellowship with us. As God's children ourselves, we can appreciate the provision of such a path when we have to return to the Lord after we've messed up. Both us and our kids need the reassurance that home is still home. We will find that sticking close to home – either by honoring our parents or by honoring God—and abiding by His council brings nothing but good to our lives. Psalm 16:11 says it this way: "You will show me the path of life; in Your presence is fullness of joy; at Your right hand are pleasures forevermore" (NKJ).

God's discipline does not mean He no longer loves us; it just means it's time to pull even closer so He can heal and bind up our wounds. If we follow God's parenting example, our kids need only to return; it's our job as godly parents to do the healing and binding.

#227
August 14: Our Loving Father's Compassion

Becoming parents allows us some unique glimpses into God's parental heart. We understand the awesome gift God gave us by sacrificing His Son for our sin, because we know full well we wouldn't sacrifice our children for anybody else. Thankfully, we are not called to sacrifice our children for others. In fact, we're encouraged to focus on them, carefully raising them to know and follow God, being examples to them on how to live in order to please Him. Our parenting then should mirror God's parenting of us. However, when our kids act crazy, we forget about being like God and default to allowing our feelings or our family upbringing to supersede God's ways of handling situations.

God's heart and corresponding actions toward His wayward children are revealed in Hosea, chapter 11. He says:

- For my people are determined to desert me. (The NKJ version says, "My people are bent on backsliding.) They call me the Most High, but they don't truly honor me.
- Oh, how can I give you up, Israel? How can I let you go? How can I destroy you like Admah or demolish you like Zeboiim? My heart is torn within me, and my compassion overflows.
- No, I will not unleash my fierce anger. I will not completely destroy Israel, for I am God and not a mere mortal. I am the Holy One living among you, and I will not come to destroy.

- For someday the people will follow me. I, the LORD, will roar like a lion. And when I roar, my people will return trembling... And I will bring them home again. Hosea 11:7-11 (NLT)

God knows His children. Although they seem determined or bent on doing everything opposite from what He's taught or shown them, His compassion is constant. His children deserve His fierce anger. He is well able to completely destroy them. He would be well within His rights to simply give up on them. However, He knows one day they will be back. He knows, one day they will realize how much they need Him, and He'll be there when they turn around. He may have to roar to get their attention, but when they head back, He'll be there as He always has been, and not with an I-told-you-so attitude.

We know our children too. Although they seem determined or bent on doing everything opposite from what we've taught or shown them, our compassion must remain constant. Our children deserve our fierce anger. We are well able to completely destroy them. We would be well within our rights to simply give up on them. However, we know one day they will be back. We know, one day they will realize how much they need us, and we ought to be there when they turn around. We may have to roar to get their attention, but when they head back, we ought to be there as we always have been, and not with an I-told-you-so attitude.

Let's follow God's example with kids who have made mistakes. They've heard us as we've roared. There comes a time to let our compassion overflow like God's did to kids who have suffered under the weight of their errors.

#228
August 15: Memorable

Having people reach the level of being considered famous is not new. There have always been memorable individuals. In the past, people's fame grew naturally out of their accomplishments. Nowadays, without a publicist, a slick advertising campaign, and a recognizable brand, accomplishments are likely to be drowned out in the noise of everyone else trying to be recognized, unless of course, you are the absolute best at what you do. We know of Charles Dickens because of his masterful way of crafting stories that taught us many lessons of what's really important in life. We know of Bill Gates because Microsoft® set the standard in the computer world. We know of Steve Jobs because Apple® products have taken us all to new heights of hand-held technology. Yes, advertising got the word out, but the excellence of the products has kept their work around and has made them memorable.

God is the very best at what He does, and because of that Hosea 12:5b is able to say, "The LORD is His memorable name" (NKJ). As you go through your day today, take time to observe God's accomplishments, i.e. His "products." Then remember the name of the One who created them. For example, as I write this piece, I'm gazing out my office window on the fertile lemon tree in our back yard. God made that tree and placed within it the ability to produce the tart fruit. In this instance, God's memorable name is Creator. I'm also looking at power lines that stretch from a major source somewhere, to our local power sub-station, to the poles on my block, and to our house. God's memorable name is Supplier. Or I consider my life, my breath, my beating heart, and know that even when my heart stops, my life will continue in heavenly realms. God's memorable name is Eternal Sustainer. And in every case, God's the best at what He has done.

How many different memorable names of God can you find through your observations of His excellence in just this one day? Make it a regular habit to call forth His memorable name every day.

#229
August 16: God's Ways

When we come across people who do not quite fit our idea of the norm, we say things about them like, "She has funny ways," or "He has a strange way about him," or "They have a bizarre way of looking at things." In these phrases, we are using the definition of the word "way" to mean "a characteristic manner of acting or doing, a particular style."

Although we may evaluate the "way" others act or see things in comparison with our "way" of acting or seeing things, there is a standard that exists that exemplifies for us the "way" we should live. Hosea 14:9 tells us, "For the ways of the LORD are right; the righteous walk in them, but transgressors stumble in them" (NKJ). The Hebrew word translated "ways" in this verse is "derek" which figuratively means "a course of life or mode of action." In other words, this verse is talking about the manner in which God acts. It's telling us how God does things. And what are we told about how God acts and does things? His manner and His actions are always right.

So what does that mean for us? The rest of the verse makes that clear. Since God's ways are right, we can know that we are right (or righteous) as we duplicate how He does things. This is not rocket science, it's Barney-simple: the righteous act like God acts. When we balk at doing things God's way, we are showing ourselves up as transgressors, rebels who want to revolt, break away, and act in an opposite "way."

It's hard to come face-to-face with our own depravity, to actually admit that our ways don't line up with God's ways. However, when once we face our sin nature head-on, identify it and all it produces as such, and surrender that sick, inky slime to God, He will wash it away. He'll then begin to show us His ways and He'll give us the strength and direction to start walking in them. The benefits are astounding, for example:

- You may have a walk worthy of the Lord, fully pleasing Him, being fruitful in every good work and increasing in the knowledge of God. Colossians 1:10 (NKJ)
- And whatever we ask we receive from Him, because we keep His commandments and do those things that are pleasing in His sight. First John 3:22 (NKJ)
- When a man's ways please the LORD, he makes even his enemies to be at peace with him. Proverbs 16:7 (NKJ)

Be encouraged today to walk in God's ways.

#230
August 17: <u>A Report that Matters</u>

My husband reads through the newspaper every day, then in the evening, we watch the evening news, which airs at 6:30pm our time and broadcasts for 30 minutes. Later each night, we tune in to the 11:00pm news for another half hour. On Sundays, we also enjoy catching *60 Minutes* and we usually end up discussing some of the stories explored by the investigators and journalists of that program. Be it the newspaper, a news broadcast, or a news magazine, in every case, we are taking in information being reported to us about people, places, and events usually separate from our personal space and experience.

All told, my husband and I spend 6 – 8 hours a week engrossed in news reports. A little parenthetical statement in Scripture caught my eye this morning and caused me to think about all the news we watch. Obadiah 1b says, "...We have heard a report from the Lord..."

This made me think. Hearing a report from the Lord every day is much more important that hearing what our favorite commentator has to say about Wall Street, the weather, the H1N1 virus, or the latest celebrity who has taken a fall from grace. I immediately did a self-evaluation that I recommend for each of us. Compare how much time is spent reading and listening to news or other forms of information with how much time is spent in a position to hear reports from the Lord. To discover the answer, add up the hours spent with TV, internet, newspaper, or radio information, then count the hours (or minutes) spent with God. For the spiritual side of the ledger, add the time spent in daily Bible reading, daily prayer, journaling, and church attendance. It's also fair to include your attendance at Bible studies and prayer meetings.

Are you pleased with the outcome? Let's consider spending more time with the reports that really matter.

#231
August 18: Saying No to God

Jonah is the classic example of what can happen to a child of God who decides to say no to God. There Jonah was – a prophet of the Lord – with a clear directive. He didn't even have to study the Hebrew to write his own sermon nor advertise for an audience. God told Jonah where to go – to Nineveh, a city of over 120,000 – and what to say – cry out against their wickedness. Seems like a simple enough task for a prophet.

But oh no, Jonah's response to his call was far from agreeable. Jonah 1:3 says, "But Jonah arose to flee to Tarshish from the presence of the LORD. He went down to Joppa, and found a ship going to Tarshish; so he paid the fare, and went down into it, to go with them to Tarshish from the presence of the

LORD" (NKJ). Jonah said no to God. Nineveh was 500 miles east of Israel (it's actually present-day Iraq) and Tarshish is 2,000 miles west of Israel, so Jonah was trying to put a 2,500 mile distance between himself and where God wanted him to go. Among the many lessons we can learn from Jonah about saying no to God, let's look at just three of them here.

#1: Your running is of no consequence to God. Psalm 139:7 asks, "Where can I go from Your Spirit? Or where can I flee from Your presence?" (NKJ) God is omnipresent (everywhere present) so there's no place we can go where we can hide from Him. God knows where our "Tarshish" is, and as embarrassing as it will be, when we run there, He'll be there waiting for us when we arrive.

#2: Your ruin affects those around you. Jonah's disobedience caused God to have to discipline him, but that discipline spilled over onto the other passengers of the ship Jonah was using for his escape. Thanks to Jonah, the men aboard the ship lost their cargo which meant a significant financial loss for them. When we disobey God, others around us could be hurt.

#3: Your responsibility will be fulfilled. After all that trouble, Jonah ended up on the shores of Nineveh anyway, right where God had originally told him to go. When God calls us, He intends for us to do exactly that. Running and complaining won't get us off the hook and God will use any means necessary – even if it takes a three-day ride in fish acid – to get us where He intends for us to be, doing what He intends for us to do.

One of the biggest blockbuster books of the past few years was Rick Warren's *The Purpose Driven Life*. What more accurate purpose could there be than to do what God has called us to do, so why do we "pull a Jonah" and run from God's clear direction? Start anywhere in God's word and you'll find your purpose. For example, Romans 13:9 is a clear verse with which we can begin to live out God's purpose for our lives. "For the commandments, 'You shall not commit adultery,' 'You shall not murder,' 'You shall not steal,' 'You shall not bear false witness,' 'You shall not covet,' and if there is any other commandment, are all summed up in this saying, namely, 'You shall love your neighbor as yourself'" (NKJ).

Let's not run toward ruin, but fulfill the responsibility of God's call. Say yes to God.

#232
August 19: Reverse Fisherman

I've never gone fishing, but I've seen people fishing and have heard stories about fishing. I understand that the fisherman goes out onto the water in a boat, or stands on the bank or bridge, or positions him or herself in the water for the purpose of catching some sort of water creature. Lines, poles, hooks, and nets are used to pull said creatures from the water. I also understand that there can be good fishing days and bad fishing days. Sometimes the fisherman brings in a great catch; at other times, not so much if any.

Rarely though do I hear of fishermen doing all that preparatory work only to throw back what they have caught. However, In Micah, chapters 6 and 7, God shows Himself to do just that. He's somewhat a "reverse fisherman." After all the work He'd done to love His people, they still turned their backs on Him. His anger burned against them and He allowed sickness, hunger, and their enemies to ravish them. Nevertheless, His great love for them won out. The prophet writes, "Who is a God like You, pardoning iniquity and passing over the transgression of the remnant of His heritage? He does not retain His anger forever, because He delights in mercy. He will again have compassion on us, and will subdue our iniquities. You will cast all our sins into the depths of the sea" Micah 7:18-19 (NKJ).

God is still reverse fishing. He has gone to great lengths to gather us in from the sea of our sin, but then He tosses that sin right back out to sea. First John 4:10 says, "In this is love, not that we loved God, but that He loved us and sent His Son to be the propitiation for our sins" (NKJ). The tossing of our sin into the sea was accomplished by Jesus on the cross—all out of God's amazing love for us.

#233
August 20: Love and Wrath

Folks seem to have a hard time reconciling the fact that God is both a God of love and a God of wrath. This is not a difficult concept. Look at any good mother. She dotes on her children, hugs them, kisses them, works hard to provide for their needs, attends their activities, cheers louder than anybody else at their games, prays for their success, thinks of ways to surprise them, etc. She loves them. On the other hand, however, let someone come against those kids and that same amazingly loving mother will attack like a hurricane, a tsunami, a tornado, and an earthquake all rolled into one. Love and wrath combined in the same person.

The prophet Nahum tells us that both love and wrath abide in our God. Nahum 1:7-8 says, "The LORD is good, a stronghold in the day of trouble; and He knows those who trust in Him. But with an overflowing flood he will make an utter end of its place, and darkness will pursue His enemies" (NKJ).

It's actually impossible to have love without wrath. The mother who truly loves her children is wrathful against anyone or anything that would hurt them. God who loves us is wrathful against anyone or anything—be it the devil, an enemy, or our own sin—that would hurt us.

#234
August 21: Not the Idol

A very funny television series was called *Dinosaurs*. Each week, a family of dinosaurs would point out, in a very clever satirical manner, some fault of human nature we could all do well to consider and change. The family consisted of the father and mother, a teen son, a teen daughter, and a baby. An ongoing gag was how the baby related closely to the nurturing of its mother, but referred to the father as Not-the-Momma. Although the father loved the baby very much and would do anything for it, the baby rarely gave the father the attention he rightly deserved. One particular episode made that poignantly clear when Earl (the father) accidentally fell into radioactive water and became a superhero. Baby became enamored with the superhero by watching him on TV, idolizing the superhero, never realizing the good being done should actually be attributed to his own dad.

We do the same thing to God.

Oh, we would never call it "idol worship," but we're pretty good at placing things and even other people before God in our lives. It's as if we look to those things or those people to meet our needs, and then turn to God and call Him "Not-the-Idol."

Well, let's get it straight: God indeed is not the idol. He's real and able to move in our lives. How dare we trust in anyone (spouses, children, employers) or anything (money, education, status) more than or instead of trusting in God! The prophet Habakkuk spoke of this saying, "What profit is the image, that its maker should carve it, the molded image, a teacher of lies, that the maker of its mold should trust in it, to make mute idols?

Woe to him who says to wood, 'Awake!' To silent stone, 'Arise! It shall teach!' Behold, it is overlaid with gold and silver, yet in it there is no breath at all. But the LORD is in His holy temple. Let all the earth keep silence before Him" Habakkuk 2:18-20 (NKJ).

Trust God first, last, only, and always.

#235
August 22: Recession Proof-er

Some years are better than others. When exiting a particularly tough year, we'd like to think things will get better in the new one. The reality is that we don't know what the new year may hold. We're good when we can see a light at the end of the tunnel, but what about if the tunnel has some twists and turns? Light tends not to bend around corners. Even if we can't see the end of the road or the breaking of day, there's still hope. We can't see oxygen, but we keep on breathing. Take the attitude of the prophet Habakkuk:

- Though the fig tree may not blossom, nor fruit be on the vines; though the labor of the olive may fail, and the fields yield no food; though the flock may be cut off from the fold, and there be no herd in the stalls—Yet I will rejoice in the LORD, I will joy in the God of my salvation. Habakkuk 3:17-18 (NKJ).

One thing stands sure—at the end of a bad year, or at the beginning of a questionable one—God is on His throne. He is in control, He is our Father, and therefore, He is the recession-proofer. No matter what it looks like all around, trust Him and rejoice in Him. He can and will make a way.

#236
August 23: Foot Doctor

When we go sailing, it may be necessary to get our sea legs under us. Having "sea legs" means we have made a bodily adjustment to the motion of the ship indicated especially by the ability to walk steadily and by freedom from seasickness. In other words, no matter what havoc the sea decides to throw at our boat, we will be able to function securely.

Now think of the sea as life's vicissitudes. The wave of financial reversal may wash across the deck. The wind of the unexpected death of a family member or close friend may threaten to blow you off course. And the lightning strike of a failed relationship might blind you momentarily and come menacingly close to burning down your main mast. In the midst of the storm, when there's nothing else you can do, trust God to supply you with sea legs.

Habakkuk 3:19 says, "The LORD God is my strength; he will make my feet like deer's feet, and He will make me walk on my high hills" (NKJ). Certain types of deer inhabit rocky hillsides. The only way they can climb up and down and survive in their habitat is because God has formed them with specially-designed feet. No matter what they face, they are able to function and walk effortlessly among stony obstacles.

Those deer's feet are like sea legs. Look to God as your source of strength. Today, let Him give you the feet you need to walk effortlessly among your obstacles and the sea legs you need to stand steadily until you reach a friendly port.

#237
August 24: God in Our Midst

One of the best things God allows in my life is the opportunity to speak and teach His Word. Most of the time, I'm speaking at conferences and churches where the majority of the people don't know me personally. Someone will be assigned to introduce me, and since that person isn't familiar with me, I provide a little information sheet about myself. This allows that person to feel comfortable and have accurate facts. She doesn't have to conduct a quick interview and hurriedly put something together.

Sometimes though, I'm introduced either by someone who knows me well, or by an MC who has taken the time to talk with me and form her own opinion. In those instances, I have always followed those comments in renewed humility and gratefulness because those introductions have been so touching. Many times, they will mention characteristics God has been developing in me, or character qualities I had no idea anyone was paying much attention to. Hearing their words is affirming and I carry them close in my heart, keeping them on reserve for times when the adversary wants to discourage me.

As great as a flattering introduction may be, the ultimate compliment comes only when God is pleased. Zephaniah tells us how God feels about the remnant who will continue to follow and trust Him no matter what. "The LORD your God in your midst, the Mighty One, will save; he will rejoice over you with gladness, he will quiet you with His love, he will rejoice over you with singing" Zephaniah 3:17 (NKJ). Better than sitting and hearing a great introduction is the realization that God is dwelling in our midst, saving us, quieting us with His love, and rejoicing over us with singing. God is excited about us and He doesn't mind telling it.

Let's be sure to conduct ourselves in such a way that when God speaks and sings of us, it's a good introduction.

#238
August 25: Don't Play God Cheap

We really do need to take God more seriously. He's the creator and sustainer of the universe, the One who holds our very breath in His hands, yet we sometimes function as if He has no say in the decisions we make. In Old Testament times, even though He spoke His will to people directly and through the prophets, most of His people refused to listen. The Israelites went about doing their own thing, worshipping the gods of the nations they were supposed to have overthrown. Regardless of the warnings God sent, they shunned Him. Then when God removed His hand of blessing and they felt some suffering, they cried for relief from the very God they had so easily ignored.

Over and over, God forgave and restored; yet, over and over, the people went right back to their old, sinful ways. Finally, even God had had enough. Zechariah 7:13 says, "Therefore it happened, that just as He proclaimed and they would not hear, so they called out and I would not listen," says the LORD of hosts (NKJ). God went on to scatter them and let their pleasant land become desolate.

Take a warning. Today God continues to speak to us and let us know His will. Hebrews 1:1-2 tells us, "God, who at various times and in various ways spoke in time past to the fathers by the prophets, has in these last days spoken to us by His Son, whom He has appointed heir of all things, through whom also He made the worlds" (NKJ).

Let's not make the same mistake our Old Testament predecessors made. If we expect God to continue to listen to us, we need to continuously listen to Him. Don't play God cheap.

#239
August 26: Refiner and Tester

My job as a high school English teacher was to get my students ready for college. I knew they would be called upon in their universities and in their careers beyond to be able to communicate clearly both verbally and in written form. If they could not prove their knowledge and express their thoughts, they would not earn their degrees or land their jobs. Their knowledge of the language was crucial to their future success. So to get them where they needed to be, I taught them lessons daily, and quizzed and tested them on their retention of and ability to effectively use the English language. Although my students complained that I was tough on them, time and time again they've returned or contacted me to tell me how appreciative they were of my classes. I was hard on them because I wanted them to be the best—like solid gold.

Our God is a refiner and tester too. He knows what's in store for us and what we need in our character to be ready to handle it. When speaking of the remnant of Israel, God reveals His zeal for bringing His people up to His standard. Zechariah 13:9 reads, "I will bring the one-third through the fire, will refine them as silver is refined, and test them as gold is tested. They will call on My name, and I will answer them. I will say, 'This is My people'; and each one will say, 'The LORD is my God'" (NKJ).

To be refined (tsaraph in Hebrew) is to have the impurities purged away, and to be tested (bachan in Hebrew) is to be investigated and examined by trial. Granted, sometimes we may feel like we're in high school English class being drilled by a hard taskmaster like Mrs. Elliott when God is refining and testing us. However, without such refining and testing, we won't be able to progress, succeed, and overcome in our Christian walk.

Only after my students successfully completed the requirements of all four years of high school English were they able to be called "graduates." Graduation in our Christian lives means we will be able to be called by God's name. We will be His people and He will be our God.

God is the master craftsman. Yield to the process. His refining and testing yields only the best—vessels of pure, solid gold.

#240
August 27: Bait and Switch

According to InvestorWords.com, the scheme of bait and switch is, "An illegal tactic in which a seller advertises a product with the intention of persuading customers to purchase a more expensive product. When a seller uses this tactic, they frequently tell the customer that the original product is sold out or no longer available (even if the product is indeed still available), and push hard for the customer to purchase the costlier product. This tactic can be considered false advertising if the seller is not actually providing the original product."

We get pretty upset; some of us even get downright mad, when bait and switch happens to us. *How dare that retailer play me like that*, we probably think. We're incensed. We may even consider reporting the company to the Better Business Bureau, and we definitely tell all our friends never to shop at that store again.

Why then do we bait and switch on God?

We are the business owners of our bodies, our minds, and our actions. We "advertise" to God that we are offering Him our best, but then we try to get Him to accept, not a costlier offering, but a cheaper one. For example, we could bring Him complete honesty; yet, we hold back what we think we can hide from Him

("...You desire truth in the inward parts," Psalm 51:6). We could bring Him our holiness, but we'd much rather sin during the week and ask for forgiveness on Sunday ("...to obey is better than sacrifice," First Samuel 15:22).

We are guilty of bait and switch with God when we give our best to someone else and substitute it for something cheaper that we'll offer to God. Malachi 1:14 tells us that God feels the same way we do about bait and switch. "'But cursed be the deceiver who has in his flock a male, and makes a vow, but sacrifices to the Lord what is blemished-- for I am a great King,' says the LORD of hosts, 'And My name is to be feared among the nations'" (NKJ).

God is not one who will accept the bait and switch. The best He's given us is what He deserves back. Let's not offer God junk when He's given us jewels.

Part 4

Glimpses of God

In the

Gospels

(60 Devotions)

#241
August 28: God's Job for You

In Matthew chapter 10, Jesus sent His disciples out to do a job. They were to go to a specific audience: "Do not go into the way of the Gentiles, and do not enter a city of the Samaritans. But go rather to the lost sheep of the house of Israel" (vss.5 – 6), with a specific message: "And as you go, preach, saying, 'The kingdom of heaven is at hand" (vs.7). They would have specific results: "Heal the sick, cleanse the lepers, raise the dead, cast out demons" (vs. 8a), and they would be provided for in a specific way: "Provide neither gold nor silver nor copper in your money belts, nor bag for your journey, nor two tunics, nor sandals, nor staffs; for a worker is worthy of his food" (vss. 9-10). In verses 11-15, Jesus even gave them specific instructions as to how to handle themselves whether they were welcomed or not.

Jesus ended His instructions to His disciples with specific precautions: First, "Behold, I send you out as sheep in the midst of wolves. Therefore be wise as serpents and harmless as doves" (vs. 16), and second, "But beware of men, for they will deliver you up to councils and scourge you in their synagogues. You will be brought before governors and kings for My sake, as a testimony to them and to the Gentiles" (vss. 17-18). Finally, Jesus gave them specific peace: "But when they deliver you up, do not worry about how or what you should speak. For it will be given to you in that hour what you should speak; for it is not you who speak, but the Spirit of your Father who speaks in you" (vss. 19-20).

Since "Jesus Christ is the same yesterday, today, and forever" (Hebrews 13:8 NKJ), He is still sending us out as His disciples today. Jesus even prayed to the Father about us when He said, "As You sent Me into the world, I also have sent them into the world" John 17:18 (NKJ).

Sit down some time today at your computer or with a pen and paper. Down one side of the page, number from one to seven, then write this list:
1. specific audience
2. specific message
3. specific results
4. specific provision
5. specific instructions
6. specific precaution
7. specific peace

As you pray, beside each item, write down what God tells you about the specific job He has for you to do. Be steadfast about filling in every line, even if it takes searching the Scriptures and asking advice from your pastor or a mature Christian friend. Then immediately get busy being about your Father's business.

What a joy it is to live and operate in the center of God's will.

#242
August 29: A Father and His Love

As I look back at my relationship with my father, I realize how much he loved me. Although he'd tell me 'no' occcassionally, that never deterred me from returning with a new request the next time I wanted something. Daddy would always figure out a way the make the really important things happen, and he'd do it with style. For example:

- I graduated from recorder band to the elementary school orchestra in the fourth grade and decided I wanted to play the flute. Instead of having me borrow the instrument from the school, Daddy searched through the Sears catalog (everything was available through the Sears catalog in those days) to find one for me. The other kids had instruments in the ugly brown school cases with the school name stenciled on in white. I proudly carried my sleek, navy blue case with the shiny silver metal studs and red velvet lining.
- When I was about 11-years-old I wanted my own grown-up Bible. Back we went to the Sears catalog. I'll never forget the day he and I went to the catalog department of the store to pick up the precious new volume with the white leather cover and pictures from the Sistine Chapel throughout. (Yes, I still have it.)
- When I was 15 and entering high school, Daddy was the senior pastor of a large, influential church in our city. The high school I longed to attend was outside of our district and permits to attend were hard to come by. Daddy to the rescue once again. He attended the first P.T.A. meeting of the year and got himself elected as P.T.A. president. The school had a prominent pastor serving in that position so it

was a good idea to them to issue his daughter a permit to attend the school. Even with his many duties at the church, Daddy served my high school that year for me.

My daddy loved me and so he wanted to see me happy. He wanted to provide things and opportunities for me that would help me grow, succeed, and receive joy. With the perfect mix of love and discipline, my daddy's life as a father drew me to the love of the Lord. Matthew 7:11 says, "If you then, being evil, know how to give good gifts to your children, how much more will your Father who is in heaven give good things to those who ask Him!" (NKJ)

The exciting thing to know is that even when we don't have earthly fathers to correct and to bless us, God our heavenly Father is there to take up that slack. Some fathers abdicate their positions, some are physically incapable, and all will eventually leave us in death. Still, God will always be there in that Father role. The Psalmist put it this way, "How precious also are Your thoughts to me, O God! How great is the sum of them!" Psalm 139:17 (NKJ).

Why not spend the day just basking in the love of God!

#243
August 30: On Knowing Who Jesus Is

In Matthew chapter 8, we read two accounts that show a stark contrast in how Jesus can be approached. Right after witnessing Jesus heal a leper, the centurion's servant, Peter's mother-in-law, and many other demon-possessed and sick people, the disciples boarded a boat with Him and found themselves in a severe, unexpected storm. Even Peter, Andrew, James, and John – the skilled fishermen of the group – couldn't control the boat and they judged that the waves were about to kill them. Meanwhile, Jesus was down in the boat taking a nap. They all woke Him up, frantically pleading, "Lord, save us! We are perishing!" (Matthew 8:25 KJV)

Jesus' response and corresponding actions took them totally by surprise. "'Why are you fearful, O you of little faith?' Then He arose and rebuked the winds and the sea, and there was a great calm. So the men marveled, saying, 'Who can this be, that even the winds and the sea obey Him?' Matthew 8:26-27 (NKJ).

Immediately following this incident, they arrived to the other side of the sea and met two demon-possessed men who, upon seeing Jesus, suddenly cried out, "What have we to do with You, Jesus, You Son of God? Have You come here to torment us before the time?... If You cast us out, permit us to go away into the herd of swine" Matthew 8:29 and 31 (NKJ).

The disciples – those who walked with Jesus regularly and witnessed His power consistently – panicked in their crisis. Instead of approaching Him by virtue of the power they had seen Him display, they questioned what kind of man He was to be able to command even the wind and waves. By contrast, the demons immediately recognized who He was and responded, knowing what He was capable of doing and what He would tolerate.

Colossians 1:16-17 says, "For by him all things were created: things in heaven and on earth, visible and invisible, whether thrones or powers or rulers or authorities; all things were created by him and for him. He is before all things, and in him all things hold together." (NIV)

What will it take for us to recognize Jesus' power? Do we know Him for who He really is? Do we trust Him for *all* He can do? We should be ashamed of ourselves for letting the demons exhibit more faith in Jesus than we do.

#244
August 31: Jesus' Mission Statement

Both in business and in personal life, it is all the rage to formulate a mission statement. A mission statement provides clarity and focus to your life and business. It is a declaration of the needs that must be addressed, how the person or organization will address those needs, and what principles guide the work. It is an unambiguous announcement of purpose.

Jesus proclaimed His mission statement to us in two distinct verses in Luke and Matthew. Luke 19:10 says, "For the Son of Man has come to seek and to save that which was lost" (NKJ). Matthew 9:12-13 says, "...Those who are well have no need of a physician, but those who are sick... For I did not come to call the righteous, but sinners, to repentance" (NKJ).

- What were the needs to be addressed? People were sick and needed a physician; lost and needed to be found.

- How would Jesus address those needs? He would seek and save the lost.
- What principle guided the work? Sinners (the lost and the sick) were in need so He pointed them to the antidote of their lost-ness and illness – repentance.

Jesus knew and verbalized His mission. The success of His mission is the beginning of ours, but before we can launch fully into the mission God has for us, we must humble ourselves before Him. Matthew Henry's Commentary says, "Christ came not with an expectation of succeeding among the righteous, those who conceit themselves so, and therefore will sooner be sick of their Savior, than sick of their sins, but among the convinced humble sinners; to them Christ will come, for to them he will be welcome."

Are we sick enough of our sins to make an appointment with the Great Physician, show up at the "office" found by worshipping at His feet, accept the diagnosis of our own sin-sickness, and take the prescription of repentance for our soul's healing? If so, we can be assured that we are the ones for whom Christ came. His mission will be accomplished in us and can then be continued through us.

#245
September 1: God's Job for You

In Matthew chapter 10, Jesus sent His disciples out to do a job. They were to go to a specific audience: "Do not go into the way of the Gentiles, and do not enter a city of the Samaritans. But go rather to the lost sheep of the house of Israel" (vss.5 – 6), with a specific message: "And as you go, preach, saying, 'The kingdom of heaven is at hand" (vs.7). They would have specific results: "Heal the sick, cleanse the lepers, raise the dead, cast out demons" (vs. 8a), and they would be provided for in a specific way: "Provide neither gold nor silver nor copper in your money belts, nor bag for your journey, nor two tunics, nor sandals, nor staffs; for a worker is worthy of his food" (vss. 9-10). In verses 11-15, Jesus even gave them specific instructions as to how to handle themselves whether they were welcomed or not.

Jesus ended His instructions to His disciples with specific

precautions: First, "Behold, I send you out as sheep in the midst of wolves. Therefore be wise as serpents and harmless as doves" (vs. 16), and second, "But beware of men, for they will deliver you up to councils and scourge you in their synagogues. You will be brought before governors and kings for My sake, as a testimony to them and to the Gentiles" (vss. 17-18). Finally, Jesus gave them specific peace: "But when they deliver you up, do not worry about how or what you should speak. For it will be given to you in that hour what you should speak; for it is not you who speak, but the Spirit of your Father who speaks in you" (vss. 19-20).

Since "Jesus Christ is the same yesterday, today, and forever" (Hebrews 13:8 NKJ), He is still sending us out as His disciples today. Jesus even prayed to the Father about us when He said, "As You sent Me into the world, I also have sent them into the world" John 17:18 (NKJ).

Sit down some time today at your computer or with a pen and paper. Down one side of the page, number from one to seven, then write this list:

1. specific audience
2. specific message
3. specific results
4. specific provision
5. specific instructions
6. specific precaution
7. specific peace

As you pray, beside each item, write down what God tells you about the specific job He has for you to do. Be steadfast about filling in every line, even if it takes searching the Scriptures and asking advice from your pastor or a mature Christian friend. Then immediately get busy being about your Father's business.

What a joy it is to live and operate in the center of God's will.

#246
September 2: God Knows Every Detail

My husband and I like to watch the police dramas on television. We're fans of NCIS (both cities), CSI (all cities), The Mentalist, Blue Bloods, and the like. The crime labs depicted on these shows are so sophisticated that a criminal is doomed from the start if he but breathed the air in the vicinity of the crime. Every minute detail – fingerprints, hair, clothing fibers, shoe impressions, soil samples, paint chips, gunshot residue, voice recognition software, blood stains, the ever-popular DNA evidence, and even bugs at the scene – all conspire to catch the crook.

In comparison, we have a God who is even better at keeping up with every detail of our lives than the most well-equipped crime lab ever could. Matthew 10:30 says, "But the very hairs of your head are all numbered" (NKJ). And Psalm 56:8 says, "You number my wanderings; put my tears into Your bottle; are they not in Your book?" (NKJ)

The neat thing about God knowing every detail is that He's not gathering up evidence to destroy us. The evidence He compiles is for our protection. He knows each hurt, so he gathers our tears to comfort us. He knows each trial we'll face, so He assures us that He's so close that not a hair from our heads will fall without His watchful and defensive eye. Every other possible detail about our life we can imagine, God gathers, knows about, and cares about. Now that's a lab about which to be glad.

#247
September 3: The Rescuer

I suppose there's nothing quite like being rescued. We watch on the news as rescue workers string lifelines across swollen rivers to prevent someone from being swept away by the current. We read of daring helicopter teams as the pilot hovers over a canyon and his partner lowers himself with a basket in order to pluck a stranded and injured hiker from a precipice. We look on as firefighters dash through burning buildings to save those trapped inside. Whether we know the people or not, all of us smile and heave a sigh of relief upon receiving the good news that a rescue has gone well.

In 1912, James Rowe wrote a hymn that captures this idea of rescue as it relates to us and Jesus. The first and the third stanzas of *Love Lifted Me* say:

I was sinking deep in sin, far from the peaceful shore,
Very deeply stained within, sinking to rise no more,
But the Master of the sea heard my despairing cry,

From the waters lifted me, now safe am I.

Souls in danger, look above, Jesus completely saves,
He will lift you by His love, out of the angry waves.
He's the Master of the sea, billows His will obey,
He your Savior wants to be, be saved today.

Yes, Jesus is our Rescuer. Just as He reached out to save Peter as he began to sink in the boisterous waves during that water-walking experience (see Matthew 14:28-31), He'll reach out to save us too. Our life-threatening situation may not be a raging river, a perilous cliff, a burning building, or an angry sea. We may be plunging into a bad relationship, sinking in overwhelming debt, or facing a lay-off. Perhaps we've succumbed to peer pressure or denied our own better judgment and have found ourselves on the wrong side of the law. Or maybe, finally, we're simply realizing that we're living in sin and are in need of a Savior.

We need but cry out, "Lord save me!" as Peter did. The Rescuer's response will be the same, "And immediately Jesus stretched out His hand and caught him, and said to him, 'O you of little faith, why did you doubt?' And when they got into the boat, the wind ceased" Matthew 14:31-32 (NKJ). Don't doubt. Get in the "rescue boat" Jesus is sending your way.

#248
September 4: House of Prayer

When we move into a new space that has before been occupied by another, the first thing we do is clean house. We move all the old stuff out, get rid of the cobwebs, and clean things up so we can start fresh. If it's a job situation wherein we have our own desk and office, we'll replace the name on the door and the desk plate to reflect our own, the one who now holds the position. Only after the housecleaning has been done do we feel comfortable and effectually get on with the work at hand.

Jesus did much the same thing after His triumphal entry into Jerusalem. It's not that He was new to His position, but the people were finally acknowledging Him as "the Son of David" and "He who comes in the name of the Lord" Matthew 21:9 (NKJ). The very next thing He did was clean house.

Then Jesus went into the temple of God and drove out all those who bought and sold in the temple, and overturned the tables of the money changers and the seats of those who sold doves. And He said to them, "It is written, 'My house shall be called a house of prayer,' but you have made it a 'den of thieves.'" Matthew 21:12-13 (NKJ).

Yes, Jesus moved all the old stuff out – the money changers and the seats of those who sold doves – and put His name up on the door – "*My* house…". Once the housecleaning was done, He effectively got on with the work at hand. "Then the blind and the lame came to Him in the temple, and He healed them" Matthew 21: 14 (NKJ).

We are the temple of God today. Our very bodies are where God has chosen to tabernacle with us. Revelation 21:3 says, "And I heard a loud voice from heaven saying, 'Behold, the tabernacle of God is with men, and He will dwell with them, and they shall be His people. God Himself will be with them and be their God'" (NKJ). And First Corinthians 6:19 reads, "Or do you not know that your body is the temple of the Holy Spirit who is in you, whom you have from God, and you are not your own?" (NKJ).

God has moved in; allow Him to clean house. Nothing has changed; His message is the same in the temple that is your body: "My house shall be called a house of prayer." Communion with you is a joy to the Lord, but the "money changers" must go.

In the devotional book entitled *Magnificent Prayer* by Nick Harrison, the February 1st entry states, "There's a special place in the heart of God that only *you* can fill. God is more than willing to be with you today. More than willing to hear your voice." Only by remaining in communion with Him will we see our work for Him effectively achieved.

#249
September 5: Forsaken for Us

Matthew 27:45-46 presents the most pivotal point of history for the Christian. "Now from the sixth hour until the ninth hour there was darkness over all the land. And about the ninth hour Jesus cried out with a loud voice, saying, 'Eli , Eli , lama sabachthani ?' that is, *"My God, My God, why have You forsaken*

Me?" (NKJ) In that very instant, God the Father's point of view shifted. You see, the wrath of our holy God had held us squarely in its crosshairs. There was no permanent escape from sin. Sure, the children of Israel could offer their sacrifices to receive temporary forgiveness, "but in those *sacrifices there is* a reminder of sins every year. For *it is* not possible that the blood of bulls and goats could take away sins" Hebrews 10:3-4 (NKJ).

So what does this forgiveness stuff have to do with God forsaking Jesus on the cross? It means everything. The moment in which God turned His eyes from His Son was the moment when all our sin crashed in upon Jesus. The debt we owed because of our inherited sin nature was wiped clean and stamped "paid in full" when our sin was transferred onto Him and nailed to that cross. That debt we never could have paid would have resulted in complete, utter, and eternal separation from God, the true death from which there is no resurrection. When God the Son shouted out His despair about being forsaken by God the Father, He was heralding of our freedom. Jesus' death meant our life. In essence, God the Father looked from Jesus to us, and for the first time, God could see us without sin.

Jesus already knew the answer to the question He asked that dark afternoon. Why had God forsaken Him? Jesus Himself had answered years before, "I am the good shepherd; and I know My *sheep,* and am known by My own. As the Father knows Me, even so I know the Father; and I lay down My life for the sheep." John 10:14-15 (NKJ). And Second Corinthians 5:21 gives us the great news too. "For He (God) made Him (Jesus) who knew no sin *to be* sin for us, that we might become the righteousness of God in Him" (NKJ).

The whole reason for the incarnation was summed up in that anguished cry from the cross. Jesus was forsaken so we would never have to be. Hallelujah, what a Savior!

#250
September 6: On God and Cemeteries

For me, the hardest part of any funeral is walking away at the end. Seeing the casket lowered into the ground or slid into the crypt, and watching the workers dump dirt on it or seal it behind the concrete slab is all so very final. My mind says, "Well, that's it," and the tone of my thought comes across as cold and, well, final. Driving away makes me feel like I'm cruelly leaving my loved one all alone.

So much is left at cemeteries. Every grave into which someone's remains were placed represents the end of memories to be built, words to be said, and experiences to enjoy. Every grave, that is, except one.

Jesus was laid in a borrowed tomb, not just because He was never encumbered by property ownership, but because He wasn't going to need it for long. I suspect that people left Golgotha, and Nicodemus and Joseph of Arimathaea walked away from that cemetery after preparing His body, feeling much the same as I feel when a funeral ends. But for them, that feeling only lasted until Sunday morning. Visitors to that tomb from then until today have been reminded, "He isn't here! He is risen from the dead, just as he said would happen. Come, see where his body was lying" Matthew 28:6 (NLT).

From now on, I'll be taking something new away from our Easter celebration. From now on, whenever I leave the cemetery after the funeral of a Christian, I'm going to remember that that person is not there. In a very real sense, the true essence of my friend—his or her born-again spirit—is very much alive.

Any visit back there to place memorial flowers should be like the celebration we have on every Easter Sunday morning. As we joyously proclaim of Christ, "He is risen. He is risen indeed," let us just as joyously proclaim of our loved one, "He's in glory. I will see him again," or "She's with Jesus. She's still living indeed."

Have a happy Resurrection Day every day! He is risen. He is risen indeed!

#251
September 7: The Holy Spirit Difference

The Holy Spirit is mentioned three times in the first chapter of Mark's gospel. First, John the Baptist tells the people, "I indeed baptized you with water, but He will baptize you with *the Holy Spirit*" Mark 1:8 (NKJ). Second, when John baptized Jesus we're told, "And immediately, coming up from the water, He saw the heavens parting and *the Spirit* descending upon Him like a dove"

Mark 1:10. Finally, verse 12 says, "And immediately *the Spirit* drove Him into the wilderness" where Jesus was tempted for 40 days by the devil and ministered to by the angels.

This infusion of the Holy Spirit's participation made the difference in Jesus' ministry. "John came baptizing in the wilderness and preaching a baptism of repentance for the remission of sins... but He will baptize you with the Holy Spirit" Mark 1:4 and 8. After his baptism, Jesus began "preaching the gospel of the kingdom of God, and saying, 'The time is fulfilled, and the kingdom of God is at hand. Repent, and believe in the gospel'" Mark 1:14-15. The reaction to John's teaching was that people got baptized. The reaction to Jesus' teaching was markedly different. Mark 1:22 tells us, "And they were astonished at His teaching, for He taught them as one having authority, and not as the scribes."

Jesus' ministry points us to the fact that living a life pleasing to God requires reliance upon the Holy Spirit. Acts 10:38 tells us that "...God anointed Jesus of Nazareth with the Holy Spirit and with power, who went about doing good and healing all who were oppressed by the devil, for God was with Him." When Jesus was about to leave for Heaven after His resurrection, He told His disciples "not to depart from Jerusalem, but to wait for the Promise of the Father, 'which,' He said, 'you have heard from Me; for John truly baptized with water, but you shall be baptized with the Holy Spirit not many days from now'" Acts 1:4-5. The disciples obeyed and in Acts 2:4, Jesus' words were fulfilled to them: "And they were all filled with the Holy Spirit and began to speak with other tongues, as the Spirit gave them utterance." The Promise of the Father was the presence of the Holy Spirit.

So what's the point? Simply this: the Holy Spirit's presence, participation, and power make a difference and that difference in available to us as believers. Today, acknowledge His presence, yield to His participation, and be amazed by His power in your life.

#252
September 8: From Him to You

Evangelist Kim Heidelberg delivered a masterful, anointed message at a women's retreat I attended. She preached about the woman with the issue of blood, a story I've heard many, many times. In short, this woman had suffered with her illness for 12 long years. She'd seen every possible doctor, had spent all her money, and got worse instead of better. When she heard Jesus was coming to town, she ventured one more try. Mark 5:27-34 takes up the story:

> When she had heard of Jesus, came in the press behind, and touched his garment. For she said, If I may touch but his clothes, I shall be whole. And straightway the fountain of her blood was dried up; and she felt in her body that she was healed of that plague.
> And Jesus, immediately knowing in himself that virtue had gone out of him, turned him about in the press, and said, Who touched my clothes?
> And his disciples said unto him, Thou seest the multitude thronging thee, and sayest thou, Who touched me?
> And he looked round about to see her that had done this thing.
> But the woman fearing and trembling, knowing what was done in her, came and fell down before him, and told him all the truth. And he said unto her, Daughter, thy faith hath made thee whole; go in peace, and be whole of thy plague. (KJV)

Evangelist Heidelberg asked, "How did Jesus pick the woman who touched Him out of the crowd?" An obvious answer we may immediately think would be, "Well, He knew because He's God." That's true; however, the preacher suggested an even more profound thought.

Notice that "virtue had gone out of him" when the woman touched the hem of His robe. In other words, something from inside of Him passed into her. When Jesus looked around in the crowd, He recognized the woman who touched Him because He saw something of Himself in her.

What comfort there is in realizing that God knows us! Second Timothy 2:19 confirms, "Nevertheless the solid foundation of God stands, having this seal: "The Lord knows those who are His," and, "Let everyone who names the name of Christ depart from iniquity" (NKJ). Why is the second part of this verse added? Because when Christ has poured Himself into us ("Christ in you, the hope of glory" Colossians 1:27, KJV), it is our responsibility to keep that image clean and clear.

Let's take joy today in knowing that Christ is in us. He can see Himself in us and so can others.

#253
September 9: Hear and Understand

Mark 7:14 says, "When He had called all the multitude to Himself, He said to them, "Hear Me, everyone, and understand" (NKJ). Over and over again throughout the Gospels, Jesus teaches people who have gathered together to hear Him. Sometimes He taught using parables – earthly stories with Heavenly meanings. But this time, Jesus is teaching the people plainly. Either way Jesus taught, plainly or by using parables, the goal was the same: He meant for the people to hear and understand.

Nothing has changed. God still intends for us to hear and understand. By implication, that which we understand, we will heed. For example:

- When I hear and understand that I am "the light of the world," then I will let my light shine so that others can see my good works and glorify my Father which is in Heaven. (See Matthew 5:14-16.)
- When I hear and understand that "the wages of sin is death," I will do my very best to steer clear of sin. (See Romans 6:23)
- When I hear and understand that I should love my wife as Christ loves the Church, or that I should submit to my husband as unto the Lord and reverence him, I will follow those admonitions in my marriage. (See Ephesians 5:21-33.)

Either by precept or principle, God's word is clear on every issue imaginable. He has made it so because He wants us to hear and understand. Let's be encouraged to read the word, hear it, understand it, be honest with what the message intends for us to do, and get busy doing it.

#254
September 10: Compassion on the Multitude

I'm glad Jesus has enough love to go around. Consider His reaction to the large crowd of people who had followed Him for three days in Mark, chapter eight. They undoubtedly couldn't get enough of His wonderful teaching. I'm sure they were also enamored by Him and astonished at His ability to heal. On the third day, Jesus realized the people hadn't been eating. The Scripture tells the story:

> In those days, the multitude being very great and having nothing to eat, Jesus called His disciples to Him and said to them, "I have compassion on the multitude, because they have now been with Me three days and have nothing to eat. And if I send them away hungry to their own houses, they will faint on the way; for some of them have come from afar."
> Then His disciples answered Him, "How can one satisfy these people with bread here in the wilderness?"
> He asked them, "How many loaves do you have?" And they said, "Seven."
> So He commanded the multitude to sit down on the ground. And He took the seven loaves and gave thanks, broke them and gave them to His disciples to set before them; and they set them before the multitude. They also had a few small fish; and having blessed them, He said to set them also before them. So they ate and were filled, and they took up seven large baskets of leftover fragments.
> Mark 8:1-8 (NKJ)

Jesus fed the whole crowd—all four thousand—with seven loaves and a few small fish! We can learn a few things about God's amazing compassion from this story:

1. God knows our needs even before we have a chance to grumble about them. Notice that the multitude hadn't complained of being hungry.
2. God can stretch what we already have to meet our need. No one went shopping; Jesus simply filled them sufficiently with what they already had.

3. God can use who is already there to help Him help us, even if the helpers don't realize what they're doing. The disciples were clueless as to how Jesus would feed all those folks, but He used them to accomplish the task anyway.
4. If we do what God tells us to do, we'll end up being filled with blessing.
   a. The people sat down and were served.
   b. The disciples served and gathered more than enough for themselves at the end.
5. We don't have to understand how God will accomplish a thing; we must simply have enough faith in His word that He *can* get it done.

The disciples were a part of the multitude on which Jesus had compassion that day. Both the servers and the served were partakers of Jesus' compassion. Know that whether we need to be served or if we're in the position to serve, God's compassion reaches equally to both. Like I said at first, I'm so glad Jesus has enough love to go around; aren't you?

#255
September 11: Do You Know Who You're Dealing With?

Recently, I made two significant location changes. I moved my membership to a new church and I got a new job. In both cases, although everyone I've dealt with is great, as I get to know more and more people, I'm discovering that I'd better be careful in both locations about what I may say about folks. Why? Because there are family ties everywhere. For example, at church, the woman who taught my New Members' class is the mother of the Sunday School superintendent, who is the wife of the deacon, whose sister is an usher, and the usher's daughter was in my Vacation Bible School class. At work, my department head's dad teaches science and her mom runs one of the offices, while the lunch lady and the principal's assistant both have kids in my classes, and the nice math teacher is the father-in-law of the Vice Principal. All these familial connections make me want to follow every introduction with, "exactly who are you and to whom are you related?"

Jesus had His disciples identify exactly who He was and then He made it clear to whom He was related. The conversation recorded in Mark chapter 8 goes like this:

> Now Jesus… asked His disciples… "Who do men say that I am?"
>
> So they answered, "John the Baptist; but some say, Elijah; and others, one of the prophets."
>
> "But who do you say that I am?"
>
> Peter answered and said to Him, "You are the Christ."
>
> Then He charged them that they should tell no one about Him. And He began to teach them that the Son of Man must suffer many things, and be rejected by the elders and chief priests and scribes, and be killed, and after three days rise again.
>
> When He had called the people to Himself, with His disciples also, He said to them, "Whoever desires to come after Me, let him deny himself, and take up his cross, and follow Me… For whoever is ashamed of Me and My words in this adulterous and sinful generation, of him the Son of Man also will be ashamed when He comes in the glory of His Father with the holy angels" Mark 8:27-31, 34-38 (NKJ).

You see, once the disciples knew His name and His title—Jesus, the Christ—He further explained to them to whom He was connected. Jesus was the One so closely connected with God the Father that He would be coming "in the glory of His Father with the holy angels." By this phrase (and many others on different occasions), Jesus declared Himself to be equal with God.

Jesus needed the disciples to know exactly who they were dealing with. He wasn't just some good teacher; He wasn't a reincarnation of John the Baptist; He wasn't just another prophet in the long line of prophets. Jesus was the Son of Man—the One who had come to show us the Father. Let's not be flippant when talking to or about Jesus. Let's be careful to remember who we're dealing with.

#256
September 12: The GPS

My friend Sandi was scheduled to pick me up from the Baltimore/Washington airport the other day when I arrived in town to conduct a seminar. As we were going over our last minute details on the phone the day before I left home, for some reason, I asked her if I needed to bring my portable GPS (global positioning system) to help us get from the airport to the conference center. I don't know why I asked. Sandi lives in the area and has driven to the place before. Nevertheless, we casually agreed that it couldn't hurt to have it. "Perhaps," Sandi mused, "it may show us a shorter route." With that idea in mind, I threw the little case in my suitcase as I packed.

Upon arrival at BWI, when I turned my cell phone on, I had a message from Sandi. Her car had broken down. She was at a gas station 30 minutes from the airport with no way to get to me. I was able to rent a car, click on the little GPS, type in the address where she was, and drive directly to her and then directly to the conference center with ease, just as if I had grown up in Maryland totally familiar with every twist and turn of the roadways. All I had to do was follow the directions calmly being given to me by the lady's voice from the satellite. Even when road construction caused us to pass one off ramp, the satellite voice didn't get excited or worried so neither did we. We just followed her recalculated route and made it to our destination just the same.

If only we'd follow the leading of the Lord that readily.

I believe I'm catching on. The "random" idea to ask about the GPS in the first place was indeed a prompting of the Holy Ghost. After all, He already knew I'd need it because He already knew Sandi's car would break down. His "voice" is in those random ideas. He leads us as we walk through life. The nudge to "turn here," or "book that particular flight," or "mention this need," or "pack that item:" all of these are God's voice seeking to place us exactly where we need to be, or to provide for us exactly what we are going to need.

How do we get to the place of keen hearing? Start by following His simple spiritual GPS instructions found in Mark 8:34, "Whoever desires to come after Me, let him deny himself, and take up his cross, and follow me" (NKJ). As explained in Matthew Henry's Commentary, these three simple turns will result in getting us where we want to be:

1. Deny self: "live a life of self-denial, mortification, and contempt of the world... renounce all confidence in [yourself] and [your] own righteousness and strength..."
2. Take up your cross: "conforming [yourself] to the pattern of a crucified Jesus, and accommodating [yourself] to the will of God in all the afflictions [you] lie under"
3. Follow Jesus: "attend on him, converse with him, receive instruction and reproof from him, as those did that *followed* him, and resolve [to] never forsake him."

Let's trust the GPS – God's Positioning Statements. Following this, we'll never go wrong.

#257
September 13: The Transformer

There are toys kids play with that look like regular little cars, but when manipulated in a certain way, they turn into muscular, armored, fighting men. The toys are called *Transformers*. These playthings caught the eye of the movie industry and now major motion pictures have been produced featuring these creatures that can alter their form to fight when necessary.

Thinking of these toys reminded me that when God's power is present, transformation takes place. It happened to Jesus in Mark, chapter nine. He said to His disciples, "'Assuredly, I say to you that there are some standing here who will not taste death till they see the kingdom of God present with power.' Now after six days Jesus took Peter, James, and John, and led them up on a high mountain apart by themselves; and He was transfigured before them" Mark 9:1-2 (NKJ). Those three disciples witnessed God's power to transform Jesus into His glorified body.

That word "transfigured" is the Greek word "metamorphoo" which means "to transform or change." It's the same word used in Romans 12:2 when Paul admonishes us, "And do not be conformed to this world, but be **transformed** by the renewing of your mind, that you may prove what is that good and acceptable and perfect will of God" (NKJ, emphasis added). God, the ultimate Transformer, shows us how to become transformers ourselves. As we renew our minds by focusing on God's good, acceptable, and perfect will, and stop conforming to the standards of the world, we'll be transformers too. We may look like harmless, everyday people, but we're actually authoritative saints of the most high God, able to stand against the onslaughts of this sinful world emboldened by the power of Heaven.

#258
September 14: Avoid the Hindrances: Receive from God

The story in the Bible of blind Bartimaeus gives us five hindrances to avoid when we need to receive that which God has for us. Here's the story:

> As He went out of Jericho with His disciples and a great multitude, blind Bartimaeus, the son of Timaeus, sat by the road begging. And when he heard that it was Jesus of Nazareth, he began to cry out and say, "Jesus, Son of David, have mercy on me!" Then many warned him to be quiet; but he cried out all the more, "Son of David, have mercy on me!" So Jesus stood still and commanded him to be called. Then they called the blind man, saying to him, "Be of good cheer. Rise, He is calling you." And throwing aside his garment, he rose and came to Jesus. So Jesus answered and said to him, "What do you want Me to do for you?" The blind man said to Him, "Rabboni, that I may receive my sight." Then Jesus said to him, "Go your way; your faith has made you well." And immediately he received his sight and followed Jesus on the road. Mark 10:46-52 (NKJ)

Now don't allow any of these hindrances to keep you from receiving God's best for your lives:

1. **Don't let your crippling issues stop you.** Blind Bartimaeus (we'll call him B.B. for short) couldn't see, but he could hear. He used what he did have to compensate for what he didn't have, so when he *heard* that Jesus was coming, he sprang into action. Identify that which is crippling you and then work around it to make the necessary connections with Jesus.

2. **Don't let the crowd stop you.** As B.B. cried out his need, the crowd tried to stop him. There will usually be people around who will have another agenda for you when you are trying to reach the Master. Like B.B., cry to God all the louder.

3. **Don't let the call stop you.** Jesus actually stopped and sent out a call for B.B. Sometimes we have no problem hearing and crying out, but we shrink back when we are actually called. Perhaps deep down we weren't really expecting God to answer. Or maybe even more likely, we weren't expecting the specificity and pointed, individual nature of the call. God is extremely personal, and when you sincerely cry out for Him, He's very likely to respond with a specially-designed call, tailor-made just for you. Be ready.

4. **Don't let the clothes stop you.** B.B. had some old stuff he had to throw away first, namely, his clothes. Those clothes were the garments of a beggar. He was readily recognizable and identified by them. Approach Jesus expectantly; already decidedly ready to shed all you used to be in favor of whatever He would decide to do.

5. **Don't let the question stop you.** B.B. was asked a very direct question. "What do you want Me to do for you?" Know and own the problem you want to get rid of. Until you realize you have a need, you won't even know what to ask for. For example, if you're broke, you may not need money. Your problem is financial irresponsibility and what you need is restraint and the ability to manage what you already have. Ask for that. If you're lonely, you don't need a mate. Your problem is your inflexible personality and what you need is a character adjustment and humility which will make you attractive to the opposite sex. Ask for that.

Blind Bartimaeus knew exactly what he needed and when it came time for him to express that need to the questioning Savior, he clearly stated, "Rabboni, that I may receive my sight." Result? Immediately he could see and he followed Jesus. B.B. didn't let anything stop him. Don't let any of the hindrances stop you either. Be honest about your real issues and then hear Jesus asking you, "What do you want Me to do for you?"

#259
September 15: Words We Can Know For Sure

A popular talk show host began using the phrase, "One thing I know for sure." Whenever this statement was uttered, it would be followed by the host's declarations of the wisdom she had learned over the years of her life. Millions of viewers hung on her comments, taking them into their lives as words to live by.

Well, as those viewers soak in their favorite TV personality's thoughts, we can be glad that our God has given us a book full of something we can know for sure. Mark 13:31 says, "Heaven and earth will pass away, but My words will by no means pass away." (NKJ)

Yes, everything in God's word we can know for sure. Among other things are these amazing gems of truth:

- For God so loved the world that He gave His only begotten Son, that whoever believes in Him should not perish but have everlasting life. John 3:16 (NKJ)
- But God demonstrates His own love toward us, in that while we were still sinners, Christ died for us. Romans 5:8 (NKJ)
- Salvation is found in no one else, for there is no other name under heaven given to men by which we must be saved. Acts 4:12 (NIV)
- That if you confess with your mouth, "Jesus is Lord," and believe in your heart that God raised him from the dead, you will be saved. For it is with your heart that you believe and are justified, and it is with your mouth that you confess and are saved. Romans 10:9-10 (NIV)
- Look, he is coming with the clouds, and every eye will see him, even those who pierced him; and all the peoples of the earth will mourn because of him. So shall it be! Amen. Revelation 1:7 (NIV)

You've just read a very condensed version of the Gospel (the Good News) of God in Jesus Christ. These are indeed words you can know and count on for sure. If you've never done so, confess Christ as Lord of your life right now! If you have, forward this devotion to someone who perhaps has never read this message so succinctly. We can keep this devotion circulating around the world! Feel free to comment on the blog when you confess Christ as Lord, rededicate your life to Him, or use this to share God's good news with your friends!

#260
September 16: I Told You So

Years ago there was a TV drama entitled *Lost in Space*. The Robinson family had ventured from Earth and couldn't get back. Week after week they faced harrowing obstacles portrayed by primitive special effects. Whenever trouble was about to strike, the robot would flail its arms and shout, "Danger, Will Robinson! Danger, danger!"

We could all use a *Lost in Space* robot from time to time. Just recently, an elderly TV preacher predicted (again) the Rapture and the end of the world on a specific date. Lots of people got all excited, even to the point of quitting their jobs and selling their homes. In response to the man's announcement, others thumped their Bibles pointing out the verse where Jesus says not even He knows the hour of this occurrence. (See Matthew 24:36.)

Predictions are going to be made (that guy mentioned above has said his calculations were off and has already set another date), and imposters are going to attempt to trick us into believing they are the returned Christ. But read Jesus' words, "Then if anyone says to you, 'Look, here *is* the Christ!' or, 'Look, He *is* there!' do not believe it. For false christs and false prophets will rise and show signs and wonders to deceive, if possible, even the elect. But take heed; see, I have told you all things beforehand" Mark 13:21 – 23 (NKJ).

Basically, when we hear these predictions and see these imposters, avoid the danger of falling for their lies. Chill out and remember that Jesus has said, "I told you so;" that is, don't believe it when you hear these things. Relax.

Blink your eyes. That's how quickly we'll be translated into Glory. We can't even live like He's coming back tomorrow. We must conduct ourselves in the present realizing He could return at any moment. Live joyously knowing that any twinkling of an eye could be the twinkling of His return. When we're eye-to-eye with the Master, will He be smiling and saying, "Well done," because He caught us in the center of His will? Or will He be shaking His head saying, "I told you so," as we embarrassingly face Him coming from a compromising situation?

#261
September 17: God when Disaster is Coming

We got the news the previous week that my brother Nick's loving wife, Lelar, had been moved into hospice care. The past year filled with chemotherapy treatments had been fraught with highs and lows, hopes raised then dashed over and over again. Now, barring a miracle, we were forced to face the ultimate earthly reality, her death that would probably be soon.

Mentally, I prepared. *Lelar has suffered and will be released from the ravishes of the horrors that cancer has brought to her body*, I reasoned. I further comforted myself with the thought, *Lelar knows Jesus as her Savior, so cessation of life here is the beginning of her eternal life in Glory with Him. She'll be much better off than any of us.* I kept my cell phone by my side so that I could get the call I knew was coming.

Sure enough, several days later, the dreaded call came. Early on the morning of March 16th, Lelar left our arms and landed safely in God's. Then I discovered something: no amount of mental preparation had gotten me ready for that moment. My human mind was unable to control the raw emotions of my soul which acutely felt the wrenching separation that the death of a loved one brings. I didn't love Lelar intellectually; I loved her spiritually, from my insides, from my heart. And mental gymnastics cannot heal a broken heart. Only the deep-seated, soul dedication to a Strength beyond ourselves can get us through times like these.

Even Jesus struggled in this same way. We're told that in the garden of Gethsemane, just before He knew the arresting posse would come and start the process that would lead to the Cross, He felt this same emotion. Mark 14:35-36 reads, "He went a little farther, and fell on the ground, and prayed that if it were possible, the hour might pass from Him. And He said, 'Abba, Father, all things are possible for You. Take this cup away from Me; nevertheless, not what I will, but what You will'" (NKJ). Jesus was so agonized at this moment that in Luke's record, we read, "And being in agony, He prayed more earnestly. Then His sweat became like great drops of blood falling down to the ground" Luke 22:44 (NKJ).

Looking forward to disaster is always painful. If even Jesus had His moment losing it, we're entitled to mourn and cry as well.

Yet, if we cry as He did, we should also recover as He did. The strength He received to go through the disaster came from that deep-seated, soul dedication that yields to the Father's will. As we bury our heads into His shoulders, our heart's cry must be "nevertheless, not what I will, but what You will." God alone will then give us the fortitude, comfort, and support we need to face the coming storm.

#262
September 18: In Contact with Christ

It is impossible to come in contact with Christ and remain the same. Jesus started making a profound impact on people's lives from the moment of the incarnation.

- Mary's life was completely re-routed by Gabriel's announcement, "And behold, you will conceive in your womb and bring forth a Son, and shall call His name Jesus... The Holy Spirit will come upon you, and the power of the Highest will overshadow you; therefore, also, that Holy One who is to be born will be called the Son of God" Luke 1:28-35 (NKJ).
- Joseph started to receive revelations in the form of divine dreams that gave him direction.
  - "...Joseph, son of David, do not be afraid to take to you Mary your wife, for that which is conceived in her is of the Holy Spirit" Matthew 1:20 (NKJ).
  - "...Arise, take the young Child and His mother, flee to Egypt..." Matthew 2:13 (NKJ).
  - "Arise, take the young Child and His mother, and go to the land of Israel..." Matthew 2:19-20 (NKJ).
  - "But when he heard that Archelaus was reigning over Judea instead of his father Herod, he was afraid to go there. And being warned by God in a dream, he turned aside into the region of Galilee. And he came and dwelt in a city called Nazareth, that it might be fulfilled which was spoken by the prophets, "He shall be called a Nazarene" Matthew 2:22-23 (NKJ).
- In the sixth month of her pregnancy, Elizabeth and her unborn baby felt Jesus enter the room when He was barely

still developing His human body inside of Mary's womb. The story reads, "Now Mary arose in those days and went into the hill country with haste, to a city of Judah, and entered the house of Zacharias and greeted Elizabeth. And it happened, when Elizabeth heard the greeting of Mary, that the babe leaped in her womb; and Elizabeth was filled with the Holy Spirit. Then she spoke out with a loud voice and said, "Blessed are you among women, and blessed is the fruit of your womb! But why is this granted to me, that the mother of my Lord should come to me?" Luke 1:39-43 (NKJ).

- Simeon, a just and devout man full of the Holy Spirit, was waiting to see the Lord's Christ and had been told by God he wouldn't die until he did. He recognized the 8-day-old infant Savior when His parents took Him to the temple to be circumcised. Simeon took Jesus in his arms and proclaimed, "Lord, now You are letting Your servant depart in peace, according to Your word; For my eyes have seen Your salvation" Luke 2:29-30 (NKJ).

- On the heels of Simeon's recognition of Jesus came Anna's acknowledgement. Anna was an elderly prophetess "who did not depart from the temple, but served God with fastings and prayers night and day. And coming in that instant she gave thanks to the Lord, and spoke of Him to all those who looked for redemption in Jerusalem" Luke 2:36-38 (NKJ).

Mary saw the power of God to do miraculous things in her life. Joseph saw the direction of God to lead him in even the minutest of details. Elizabeth saw how the Holy Spirit can grant favor. Elizabeth's yet unborn baby, John, saw the need to leap and praise God just because of His presence. Simeon saw God's salvation. (Notice that salvation is not a thing but a Person.) And Anna saw that a lifetime of dedicated service is rewarded spectacularly because she was able to set her eyes upon the redemption of Jerusalem.

What do you see in Jesus when you come in contact with Him? How is He impacting your life? May His presence in your life make a marked difference today and always.

#263
September 19: Feel Him Move

Most women who have birthed a baby have had the same experience, excitement upon first feeling the baby move. I remember exactly where I was when I first felt my first baby move. I was working a temp job at a camera company in Hollywood, CA. While sitting at that receptionist's desk, I felt a little flutter ripple across my growing tummy. From that time forward, Matthew's movements became more and more distinct. The larger he grew and the closer I got to my delivery date, the more I felt him. He finally became so big that I could no longer carry him inside of me. Because of his movements, I knew without a shadow of a doubt when the time came for him to be born, and everything within me participated in making that happen.

I'm sure it was no different for Mary, the mother of Jesus. I had a much smoother ride during labor to the hospital than she had riding a donkey to the place where she would deliver her child; however, her physical discomfort was the same. Her birthing story happened when "Caesar Augustus issued a decree that a census should be taken of the entire Roman world" Luke 2:1 (NIV). Probably to her chagrin, she learned that at nine months pregnant, she and Joseph would have to travel all the way from Nazareth in Galilee to Bethlehem in Judea and "while they were there, the time came for the baby to be born" Luke 2:6 (NIV).

Yes, because He was big enough within her, and because of His movements, Mary knew without a shadow of a doubt that the time had come for Jesus to be born. No matter where she was, His movements within her moved her to let Him out.

How big is Jesus in you? Is His presence in your life growing so much that you can feel Him move? The larger He grows in you, the more you will feel Him move. The mystery of this birthing analogy is that He will never leave us, He'll continue to grow within us, but we're also obliged to let Him out so others can see Him.

#264
September 20: The Lamb

To whom did God first announce the birth of His Son? He announced Christ's birth to shepherds. It's a beautiful story, worth reading over and over again:

- Now there were in the same country shepherds living out in the fields, keeping watch over their flock by night. And behold, an angel of the Lord stood before them, and the glory of the Lord shone around them, and they were greatly afraid. Then the angel said to them, "Do not be afraid, for behold, I bring you good tidings of great joy which will be to all people. For there is born to you this day in the city of David a Savior, who is Christ the Lord. And this will be the sign to you: You will find a Babe wrapped in swaddling cloths, lying in a manger."
- And suddenly there was with the angel a multitude of the heavenly host praising God and saying: "Glory to God in the highest, and on earth peace, goodwill toward men!"
- So it was, when the angels had gone away from them into heaven, that the shepherds said to one another, "Let us now go to Bethlehem and see this thing that has come to pass, which the Lord has made known to us." And they came with haste and found Mary and Joseph, and the Babe lying in a manger.
- Now when they had seen Him, they made widely known the saying which was told them concerning this Child. And all those who heard it marveled at those things which were told them by the shepherds. Luke 2:8-18 (NKJ)

Why would God announce the birth of His Son to shepherds? It's obvious. That special announcement was made to the people who would recognize a lamb when they saw one. It is rumored that these weren't just any shepherds; these were possibly the shepherds who guarded the temple sheep—the sheep that were used for sacrifice for the sins of the people. When the angel told them there was born "a Savior, who is Christ the Lord," they immediately put it together through the sieve of their understanding as shepherds. Savior means deliverer, Christ means the anointed Messiah, and Lord means master and supreme in authority. Shepherds understood that sacrificial lambs stood for being delivered from sin. They represented that for which they awaited, the Messiah who would ultimately stand in supreme authority.

The word "lamb" may not be used in this message to the shepherds, but a lamb by any other name is still a lamb. John the

Baptist introduced Jesus 30 years later as the Lamb of God (see John 1:29 and 36), and the apostle John saw Jesus as the Lamb who had been slain but who now stood "worthy to take the scroll and to open its seals" Revelation 5:9 (NKJ). For indeed, John heard "...the voice of many angels around the throne, the living creatures, and the elders; and the number of them was ten thousand times ten thousand, and thousands of thousands, saying with a loud voice: 'Worthy is the Lamb who was slain to receive power and riches and wisdom, and strength and honor and glory and blessing!'" Revelation 5:11-12 (NKJ).

This is the Lamb those shepherds saw that night!

#265
September 21: When God's Home

Jesus didn't travel far and wide in His lifetime while on Earth. For the short 3½ years of His public ministry, He walked from city to city in the tiny area of the Middle East, never really too far from His own hometown. In Luke 4:16, we read of one of the times (after His name and exploits were becoming known, see verse 14) when He passed through home. "So He came to Nazareth, where He had been brought up. And as His custom was, He went into the synagogue on the Sabbath day, and stood up to read" (NKJ).

Lots of times when people get famous, they don't act the same as they used to act. They return to their hometowns with an entourage and demands for special treatment. Not Jesus. He returned to where He grew up and followed His same custom of going to the synagogue and reading the Scriptures.

On this side of Calvary, we're told that we are the synagogue, we are the church, we are the place in which Christ dwells. Second Corinthians 6:16 says, "For we are the temple of the living God. As God has said: 'I will live with them and walk among them, and I will be their God, and they will be my people'" (NIV). And Ephesians 2:22 explains, "And in him you too are being built together to become a dwelling in which God lives by his Spirit" (NIV).

Is Jesus at home in you? It is His custom to stand up in you and expound upon the Scriptures. Do you give Him the floor? As you go about your daily life, are you listening for His voice on your every move? You see, the Bible contains the word of God, and the Word of God is Jesus; therefore, everything in the Bible is alive, as real as Jesus Himself. When the Word of God is in you, the very presence of Jesus is there. He is literally present in the synagogue of your heart. Let him stand up to read.

#266
September 22: The Touch

Cell phones, computerized copy machines, microwave ovens, global positioning system devices, even automatic teller machines – many gadgets are made with touch screens. No longer is there a need to push buttons; now just touch the magic screen in the right places, and the device does your bidding.

Well, I'm here to tell you that touch technology is nothing new. Jesus introduced touch technology long before the computer was ever even invented. In Luke chapter 8, we read of a woman who had been ill with a bleeding disorder for 12 years. She slipped into the crowd one day as Jesus was passing by and "touched the border of His garment, and immediately her flow of blood stopped" Luke 8:44 (NKJ). Later in that same chapter, Jesus arrived at Jairus' house where the man's little 12-year-old daughter had just died. Jesus touched the little girl by taking her by the hand. He then "called, saying, 'Little girl, arise.' Then her spirit returned, and she arose immediately" Luke 8:54 (NKJ).

Notice something about the touch technology of Jesus: when the woman touched Him and when He touched the little girl, the results were immediate. The woman's blood flow ceased right then. The little girl came back to life instantly. Not only were the results immediate, they were also astonishing. A twelve-year disease that had stumped the medical community was simply gone; a dead twelve-year-old girl lived again.

You might think a touch screen is cool, but I dare you to experience Jesus' touch. The Greek word for touch (haptomai) means 'to attach oneself to.' Reach out and touch Jesus or be still and let Him touch you. It doesn't matter which way the touch flows; the difference will be immediate and astonishing.

#267
September 23: Jesus Rejoiced

We don't generally think of Jesus as rejoicing. We picture Him teaching the people, healing the sick, chastising the religious leaders, comforting the downtrodden, and explaining things to His disciples. Our mind's eye also sees Him trudging down the Via Delarosa, hanging on the Cross, suffering the agony of Calvary, and dying for our sins. We then remember His resurrection, ascension, and continuing work as our advocate before the Father. Even in all of this, we may end up rejoicing, but we would still probably use adjectives other than "rejoicing" to describe Jesus in any of these situations.

That's why a little phrase in Luke 10:21 jumped out at me. That verse starts by saying, "In that hour Jesus rejoiced in the Spirit..." (NKJ). How cool is that? What made Jesus rejoice? Well, Jesus had sent seventy of His followers out into cities where He was about to go. They were to heal the sick and carry the message that the kingdom of God had come near to them. Those seventy had returned with joy and reported to their amazement, "Lord, even the demons are subject to us in Your name" Luke 10:17 (NKJ).

Jesus' response to that was, "That's no big deal. Satan is an easy fix. I was there when he got thrown out of heaven and I've given you the authority to take out the power of the enemy. He's the least of your worries; nothing he can throw your way can hurt you. Even so, don't be so excited about that. Be excited because Satan's out of heaven and you're in" (Paraphrased from Luke 10:18-20).

We're then told that Jesus rejoiced while talking to His Father about this. Jesus smiled as He thought about how His followers "got it." His disciples understood that God was in control. Healing the sick and casting out demons was no big deal or hard task because these phenomena pointed glory to God. Submission to the Father was all they needed to overcome any problem they would ever face. That was the whole point of Jesus coming to earth in the first place; to turn our eyes upon God.

Do we "get it?" Can Jesus smile over us because we understand that God is in control and can be trusted with all of our issues? Whatever we're dealing with that's troubling us, let's fully turn it over to God and make Jesus rejoice.

#268
September 24:
God the Provider (and Our Response)

Read Joshua 17 – 18 and you'll find the Promised Land being divided up among the tribes. This is the land God was providing for the Children of Israel. Then read Luke 12:1-31 and you'll read Jesus' words as He talks about not worrying about material things. The end of that passage says, "And do not seek what you should eat or what you should drink, nor have an anxious mind. For all these things the nations of the world seek after, and your Father knows that you need these things. But seek the kingdom of God, and all these things shall be added to you" Luke 12:29-31 (NKJ). You see, be it land, food, or clothing, God is perfectly able to provide for us.

In response, I surveyed my life and stopped to thank God for all the ways He provides for me. He sent me my husband, He provided me with my job, and He gave me my gifts that are now supplying me with income as well. All of these provisions work together to meet all of my personal needs. Most of all, some of what He gives me, I can give to others, and the blessings just keep flowing.

When it comes to God's provisions, be a pipeline, not a dam.

#269
September 25: Blessed Insurance

We spend lots of money on insurance, don't we? We have life insurance, health insurance, homeowners' insurance, and car insurance. Those categories are broken down even further for the sake of specificity. Life insurance is carried on each child with death benefits (I never quite understood the nomenclature of that one) and burial insurance. We pay itemized amounts within our health insurance premiums as we add such essentials as eye care, dental care, chiropractic care, and prescriptions. Depending upon what area of the country we live in, we can tack on earthquake and flood coverage to our homeowners' policies (why those things are "extra" I can't figure). And our vehicle policies are figured as we add up liability, collision, comprehensive, uninsured motorist, and medical coverage amounts.

The funny thing to me is that insurance is basically a bet. We are betting that something is going to happen to us so we pay into the system, gambling that when calamity strikes, we will have paid less than the disaster actually costs. In the meantime, the insurance companies are betting that nothing will happen so that they'll keep getting paid. Their gamble is that more people paying in will stay healthy, alive, and safe, than those they need to pay.

It's a good thing that our Heavenly insurance doesn't work that way. We pay in by living for the Kingdom, but the Company pays out in regular dispersals both now and in the life to come. Jesus explained the policy when Peter commented that he and the other disciples had left all to follow Him. Jesus said, "Assuredly, I say to you, there is no one who has left house or parents or brothers or wife or children, for the sake of the kingdom of God, who shall not receive many times more in this present time, and in the age to come everlasting life" Luke 18:29-30 (NKJ).

Talk about being in good hands! Now that's a policy we can afford!

#270
September 26: Ask

Ry Cooder wrote a traditional gospel chorus that says, "Jesus is on the main line, tell Him what you want. Call Him up and tell Him what you want." This song was written back in the days when there were such things as "main lines" and "party lines" on the telephone. You received your major messages via the main line, but every now and then, you could get hooked into a party line, a slip-up when multiple customers were connected to the same phone line. You can imagine the confusion that could ensue if several conversations were going on at the same time. Cooder's song points out that you can talk directly to Jesus with no interference, having His complete attention when asking for what you need.

The blind man on the Jericho road found out about the main line to Jesus. Here's the account:

Then it happened, as He was coming near Jericho, that a

certain blind man sat by the road begging. And hearing a multitude passing by, he asked what it meant. So they told him that Jesus of Nazareth was passing by. And he cried out, saying, "Jesus, Son of David, have mercy on me!" …So Jesus stood still and commanded him to be brought to Him. And when he had come near, He asked him, saying, "What do you want Me to do for you?" And he said, "Lord, that I may receive my sight." Then Jesus said to him, "Receive your sight; your faith has made you well." And immediately he received his sight, and followed Him, glorifying God. And all the people, when they saw it, gave praise to God. Luke 18:35-43 (NKJ)

Such a simple story with such a profound lesson for us. We make prayer so complicated when it's really quite the opposite. Here are our lessons on prayer from this narrative:

1. **Be where Jesus is.** This man was sitting on the road Jesus was walking down. Realize that our prayers won't be heard if we're not in the place we should be.
2. **Ask for mercy.** Mercy is *not* getting what we do deserve. Involve confession in our times of prayer. Realize there will need to be a turning from some old ways.
3. **Make specific requests.** Be explicit and unambiguous with what we're asking Jesus to do or supply. Looking Jesus in the face with our requests will temper what we ask of Him. We're liable not to ask for stupid stuff.
4. **Accept Jesus' answer by faith.** God delights in answering the prayers of the saints. Accept His answer.
5. **Immediately operate in the answer.** Instantly begin operating in the new way. If we couldn't see before, we now should walk like we can see. If we were broke before, we now should operate like people with good financial sense. Etc.
6. **Follow Jesus in the strength of that answered prayer.** Let's not take our blessings and run off with them. Use our answered prayers to be even better Christians.
7. **Glorify God.** Give God His props for the answer to our prayers.
8. **Let people see what God has done.** Testify. Let others know what God has done.

Prayer doesn't take all day and lots of words. Just call Him up and tell Him what you want. Try it.

#271
September 27: Hide and Seek

Do you remember playing Hide and Go Seek? That was one of my favorite games when I was a kid. I didn't like being the seeker, though. I always wanted to be one of the hiders. It was easy to hide. I could find slick places to hide from which I could see the seeker yet elude him until I felt like exposing myself. We hiders actually received pleasure from evading the seeker and causing him to fail at his attempt to find us before we popped out of hiding and touched the base.

A purpose statement for the coming of Christ is found in Luke 19:10. "For the Son of Man has come to seek and to save that which was lost" (NKJ). How much hiding are we doing from the One sent not only to seek us, but also to save us? Have we found what we deem to be "slick hiding places" from which we peer out at God, yet refuse to expose ourselves so as to be seen fully by Him? Do we receive smug pleasure from evading Him and then blame Him for not finding us before we touch the base things of life?

Being found is not just a one-time occurrence. God wants to find us to save us from sin, but He's also continuing to look down inside of us to save us on an ongoing basis from any trails we walk on which we can find ourselves lost. Let's come out of hiding and allow Jesus – the Seeker of our lost hearts and souls – to find us and save us in every way.

#272
September 28: On His Prayer List

Although I don't consider myself to be a prayer warrior, I'm one of those Christians who has a prayer list. I actually keep my prayer list on index cards and each person and family has their own card. Whenever these people request prayer (and even when they don't ask) I jot down the request or concern on the card.

Each time I look at that card, I'm reminded of the specific issue and I pray about it.

I'm in good company as a pray-er for my friends. In Luke 22:31-32, we find that Jesus prayed for His friends too. "And the Lord said, 'Simon, Simon! Indeed, Satan has asked for you, that he may sift you as wheat. But I have prayed for you, that your faith should not fail; and when you have returned to Me, strengthen your brethren'" Luke 22:31-32 (NKJ).

Jesus prayed very specifically and purposefully for Peter*. We can learn five things about praying for our friends from Jesus' brief comment here.

- First, Jesus knew what was going on in Peter's life and was attuned to his spiritual struggle. We too should be able to discern when Satan is attacking our friends. With Biblical truth as our guide, we can help our friends see the true source of their problem.
- Second, Jesus took it upon Himself to pray for Peter. There's no need to wait for an invitation to pray for our friends.
- Third, Jesus prayed that Peter's faith would not fail. When I was young, I didn't understand what they meant when the old saints at my church used to say, "Pray my strength in the Lord." Now I get that. It's our duty as Christian friends to pray for our buddies' spiritual strength as they must stand against the onslaught of the devil and temptation.
- Fourth, Jesus prayed that Peter be restored. Like us, our friends will fall and fail sometimes. We still need to be there for them, praying that they regain their place of fellowship with the Lord.
- Finally, Jesus prayed for Peter's outreach. Let's get behind our friends and pray earnestly for them as they step out into their purpose.

Hebrews 7:25 says, "Therefore He is also able to save to the uttermost those who come to God through Him, since He always lives to make intercession for them" (NKJ). Peter was on Jesus' prayer list and so are we. Mimic the Savior as you dedicate yourself to pray for your friends.

*See Matthew 16:17-18 and keep reading the Luke 22 passage and you'll see that "Simon" is Peter's other name.

#273
September 29: The Autobiography

What would we tell about ourselves if we were to write our autobiographies? We'd probably include the basic life facts—where and when we were born, where we grew up, houses we lived in, schools we attended. We'd tell of our hopes and dreams—some dashed, others fulfilled. We'd share exciting times as well as sorrowful ones with the view to pass on what we'd learned from it all. We'd also undoubtedly speak of all the significant things we'd done in life. Hopefully, through the divulgence of our entire story, our readers would come away from our book knowing the real us.

After Jesus' resurrection, He talked with some guys who were walking along the road to Emmaus. He caused them not to recognize Him and they engaged the Stranger in a conversation about all that had happened over the past few days. When the men told Him of their dismay over Jesus of Nazareth's death because "we were hoping that it was He who was going to redeem Israel," Jesus said to them, "O foolish ones, and slow of heart to believe in all that the prophets have spoken" ... And beginning at Moses and all the Prophets, He expounded to them in all the Scriptures the things concerning Himself. Luke 24:25 and 27 (NKJ)

Whenever we read the Bible, we are delving into Jesus' autobiography. (Now you English purists are saying, "Gotcha! An autobiography is written by the person himself. The Bible was written by others so technically it should be called a biography." Okay, but gotcha back, because the Bible is the uniquely inspired Word of God—God-breathed directly into the writers, so in a very real sense, He did write the book about Himself.) So as I was saying, the Bible is Jesus' autobiography. He's told us where and when He came into existence (He's eternal and then came into His own created history through a virgin). He's shared with us exciting times (the parting of the Red Sea, the Jericho wall falling, and the Mount Carmel contest, just to name a few), as well as sorrowful ones. He's even proclaimed His hopes for us ("And the glory which You gave Me I have given them, that they may be one just as We are one" John 17:22, NKJ).

By including in His book a detailed account of His activities, Jesus has revealed to us His real and true self.

- In the beginning God created the heavens and the earth. Genesis 1:1 (NKJ)
- And God said, Let us make man in our image, after our likeness... Genesis 1:26 (KJV)
- In the beginning was the Word, and the Word was with God, and the Word was God. John 1:1 (NKJ)
- And the Word became flesh and dwelt among us... John 1:14 (NKJ)
- All things were made through Him, and without Him nothing was made that was made. John 1:3 (NKJ)
- For by him all things were created: things in heaven and on earth, visible and invisible, whether thrones or powers or rulers or authorities; all things were created by him and for him. He is before all things, and in him all things hold together. And he is the head of the body, the church; he is the beginning and the firstborn from among the dead, so that in everything he might have the supremacy. For God was pleased to have all his fullness dwell in him, and through him to reconcile to himself all things, whether things on earth or things in heaven, by making peace through his blood, shed on the cross. Colossians 1:16-20 (NIV)

Enjoy the Bible, Jesus' autobiography, on a regular basis!

#274
September 30: The Scars are Proof

I have a scar at the base of my right thumb. Whenever I see it, I'm reminded of how it got there. That scar is the reason why I only submerge glasses into sudsy dishwater one at a time and then I wash each one very gingerly. I couldn't see the wicked crack under all those suds when I began to push the dishcloth around the inside of that glass almost 20 years ago. That broken glass made a slice in my hand that required about 5 stitches at the emergency room.

Scars serve not only as reminders of the hurts we've been through, but also as identification. No one else has the exact same scars I have. In the same way, Jesus' scars remind us not only of the hurt he went through for us, but also of who He is. After

His resurrection, He told His disciples, "Behold My hands and My feet, that it is I Myself. Handle Me and see, for a spirit does not have flesh and bones as you see I have" Luke 24:38-39 (NKJ).

Usually our scars are obtained accidentally, but Jesus obtained His scars on purpose. Only He has the scars that represent our release from being subject to God's wrath. His scars are proof of His Lordship, and glorious reminders of His amazing love.

#275
October 1: Comprehension Opener

"I just don't understand." We've all said it. We've all had stuff happen to us that we don't understand. It's especially difficult when we are doing our best to concentrate on pleasing God with our lives.

After Jesus was crucified, the disciples felt this way. I'm sure each one said to himself, "I just don't understand." After all, they had concentrated on Jesus for 3 ½ years. They had literally walked with Him. He had taught them to pray, allowed them to heal the sick, and they experienced having the demons be subject to them. They'd watched as Jesus fed multitudes, commanded nature to obey, and raised the dead. They were convinced that they had found the Messiah and were determined to go with Him all the way. And then Jesus was murdered. The disciples' hearts were in the right place. To the best of their ability, they had done almost everything right. Yet now all their hopes and dreams were shattered.

Then came resurrection morning and the following days.

Jesus had risen from the dead and He appeared to talk with His disciples. He asked them, "Why are you troubled? And why do doubts arise in your hearts? Luke 24:38 (NKJ). Then after showing them His scars, He reminded them that He had told them "that all things must be fulfilled which were written in the Law of Moses and the Prophets and the Psalms concerning Me" Luke 24:44. Then Luke writes a very important commentary sentence. "And He opened their understanding, that they might comprehend the Scriptures" Luke 24:45.

Here is a key point we too must grasp. When we have tried as hard as we can, to do all that we can, to be the best we can be, and things still go awry, let Jesus open our understanding so we can comprehend the Scriptures. We just may find that our losses and dry times don't have anything at all to do with us. The disciples' discouragement happened because Jesus had other work to do, but the work He was doing—leading captivity captive (Ephesians 4:8-10) and ascending to His Father, possibly to deposit His blood at His Father's feet on our behalf (John 20:17)—would ultimately be for their benefit.

Our discouragement, like everything else in the life of a believer, can be offered to Jesus for God's glory. Turn to the Scriptures and let Him help you to comprehend.

#276
October 2: Jesus' Job Description

"Behold the Lamb of God who takes away the sin of the world!" With these words in John 1:29, John the Baptist introduced Jesus and Jesus' public ministry kicked off. Jesus' entire mission and job description was to take away the sin of the world. Notice the word "sin" is singular; we're not talking here about individual "sins." Jesus' job was to remove the disposition of sin and through His act of nailing that sin to the Cross in His own body, He did so. Now we must relinquish that disposition of sin in us (with which He has already dealt), and refuse to live by its dictates any longer. This is fully accomplished in us when we repent. That's why Jesus was baptized – not for His sins because He had none, but for ours which He came to destroy. What is "necessary to fulfill all righteousness" is that sin be dealt with and put away. Our baptism is the statement of this fact in our lives.

Identify with the work of Jesus today and be grateful that He actually did the job He willingly came to do. Realize that He died that you might have life and that more abundantly. That kind of life is a life free from the dictates of sin. Believe me: living a life free from sin is way better than living a life dictated by it. Give repentance a try. I guarantee, you'll enjoy the results!

#277
October 3: A Glimpse of His Glory

Every now and then we need a pick-me-up, don't we? For whatever reason, we may feel a little down or lonely or uncomfortable. Well, before we reach for that half gallon of ice cream (or insert your favorite shouldn't-eat-it-and-you-know-it comfort food) or call the wrong person on the phone, look for a glimpse of God's glory.

In the Message Bible, John 2:11 says, "This act in Cana of Galilee was the first sign Jesus gave, the first glimpse of his glory. And his disciples believed in him." Jesus had just turned regular old everyday water into the best wine anyone had ever tasted, but it wasn't that wine that moved His disciples to a deeper belief. It was the fact that the action was a manifestation of His glory. You see, to this point, the disciples had followed Jesus simply because of the words He said to them and because He had bidden them to follow. Now they saw some evidence of who they already believed Him to be.

Our world is full of manifestations of the glory of God if we but open our eyes to deliberately look for them. I love seeing a father playing with and caring for his little children. That reminds me of the tenderness God has for me. That's a glimpse of His glory. I notice that despite the thorns on my rosebushes, my roses still bloom and smell sweet. That reminds me that my thorny issues cannot keep me from blossoming to beautify my circle of influence. That's a glimpse of His glory. A new sunrise, a rainbow, an eagle in flight, a call from a friend, a fond memory of a loved one now in Heaven: all are glimpses of His mighty work – His magnificent glory.

Miracles are happening all around us every single moment. We didn't have to wake up this morning. That friend didn't have to make it through the surgery. We were held up on that phone call just long enough to avoid being part of a major accident along the route we normally travel.

Take time today to glimpse the glory of the Lord and affirm again what the disciples found – Jesus is who we believe Him to be.

#278
October 4: Know the Author

At a Mother's Day luncheon at our church, our pastor's wife, Teresa, taught us something very profound about the Bible. She said we can read, understand, and even enjoy other books without the slightest hint of insight into the lives of their authors; however, we must have an understanding of the Author of the Bible in order to comprehend its truths. From her statement, I realized that reading the Bible and knowing God go hand-in-hand. We come to know God as we read the Bible, and we come to understand the Bible as we know God more intimately. One is not possible without the other.

Although the Bible had not been put together as we know it today, Jesus told Nicodemus essentially the same thing. Nicodemus was a Pharisee, a ruler of the Jews, who approached Jesus one evening and said, "Rabbi, we **know** that You are a teacher come from God; for no one can do these signs that You do unless God is with him" John 3:2 (NKJ). Jesus' answer is intriguing. He told Nicodemus, "Most assuredly, I say to you, unless one is born again, he cannot **see** the kingdom of God" John 3:3 (NKJ). The words "know" and "see" in the above two verses are really the same Greek word – eido – which means "to know, be aware, have knowledge, perceive, and understand." Although Nicodemus and the other Pharisees had come to a logical conclusion about who Jesus must be, Jesus clarified that true perceptive understanding could not come unless they were born again. Being born again meant becoming a part of the family, coming into a personal, intimate relationship between Father and child. Since Jesus is the Word of God in the flesh (see John chapter 1), for Nicodemus, knowing Jesus in person was the same as reading the Bible.

We must become part of the family to know the Father. You can do that easily right now. "If you confess with your mouth the Lord Jesus and believe in your heart that God has raised Him from the dead, you will be saved. For with the heart one believes unto righteousness, and with the mouth confession is made unto salvation" Romans 10:9-10 (NKJ). If you are already born again, determine today to get to know Jesus even more intimately. To better understand the Bible, get to know the Author; to better know the Author, read the Bible.

#279
October 5: The Matchmaker

A matchmaker is a person with a twinkle in her eye who lives for nothing else but to see people connect. She'll work the angles, drop hints, and orchestrate circumstances so that the two people she has in mind for each other will meet. She's slightly devious but with good intentions. Sometimes her plans work; sometimes they don't, but we can't get mad at her. She sees our need for love and companionship and has our best interest at heart.

I witnessed the Matchmaker of Heaven at work as I flew home one day and He involved me in His scheme this time. On the second leg of my flight, a woman sat next to me in my row toward the back of the plane. Our conversation started because of the Kindle (a computerized book-reading device) she had in her lap. Somehow, the topic changed to our children and our sons, almost the same age, who were facing similar challenges. It was soon evident that although we faced some of the same issues, they were affecting us in very different ways. She wondered about the peace I had, and I was delighted to introduce her to its Source.

Once she heard the Gospel and responded to it, she marveled as she began to realize it was no coincidence that she chose the seat next to me. Originally booked to fly on a later flight, she had arrived at the airport unusually early, but had been told she wouldn't be allowed to go stand-by on an earlier flight because of the sale-priced ticket she had purchased. She asked anyway, and the ticket agent said, "I don't know why I'm doing this, but go ahead." I then shared with her that it's unusual for me to stay on an extra day after a speaking event, but had decided to this time and that's why I was on a Monday, rather than a Sunday flight. We both even realized that if it hadn't been for her Kindle and our sons having the same problem, perhaps we wouldn't even have started talking.

The conversation that had started with tears of pain, ended with tears of joy. As we were landing, she said, "I'm not going to California for my son; I'm on this plane to meet you. I feel like a totally new person." I shook her hand and said, "Welcome. You were on this plane to meet Jesus!"

The Matchmaker had a twinkle in His eye on that plane. Since He lives for nothing else but to see us connect with Him, He worked the angles, dropped hints, and orchestrated circumstances so that my new friend and I would meet. He had only good intentions and His plan worked. He saw her need for love and companionship and had her best interest at heart.

"For God so loved the world that He gave His only begotten Son, that whoever believes in Him should not perish but have everlasting life" John 3:16 (NKJ).

The Matchmaker strikes again!

#280
October 6: He Still Walks on Water

Immediately following the miracle when Jesus fed 5,000 people with a little boy's lunch, He left for some alone time at the mountain. We take up the narrative in John chapter six when His disciples, seemingly tired of waiting, took off in a boat without Him.

"Now when evening came, His disciples went down to the sea, got into the boat, and went over the sea toward Capernaum. And it was already dark, and Jesus had not come to them. Then the sea arose because a great wind was blowing. So when they had rowed about three or four miles, they saw Jesus walking on the sea and drawing near the boat; and they were afraid. But He said to them, 'It is I; do not be afraid.' Then they willingly received Him into the boat, and immediately the boat was at the land where they were going" John 6:16-21 (NKJ).

How like us these disciples were! How often do we get tired of waiting for Jesus and decide to take things into our own hands? We wait, it gets dark, and still no word from Jesus. So what do we do? We strike out on our own. We get into relationship boats, business deal boats, and debt boats. As the storms arise around our boats, we do exactly what the disciples did – we row like crazy, making three or even four more decisions that do nothing but take us deeper into the tempest. Like the disciples, we never even think of Jesus; after all, we are well aware that we're the ones who left Him behind.

Ahh, but the Savior has a trick up His sleeve. He can walk on water (and why not, He created it)! Even without being asked, Jesus went to the disciples in their distress. The storm which was causing the disciples so much anguish was the very thing Jesus stepped on to get to them in order to rescue them.

My mother used to ask, "Just what have you gotten yourself into now?" What "boat" are you in today? Hebrews 13:8 tells us, "Jesus Christ is the same yesterday, today, and forever" (NKJ). Our wonderful Lord still walks on water. Even though you have gotten yourself into a mess, you left the Lord behind, and you've continued to make decisions that have only sent you farther "out to sea," I challenge you to look up. Jesus is coming to you, walking right on top of madness.

Now continue to be like the disciples at the end of the story: willingly receive Jesus into your boat. That's right, let Him step smack dab into the middle of the mess. You will find He will immediately take you to where you are supposed to be.

#281
October 7: Have Some Bread

The story is told in John chapter 6 of Jesus feeding 5,000 by multiplying a little boy's lunch. The following day, the people searched for Jesus and when they found Him, He challenged them saying that they weren't really all that interested in Him, they had just followed Him for the food. He told them, "Do not labor for the food which perishes, but for the food which endures to everlasting life, which the Son of Man will give you, because God the Father has set His seal on Him" John 6:27 (NKJ).

The people knew how to work for physical food, but they had to ask Jesus how they were expected to work for the spiritual (everlasting) food. The conversation then goes as follows:

Jesus answered and said to them, "This is the work of God, that you believe in Him whom He sent."
Therefore they said to Him, "What sign will You perform then, that we may see it and believe You? What work will You do? Our fathers ate the manna in the desert; as it is written, 'He gave them bread from heaven to eat.'"
Then Jesus said to them, "Most assuredly, I say to you, Moses did not give you the bread from heaven, but My Father gives you the true bread from heaven. For the bread of God is He who comes down from heaven and

gives life to the world."

Then they said to Him, "Lord, give us this bread always."

And Jesus said to them, "I am the bread of life. He who comes to Me shall never hunger, and he who believes in Me shall never thirst. John 6:29-35 (NKJ)

The manna from heaven God gave to the Israelites in the wilderness sustained them for 40 years. The bread Jesus gave the 5,000 sustained them that afternoon. Both instances were but shadows of the true bread from heaven which is Jesus Christ come in the flesh. We have but to believe on Him, which encompasses taking His life into us in the same way in which we eat bread, and the nutrition which He is becomes our eternal sustenance.

Had God not given the manna in the wilderness, the wandering Israelites could not have eaten and could not have survived. Had Jesus not given the bread to the 5,000, the crowd could not have eaten and could not have made it through the evening. Had the Savior not given Himself on the cross, we could not have "eaten" – could not have believed – and could not have everlasting life.

Have some bread!

#282
October 8: True Communion

One of my Sunday School children was visibly upset in the church service one Sunday. I put my arm around her and asked what was wrong. She snuggled close to me and said, "I don't want to drink blood." The pastor was preparing the congregation for the Communion meal we were about to take. When he held up the cup and quoted Jesus saying, "This is My blood," that was just too much for my little learner. She wanted to obey and participate, but she knew what she heard, and it all seemed like a barbaric practice in her innocent mind. I recognized a teachable moment when I saw one. She was okay once I whispered that the cup actually contained grape juice that *represented* the blood of Christ and in class the following Sunday, I explained the sacrament to all the kids.

Jesus used the feeding of the 5,000 as a teachable moment. The people were excited over being fed physical food, so He captured that instant and flipped the meaning to the spiritual. He talked of someone else they knew who had fed folks: Moses. Had not Moses prayed and bread – manna – literally dropped from Heaven to feed the children of Israel in the wilderness? Jesus then compared Himself to that incident saying, "...Moses did not give you the bread from heaven, but My Father gives you the true bread from heaven. For the bread of God is He who comes down from heaven and gives life to the world... I am the bread of life. He who comes to Me shall never hunger, and he who believes in Me shall never thirst" John 6:32-35 (NKJ). And later in the passage He gets even more graphic. "He who eats My flesh and drinks My blood abides in Me, and I in him. As the living Father sent Me, and I live because of the Father, so he who feeds on Me will live because of Me" John 6:56-57 (NKJ).

Jesus is giving us a metaphor: using something we understand to get us to grasp the meaning of something He's trying to teach us. We understand the importance of eating and drinking for our physical survival. Jesus here teaches us that in the same way, we must "eat and drink" of Him for our spiritual survival. We must literally take Him in: how He lived and moved (His body), and how He was vitally connected to God (His blood). To become God's children means we are "born" into His family (thus the term "born again") and we have new DNA – Divine New Attributes.

Let's make the practice of eating His flesh and drinking His blood – taking on Christ's character and way of life – our daily modus operandi.

#283
October 9: He Is Who He Says He Is

Have you ever known people who said they were something and then acted totally different? A person like that is called a "perpetrator." Some people "perpetrate" to make you think they are rich. Others "perpetrate" to make you think they are smart. Still others "perpetrate" to make you think they have more influence than they really have. However you cut it, a perpetrator is a fake.

Not so with Jesus Christ. Look at just the Scriptures in the book of John in which He tells us point blank who He is:

- John 6:35a "I am the bread of life..."
- John 8:12 "I am the light of the world..."
- John 10:7 "I am the door of the sheep."
- John 10:11 "I am the good Shepherd..."
- John 14:6 "I am the way, the truth, and the life..."
- John 15:5 "I am the vine, ye are the branches..."
- John 11:25 "I am the resurrection, and the life..."

Since Jesus is who He says He is, He acts in accordance with His identity. For example, as the Bread, He feeds us; as the Light, He shows us our way; as the Vine, He passes needed nourishment to us, the branches; and so forth. Knowing that Jesus is not a perpetrator should embolden our faith. When the hungry multitude needed Him, He was their Bread. When Mary and Martha grieved over the death of their brother, He was the Resurrection. Jesus is what we His children need Him to be because He is who He says He is. Trust.

#284
October 10: He's Good for It

A friend of mine wanted to obtain autographed copies of my books but she didn't have her checkbook or cash with her at the time. We lived in different cities and I had no idea when we were going to see each other again. I didn't want to have to package the books and send them in the mail, so I signed them and gave them to her saying, "Just mail me the payment." She was grateful and replied, "I'll send you a check when I get home; you know I'm good for it."

Martha didn't trust Jesus' word like I trusted my friend's. When her brother Lazarus took sick, she and her sister Mary sent for Jesus. The family had befriended the Master and commentators believe He even stayed at their home whenever He traveled through Bethany. They had witnessed Him healing dozens, maybe even hundreds, of people throughout His ministry; surely He would come over and heal His friend. However, Jesus took too long and Lazarus died. By the time He arrived, Lazarus had been in the tomb for four whole days. As soon as Martha heard that Jesus was close, she ran out to meet Him. Here we'll take up the narrative from John, chapter 11.

> Then Martha said to Jesus, "Lord, if You had been here, my brother would not have died. But even now I know that whatever You ask of God, God will give You."
> Jesus said to her, "Your brother will rise again."
> Martha said to Him, "I know that he will rise again in the resurrection at the last day."
> Jesus said to her, "I am the resurrection and the life. He who believes in Me, though he may die, he shall live. And whoever lives and believes in Me shall never die. Do you believe this?"
> She said to Him, "Yes, Lord, I believe that You are the Christ, the Son of God, who is to come into the world."
> And when she had said these things, she went her way..." John 11:21-28a (NKJ).

Notice that Martha did *not* believe what Jesus said. When asked if she believed that Jesus was the resurrection and the life, and that whoever lives and believes in Him would never die, Martha responded by saying something totally different. Although she started her response with "yes," what she said she actually believed was different from what Jesus had said to her. Martha said she believed Jesus was the Christ; she did *not* believe He was the resurrection. In other words, she did not believe that Jesus was what she needed most at the time.

Do we trust Jesus like Martha trusted Him, or do we trust Jesus like I trusted my friend? Do we take Jesus' word for who He is and for what He can do only so far, or do we read His word and even if we don't understand it, say, "Lord, You're good for it"? Do we truly believe that Jesus is everything we need most?

Jesus is who He says He is. Jesus can do what He says He can do. Our only responsibility to make His person and His presence real in our lives is to believe who He is and what He says. All the riches of Heaven are then opened to us. Trust Him. He's good for it.

#285
October 11: Three Things Jesus Knew

John records quite a bit about the happenings during the last Passover meal (which we call The Last Supper) Jesus shared with His disciples. (See John chapters 13 – 17.) Before Jesus begins to elucidate His final words to them, we read about three things Jesus knew. "…Jesus knew that His hour had come that He should depart from this world to the Father… knowing that the Father had given all things into His hands, and that He had come from God and was going to God, rose from supper and laid aside His garments, took a towel and girded Himself" John 13:1-4 (NKJ).

The three things Jesus knew at this most critical time in His earthly life, and His corresponding action hold a lesson for us.

- **#1: Know your duration.** "Jesus knew that His hour had come that He should depart from this world to the Father." Jesus knew the duration of His earthly ministry was coming to an end and He was fine with that. We need to hold loosely to our places in ministry so when God wants to bring their duration to an end, He can, without our grabbing at them to keep ourselves involved past our designated time of effectiveness.
- **#2: Know your design.** "…knowing that the Father had given all things into His hands." Jesus was clear about what God had given Him to accomplish. What are our God-given gifts, talents, purposes, and passions? Are we certain of them and operating fully in them?
- **#3: Know your destination.** "…and [knowing] that He had come from God and was going to God." Jesus had no doubt about where He came from and where He was going. With the assurance of being God's children and of ultimately going to Heaven, there should be no hesitancy in carrying out God's business day by day.

Having complete knowledge of our duration, design, and destination frees us up to do exactly what Jesus did with the same knowledge—to serve. Jesus was God, yet He washed His disciples' feet.

Okay, children of God, now that we know what Jesus knew, what service has God called us to do?

#286
October 12: Accurate Information

I had an opportunity to speak with members of a women's book club regarding my book *Power Suit: The Armor of God Fit for the Feminine Frame*. After a lovely lunch and some small talk, we got down to the business at hand of discussing the book. I answered the opening question about my initial inspiration to write the book, and then one of the women asked me about some points I had made in one of the chapters. As I prefaced each of my comments with, "Well, the Bible says...," I noticed that several of the women were not only quiet, but seemed a bit distant. Soon the reason was disclosed.

Very politely, one of the women said, "I don't want to offend you, but I stopped reading the book at page 42." You see, page 42 lays out the Gospel truth that all religions do not lead to the same God. The book states:

No matter what name is on the marquee, churches that teach the fundamental truths of the Bible, acknowledging first and foremost the deity of Jesus Christ, are leading their parishioners to the God of Christianity. However, any religion not willing to assert that Jesus Christ is God – and the coming to Him in faith for eternal life – is not leading its followers to the same God we serve.

A discussion ensued about the veracity of the Bible, the identity of the person of Jesus Christ, and the existence of absolute truth. The question was asked, "How can you say that this viewpoint is "right" and all other religions in the world are "wrong"?

Again, I pointed to Jesus' own words. I answered, "In John 14:6, Jesus Christ Himself asserted, 'I am the way, the truth, and the life. No one comes to the Father except through Me.' By saying this, either Jesus is lying, He's a lunatic, or He actually is the Lord stating the truth about Himself. And we are responsible regarding what we do with that truth."

That comment forced the next retort. "How can you judge everyone in the world like that?"

My heart was racing now because I realized I was literally on the battlefield for which my book instructed me to suit up. I relished the conversation because I knew that in the armor, I could confidently wield the sword of the Spirit, which is the Word of God, and know that each strike would make its point.

My answer was that there's a difference between "judgment" and "stating a fact." I could confidently and unapologetically say that Jesus Christ is the only way to God because that is a fact stated in the Bible. If we believe the Bible to be true, we have to believe all of it. We can't pick and choose the parts we like – the parts that hold no consequence – and toss out the parts that make us uncomfortable or require us to change. By stating what the Bible says, I am not judging. If people feel judged or criticized, it's God's word that's doing the judging.

People probably will be defensive at first when they hear the truth of the Gospel clearly proclaimed. John 3:19-20 says, "And this is the condemnation, that the light has come into the world, and men loved darkness rather than light, because their deeds were evil. For everyone practicing evil hates the light and does not come to the light, lest his deeds should be exposed" (NKJ). However, don't be scared to share the truth of the Word of God, but do so gently and lovingly. Peter instructs us to have Christ so set apart in our hearts that at any and every moment we should "always be prepared to give an answer to everyone who asks [us] to give the reason for the hope that [we] have. But do this with gentleness and respect" First Peter 3:15 (NIV).

Eternity hangs in the balance. Give out accurate information about God.

#287
October 13: God's If/Then Proposition

God is love; there is no doubt about that (First John 4:8). Our response to that love is well stated in Matthew Henry's Commentary on First John 4:17-21, paragraph 5, it reads:

We love him, because he first loved us, v. 19. His love is the incentive, the motive, and moral cause of ours. We cannot but love so good a God, who was first in the act and work of love, who loved us when we were both unloving and unlovely, who loved us at so great a rate, who has been seeking and soliciting our love at the expense of his Son's blood; and has condescended to beseech us to be reconciled unto him. Let heaven and earth stand amazed at such love! His love is the productive cause of ours..."

If we're responding to God as we should, we are remiss if

we keep His love bottled up inside of us, selfishly hoarding it all for ourselves. So exactly how are we to exercise this over-flowing love? Simple. Jesus says, "If you love Me, keep My commandments" John 14:15 (NKJ).

Easier said than done, you might say. Jesus understands that it may not be the easiest thing in the world for us to keep His commandments, so He has provided assistance. Immediately after giving us the if/then proposition (*If* you love me, *then* keep my commandments), Jesus says, "And I will pray the Father, and He will give you another Helper, that He may abide with you forever—the Spirit of truth, whom the world cannot receive, because it neither sees Him nor knows Him; but you know Him, for He dwells with you and will be in you" John 14:16-17 (NKJ).

A true if/then proposition also means its opposite. By giving us this if/then statement in John 14:15, Jesus is also saying, "If you don't keep My commandments, you don't love me." That sounds harsh, but that's how the logic of an if/then proposition works. We can't say we love Jesus if we are participating in actions that are contrary to His commandments. Living out God's love starts by the total surrender of our will to His. In The Message Bible, Eugene Peterson translates Romans 12:1-2 as follows:

"So here's what I want you to do, God helping you: Take your everyday, ordinary life—your sleeping, eating, going-to-work, and walking-around life—and place it before God as an offering. Embracing what God does for you is the best thing you can do for him. Don't become so well-adjusted to your culture that you fit into it without even thinking. Instead, fix your attention on God. You'll be changed from the inside out. Readily recognize what he wants from you, and quickly respond to it. Unlike the culture around you, always dragging you down to its level of immaturity, God brings the best out of you, develops well-formed maturity in you."

Our only right response to God's love is to love Him back by conforming to what He wants us to be. This type of conformity will be opposite to everything our flesh and feelings want to do on their own. Keeping His commandments means giving up our right to relish in how we feel. As we are stamping our puny feet and shaking our puny fists at God demanding our rights to follow our feelings, what we fail to realize is that when we submit our willingness to do whatever He says, the way He says to do it, God promises to reveal Himself to us (see John 14:21). And as the above passage points out, He will make any necessary changes in us from the inside out.

#288
October 14: How to Get God to Show Up

There is no secret to getting God to show up in your life.
Read John 14:21-23:

> He who has My commandments and keeps them, it is he
> who loves Me. And he who loves Me will be loved by My
> Father, and I will love him and manifest Myself to him."
> Judas (not Iscariot) said to Him, "Lord, how is it that You
> will manifest Yourself to us, and not to the world?"
> Jesus answered and said to him, "If anyone loves Me, he
> will keep My word; and My Father will love him, and We will
> come to him and make Our home with him. (NKJ)

Did you see it? Jesus says He will manifest Himself to
those who love Him, and will make His home (along with God the
Father) with those who keep His word. The Greek word for
manifest is "emphanizō" and it means to exhibit (in person) or
disclose (by words). The phrase "make His home" means to take
up residence.

So it's simple: When we love God and obey Him, we can
be assured that He not only shows up, but also He has moved in.
We really don't have to get God to show up. He's already at home
in those of us who love Him and keep His word.

Be determined today to keep every word God's given and
bask in the assurance of His presence.

#289
October 15: He Moves In

Not long after one of my friends got married, she and her
new husband moved into a lovely home in one of the classiest
neighborhoods in our city. The streets are lined with great trees
and each home is distinctively different. However, no sooner did
she and her husband move in that she started making plans to
remodel. She appreciated the house, but she wasn't completely
comfortable. First she redid a small bathroom, then she had the
kitchen gutted and renovated. When she expressed plans to tear
out a wall in the living room area, her husband said, "This isn't the

house for you." They soon moved to another home already designed as she liked it to be.

Jesus has said, "If anyone loves me, he will obey my teaching. My Father will love him, and we will come to him and make our home with him" John 14:23 (NIV). Think of that: Jesus and His Father actually take up residence in us! That's an amazing concept, but as I pondered it, I began thinking that I suppose Jesus feels the same way when He moves in to live with us as my friend felt when she moved into that first house. It's not that Jesus doesn't appreciate His new digs in our heart; it's just that there are a few things that need renovation in order for Him to be completely comfortable. He may start with something small and easy to manage like curbing our desire to spend so much time on the internet. Then he may move to revising our vocabulary by eradicating those curse words. His third project may be the slower renovation of our thought life or eating habits. Bit by bit, His goal is to remodel us into a place that is really made for Him.

We're okay with the small stuff, but when Jesus starts tearing down walls, we tend to get nervous. We really like the walls we've built. In fact, we've wallpapered them and hung photos of our dearest relatives on them, forcing them to take part in maintaining our walls. It's time for an attitude adjustment and a re-evaluation of our thinking process. Once Christ moves in, "your body is a temple of the Holy Spirit, who is in you, whom you have received from God? You are not your own; you were bought at a price. Therefore honor God with your body" First Corinthians 6:19-20 (NIV).

Know today that when Jesus moves in, He owns the place. The old landlord (that's us) has no say in what the new Owner decides to do. Allow Him free reign with home improvement. (Hint: He's God so He's used to living in splendor!) Hands off and let God do an extreme makeover.

#290
October 16: The Gardener

I love roses, so my husband has planted seven rose bushes for me around the front of our home. The red, yellow, white, pink, and lilac blooms adorn our home and bring me joy especially when I can bring them in the house and place them in vases in my office or on the kitchen table.

From time to time though, I have to prune back my rose bushes. I snip off the branches that no longer yield buds and cut away the dead leaves and sucker shoots (those branches that seem healthy, but are nothing more than wild growth that "sucks" nutrients from the productive branches). After my pruning times, my rose bushes look pitiful and almost dead; however, I know better. Given time, the rest and relief that have been produced by the pruning will allow the strong core of the bush to revive, and soon I'm enjoying my beautiful blooms again.

We are God's rose bushes and He is the Gardener. Jesus explains that to us in John 15:1-2 when He states, "I am the true vine, and My Father is the vinedresser. Every branch in Me that does not bear fruit He takes away; and every branch that bears fruit He prunes, that it may bear more fruit" (NKJ).

God deals with us in exactly the same way in which I deal with my rose bushes. He's interested, as I am, in seeing beautiful, productive fruit (blooms). In order to keep us healthy and ward off the possibility of our energy being sapped, He will get rid of sucker shoots. Branches that are not bearing fruit, He will prune; that is, He will *kathairo*, which comes from the Greek word that means to cleanse or expiate. This is the root from which we get the word catharsis which we know to describe a thorough decontamination.

When we're in God's garden, He has the right to do whatever is necessary to keep us healthy so we can grow and produce. The pruning process doesn't feel good at the time, and we may look a little jagged immediately afterward, but just stay rooted and attached to the main Vine, Jesus Christ. In due season, we will sprout again.

#291
October 17: Jesus is Divine

A line in an old Steve Green song said, "He is divine, and you are de-branch." Of course, the songwriter was using a play-on-words from John 15:4-5 which says, "Abide in Me, and I in you. As the branch cannot bear fruit of itself, unless it abides in the vine, neither can you, unless you abide in Me. <u>I am the vine, you *are* the branches.</u> He who abides in Me, and I in him, bears much fruit; for without Me you can do nothing." (Underlining added.)

Yes, Jesus is divine ("theios" in Greek meaning to be in every way like God [because He *is* God], see Second Peter 1:2-3), but He is also de-Vine, the wellspring of all our strength and ability. We cannot draw on the nutrients of this Vine simply by hanging around near it. We can't just dress in leafy clothes and speak leafy language and expect to soak in its life-giving energy. No, we must be literally grafted in, completely detached from every other root and totally attached to the Vine that is Christ. Then and only then will that wonderful, divine (de-Vine) sustenance run through our veins.

Don't be scared. Abide (from the Greek verb *ménō* which means to remain) in de-Vine and watch the growth and multiplication in your life of both the fruit of the Spirit (Galatians 5:22-23) and the fruit of the works of your hands.

#292
October 18: Our Keys to God

In order to get into a safety deposit box at a bank, two keys are required. The bank has one key and the owner of the box has the other. After checking in at the teller window, a bank representative will retrieve the first key that opens the space holding the box, granting the owner access to it. Then the box owner can take the box out of the space to a private area and use the second key to open the box and review its treasures.

In much the same way, there are two keys to God. In John 16:26-27, Jesus says, "In that day you will ask in My name, and I do not say to you that I shall pray the Father for you; for the Father Himself loves you, because you have loved Me, and have believed that I came forth from God" (NKJ).

You see, we have access to God directly ("in that day you will ask in My name") thanks to two keys. Key number one, like the banker's key, is the Father's personal love for us ("for the Father Himself loves you). This opens the door. Let's not get it twisted, "In this is love, not that we loved God, but that He loved us and sent His Son to be the propitiation for our sins" First John 4:10 (NKJ). Key number two is our love for Jesus. The John 16 verse says that the Father loves you "because you have loved Me [Jesus]." This key—our love for Jesus—grants us access to all the treasures to which we are entitled: salvation, security, love, joy, peace, heaven, etc.

How thankful I am for the keys God has provided for us to have access to Himself and His blessings! Rejoice that those keys hang on your key ring today.

#293
October 19: Life Begins at Conception

The moment in which egg and sperm come together, life begins. I remember the April 30, 1965 groundbreaking LIFE magazine pictorial entitled "The Drama of Life before Birth" which showcased the amazing photos taken by Lennart Nilsson of a pre-born baby. Using macro-lenses and endoscopes, the pictures took us inside of the womb to see life developing. I was further amazed years later when ultrasound technology enabled me to see my own baby growing inside of me. These pictures alone—even apart from the Biblical evidence stating that God knew us as real, living people in the womb—are rock-solid proof that life begins well before the moment of birth.

In the same way, God has designed that our eternal life begins well before the moment of our being ushered into Glory through our earthly death. Our eternal life begins at our conception, at the moment in which we are born again. What moment is that? We are born again at the moment in which we come to know God and Christ as our personal Lord and Savior. In John 17:3, Jesus succinctly explains, "And this is eternal life, that they may know You, the only true God, and Jesus Christ whom You have sent" (NKJ).

It's easy for us to understand the nine months of pregnancy as the developmental time for a baby, so let's start understanding our earthly lives for what they truly are: simply the gestational period that is getting us ready for Heaven. Proper nourishment now—a steady diet of the Word of God, prayer, and Christian service—will make us strong when we break through into Life. Death is merely our trip through the birth canal. A far better and entirely new existence awaits us forever in the presence of God. Hallelujah!

#294
October 20: The Grand Merger

Unfortunately, from time to time, we hear of churches splitting. One group is ticked off by what another group has done, the older folks like hymns while the younger folks like praise choruses, or the pastor makes a decision that sends a faction into a tizzy. This shameful phenomenon is nothing new; we've been separating almost as long as we've been the Church. According to an internet article entitled "Christian Denominations: The History and Evolution of Christian Denominations and Faith Groups," author Mary Fairchild says:

- There are numerous ways to dissect the many Christian faith groups. They can be separated into fundamentalist or conservative, mainline and liberal groups. They can be characterized by theological belief systems such as Calvinism and Arminianism. And lastly… Christians can be categorized into a vast number of denominations.

Yes, the Eastern Orthodox folks broke away from the Roman Catholic Church. Then the Protestant Reformation came along and the Lutherans started. The Methodists separated from them and the Baptists separated from them and on and on it goes. I'm sure the people who orchestrated each split felt they had sound reasons to do so, but any way you cut it (no pun intended), the final outcome was division.

Just before Jesus went to the Cross, He prayed for us. One of the key points He made to the Father was about unity. He prayed:

- "Now I am no longer in the world, but these are in the world, and I come to You. Holy Father, keep through Your name those whom You have given Me, *that they may be one* as We are… I do not pray for these alone, but also for those who will believe in Me through their word; *that they all may be one*, as You, Father, are in Me, and I in You; *that they also may be one* in Us, that the world may believe that You sent Me. And the glory which You gave Me I have given them, that *they may be one* just as We are one: I in them, and You in Me; *that they may be made perfect in one*, and that the world may know that You have sent Me, and have loved them as You have loved Me" John 17:11, 20-23 (NKJ, emphasis added).

Look at that: five times Jesus emphasized His desire for our unity with one another and with Him and His Father. This is important stuff.

For the past couple of weeks, I've seen the beginnings of what unity looks like here on earth. Instead of splitting, my church has merged with another church. Folks from the two congregations are getting to know one another and we're looking forward to growing together as believers and to working together as a family in the Lord's vineyard. I consider this to be one small example of what Heaven's going to be like. John saw it in the Revelation:

- "...the four living creatures and the twenty-four elders fell down before the Lamb... And they sang a new song, saying: "You are worthy to take the scroll, and to open its seals; for You were slain, and have redeemed us to God by Your blood out of every tribe and tongue and people and nation..." Revelation 5:8-9 (NKJ).

Do you see that? Jesus has redeemed folks "out of every tribe and tongue and people and nation." There will be no denominational flag-waving marches in Glory. Jesus' blood unites all believers. We might as well get used to it down here because we'll all be in Heaven together – forever.

#295
October 21: The Bitter and the Sweet

We're great at accepting pleasantries from God, but we pretty much stink at receiving negative circumstances from His hand. We've come to love a gospel that only teaches us about comfort, and we'd just as soon skip the verses about persecution and suffering. We want to bask with Jesus in His triumph, but skip identifying with Him in His tests.

Well, if we really want to be like Jesus, like Him we'll have to man-up and learn to take the bitter with the sweet. He did it. While Jesus was being arrested, Peter jumped up and was ready to take on the whole arresting mob. He got to one of the guys and sliced off his ear, but Jesus stopped him and said, "Put your sword into the sheath. Shall I not drink the cup which My Father has given Me?" John 18:11 (NKJ)

If Jesus could submit Himself to a hard situation, we must do so as well. Jesus said, "All men will hate you because of me, but he who stands firm to the end will be saved... A student is not above his teacher, nor a servant above his master. It is enough for the student to be like his teacher, and the servant like his master. If the head of the house has been called Beelzebub, how much more the members of his household!" Matt 10:22-25 (NIV)

God has something in mind when he allows us to confront the tough stuff we face. Jesus' bitter circumstance was the Cross that led to the sweet offering of our salvation. As for us, Romans 8:28-29 proclaims, "And we know that all things work together for good to those who love God, to those who are the called according to His purpose. For whom He foreknew, He also predestined to be conformed to the image of His Son, that He might be the firstborn among many brethren" (NKJ). No pain, no gain. No test, no testimony. No cross, no crown.

Trust me; I am not making light of the pain associated with bitter circumstances. Let's keep the truth in mind though that every bitter circumstance has one overarching goal in mind – to make us more like Christ. That is the sweet end of it all.

#296
October 22: Born to Die

The religious leaders were bent on killing Jesus but they couldn't do so legally because they were under Roman control. They had to take Jesus to Pilate, the representative of the Roman government in the region, to get him to pass down the judgment. Naturally, Pilate needed to interrogate Jesus to find just cause for putting Him to death. During that cross-examination, Pilate asked Jesus if He was a king. Jesus replied, "You say rightly that I am a king. For this cause I was born, and for this cause I have come into the world, that I should bear witness to the truth. Everyone who is of the truth hears My voice" John 18:37 (NKJ).

Pilate never did find a just cause to put Jesus to death and ended up literally washing his hands of the whole ordeal. Jesus, however, did speak to the cause or reason for His death. Look at the above verse again. Jesus says, "For this cause I was born, and for this cause I have come into the world." The cause Jesus was speaking of was His death. Jesus was saying, "In order to die is why I was born, and in order to die is why I have come into the world, that I should bear witness of the truth." The truth is that we have sinned, have missed the mark, have fallen short of the glory of God, and are all in desperate need of a Savior.

Jesus was born – sent into this world from His home in Heaven – to die. He was born to be our Savior. Isaiah prophesied to this fact. "But He was wounded for our transgressions, he was bruised for our iniquities; the chastisement for our peace was upon Him, and by His stripes we are healed. All we like sheep have gone astray; we have turned, every one, to his own way; and the LORD has laid on Him the iniquity of us all" Isaiah 53:5-6 (NKJ). The writer of the book of Romans reiterates this truth. "He was delivered over to death for our sins and was raised to life for our justification" Romans 4:25 (NIV). And Titus says it again. "[Jesus] gave himself for us to redeem us from all wickedness and to purify for himself a people that are his very own, eager to do what is good" Titus 2:14 (NIV).

That verse in Titus brings home how we should respond to Jesus' sacrifice. Since He carried out the purpose of His earthly life and died for our sins, we really should have no problem living our earthly lives in obedience to Him, joyfully realizing we are "his very own" and being "eager to do what is good." Thanks to Jesus being born to die for us, we were born to live for Him.

#297
October 23: Jesus Our Personal Savior

If you are a regular customer at Nordstrom, a fine department store, you can choose one of the salespeople to be your personal shopper. She will get to know you, your style preferences, and your career and lifestyle needs. Then whenever you are ready to shop, you can call her in advance, and she will have some choices waiting for you when you arrive. She'll also call you with a heads-up on sales and new arrivals. What a service!

In John, chapter 20, Jesus shows Himself to be, not our personal shopper, but our personal Savior. He knew Mary Magdalene's need as she stood outside His empty tomb, longing to know where He was. He stopped on His way to Heaven to comfort her. (See John 20:11-17.) Jesus also made a special trip to assure Thomas who would only believe Jesus was alive if he could see and touch the scars for himself. (See John 20:26-29.)

Like Mary and Thomas, sometimes, especially after traumatic events (they had seen the Lord die), we too need to be assured of His presence. The Lord may seem to us to be dead – unaware of our situation, unconcerned about our plight, or just plain gone. Take heart from what He did for Mary and Thomas. Know that He loves us so much, that He will stop what He's doing to show Himself to us.

Be on the lookout for your personal Savior's appearance. Jesus promised to always be with you (Matthew 28:20), He's living to intercede for you (Hebrews 7:25), and Second Corinthians 9:8 says, "And God is able to make all grace abound to you, so that in all things at all times, having all that you need, you will abound in every good work" (NIV). Since He knows your needs, He's on the lookout for you. What a service!

#298
October 24: Expect the Unexpected

Mary Magdelene approached the garden tomb with spices, expecting to anoint the body of her Lord. She brought something to give Him. He had done so much for her; she expected to do something for Him. She knew where to find Him, and she expected Him to be there in the same way she had seen Him last – still and dead.

She saw Him all right. She was in the right garden and He indeed He was there, but she saw Him in a way she didn't expect. We read of the scene in John chapter 20.

But Mary stood outside by the tomb weeping, and as she wept she stooped down and looked into the tomb. And she saw two angels in white sitting, one at the head and the other at the feet, where the body of Jesus had lain. Then they said to her, "Woman, why are you weeping?"
She said to them, "Because they have taken away my Lord, and I do not know where they have laid Him."
Now when she had said this, she turned around and saw Jesus standing there, and did not know that it was Jesus. Jesus said to her, "Woman, why are you weeping?

319

Whom are you seeking?"

She, supposing Him to be the gardener, said to Him, "Sir, if You have carried Him away, tell me where You have laid Him, and I will take Him away."

Jesus said to her, "Mary!"

She turned and said to Him, "Rabboni!" (which is to say, Teacher).

Jesus said to her, "Do not cling to Me, for I have not yet ascended to My Father; but go to My brethren and say to them, 'I am ascending to My Father and your Father, and to My God and your God.'" John 20:11-17 (NKJ)

Jesus was outside of the tomb and very much alive! What Mary had brought was well-intentioned and no doubt even appreciated, but on this morning, her gift was not needed. Instead, Jesus had something extra-special in store for her — Himself.

Let's approach church and devotional times expecting to see the Lord. But don't be surprised: He's liable to show up with something extra-special in store for you too. Be ready to meet the resurrected Lord daily. Hallelujah, He is risen. He is risen indeed!

#299
October 25: Enough Proof

I teach at a Christian high school where we have 1300 students, yet not all of our students have a saving faith in Jesus Christ. Interestingly, our academic program is so strong that families of other faiths (Hindu, Muslim, Jewish, etc.) send their children there. In a conversation with one of those children, I asked, "What are your thoughts about Jesus Christ." She answered, "I respect what this school believes; however, I lean more toward the scientific and I don't believe in people coming back from the dead."

Thankfully and all things being equal, we have two more years with this young lady to present our Christian case. And thankfully, we do so prayerfully, day by day, in every class, and in chapel services. As Christians, we need to realize that the case for Christianity is strong and there are many arguments to prove its truth. Although the Biblical record is enough, proof outside of the Bible exists as well. Take, for example, the record left by

Flavius Josephus, a historian who lived at the time of Christ. Information found at www.josephus.org/#testimonium discusses *The Testimonium Flavianum*, which contains Josephus' account of Jesus:

> In Rome, in the year 93, Josephus published his lengthy history of the Jews. While discussing the period in which the Jews of Judaea were governed by the Roman procurator Pontius Pilate, Josephus included the following account:

> About this time there lived Jesus, a wise man, if indeed one ought to call him a man. For he was one who performed surprising deeds and was a teacher of such people as accept the truth gladly. He won over many Jews and many of the Greeks. He was the Messiah. And when, upon the accusation of the principal men among us, Pilate had condemned him to a cross, those who had first come to love him did not cease. He appeared to them spending a third day restored to life, for the prophets of God had foretold these things and a thousand other marvels about him. And the tribe of the Christians, so called after him, has still to this day not disappeared.

Proof of the existence of God abounds already. Romans 1:19-20 tells us that "what may be known about God is plain to them, because God has made it plain to them. For since the creation of the world God's invisible qualities—his eternal power and divine nature—have been clearly seen, being understood from what has been made, so that men are without excuse" (NIV). Still, God took the time to pad the proof with sources like the writings of Josephus, outside of the Biblical record. Those proclaiming to have more rational or scientific minds, must then deal with the existence of historical evidence.

When Thomas, one of Jesus' own disciples, requested proof of His resurrection, Jesus appeared to Him and replied, "Thomas, because you have seen Me, you have believed. Blessed are those who have not seen and yet have believed" John 20:29 (NKJ). John's passage continues with the following commentary, "And truly Jesus did many other signs in the presence of His disciples, which are not written in this book; but these are written that you may believe that Jesus is the Christ, the

Son of God, and that believing you may have life in His name"
John 20:30-31 (NKJ).

Certainly there is enough both inside and outside of the
Bible to authenticate the existence, death, burial, and resurrection
of Jesus Christ. The question is, what are you going to do with
that evidence?

#300
October 26: You Follow Me

A group of acquaintances and I recently engaged in a
conversation about commitment to the dictates of the Bible. When
the discussion turned to tithing, one young lady said, "Miss me
with that. What about you?"
One of the classic dodges used when folks start feeling
convicted is to try to redirect the conversation. They think that the
revelation of your shortcomings excuses theirs. Buzz. Wrong
answer!
Jesus dealt with this very deflection technique with Peter.
After His resurrection, Jesus visited with some of His disciples and
found they had decided to return to fishing. After challenging
Peter's love for Him and telling Peter about the kind of death he'd
die for the glory of God, Peter tried to shift the focus. John 21:20-
22 records the conversation:

- Then Peter, turning around, saw the disciple whom Jesus
  loved following, who also had leaned on His breast at the
  supper, and said, "Lord, who is the one who betrays You?"
  Peter, seeing him, said to Jesus, "But Lord, what about this
  man?"
- Jesus said to him, "If I will that he remain till I come, what
  is that to you? You follow Me." (NKJ)

We need to quit worrying about everybody else. Judgment
Day has no pinch hitters. Each one of us will stand before God for
ourselves. No matter how God communicates His truth to us, and
no matter who says it, the bottom line is still the same. Jesus
says, "*You* follow Me."

Part 5

Glimpses of God

In the

Letters (Epistles)

And

The Revelation

(66 Devotions)

#301
October 27: Ten Key Facts about Jesus

The book of Acts is part two of the testimony of Luke about the life of Jesus. After starting the book by telling about Jesus' ascension into heaven (see Acts 1:9), Luke tells about the Day of Pentecost when the Holy Spirit first filled all those initial followers of Jesus (see Acts 2:4). Pouring out of the room where they were assembled, those filled followers were heard speaking about the "wonderful works of God" in the languages of people from all over the known world (See Acts 2:5-11). When it was noted that all of those speakers were Galilean, Peter stood up to explain what was going on. His talk—the initial sermon of the Church—began with a list of 10 key facts about Jesus:

1. Jesus is from Nazareth.
2. He is a Man attested by God... by miracles, wonders, and signs which God did through Him.
3. He was delivered by the determined purpose and foreknowledge of God... taken by lawless hands... crucified, and put to death.
4. The pains of death couldn't hold Him.
5. David... being a prophet... spoke concerning the resurrection of the Christ, that His soul was not left in Hades, nor did His flesh see corruption.
6. God has raised [Jesus] up.
7. [Jesus is] exalted to the right hand of God
8. And having received from the Father the promise of the Holy Spirit, He poured out this [all the believers speaking in other languages] which you now see and hear.
9. Jesus is sitting at God's right hand until God makes all of Jesus' enemies His footstool.
10. God has made this Jesus... both Lord and Christ. Acts 2:22-36 (NKJ)

What a marvelous list! This is by no means an exhaustive inventory. Our Bible is full of life-changing facts about our Savior. However, the beginning of Peter's sermon here is a great way to start a day—bringing to mind these wonderful truths about our Lord.

#302
October 28: Identity

I read through the Bible each year using *My Utmost Devotional Bible.*[3] Each day's reading is divided into four parts, so I read a selection each from the Old Testament, Psalms, Proverbs, and the New Testament. The selections are in order, Genesis to Revelation, and it's amazing how on many days, the readings from the different sections of the Bible still carry a consistent message and give parallel insight.

Such was the case again when First Chronicles chapters 1 and 2 were coupled with Acts chapter 4. In what could have been a very boring list of names in the Old Testament chapters, I noticed the women who were mentioned. Their distinction was who their fathers were, who their husbands were, or who their sons were. In other words, they received their identity from the men in their lives.

As I pondered that, I read the New Testament selection, Acts 4:1-22. In this account, the Sadducees and the rulers of the synagogue faced off with Peter and John after the healing of the lame man. Those leaders couldn't deny the miracle, took note of the apostles' boldness, "and they realized that they had been with Jesus" (Acts 4:13d).

Wow! Do you see it? Identity comes not from who we are, but from with whom we are associated. We would know nothing about the women in the Bible had they been pushing to make a name for themselves. We know their identity and their influence because of their connections with the men in their lives. The synagogue leaders would probably have ignored Peter and John had it not been for their identity as followers of Jesus.

Regardless of our gender or earthly marital status, as believers, we should still draw our identity from the Man in our life. What is your identification with the God-man, Jesus Christ?

#303
October 29: The Whole Package

If you give someone a wallet as a gift, the customary thing to do is to also put some money in it. Since wallets are supposed

---

[3] My Utmost Devotional Bible. Thomas Nelson, Inc., 1992.

327 GLIMPSES OF GOD

to hold money, when the receiver opens the gift and looks through it, she will realize she's received the whole package. With that philosophy in mind, I guess we should follow that line of reasoning with other gifts.

- When we give a new suitcase, we should fill it with clothes.
- When we give a coffee mug, place a package of coffee beans in the box.
- When we give a toiletry bag, include travel-sized products.
- And when we give a car, fill it with gas.

Peter realized that God was this kind of giver. When addressing the council who had commanded him not to teach in the name of Jesus, Peter answered that he'd keep doing so since he and the other apostles were "...His witnesses... and so also is the Holy Spirit whom God has given to those who obey Him" Acts 5:32 (NKJ).

You see, Peter knew that as one of God's obedient children, he had received the whole package—God, Jesus Christ, and the Holy Spirit—upon which he could rely. The three (the Trinity) are one gift, fully ours at the moment of salvation. Just as wallets are places that hold money, so we—the children of God—are vessels that house the Holy Spirit. The money in our wallets allows us to do the things we need to do; the Holy Spirit in our lives allows us to do the things for God we need to do; i.e., carry and live out His plan in our sphere of influence.

God sure knows how to fill a gift bag!

#304
October 30: Can't Touch This

Wikipedia tells us that "U Can't Touch This," MC Hammer's 1990 hit signature song, was the primary reason the singer's album that year sold more than 10 million copies. The lyrics describe the rapper as having "toured around the world, from London to the Bay" and as being "magic on the mic." The point of the song was to say that no one else was as good or could come even close to rapping like he did. The catchphrase "can't touch this" became a part of the culture, expressed whenever you wanted to claim superiority at whatever you were doing.

If M.C. Hammer had been around during the time of the

early church, Gamaliel may have used the phrase as he talked some sense into the religious leaders who were trying to stop the apostles from teaching in Jesus' name. After being sternly commanded not to teach of Christ anymore, Peter and the other apostles persisted anyway. In Acts chapter 5, the leaders tried throwing them in prison, but God busted them out, and they went right back to preaching. When rearrested, Peter boldly proclaimed, "We ought to obey God rather than men. The God of our fathers raised up Jesus whom you murdered by hanging on a tree. Him God has exalted to His right hand to be Prince and Savior, to give repentance to Israel and forgiveness of sins. And we are His witnesses to these things, and so also is the Holy Spirit whom God has given to those who obey Him" Acts 5:29-32 (NKJ).

Needless to say, this didn't sit too well with those leaders. They were furious and decided to find a way to kill the apostles too. That's when Gamaliel, described as "a teacher of the law held in respect by all the people" (verse 34), stepped in. He reminded the leaders that others had presented themselves, gained a following, and then in time the excitement wore off and things got back to normal. He ends his discourse by saying, "And now I say to you, keep away from these men and let them alone; for if this plan or this work is of men, it will come to nothing; but if it is of God, you cannot overthrow it-- lest you even be found to fight against God" Acts 5:38-39 (NKJ).

Gamaliel realized you "can't touch this" when something is of God. Be encouraged today in what you are doing for God. Keep in mind that no matter how hard others may try to stop you – including the devil in hell – nothing that God wants done will ever be left undone.

Everything that God has established for you to accomplish will indeed be accomplished by you. Just look the haters in the face and say, "Can't touch this!"

#305
October 31: Rest Stops

When James and I take road trips, we enjoy cruising along the highways, taking in the scenery, discussing various topics, and speculating about what's going on in various locations we pass. Even though we take just as much pleasure in covering the miles as we do in reaching our destination, we still have to stop periodically for rejuvenation. The highway designers realized this necessity and added rest stops along the road every so many miles.

This isn't a new idea. God provides rest stops all along our life's journey. To every busy day, He gives a night. We're to stop, sleep, and allow our bodies to recharge. To every week, He gives a Sabbath. We're to stop working, rest, and turn our minds and hearts to Him. To every year, He gives seasons: times in which the earth itself goes through its cycles of growth and rest. And to every trial, He gives an end: the end that He deems best, and the end that always leads to some new beginning.

One Biblical example of a rest stop happened for the early Church after the conversion of Saul, who would later be known as the Apostle Paul. This Saul had been the one guarding the coats of those who stoned Stephen (see Acts 7:58 and 8:1), and chasing down Christians to arrest and kill them (see Acts 9:1). Once Saul was converted, God provided a rest stop. Acts 9:31 tells us, "Then the churches throughout all Judea, Galilee, and Samaria had peace and were edified. And walking in the fear of the Lord and in the comfort of the Holy Spirit, they were multiplied" (NKJ).

Several things happen during God's rest stops. First, there's peace. Thanks to that peace, the second happening is edification. The rest stop is the time to be nourished and fortified by the Word of God so we can grow strong. (We'll need this strength for the next trial.) Third, because of our remembrance of the trial and our thankfulness of God's deliverance, we should be caught "walking in the fear of the Lord." In other words, we should emerge from a trial with a deeper respect for God.

The fourth thing that happens during God's rest stops blew me away! We reach a place of receiving "comfort of the Holy Spirit." The Greek word for comfort used here is "paraklesis (par-ak'-lay-sis)" which comes from another Greek word meaning "imploration, hortation, and solace." To implore means to ask or beg, and something that is hortatory serves to encourage, gives advice, exhorts, and urges to good deeds. Solace is relief; an easing of grief, loneliness, and discomfort. When we combine all of this, we see that the Holy Spirit is much more than the much-needed listening ear or shoulder as we pour out our hearts about the difficulty of our trial. He serves to literally usher into our lives the perfect relief to our struggle, sorrow, or pain. Additionally, He then encourages us to move forward, giving us divine instruction (remember, the Holy Spirit is a member of the Trinity) on exactly how to do just that. Wow! Talk about filling up the tank!

Finally, at God's rest stops, our lives are multiplied. For the early Church, that meant more converts. For us, it may mean anything: renewed health, a refurbished lifestyle, a restocked refrigerator, restored character, a re-energized following, a refilled bank account. God's multiplication can be applied to any area of our lives.

So what's the bottom line? When we're in or facing a trial, know that rough spots are part of the journey, but rest stops are provided all along the way.

#306
November 1: God is not Racist; Why are We?

One of the clearest passages in the Bible against racism is the story of Peter and Cornelius the centurion. The Bible describes this Roman soldier as "a devout man and one who feared God with all his household, who gave alms generously to the people, and prayed to God always" Acts 10:2 (NKJ). Read all of Acts, chapter 2, for the complete story, but in a nutshell, Cornelius received a message from God to have Peter come to his house and tell him what he had to do. In the meantime, God prepared Peter, a devout Jew who would have no kind of personal or social relationship with any Gentile, to preach the Gospel to Cornelius. God did this by presenting Peter the option to eat some animals the Jews had come to know as "unclean." When Peter protested, God told him, "What God has cleansed you must not call common" Acts 10:15. When Cornelius' messengers arrived moments later to summon him, Peter got the clue. Upon arrival at Cornelius' home, Peter announced, "You know how unlawful it is for a Jewish man to keep company with or go to one of another nation. But God has shown me that I should not call any man common or unclean" Acts 10:28.

We do a lot of talking about being changed and becoming like Christ once we are believers. We agree with verses like the following:

- Romans 8:29 – "For whom He foreknew, He also predestined to be conformed to the image of His Son, that He might be the firstborn among many brethren" (NKJ).
- Romans 12:2 – "And do not be conformed to this world, but be transformed by the renewing of your mind, that you may prove what is that good and acceptable and perfect will of God" (NKJ).
- Romans 13:14 – "But put on the Lord Jesus Christ, and make no provision for the flesh, to fulfill its lusts (NKJ).
- Second Corinthians 3:18 – "But we all, with unveiled face, beholding as in a mirror the glory of the Lord, are being transformed into the same image from glory to glory, just as by the Spirit of the Lord" (NKJ).

If we are truly going to manifest the likeness of Christ in our lives, we are going to have to emulate His point of view on every subject, including racism. God's word on race relations never applied to skin color, social status, or country of origin. God's only restriction in doing business, in forming military alliances, or even in getting married had to do with a spiritual component. "Do not be unequally yoked together with unbelievers. For what fellowship has righteousness with lawlessness? And what communion has light with darkness?" Second Corinthians 6:14 (NKJ)

What do we think Ephesians 4:24 means when it says, "and that you put on the new man which was created according to God, in true righteousness and holiness" (NKJ)? Being like God and thinking in a righteous and holy manner means we conform ourselves to think like He thinks, regardless of our upbringing, our past experiences, and definitely despite our own prejudices. All of that changes at the Cross.

Once Peter heard the word of the Lord, he obeyed and immediately changed his way of thinking. He crossed the prejudicial lines of his culture because God had clearly shown him that racism was wrong. Other people's views are not our responsibility. We are held accountable by God to God as to whether or not we operate according to God's views. Since God is not racist, we cannot justify racist views within ourselves.

#307
November 2: God's Story in a Nutshell

It has been said that the Bible is a history book. That's true: the Bible is His-story. During the early days of the Church as recorded in the book of Acts, the apostles took occasion to tell and retell how the Old Testament record connected with their present-day happenings in the person of Jesus Christ. If Paul had to put a title on the message he gave in Acts 13, I believe he may have called it "How the Old and the New Collide." Here's the transcript:

"Men of Israel, and you who fear God, listen: The God of this people Israel chose our fathers, and exalted the people when they dwelt as strangers in the land of Egypt, and with an uplifted arm He brought them out of it. Now for a time of about forty years He put up with their ways in the wilderness. And when He had destroyed seven nations in the land of Canaan, He distributed their land to them by allotment.

"After that He gave them judges for about four hundred and fifty years, until Samuel the prophet. And afterward they asked for a king; so God gave them Saul the son of Kish, a man of the tribe of Benjamin, for forty years. And when He had removed him, He raised up for them David as king, to whom also He gave testimony and said, 'I have found David the son of Jesse, a man after My own heart, who will do all My will.'

"From this man's seed, according to the promise, God raised up for Israel a Savior—Jesus—after John had first preached, before His coming, the baptism of repentance to all the people of Israel. And as John was finishing his course, he said, 'Who do you think I am? I am not He. But behold, there comes One after me, the sandals of whose feet I am not worthy to loose.'

"Men and brethren, sons of the family of Abraham, and those among you who fear God, to you the word of this salvation has been sent. For those who dwell in Jerusalem, and their rulers, because they did not know Him, nor even the voices of the Prophets which are read every Sabbath, have fulfilled them in condemning Him. And though they found no cause for death in Him, they asked Pilate that He should be put to death. Now when they had fulfilled all that was written concerning Him, they took Him down from the tree and laid Him in a tomb.

"But God raised Him from the dead. He was seen for many days by those who came up with Him from Galilee to Jerusalem, who are His witnesses to the people. And we declare to you glad tidings—that promise which was made to the fathers. God has fulfilled this for us their children, in that He has raised up Jesus...

"Therefore let it be known to you, brethren, that through this Man is preached to you the forgiveness of sins; and by Him everyone who believes is justified from all things from which you could not be justified by the law of Moses" Acts 13:16-39 (NKJ).

Amen; preach it, Paul!

#308
November 3: You Need Jesus; I'm Just Sayin'

One of my favorite t-shirts says, "You Need Jesus; I'm Just Sayin'." When I saw the shirt, I knew I had to have it because that's the message my life is all about. The importance of this message is so very clear that I don't want anyone to miss it. Without Jesus, you are living your life in vain. Oh, you may be the most philanthropic person others ever meet, giving away your last dime if another human being can be helped. But in the end, those acts of kindness will be isolated incidences that flashed beautiful like fireworks then faded into smoke. You may be one who has shunned the comforts of this world, choosing instead to pass through life quietly and unobtrusively in an effort to bring no pain on anyone else. That's lovely, but again, hurting no one is not the qualification of entering into eternal rest when you die.

This life on Earth is fleeting. At the most, some people nowadays can live to be about 110. That sounds like a lot of years until you hold that up against all time since Creation. What's 110 years? But hold on; that 110 years are merely the starting point, the dress rehearsal for what is to come. Once conceived, your eternity began. Yes, be concerned about what you'll do with your years on this planet, but it makes sense to be even more concerned about where you'll spend the rest of your eternity. Regarding that issue, there are only two choices: heaven or hell. Of those two choices, only one makes sense: heaven. And to get into heaven, there's only one passage: through Jesus Christ whose death and resurrection affected the forgiveness of our sins. Consider the following proof texts:

- Therefore, my brothers, I want you to know that through Jesus the forgiveness of sins is proclaimed to you.

Through him everyone who believes is justified from everything you could not be justified from by the law of Moses. Acts 13:38-39 (NIV)

- ...God anointed Jesus of Nazareth with the Holy Spirit and power... All the prophets testify about him that everyone who believes in him receives forgiveness of sins through his name." Acts 10:38 and 43 (NIV)
- Then Jesus said to them again, "Most assuredly, I say to you, I am the door of the sheep. John 10:7 (NKJ)
- Salvation is found in no one else, for there is no other name under heaven given to men by which we must be saved." Acts 4:12 (NIV)
- For Christ died for sins once for all, the righteous for the unrighteous, to bring you to God. He was put to death in the body but made alive by the Spirit. First Peter 3:18 (NIV)
- No one who denies the Son has the Father; whoever acknowledges the Son has the Father also. First John 2:23 (NIV)
- And I saw in the right hand of Him who sat on the throne a book written inside and on the back, sealed up with seven seals. And I saw a strong angel proclaiming with a loud voice, "Who is worthy to open the book and to break its seals?" ...the Lion that is from the tribe of Judah, the Root of David, has overcome so as to open the book and its seven seals." And when He had taken the book, the four living creatures and the twenty-four elders fell down before the Lamb... And they sang a new song, saying, "Worthy art Thou to take the book, and to break its seals; for Thou wast slain, and didst purchase for God with Thy blood {men} from every tribe and tongue and people and nation. Rev 5:1-2, 5, 8-9 (NAS)
- If anyone's name was not found written in the book of life, he was thrown into the lake of fire. Revelation 20:15 (NIV)
- Jesus said..., "I am the way, the truth, and the life. No one comes to the Father except through Me. John 14:6 (NKJ)

If as of yet, you haven't gotten right with Jesus, what are you waiting for? As my t-shirt proclaims, "You need Jesus; I'm just sayin'.

(Read Romans 3:23, Romans 5:8, Romans 6:23, and Romans

10:9-10 to get right with Jesus. Then please send me a note on this blog to let me know that your name is now written in the Lamb's Book of Life!)

#309
November 4: Sit Beside the Source

I remember playing the telephone game as a kid. My friends and I would sit around the room and the first person would whisper a message into the ear of the person next to her. Then that person would whisper the message to the next person, and so on. The rules were that you could say the message only once and you had to pass along exactly what you thought you heard. The last person to receive the message would report it out loud. Inevitably, the final message would be vastly different from the original one. Sometimes the last message was so distorted that it was completely nonsensical and often even unintelligible.

We'd all have a good laugh at how far from the original the final message became. Then we'd try to figure out where the message got screwed up. The people near the end the chain would swear they heard what they heard, while the people near the source of the message insisted they communicated the right thing clearly. All in fun, we'd point out the blame, and then we'd play our next round, determined to get it right this time. We never did.

I think it's possible for this to happen to us when it comes to the Word of God. When we are not praying and reading the Bible for ourselves, we rely on others to communicate God's message to us. How do we know they heard it right? There's only one way to know: sit beside the Source. I'm not saying don't go to church, or listen to Christian speakers, or read Christian books. What I am saying is that we should be like the Bereans who God calls "of noble character" because "they received the message with great eagerness and examined the Scriptures every day to see if what Paul said was true" Acts 17:11 (NIV).

What is God whispering directly into your ear today?

#310
November 5: Let Me Explain

Sometimes, we may feel a bit intimidated in the company of people who seem more educated than we are. We may feel especially so if the conversation turns to philosophy and religion. Just about everybody has his or her ideas about right and wrong and who God is. And lots of people enjoy a good debate about these subjects; that is, until it gets personal.

Debate gets us no where but to the valley of frustration unless it can lead to the truth. No matter what anyone says or believes, there is such a thing as truth, of which the Bible says it has the power to set us free (see John 8:32). Paul shows us a great example of how to turn a philosophical conversation around and head it toward the truth. Feel free to use his argument the next time you find yourself in a debate about the true and living God.

Men of Athens [insert the name of the group or person you are addressing], I perceive that in all things you are very religious; for as I was passing through and considering the objects of your worship, I even found an altar with this inscription: TO THE UNKNOWN GOD. Therefore, the One whom you worship without knowing, Him I proclaim to you:

God, who made the world and everything in it, since He is Lord of heaven and earth, does not dwell in temples made with hands. Nor is He worshiped with men's hands, as though He needed anything, since He gives to all life, breath, and all things. And He has made from one blood every nation of men to dwell on all the face of the earth, and has determined their preappointed times and the boundaries of their dwellings, so that they should seek the Lord, in the hope that they might grope for Him and find Him, though He is not far from each one of us; for in Him we live and move and have our being, as also some of your own poets have said, 'For we are also His offspring.'

Therefore, since we are the offspring of God, we ought not to think that the Divine Nature is like gold or silver or stone, something shaped by art and man's devising. Truly, these times of ignorance God overlooked, but now commands all men everywhere to repent, because He has appointed a day on which He will judge the world in righteousness by the Man whom He has ordained. He has given assurance of this to all by raising Him from the dead. Acts 17:22-31 (NKJ)

#311
November 6: Nothing Boring about God

If there's one thing I'm sure about, it's the realization that Heaven will not be boring. Think about it: we'll be spending eternity with God almighty, the self-existent One. He's the one who came up with the idea of galaxies, universes, planets, moons, and stars. He thought up water and made bodies of it freeze from top to bottom so the fish wouldn't be in the frozen food section before they were caught. He designed the human body with the ability to fight to heal itself. He put fragrance and color in the flowers, taste in the food, and melodies and harmonies in music.

God didn't do things the same way in history either. Sometimes He allowed an army to defeat its foe, and at other times He told the army to stand still while He confused the enemy for them. At times, healing came through a word; at others, it came through a touch. He even proved that He could switch up all that we're used to and do things in a completely unusual way. Consider Acts 19:11-12: "Now God worked unusual miracles by the hands of Paul, so that even handkerchiefs or aprons were brought from his body to the sick, and the diseases left them and the evil spirits went out of them" (NKJ).

We can never put God in our little boxes. He is completely and totally sovereign. He does what He wants, when He wants, how He wants, where He wants, and to whom He wants. And I believe, with a twinkle in His all-seeing eyes, He delights in surprising us with His unusual moves from time to time. Surely a God with so much imagination will be able to schedule our eternity to be interesting enough to keep our attention.

#312
November 7: The Blessing Overflow

When returning home from a conference one Saturday, my itinerary called for me to fly from Indianapolis, IN, through Chicago's Midway airport, and then into Los Angeles. All that previous week, the Midwest had experienced wild thunderstorms. On the Friday before my trip home, I talked to my husband about how I was tired and could hardly wait to get home. He informed me that the news had reported the closure of the Chicago airports that day due to the weather.

Oh no, I thought, I have to get home. It then dawned on me that I knew Someone who could handle just such a situation. During a storm once, Jesus "arose and rebuked the wind, and said to the sea, 'Peace, be still!' And the wind (you know, the ones He created) ceased and there was a great calm" Mark 4:39 (NKJ, words in parenthesis are my own). So on Saturday morning before my flight, I prayed. "God," I said, "I need to get home today. Please do to the thunderstorms over the Midwest as you did to the storm in the Bible. Thanks."

We took off from Indianapolis on a beautiful, bright, sunny morning, but by the time we reached Chicago, the plane was rocking and rolling in turbulence. As we broke through the cloud bank, rain was hitting the windows. The stewardess even told us to watch our step as we exited the aircraft because the jetway was wet. But I knew what I had prayed.

I had a three-hour layover there in Chicago, so I bought some food and found a seat at my gate facing large windows. I settled in, plugged in my computer, and started eating my brunch. As time clicked by, I also watched the clouds. With each passing moment, the sky grew clearer and clearer. More and more blue and less and less clouds were visible. God had said, "Peace, be still," to the weather just for me. By the time my flight took off, the sky for miles was clear.

It was all I could do to keep from laughing out loud and telling everybody on the plane why they too were getting to Los Angeles right then. It dawned on me that every other plane heading anywhere out of Chicago at that time was doing so because God had heard my little prayer and loved me enough to say, "Okay, my daughter." All those people were receiving a blessing overflow. Later that night, as my husband and I watched the news, to my amazement, the report was all about the wicked thunderstorms over Chicago.

A blessing overflow also happened to people traveling with Paul in Acts. Storms were so bad during a sea voyage that survival looked pretty bleak. However, an angel of God appeared to Paul and told him, "Do not be afraid, Paul; you must be brought before Caesar; and indeed God has granted you all those who sail with you" Acts 27:24 (NKJ).

People should want to hang around us because God's dropping blessings our way. Those who stick close will have no other choice but to receive a blessing overflow.

#313
November 8: The Big Payback

Do you remember when you were a kid and someone got away with doing something to you that you didn't like? You probably yelled something like, "I'm gonna get you for that!" You then went about for days and days plotting and planning as to how you were going to pull off the big payback for whatever had been perpetrated upon you. You expended lots of mental energy thinking through each possible scenario until you came up with the perfect plan so your enemy would know she was suffering because of her actions toward you. She had it coming.

Unlike us, God is not vindictive in His retribution; He's simply acting out of either His justice or His mercy. The payback you receive from Him depends upon your response to Him. Consider Romans 2:6-11:

[God] ...will render to each one according to his deeds: eternal life to those who by patient continuance in doing good seek for glory, honor, and immortality; but to those who are self-seeking and do not obey the truth, but obey unrighteousness-- indignation and wrath, tribulation and anguish, on every soul of man who does evil, of the Jew first and also of the Greek; but glory, honor, and peace to everyone who works what is good, to the Jew first and also to the Greek. For there is no partiality with God. (NKJ)

God is not up in His heaven pacing back and forth, pounding His right fist in His left hand, gritting His teeth, and seething about how He plans to get us back for all the wrong we've done toward Him. He's not plotting and planning as He hisses, "I'm gonna get you for that!" To the contrary, through the sacrificial and atoning death of His very own Son, Jesus Christ, God's mercy has reached out to us to payback blessing for our evil. "To each according to his deeds...to everyone who works what is good," the big payback is eternal life, glory, honor, and peace. The payback of indignation, wrath, tribulation, and anguish—paid from the account of justice—is the alternate payment meted out "on every soul of man who does evil."

There will be a big payback for both the evil and the good. Here's the question: which pay-out group are you in?

#314
November 9: In Context

It is important to understand the context in which any comment is made. Many a misunderstanding has happened thanks to taking comments out of context. The same is true regarding the Word of God. Many a misunderstanding about spiritual things has happened because of taking Scripture out of context.

A very common mistake is made with the part of Romans 4:17 that says, "...calleth those things which be not as though they were" (KJV). Folks take this personally and say in prayer that they will make things happen by calling what they want into existence. That would be great if it were true, but it's not. The context of this verse is a discussion about justification by faith. Abraham was declared righteous by God, not because of the Law, but because of his faith. The promise passes down to us because "God, who gives life to the dead ...calls those things which do not exist as though they did" (NKJ).

Notice two things: first, God is the one calling things into existence, not us. Second, this verse isn't about getting stuff we want. It's about God turning us into what we weren't before.

So keep this in mind: Read Scripture for what it actually says. "The main thing to keep in mind here is that no prophecy of Scripture is a matter of private opinion. And why? Because it's not something concocted in the human heart. Prophecy resulted when the Holy Spirit prompted men and women to speak God's Word" Second Peter 1:20 (The Message).

God wrote us a book, so He obviously meant for His words to be understood. Let's not only understand that Romans 4:17 tells us that God is the only One—the Creator—able to call something out of nothing; but let us also understand all of Scripture in context. That way, we'll be able to apply the whole counsel of God accurately and effectively to each of life's circumstances.

#315
November 10: Dark Room Development

In my senior year of high school, I worked on yearbook staff and was editor of one of the sections of the volume. Our student photographers on staff not only took the pictures, but developed them right there at the school in our darkroom. Using only the illumination of a special red light, the film would be transferred somehow to the paper and then the paper would be dipped in several different trays holding chemical solutions. As the photos were moved from tray to tray, the image began to emerge. The process took a considerable amount of time and care and seemed almost magical.

Understandably, our teacher and those photographers would get quite upset if someone opened the dark room door while they worked. Too much light would flood in and mess up every piece of film on which they had been painstakingly laboring. More than those pictures would be ruined. All the money for the film and the time those photographers had logged on their assignments had been a waste. Deadlines for getting the yearbook pages designed were pushed back without those photos. And suppose those pictures had been of the miraculous catch that won the homecoming game, the photo-finish at the swim meet, or the principal's surprise 50th birthday party thrown by the whole school? The photographic memories of those events could never again be recaptured. The darkness of that dark room made the proper development of those pictures possible so that everything else necessary to produce a memorable yearbook could happen.

God allows dark rooms to develop us. When we are experiencing the darknesses of financial reversals, failures, job losses, strenuous challenges, sicknesses, disappointments, loneliness, separations, and deaths; we need to look at things through the "red" of the blood of Jesus. Like the photographers, wait patiently inside the dark room and watch as God takes time and care to develop the picture of your life that He's taken. Don't rush through any of the stages; endure every "chemical." Only when the process is complete will you be fully developed. You'll only be ready for use on just the right "pages" of life when His image emerges through you.

Be encouraged by the following verses of Scripture as you face your dark rooms:

- Romans 5:3-5 – Not only so, but we also rejoice in our sufferings, because we know that suffering produces perseverance; perseverance, character; and character, hope. And hope does not disappoint us, because God has poured out his love into our hearts by the Holy Spirit, whom he has given us. (NIV)

- Second Corinthians 4:17-18 – For our light and momentary troubles are achieving for us an eternal glory that far outweighs them all. So we fix our eyes not on what is seen, but on what is unseen. For what is seen is temporary, but what is unseen is eternal. (NIV)

- Hebrews 12:6 and 11 – For whom the Lord loves He chastens, and scourges every son whom He receives. Now no chastening seems to be joyful for the present, but painful; nevertheless, afterward it yields the peaceable fruit of righteousness to those who have been trained by it. (NKJ)

#316
November 11: God Knows Your Name

Having taught school for over 27 years, there are a lot of previous students in my past. From time to time, I meet them at an event or in a store. Inevitably I usually know their faces but I can't remember their names and they always expect me to. I'm thinking, *Come on, now. The mathematical comparison is completely lopsided between how many teachers' names you had to remember in 13 years and how many students' names I had to remember in 27.* Numerous memories of the great times we shared are indelibly printed, but I humbly request that they please don't hold it against me if I can't remember every name.

On the rare occasion when I can remember a former student's name, I see an amazing grin flash across his or her face. That smile reminds me of how special I feel knowing that this child remembered me fondly. And that special feeling speaks to the worth of what I do as an educator and mentor of young people, which in turn encourages my worth as a human being and a Christian.

I get it; it's nice to be remembered by name. In chapter 16 of the book of Romans, Paul impressed me by giving shout-outs to people he knew by name. And he had some names to remember like Priscilla and Aquila, Epaenetus, Andronicus, Junia, Amplias, Urbanus, Stachys, Apelles, Aristobulus, etc. But not only that, Paul remembered something about each one of them as well:

- Greet Priscilla and Aquila, my fellow workers in Christ Jesus who risked their own necks for my life, to whom not only I give thanks, but also all the churches of the Gentiles. Likewise greet the church that is in their house. (verses 3-5a)
- Greet my beloved Epaenetus, who is the firstfruits of Achaia to Christ. (verse 5b)
- Greet Mary, who labored much for us. (verse 6)
- Greet Andronicus and Junia, my countrymen and my fellow prisoners, who are of note among the apostles, who also were in Christ before me. (verse 7)
- Greet Amplias, my beloved in the Lord. (verse 8)
- Greet Urbanus, our fellow worker in Christ, and Stachys, my beloved. (verse 9)
- Greet Apelles, approved in Christ. (verse 10a)
- Greet Herodion, my countryman. (verse 11a)
- Greet Tryphena and Tryphosa, who have labored in the Lord. Greet the beloved Persis, who labored much in the Lord. (verse 12)
- Greet Rufus, chosen in the Lord, and his mother and mine. (verse 13)

Charge it to my head and not my heart that I can't remember the names of all my former students, but be encouraged today to know that once you're a part of God's family, He will never forget your name. He's smart. He writes them all down in a book, the Book of Life. And He keeps a record there of stuff about you (see Revelation 20:12-15). Be encouraged by Luke 10:20b which says, "...rejoice because your names are written in heaven."

Hmmm. Writing things down to remember them. What a novel idea. Now if only I could remember where I put my pen...

#317
November 12: The Holy Spirit: Our HR Coordinator

A great job usually comes with a benefit package. Besides medical, dental, and vision care, you may be offered profit sharing whereby you end up owning some of the company stock. Little day-to-day advantages are yours as well. Maybe you are given a set of keys, the security code, and a special parking space. Other perks could be some clothing with the company emblem, an expense account, a company car, and personal technology like a business cell phone or other computer device. Whatever you receive, the HR (Human Resources) coordinator is probably your point man or woman who apprises you of all the advantages you have now that you are a new employee.

Well, consider the Spirit of God to be your HR coordinator. As believers, we have a benefit package. The manual is 66 books long and the perks are written throughout. God (the CEO) has assigned the Spirit to help us interpret the manual. First Corinthians 2:12 states, "Now we have received, not the spirit of the world, but the Spirit who is from God, that we might know the things that have been freely given to us by God" (NKJ).

Once we've been "employed" by the company of Heaven, every benefit is available for our use and enjoyment. All we need to do is consult the manual and the Holy Spirit for full understanding. Then, for example, we can park in our space (operate in our talent), wear our shirts with the company logo (witness and let others know for whom we work), and use our company e-mail (talk to God in prayer).

God has given us the Spirit whose job it is to help us fully understand all that has been freely given to us. Rely on the Spirit for that information and then start enjoying the wonderful benefit package Christianity offers.

#318
November 13: The Holy Spirit's Address

Some people clamber to get into certain neighborhoods. Living in the "right" area equals status. A popular TV series was based on this premise. The show entitled simply 90210 highlighted the prestigious city of Beverly Hills, CA, which boasts that zip code. To be from B.H. meant you were successful, beautiful, and high favored. Your address spoke for you.

The Spirit of God has an address. First Corinthians 6:19-20 directs us to His abode. "Or do you not know that your body is the temple of the Holy Spirit *who is* in you, whom you have from God, and you are not your own? For you were bought at a price; therefore glorify God in your body and in your spirit, which are God's" (NKJ). With your body as His house, what kind of neighborhood is He living in? Would your name be the title of a TV show about a prestigious zip code or a slum? Is the Holy Spirit proud He lives in you, or would He rather not say (or have you boast) that He abides there? Is His "neighborhood" (your body) experiencing success, beauty, and favor; or is it in a constant state of disrepair?

God the Holy Spirit deserves to live in style. He has paid a high price – Jesus's blood – for the deed to the property that is you. His payment for it means it's no longer yours to do with as you please. The new Owner has major renovations in His mind starting with your mind:
- "Be transformed by the renewing of your mind." Romans 12:2 (NKJ)
- "Let this mind be in you which was also in Christ Jesus." Philippians 2:5 (KJV)

The Sovereign Property Owner – the One who has paid for the land and the structures – has the right to remodel to make His home comfortable for Himself. As children of God, we can't make the Spirit move out. Once in, He declares imminent domain. "He Himself has said, *I will never leave you nor forsake you*" Hebrews 13:5 (NKJ).

#319
November 14: His Grace toward Me

We think quite a lot of the apostle Paul and well we should. Here was a man who humbled himself so completely to God's service that he ended up writing most of what we now have as the New Testament. He suffered many things for the sake of the Gospel, planted churches wherever he went, and mentored young preachers. If some of us could dedicate ourselves to God even a fraction of as much as Paul did, we'd really make some headway. Then, knowing some of us, we'd get pretty cocky about all God was doing with and through us.

Paul, however, was very clear about himself. First Corinthians 15:9 – 10 says, "For I am the least of the apostles, who am not worthy to be called an apostle, because I persecuted the church of God. But by the grace of God I am what I am, and His grace toward me was not in vain; but I labored more abundantly than they all, yet not I, but the grace of God which was with me" (NKJ).

Let's learn some things from Paul:
1. He remembered the base-ness of his sin.
2. He acknowledged the basis of his situation.
3. He recognized the balance due to his Source.

A quick recollection of where we were when Christ finally got through to us should be enough of a memory-jogger to put us where Paul was. Paul never forgot the base-ness of his sin. He had persecuted the church. You know what happens when you threaten a man's woman, and Paul had raised his hands against the bride or Christ. Jesus had to deal with Paul personally by knocking him off his horse and temporarily blinding him to get it through his thick head that this just wouldn't be tolerated. Paul didn't forget that encounter; nor should we ever forget how bad off we were when Jesus finally got our attention.

Second, although Paul acknowledged his apostleship, he still realized that he was in the job he as in thanks to the grace of God. He didn't shun the job nor make excuses for it, but he knew he didn't deserve to be there. God's unmerited favor was allowing him to do all he was doing. So it is with us. The basis for our situation in Christ is God's grace.

Finally, Paul says, "…and His grace toward me was not in vain…" Paul continued to work realizing the balance that was due to his Source. Paul's service was a repayment of a debt, so to speak. He always felt indebted to God; his service was a perpetual thanksgiving for all God had done for him. Again, as with Paul, so it should be with us. We serve God because we owe unending thanksgiving for His marvelous grace.

Keep working and serving, but be careful not to get it twisted. Maintain the attitude Paul wrote about in another place in Scripture. "I have been crucified with Christ; it is no longer I who live, but Christ lives in me; and the life which I now live in the flesh I live by faith in the Son of God, who loved me and gave Himself for me" Galatians 2:20 (NKJ).

#320
November 15: Treasure in Our Body

People who have survived a rattlesnake bite carry precious antibodies in their blood. Because of the encounter they had with the snake, their blood can heal a newly bitten person. They may not appear so on the outside, but those formerly bitten people carry life for someone else in their blood.

The Bible tells us that all have, in a sense, been bitten by a poisonous snake—the poisonous snake of sin. (See Romans 3:23.) The remedy for this spiritually fatal "bite" is found in the blood of Jesus Christ. Because of His encounter with the "snake," our sins are forgiven. The cure was set up way back in Genesis 3:15 when God said to the serpent, "And I will put enmity between you and the woman, and between your seed and her Seed; he shall bruise your head, and you shall bruise His heel" (NKJ). Jesus put this prophesied hurting on Satan when He rose from the dead.

The great news for us is that no one has to succumb to the death that runs rampant through our veins. One acceptance of the anti-venom found in Jesus' blood instantly cures the sin disease. Second Corinthians 4:7 and 10 tell us of the wonderful treasure we now carry around in our bodies. "But we have this treasure in earthen vessels, that the excellence of the power may be of God and not of us… always carrying about in the body the dying of the Lord Jesus, that the life of Jesus also may be manifested in our body" (NKJ).

We are now responsible to conduct ourselves as "healed"

people. Romans 7:6 says, "But now we have been delivered from the law, having died to what we were held by, so that we should serve in the newness of the Spirit and not in the oldness of the letter" (NKJ). And First Peter 4:1-2 says, "Therefore, since Christ suffered for us in the flesh, arm yourselves also with the same mind, for he who has suffered in the flesh has ceased from sin, that he no longer should live the rest of his time in the flesh for the lusts of men, but for the will of God" (NKJ).

We have a wonderful treasure inside of us. Let's live in a way that attracts other dying individuals to our life-giving Savior.

#321
November 16: Builder with No Hands

Joni Eareckson Tada is able to paint beautiful pictures by holding the brush between her teeth. If we didn't know how her masterpieces were created, we'd still ohh and ahh over them, but knowing they were done by a quadriplegic just makes them ever so much more magnificent. It's amazing to imagine those paintings being done without the use of her hands.

Well, the Bible says that God builds houses without the use of hands. Second Corinthians 5:1 states, "For we know that if our earthly house, *this* tent, is destroyed, we have a building from God, a house not made with hands, eternal in the heavens" (NKJ). The "houses" being spoken of here are our bodies. You see, although God created the amazing bodies we now have—the earthly inhabiting place for our spirit—He's got something even more impressive in mind. Just think of the splendor of the "houses" God will place us in once we exit the ones we're currently occupying! The new "houses" will have no leaks, no cracks, no bug infestations, no mold growing in the walls, and no peeling paint. They won't cave in, rot, rust, decay, or slide off their foundations. In other words, our new bodies won't get sick, broken, infected, wrinkly, confused, tired, or old. And all of these new "buildings" will be built by God with no hands!

When we know that God has this plan, it kinda makes it seem not so bad to die. Exactly the point!

#322
November 17: Getting Us Ready

As a high school teacher, I am well aware that I am helping to prepare most of my students for careers away from school because very few kids want to become teachers. So every day, I am moving them closer and closer to leaving me to move on to the next level of life. We discuss how what they are learning from me is preparing them for "the real world." As a mom, I saw myself in that very same role with my children. Every day that I raised them and taught them, I was preparing them for life outside of my house—for life in "the real world." And with both my students and my children, school life or home life was much more pleasant when they followed my directions and pleased me in their assignments, chores, and attitudes.

God is basically doing the same thing with us. Life on this earth and in these bodies is just preparation, just practice, for the actual real world—our heavenly home where we'll live for eternity. Second Corinthians 5:5-9 makes this clear:

- Now He who has prepared us for this very thing *is* God, who also has given us the Spirit as a guarantee. So *we are* always confident, knowing that while we are at home in the body we are absent from the Lord. For we walk by faith, not by sight. We are confident, yes, well pleased rather to be absent from the body and to be present with the Lord. Therefore we make it our aim, whether present or absent, to be well pleasing to Him. (NKJ)

So as we live, let's keep in mind that this life, with its ups and downs, joys and sorrows, is but for a little while. We may as well get good at pleasing God here, because in that "real world" to come, at least one of our continual, delightful tasks will be to glorify and please God in person.

#323
November 18: The Judgment Seat of Christ

Second Corinthians 5:10 is often used to scare people into confessing a faith in Christ or out of making foolish lifestyle choices. It says, "For we must all appear before the judgment seat of Christ, that each one may receive the things *done* in the body, according to what he has done, whether good or bad" (NKJ). However, the context of this verse leans toward quite a different feel.

Paul has just mentioned the fact that it will be absolutely fabulous and something to look forward to, to be present with the Lord. Because he knows that day is coming, he is moved to be sure his actions please God. In other words, Paul is looking to meet God on good terms. He's not ignorant of the fact that the bad will be judged negatively, but the emphasis is on the rejoicing point that the good will be judged positively. Because of the terror that is possible, Paul is eager to persuade us to live a life that's pleasing. The confidence comes by realizing we are "well known to God" and are "well known in [our] consciences" Second Corinthians 5:11 (NKJ). This being "well known" is also a positive thing. The mention of this is implying that God is well aware of how we are living to please Him and so He's enthusiastic about rewarding us.

So, the next time you think of the judgment seat of Christ, reflect upon the positive. Let it be a reminder to you of why you are living the clean, moral, upright life you are living. You're on the podium for rewards, not punishments.

#324
November 19: God's Homies and Peeps

Every literary hero has his "boys." Beowulf had the 14 warriors who went with him to fight Grendel and Wiglaf, Hamlet had Horatio, Arthur had the knights of the Round Table, and Julius Caesar had Brutus (well, at least for a while). Down through the ages, men have surrounded themselves with other men they could trust. These guys would know each other very well and rely on each other in a pinch. Fraternities carry on this tradition. Even in the gang culture, although twisted, this drive continues. Nowadays, the warriors, knights, brothers, and friends are known as "homies" and "peeps" (slang for "people").

In Second Corinthians 5:11, Paul mentions that "we are well known to God." In other words, we are God's homies. Then in the very next chapter, he tells us we "are the temple of the living

God," and quotes God saying *"I will dwell in them and walk among them. I will be their God, and they shall be My people."* Because of our special, familial relationship with God, He goes on to tell us to *"Come out from among them and be separate... Do not touch what is unclean, and I will receive you. I will be a Father to you, and you shall be My sons and daughters, says the Lord Almighty"* Second Corinthians 6:16-18 (NKJ). Here, God Himself calls us His peeps.

In whatever era or culture we live, and by whatever name we decide to use, we can just be glad we are in God's inner circle. What a blessing to be one of God's homies, one of God's peeps, one of God's children, one of God's friends.

#325
November 20: Downcast Comforter

Everyone has a bad day now and again. It seems that even the apostle Paul was not immune to at least slight depression every now and then. And we can hardly blame him. "Are they ministers of Christ?" he says in Second Corinthians 11:23-28, "I am more: in labors more abundant, in stripes above measure, in prisons more frequently, in deaths often. From the Jews five times I received forty stripes minus one. Three times I was beaten with rods; once I was stoned; three times I was shipwrecked; a night and a day I have been in the deep; in journeys often, in perils of waters, in perils of robbers, in perils of my own countrymen, in perils of the Gentiles, in perils in the city, in perils in the wilderness, in perils in the sea, in perils among false brethren; in weariness and toil, in sleeplessness often, in hunger and thirst, in fastings often, in cold and nakedness— besides the other things, what comes upon me daily: my deep concern for all the churches" (NKJ).

Yes, Paul had reasons to get depressed; yet, he also had the hugest possible reason to pull quickly out of any depressive state. Earlier in the book, when speaking of a different matter, he identified the source of his consolation. In Second Corinthians 7:6, Paul describes God as the One "who comforts the downcast" (NKJ). The Greek word for "downcast" used here is "tapeinos" (tap-i-nos'), which means depressed or humiliated in circumstances or disposition. There's good news for times when we experience such times. James, the Lord's brother, uses this word when he says, "Let the lowly—*tapeinos*, depressed, humiliated—brother glory in his exaltation," (James 1:9, NKJ) since "God resists the proud, but gives grace to the humble—*tapeinos*, depressed, humiliated" James 4:6 (NKJ). You see, Paul could pull out of depression because he was on speaking terms with God as the One who comforts the *tapeinos*.

Jesus identifies Himself as God by introducing Himself as being "gentle and lowly (tapeinos) in heart." We can take His yoke upon us, learn from Him, and find rest in Him for our souls because He can totally identify with where we're coming from when we're down (Matthew 11:29, NKJ).

Give God an opportunity to comfort you in your depression or humiliation today. He is there to exalt you and supply you with all the grace you will need to get through it.

#326
November 21: Good to Feel Bad

Someone told me that those who debate educational philosophies have suggested we teachers stop grading children's papers with red ink. Doing so supposedly damages their psyches somehow. I have told my students I plan to continue grading their papers in red ink because I want their psyches damaged. I want them damaged in such a way that their brains block out the possibility of making those same mistakes again. I want those red marks to so stick out in their remembrance that they form a blind spot to the mistakes and see only how to correctly respond to what's being asked of them. In other words, it's good for those red marks to be making my students feel bad enough *not* to want me to mark all over their papers again.

In the same way, it's good for us to feel bad about our sin. God, through the apostle Paul, explains, "For godly sorrow produces repentance leading to salvation, not to be regretted; but the sorrow of the world produces death. For observe this very thing, that you sorrowed in a godly manner: What diligence it produced in you, what clearing of yourselves, what indignation, what fear, what vehement desire, what zeal, what vindication!" Second Corinthians 7:10-11 (NKJ).

When God produces sorrow—sadness, grief, grievous, or

heaviness—in us over something we've done, we ought to feel regret. We've hurt our loving, heavenly Father. We ought not just "buck up" and "try to get over it." No, this kind of sorrow is designed to ignite a passionate zeal that pushes us to repent and get right again with God. This is good sorrow; this is when it's good to feel bad.

#327
November 22: The Great Exchange

Lots of us give to charities. Besides giving my tithes and offerings to my church, I give money to such organizations as the Alzheimer's Association to fund research to find a cure, The Right to Life League to spread accurate information about the atrocity of abortion, and Biola University to continue the ministry of Christian higher education. But no matter how much I give to causes in which I believe, I have never been moved to give away all the money I earn to charities. I keep enough to live on, to maintain a savings, and to do things for personal enjoyment and entertainment. In fact, besides my tithes which I set aside first, I pay myself and my bills before I give to non-profits or others who are looking for financial assistance from me.

By contrast to my self-sustaining giving habits (and I dare say, yours as well), Jesus gave absolutely everything He had—down to His very life—for us charity cases. He didn't pay Himself first, put some of Himself aside for a rainy day, nor hang on to just enough of Himself so as not to lose Himself in His sacrifice. He gave it all. Second Corinthians 8:9 gives us this wonderful news. "For you know the grace of our Lord Jesus Christ, that though He was rich, yet for your sakes He became poor, that you through His poverty might become rich" (NKJ).

His life for ours. His riches to replace our poverty. Christ's riches enrich us. He emptied Himself to fill us. That marvelous exchange empowers and enables us to live for Him. Hallelujah, what a Savior!

#328
November 23: God Loves a Cheerful Giver

Second Corinthians 9:7-8 says, "So let each one give as he purposes in his heart, not grudgingly or of necessity; for God loves a cheerful giver. And God is able to make all grace abound toward you, that you, always having all sufficiency in all things, may have an abundance for every good work" (NKJ). We usually hear these verses during offering time at church. And there's nothing wrong with that. Indeed, these verses are imbedded in a context that speaks about the Corinthian Christians gathering a monetary gift to be sent to suffering saints in other regions. However, there is a broader meaning to this giving concept. Read these two verses with the immediately surrounding verses:

> But this I say: He who sows sparingly will also reap sparingly, and he who sows bountifully will also reap bountifully. So let each one give as he purposes in his heart, not grudgingly or of necessity; for God loves a cheerful giver. And God is able to make all grace abound toward you, that you, always having all sufficiency in all things, may have an abundance for every good work. As it is written: "He has dispersed abroad, he has given to the poor; his righteousness endures forever."
> Now may He who supplies seed to the sower, and bread for food, supply and multiply the seed you have sown and increase the fruits of your righteousness,
> while you are enriched in everything for all liberality, which causes thanksgiving through us to God. Second Corinthians 9:6-11 (NKJ)

When read this way, can you see how God is not only communicating the importance of giving money? Knowing that we can only harvest that which we plant, realize that this passage is also hinting at the fact that God expects us to cheerfully give—plant or sow—of everything we have. When He supplies us with "seed"—money, gifts, talents, time, etc.—He then supplies and multiplies for us that which we in turn "sow" into others' lives. He increases the fruits of our righteousness; that is, the results of our right living. We are then enriched in everything because we have been liberal with what God has given to us.

Never mind a recession; take an inventory of all God has

given you.

- Do you have some extra hours? Sow them into the lives of others. Read to little children at the library, visit a lonely, elderly person in a nursing home, or help your grandchild's teacher in the classroom.
- Do you have Godly wisdom after living through a tumultuous time? Conduct a Bible study, write a book, or do a lecture series about what you've learned.
- Can you read? Teach someone who is illiterate.
- Do you have a car you can drive? Take someone without transportation to the grocery store, the bank, or the mall.
- Do you have some free weekend evenings? Volunteer to babysit free for young, two career parents who rarely get a date night.
- Can you do minor household or car repairs. Do so without charge for a single parent.
- Teach a young boy how to tie a necktie; teach a young lady how to wear make-up.

You have lots of gifts and talents. God loves it when you give them cheerfully.

#329
November 24: The Gift of Thorns

God gives some people an abundance; Paul was one such person. Second Corinthians chapter 12 tells us that so many revelations were given to him that God deemed it necessary to supply him with one more thing: "a thorn in the flesh." Bible expositors through the years have debated about exactly what that thorn might have been, but several things about it are clear from just a cursory reading of the text. First, the thorn was "in the flesh," in other words, it was a physical problem. Second, the thorn was perpetrated by "a messenger of Satan to buffet [him]." This seems to be much like when God allowed Satan to mess with Job (see Job 1 and 2). Third, the thorn was bothersome, so much so that Paul "pleaded with the Lord three times that it might depart."

The fourth characteristic about the thorn is the most interesting; it had a purpose. After the third time Paul begged for it to be removed, God said to him, "My grace is sufficient for you, for My strength is made perfect in weakness" Second Corinthians 12:9a (NKJ).

God knows us so well that He realizes many times we can't properly handle the magnitude of His goodness to us. His blessings are so awesome that we can easily become lost in them. Because of their rich magnificence (after all, those are the only kinds of gifts God has to give), God knows our eyes and hearts will be prone to turn toward worshipping them to the exclusion of honoring Him. He, therefore, wisely provides us with the gift of thorns. He doesn't take away the other gifts, the talents, and the revelations, but He tempers them with thorns so we don't get beside ourselves.

Once God answered Paul's prayer with a "no," he understood what God was up to and responded, "Therefore most gladly I will rather boast in my infirmities, that the power of Christ may rest upon me" (verse 9b).

Giftedness comes as an amazing blessing, but so are the boundaries God builds for us, and the precautions He takes to be sure we keep our eyes steadily on Him. "For everyone to whom much is given, from him much will be required" Luke 12:48 (NKJ).

God knows what He's doing when He rewards us with thorns. We are but the stem, thorns and all, allowing the rose of His face to blossom—through the faithful use of our gifts—so others can enjoy the sweet fragrance of His presence.

#330
November 25: Bought Back

Can you imagine giving away a box of odds and ends to the Goodwill® and then realizing your grandmother's precious family heirloom ring was in the carton? You'd probably run as fast as you could to the store to get the item back. When you arrived, however, you discovered that the clerk had already placed the ring in the display case. Undoubtedly, you would happily pay whatever price there was on the tag to purchase the ring. In fact, you would be buying it back, redeeming it, from an unknown fate.

God has done the very same thing for us. We were that precious ring, tarnished and lost in the carton on this world amid all its wickedness. My fate seemed sealed, for "... I am unspiritual, sold as a slave to sin" Romans 7:14 (NIV). But thank God for Jesus. Galatians 3:13-14 proclaims, "Christ has redeemed us from the curse of the law, having become a curse for us (for it is written, 'Cursed is everyone who hangs on a tree'), that the blessing of Abraham might come upon the Gentiles in Christ Jesus, that we might receive the promise of the Spirit through faith" (NKJ).

God's love for us to this extent is not merely a New Testament thing. All the way back in the book of Isaiah, God identified Himself as the Redeemer. Isaiah introduced the Lord as the One "...who created you, O Jacob, and He who formed you, O Israel" and then he quotes the Lord saying, "Fear not, for I have redeemed you; I have called you by your name; you are Mine" Isaiah 43:1 (NKJ).

Lift up your head today. You have value. You were precious enough for God to come all the way to Earth to purchase you out of sin's bondage. He sacrificially paid the price to see you free. Make the attitudinal change necessary to match the changed reality in which you now stand. In actuality, you now have a whole new lease on life. Let new behaviors flow from your position as a blood-bought believer.

#331
November 26: The Abraham-Law-Christ Connection

The Bible is a history book; it's His-story, the story of Jesus Christ. From Genesis to The Revelation, we come to know all about God through His manifestation of Himself to us in Jesus Christ. One way to see that link is found in Paul's letter to the church at Galatia.

To explain the connection between the Old Testament character of Abraham, the Law given through Moses, and the promise fulfilled by Christ, Paul writes:

> Now to Abraham and his Seed were the promises made. He does not say, "And to seeds," as of many, but as of one, "And to your Seed," who is Christ. And this I say, that the law, which was four hundred and thirty years later, cannot annul the covenant that was confirmed before by God in Christ, that it should make the promise of no effect. For if the inheritance is of the law, it is no longer of promise; but God gave it to Abraham by promise. Galatians 3:16-18 (NKJ)

You see, the promise of the Seed—that is, the coming fulfillment of the covenant through Jesus Christ—was given to Abraham 430 years before the Law was given to Moses. The Law "was added because of transgression" (verse 19) and was in place to show us how we should be living, but the Law itself did not give us life. Life came through faith. "Therefore, the law was our tutor to bring us to Christ, that we might be justified by faith" Galatians 3:24 (NKJ).

And exactly what was this promise and covenant? We are justified by faith in Jesus. "For you are all sons of God through faith in Christ Jesus. For as many of you as were baptized into Christ have put on Christ. There is neither Jew nor Greek, there is neither slave nor free, there is neither male nor female; for you are all one in Christ Jesus. And if you are Christ's, then you are Abraham's seed, and heirs according to the promise" Galatians 3:26-29 (NKJ).

#332
November 27: The Liberator

Most of us do not like to be trapped. Being locked in a room, stuck in a stalled elevator, or even being held up in traffic gridlock: all of these and other entrapments make us extremely agitated and uncomfortable. Bondage of any kind is not positive.

Christ came to untangle us from our major entrapment—our bondage to sin. What He has done for us on the cross enables us to "stand fast...in the liberty by which Christ has made us free" and we're encouraged "not [to] be entangled again with a yoke of bondage" Galatians 5:1 (NKJ). The NIV Bible translates that verse like this: "It is for freedom that Christ has set us free. Stand firm, then, and do not let yourselves be burdened again by a yoke of slavery."

When you know that door could get jammed and lock you in, you stay out of that room. If you know that elevator is always getting stuck between floors, you take the stairs. And when you are aware that by 8am, the freeway will be bumper-to-bumper for the next hour-and-a-half, you either leave earlier than 8, stay home until after 9:30, or take an alternate route. You're smart to do what you can to avoid getting stuck, trapped, or closed in. So why do you behave any differently toward the freedom Christ provides? Paul admonishes us, "But now that you know God-- or rather are known by God-- how is it that you are turning back to those weak and miserable principles? Do you wish to be enslaved by them all over again? Galatians 4:9 (NIV)

Remember how it feels to be trapped and avoid the ambushes sin lays out for you. Rely on the Liberator to set you free and maintain that freedom as you "live as free men, but do not use your freedom as a cover-up for evil," instead, operate realizing that your freedom enables you to "live as servants of God" First Peter 2:16 (NIV).

#333
November 28: No Tricks

According to www.joe-ks.com/phrases:

In the 19th century, the status of men was often indicated by the size of their wigs... Judges often wore these poor-fitting wigs, which frequently slipped over the eyes, and it may have been that a clever lawyer who tricked a judge bragged about his deception by saying that he pulled the wool over his eyes... Street thugs would pull the wig down over the victim's eyes in order to confuse him.

Well, according to another famous saying, we may be able to pull the wool over the eyes of "some of the people, some of the time," but we can never trick God. Galatians 6:7-8 says, "Do not be deceived, God is not mocked; for whatever a man sows, that he will also reap. For he who sows to his flesh will of the flesh reap corruption, but he who sows to the Spirit will of the Spirit reap everlasting life."

Let's remember that since God knows everything, He can't be fooled. We cannot put anything over on Him. But not only that, God will make sure that what we do engage in will pay us.

#334
November 29: What God Has Done, Part 1

One of the best lists detailing what God has done for us is in the opening salutation of the book of Ephesians. In the first two chapters, Paul lays out a remarkable list that I'll let him tell you. All I've done is highlight the specifics. I guarantee you, you'll be smiling by the end of this read!

Ephesians 1:3-13
3   Blessed be the God and Father of our Lord Jesus Christ, who **has blessed us** with every spiritual blessing in the heavenly places in Christ,
4   just as He **chose us** in Him before the foundation of the world, that we should be holy and without blame before Him in love,
5   having **predestined us to adoption as sons** by Jesus Christ to Himself, according to the good pleasure of His will,
6   to the praise of the glory of His grace, by which He has **made us accepted** in the Beloved.
7   In Him **we have redemption** through His blood, **the forgiveness of sins**, according to the riches of His grace
8   which He made to abound toward us in all wisdom and

360

prudence,
9   having **made known to us the mystery of His will**,
according to His good pleasure which He purposed in Himself,
10   that in the dispensation of the fullness of the times He might
gather together in one all things in Christ, both which are in
heaven and which are on earth-- in Him.
11   In Him also we have **obtained an inheritance**, being
predestined according to the purpose of Him who works all
things according to the counsel of His will,
12   that we who first trusted in Christ should be to the praise of
His glory.
13   In Him you also trusted, after you heard the word of truth, the
gospel of your salvation; in whom also, having believed, you were
sealed with the Holy Spirit of promise,
(NKJ)

#335
November 30: What God Has Done, Part 2

        In "What God Has Done, Part 1," you read the list from
Ephesians chapter 1 detailing what God has done for us. Paul
was not finished. He continued his list in chapter 2. Again, I'll let
the word of God do the talking, and all I've done is highlight the
specifics. Again, even if you only have time to read the underlined
sections, I guarantee you once more that you'll be smiling by the
end of this read!

Ephesians 2:1, 4-22
1   And you **He made alive**, who were dead in trespasses and
sins...
4   **But God**, who is rich in mercy, because of His great love with
which He **loved us**,
5   even when we were dead in trespasses, **made us alive
together with Christ** (by grace you have been saved),
6   and **raised us up together**, and **made us sit together in the
heavenly places in Christ Jesus**,
7   **that in the ages to come He might show the exceeding
riches of His grace in His kindness toward us in Christ Jesus**.
8   For **by grace you have been saved** through faith, and that
not of yourselves; it is the gift of God,

9   not of works, lest anyone should boast.

10   For **we are His workmanship**, created in Christ Jesus for good works, which God prepared beforehand that we should walk in them...

13   But now in Christ Jesus you who once were far off have been **brought near by the blood of Christ.**

14   For **He Himself is our peace**, who has made both one, and has broken down the middle wall of separation...

18   For through Him **we both have access by one Spirit to the Father**.

19   Now, therefore, you are **no longer strangers and foreigners, but fellow citizens with the saints and members of the household of God**,

20   having been **built on the foundation of the apostles and prophets**, Jesus Christ Himself being the chief corner stone,

21   in whom the whole building, being joined together, grows into a holy temple in the Lord,

22   in whom **you also are being built together for a dwelling place of God in the Spirit.** (NKJ)

#336
December 1: God's Publishing Efforts

All authors have one ultimate goal in mind – to be published. After all, that's why we are writing. We actually think other people want to know, and indeed need to hear, what we have to say. We attend writers' retreats to get tuned in to God's voice, and we pack ourselves off to writers' conferences with proposals in hand, seeking the appropriate publisher (or at least a willing one) for our words. We're concerned about things like capturing our voice on the page, writing tight, weaving humor into serious subjects, and showing not telling. Then once we release our work to the world, we turn our attention to marketing and getting the word out there about our books so people can get the message in their hands and hearts. We pray they understand the takeaway – the main point we are trying to convey.

As an author Himself, God is concerned about these very same things. He was the Ghostwriter for the best-seller of all times, but the published works He continues to produce – those with His personal name on the cover – tend to need more of His hands-on marketing efforts. Ephesians 2:10 says, "For we are His workmanship, created in Christ Jesus for good works, which God prepared beforehand that we should walk in them" (NKJ). That word "workmanship" is poiema in Greek and it literally means "a product, fabric, and thing that is made." It's the word from which we get our English word "poem." In other words, we are literally God's poem which He is trying to publish and market.

When God reads back over His poem that is you today, has He captured His voice on the page? Can He see that He's written a tight, easy-to-comprehend message? Does His joy burst through even in these serious times? Has He accomplished the show-don't-tell goal in you because you are living what He has penned in your heart?

As the personally authored work of His hands, what's the takeaway people remember when they read you?

#337
December 2: Able

If you are sitting in a chair right now reading this devotion, I bet you didn't check the chair before you sat in it to see if it would be able hold you. You trusted that chair. Of course, you had good reason to trust that chair. Perhaps you sit in the same chair every day. It has never failed to hold you before, so you had no reason to believe it would not hold you today. Maybe you are on a sofa, a park bench, a folding chair, or a pew. Still, I would venture a guess that you didn't check the strength of the seat before you plopped into it. Why? Because the track record of seats in your experience has been exemplary. You have confident and firm faith in the capability of the seats. You are so sure of their strength and ability to hold your weight that it never crosses your mind to question their integrity.

Our faith in God needs to be no less certain. In fact, better than the strength of the chair you're sitting in right now, is His potency. Paul ends a section of his letter to the Ephesians by expressing the thought of "Him who is able to do exceedingly abundantly above all that we ask or think..." Ephesians 3:20 (NKJ).

So what do we learn about God from Paul's words?
First of all, God is able. The Greek word "dunamai" is

translated here as "able" and it means "to be of power." The word from which we get our English word "dynamite, is the same word used in Matthew 3:9 when Jesus says that "God is able to raise up children to Abraham from these stones" (NKJ). The leper who believed in Jesus' ability to heal him used this word when he said in Matthew 8:2, "Lord, if You are willing, You can [dunamai] make me clean" (NKJ).

Not only is God able, but His power can do "all that we ask or think." That little word "all" is translated from the Greek word "pas" and means "any, every, the whole, always, daily, as many as, thoroughly, whatsoever, whole, and whosoever." There is nothing too big or too small that God can't handle. Whatever we can imagine to bring to Him, He is equipped to take care of it. Nothing is out of the realm of His ability.

As a writer, I can picture Paul in my mind's eye doing some self-editing as he wrote these words. Notice that Paul doesn't just say "God is able to do all," he says God is able to do "above all." However, the more Paul thought about it, I imagine he figured that "above all" was not accurate enough, so he wrote that God is able to do "abundantly above all." Still not satisfied, I can see him adding an additional modifier, so he ended up trying to get the idea across to us that God is so very awesome, He can perform "exceedingly abundantly above all" we can ever form our mouths to request or allow our hearts to dream.

Our confidence in God will take an entirely new up-turn if we actually approach prayer with the unwavering belief that God "is able to do exceedingly abundantly above all that we ask or think." We will revolutionize our prayer lives if you take this conviction into our times with God from now on.

#338
December 3: God Guards our Hearts

One morning, I couldn't hear God as I read my Bible because there was turmoil in my life. I tried and tried to concentrate on what I was reading, but kept finding my mind drifting to my troubles. I begged God for a word from Him. Thankfully, He spoke, but not from the passages I was reading. He brought to my mind a familiar passage, perfectly fitted for my present situation.

Philippians 4:6-7 says, "Be anxious for nothing, but in everything by prayer and supplication, with thanksgiving, let your requests be made known to God; and the peace of God, which surpasses all understanding, will guard your hearts and minds through Christ Jesus" (NKJ).

I knew these verses by heart. At first, it seemed not too comforting for God to be telling me, "Just stop trippin'." How was I supposed to stop being upset when upsetting stuff was going on? Then God pulled my attention to the last phrase. That was it. I needed my heart and my mind guarded. Confusion and troubles are designed by our great enemy to turn our minds and hearts from God. When we are troubled, our thoughts dwell on ourselves and not on God. We wonder what we should do; we justify our feelings and our actions; and we worry about how things are going to turn out. I wasn't trying to operate that way; in fact, I had been in constant communication with God, but I still found my mind overwhelmed and my heart breaking and in pain.

I've figured out that it comes down to whether or not I really trust God's word. I know I do, so no matter what I'm feeling, I must put my foot down on the fact that God's Word is true – the spiritual is in control of the physical – and that's that. God's Word says that God's peace will station a guard around my feelings (my heart) and my thoughts (my mind). I didn't get what I needed from the particular passage I wanted to read in my morning Bible-reading routine, but God's Word still had a word for me – a word for where I was on my journey with Him. He then graciously led me to other words of encouragement from his heart to mine.

- Commit thy way unto the LORD; trust also in him; and he shall bring it to pass. Psalm 37:5 (KJV)
- But the meek shall inherit the earth, and shall delight themselves in the abundance of peace. Psalm 37:11 (NKJ)
- Cast your burden on the LORD, and He shall sustain you; he shall never permit the righteous to be moved. Psalm 55:22 (NKJ)
- Great peace have those who love Your law, and nothing causes them to stumble. Psalm 119:165 (NKJ)
- I pour out my complaint before Him; I declare before Him my trouble. When my spirit was overwhelmed within me, then You knew my path. Psalm 142:2-3 (NKJ)
- But glory, honor, and peace to everyone who works what is good... Romans 2:10 (NKJ)

- Rejoicing in hope, patient in tribulation, continuing steadfastly in prayer; Romans 12:12 (NKJ)
- Let us therefore come boldly to the throne of grace, that we may obtain mercy and find grace to help in time of need. Hebrews 4:16 (NKJ)

Sometimes, we just have to be determined to believe God's word even when everything around us – and even everything within us – shouts the opposite. Take refuge in the truth of the fact that you are God's child. Know that God loves and cares for you, guards your heart and mind with peace, and has no intention of allowing you or your testimony to be destroyed.

#339
December 4: Everybody Ought to Know

The first time I remember using the word "ought" was in a Sunday School song my dad taught all the kids. The chorus was simple:
Everybody ought to know
Everybody ought to know
Everybody ought to know
Who Jesus is.

The verses went on to list some of Jesus' attributes. Well, I don't think the apostle Paul knew that song, but he writes out an impressive description of who Jesus is in the first chapter of Colossians.

He is the image of the invisible God, the firstborn over all creation.

For by Him all things were created that are in heaven and that are on earth, visible and invisible, whether thrones or dominions or principalities or powers. All things were created through Him and for Him.

And He is before all things, and in Him all things consist.

And He is the head of the body, the church, who is the beginning, the firstborn from the dead, that in all things He may have the preeminence.

366

For it pleased the Father that in Him all the fullness should dwell, and by Him to reconcile all things to Himself, by Him, whether things on earth or things in heaven, having made peace through the blood of His cross. Colossians 1:15-20 (NKJ)

Every one of these attributes stems from the first point in the list: Jesus is the image of the invisible God. When Philip asked Jesus to show the Father to him and the other disciples, Jesus Himself answered, "Have I been with you so long, and yet you have not known Me, Philip? He who has seen Me has seen the Father" John 14:9 (NKJ). The above Colossians passage goes on to prove that Jesus is God by revealing to us that it was "by Him [that] all things were created that are in heaven and that are on earth." Again, "All things were created through Him and for Him. And He is before all things, and in Him all things consist."

So, since Jesus is who He is and has done what He's done (reconcile[d] all things to Himself... having made peace through the blood of His cross), in light of Colossians chapter 1 and John chapter 14, the Sunday School song was right: everybody ought to know who Jesus is.

#340
December 5: Full

Talk to anybody about relationships and you'll find that there is no such thing as a perfect one. Even in the most loving marriages, if they hadn't learned to look past the idiosyncrasies, each spouse could probably pretty easily find something about the other that's annoying. Why is that? No human is perfect. None of us will ever find another human being who will totally fill all our empty or lacking spaces.

The good news is that there does exist Someone who is so complete in Himself that He can fill in everywhere we are empty. Colossians chapter 2, verses 6 and 9-10 says, "As you therefore have received Christ Jesus the Lord, so walk in Him... For in Him dwells all the fullness of the Godhead bodily; and you are complete in Him, who is the head of all principality and power" (NKJ).

Absolutely everything we need in every area of our lives

exists in Jesus. If we're feeling empty, lonely, lost, abandoned, confused, overwhelmed, afraid, anxious, sick, incomplete, powerless—whatever we're going through—Jesus is able to handle it. He is "the fullness of the Godhead bodily." In other words, anything from God or anything that is part of God that we need, God is able to supply. He has what it takes to seal up the cracks, fill in the gaps, and give what we lack.

#341
December 6: Time for a Job Evaluation

We may not dread the annual job evaluation done by our boss, but we probably experience at least a tiny bit of nerves. We want to perform well on the day he/she shows up to watch us working. The boss trusted our abilities when we were hired, and the yearly evaluation should be nothing more than a testament to the belief originally placed in us. If we are confident in our abilities and are prepared for the day's tasks, no problem. The assessment will be positive and we can breathe easy for another year. However, if we've been messing up, shirking our responsibilities, cutting corners, and approaching the job unprepared, the boss might not like what he/she sees during the evaluation period.

The apostle Paul realized he and the other apostles were working for God as their boss. He also realized it was God who would do their evaluations. Paul tells the believers at Thessalonica, "But as we have been approved by God to be entrusted with the gospel, even so we speak, not as pleasing men, but God who tests our hearts" 1 Thessalonians 2:4 (NKJ). The apostles were "approved" or "examined and tried" (dokimazo in the Greek) when God gave them the job of taking the gospel to the world. Paul understood this and did his job, not to please people, but to please the Boss who had hired him. Paul also knew that that Boss would evaluate or test the apostles' hearts continually to be sure they were doing the job as they were supposed to do it. (The word "test" in the above verse in the phrase "God who tests our hearts," is the same Greek word used for "approved" in the first part of the verse.)

We need to understand what Paul understood: God is giving us the same kind of job evaluation today. Second

Corinthians 5:17-18 tells us that "if anyone is in Christ [this is speaking of us], he is a new creation, old things have passed away; behold, all things have become new. Now all things are of God, who has reconciled us to Himself through Jesus Christ, and has given us the ministry of reconciliation" (NKJ). We, like the apostles, have been given the job of letting people know they can be reconciled to God. That news is the gospel. We need, then, to realize that like Paul and the apostles, God will test our hearts—perform evaluations—to see that we are doing the job for which He hired us.

If God sat in on your life with His clipboard and evaluation sheet today, what would He write?

#342
December 7: God's Will is Abstinence

"God, just let me know what Your will is, and I'll do it!" This is probably the cry of many of our hearts. In fact, we'd probably agree with the Psalmist who said, "I delight to do Your will, O my God, and Your law is within my heart" Psalm 40:8 (NKJ). But do we really mean this? When we say it, I'm afraid we're waiting for some awesome sign from heaven, perhaps in the form of an audible voice, handwriting on a wall, a random comment made by a complete stranger, or some such phenomenon. However, God has given us an entire book filled with His express will for our lives. If we're looking for His will, we can start in the Bible.

One case of God telling us His perfect will for our lives is in the area of our sexual behavior. First Thessalonians 4:3 – 7 tells us plainly:

> For this is the will of God, your sanctification: that you should abstain from sexual immorality; that each of you should know how to possess his own vessel in sanctification and honor, not in passion of lust, like the Gentiles who do not know God; that no one should take advantage of and defraud his brother in this matter, because the Lord is the avenger of all such, as we also forewarned you and testified. For God did not call us to uncleanness, but in holiness. (NKJ)

(Also see First Corinthians 6:9-20; 7:2; Galatians 5:19; Ephesians

5:2-4; Colossians 3:5-6; Hebrews 13:4; Revelations 21:8; and Revelations 22:14-15.)

So if we want to live within the will of God, we must abstain from sexual immorality. That means we do not lust, do not fornicate (have sex as a single person), and do not commit adultery (have sex as a married person with someone who is not our spouse). Failure to abstain means we are in sin and we can expect dire consequences (read Romans 6:23).

With the help of the Holy Spirit, as we are controlling ourselves in the area of our sexual behavior, we should start searching the Scriptures to discover more of the will of God. Be challenged today to start looking through Scripture for passages about God's will. Find a passage, study it, understand it, and then apply it. Then move on to the next. I guarantee you, you'll be busy for quite some time, and you will have reached your goal: to live and operate in the will of God.

#343
December 8: Friends Fly Free

A certain air carrier advertised a special entitled "Friends Fly Free." When the frequent-flyer customer had racked up so many miles of travel, she could take advantage of this special program that allowed one friend to accompany her for free on any trip to any location. Such a deal!

First Thessalonians 4:14-17 outlines much the same program:

> For if we believe that Jesus died and rose again, even so God will bring with Him those who sleep in Jesus... For the Lord Himself will descend from heaven with a shout, with the voice of an archangel, and with the trumpet of God. And the dead in Christ will rise first. Then we who are alive and remain shall be caught up together with them in the clouds to meet the Lord in the air. And thus we shall always be with the Lord. (NKJ)

Jesus racked up "miles" for us on the cross, and He has future travel plans. Accompanied by the fanfare of Heaven, Jesus will come and gather the saints for the trip of a lifetime—the trip that will take us into our forever with Him.

How do you know you'll be on board? Romans 10:9-10 tells you how to take advantage of the free ticket:

> That if you confess with your mouth the Lord Jesus and believe in your heart that God has raised Him from the dead, you will be saved. For with the heart one believes unto righteousness, and with the mouth confession is made unto salvation. (NKJ)

As those who believe in His death and resurrection—as His friends—we'll fly free. Such a deal!

#344
December 9: Not Yet

Through the ages, people have predicted when Jesus would return. It doesn't seem to matter that Scripture clearly says, "But of that day and hour no one knows, not even the angels of heaven, but My Father only" Matthew 24:36 (NKJ). Even though we can't know when, God reminds us over and over again of the certainty of the event with the wise warning, "Therefore you also be ready, for the Son of Man is coming at an hour you do not expect" Matthew 24:44 (NKJ). With those things in mind, if someone were to ask us the question about the time of Christ's return, we could answer with some certainty, "Probably soon, but not yet."

Why, then, do we have to be so watchful? What is God talking about when He tells us to "be ready"? The apostle Paul gives us this answer by letting us know that some things are going to happen before Christ's return that could keep us from enjoying and participating in that day.

- Let no one deceive you by any means; for that Day will not come unless **the falling away comes first**, and **the man of sin is revealed**, the son of perdition, who opposes and exalts himself above all that is called God or that is worshiped, so that he sits as God in the temple of God, showing himself that he is God. Second Thessalonians 2:3-4 (NKJ), emphasis added

- The coming of the lawless one is according to the working of Satan, **with all power, signs, and lying wonders**, and **with all unrighteous deception** among those who perish, because they did not receive the love of the truth, that they might be saved. And for this reason **God will send them strong delusion, that they should believe the lie**, **that they all may be condemned who did not believe the truth but had pleasure in unrighteousness.** Second Thessalonians 2:9-12 (NKJ), emphasis added

You see, before Christ returns, there will be a "falling away." Matthew Henry explains that this apostasy is "in spiritual or religious matters, from sound doctrine, instituted worship and church government, and a holy life." In other words, damnable heresies will infiltrate the Church in order to deceive the people of God and cause them to turn from the truth. People we never thought would stray from solid doctrine will espouse ideas contrary to God's revealed truth. And who is behind all of this? Satan. This lawless one comes in "with all power, signs, lying wonders, and with all unrighteous deception."

Now here's the scary part. Those who fall for all Satan has put out there and turn their backs on the truth will receive "strong delusion." They will "believe the lie" and be "condemned" for two reasons. First, they "did not believe the truth," and second they "had pleasure in unrighteousness." In other words, those who fall away will put forth arguments contrary to the truth revealed in the Bible, and justify their actions being perfectly comfortable with and glorying in their new lifestyle which the Scripture defines as unrighteous.

Is it possible for us to be in that number of people who will fall away? Yes, if we aren't careful and watchful. Thankfully, Paul ends this passage with hope. "Therefore, brethren, **stand fast and hold the traditions which you were taught**... may our Lord Jesus Christ Himself, and our God and Father, who has loved us and given us everlasting consolation and good hope by grace, comfort your hearts and **establish you in every good word and work**" Second Thessalonians 2:15-17 (NKJ), emphasis added.

The way to keep from falling away is to stand fast—be stationary, persevere—and hold—seize with all your might and strength—the precepts and ordinances of the whole counsel of what Gods' word clearly teaches. We look forward to the glorious day of Christ's return, but let's not hasten it by being the ones who will fall away first.

#345
December 10: Peace

"Now may the Lord of peace Himself give you peace always in every way. The Lord be with you all" First Thessalonians 3:16 (NKJ). There is so much good news packed into these twenty words, it's crazy.

First of all, who is this Lord of peace? Isaiah introduced Him to us long before His earthly existence with words we hear every Christmas season: "For unto us a child is born, unto us a son is given: and the government shall be upon his shoulder: and his name shall be called Wonderful, Counsellor, The mighty God, The everlasting Father, The Prince of Peace" Isaiah 9:6 (KJV). No other figure in Scripture or in any other discipline for that matter is known as the Prince of Peace except for Jesus Christ. So the first piece of good news is the fact that we have a personal relationship with the Prince of Peace.

Next, what is peace? The Greek word for peace is "eirene (i-ray'-nay)" from which we get the girl's name Irene. It means quietness, rest, to set at one again, and by implication, prosperity. In other words, Jesus gives us rest, tranquility, calm, and harmony. That's the second piece of good news.

The third piece of good news is that the Prince of Peace is personally available to give that peace to us. He does not send a representative, and envoy, an ambassador, or His assistant. He Himself doles out the peace.

Good news point number four is the fact that Jesus indeed does have peace to give. One cannot give out what one does not possess. He alone possesses the peace we need because He alone is the Prince of Peace.

Good news point number five is that Jesus will give us peace "always in every way." This phrase means that peace – tranquility, calm, and harmony – is available at all times and in every possible circumstance and scenario.

- In a family crisis, peace.

- In a financial reversal, peace.
- Facing a physical or mental illness, peace.
- In a car accident, peace.
- When in need of food, clothing, and shelter, peace.
- When having to wait, peace.
- When a loved one has left, peace.
- When you don't understand, peace.
- While your children are in need or are acting crazy, peace.
- When your spouse is suffering, peace.

Jesus Himself said, ""Peace I leave with you, My peace I give to you; not as the world gives do I give to you. Let not your heart be troubled, neither let it be afraid" John 14:27 (NKJ). Take His word for it and enjoy His peace today.

#346
December 11: Jesus' Purpose Statement

If you have any kind of business or are trying to make a name for yourself in any profession, you are becoming familiar with terms like branding, tagline, logo, and purpose statement. The whole point is for you or your company to be seen above the crowd, be understood for what it is that you do or provide, and be recognized as the best in your field – someone the consumer cannot live without.

Well, Jesus is certainly branded. His brand is the Son of God, Savior of the world. His tagline is found in Isaiah 9:6, "Wonderful, Counselor, Mighty God, Everlasting Father, Prince of Peace" (NKJ). His logo is the cross.

But what about His purpose statement? Timothy stated it succinctly: "Christ Jesus came into the world to save sinners" 1 Timothy 1:15 (NKJ). That's plain and simple. If you haven't appropriated the free gift of salvation, do so today. Just confess with your mouth the Lordship of Jesus Christ and believe in your heart that God has raised Him from the dead, and salvation is yours! (See Romans 10:9-10.) If you have received this great salvation, share the news and continue to spread Christ's purpose on earth until He returns.

#347
December 12: If God Had a Website

If God had a website, it would be extremely easy to navigate. There would be three main pages: one for God the Father, one for God the Son, and one for God the Holy Spirit; but those three pages would all encompass one website. Each page would be inextricably connected to the other, yet each would be distinct. The overall name of the website would be something like www.TrueGodOfHeaven.com.

For everything pertaining to God the Father, once you hit that tab, a menu would pop up giving you choices to get to know Him better. Listed attributes would be things like: King Eternal, Immortal, Invisible, and God Who Alone is Wise (see First Timothy 1:17). Also in this list would be the "omni's": Omnipresent, Omnipotent, and Omniscient (which mean everywhere present, all powerful, and all knowing). Access would always be available directly to God and the chat line for whatever you needed to talk with Him about would always be open and available.

For everything pertaining to God the Son, once you hit that tab, the Jesus menu would read: Child born for us, Son given to us, Government Carrier, Wonderful, Counselor, Mighty God, Everlasting Father, and Prince of Peace (see. Isaiah 9:6). Also in this list would be: Seeker and Savior of the Lost (see Luke 19:10), Only Name for Salvation (see Acts 4:12), and Heavenly Defense Attorney (see Romans 8:34). Jesus too would always be available to chat with you as your Brother, your Savior, and your Friend.

Finally, for everything pertaining to the Holy Spirit, once you hit that tab, the pull-down menu would read: Comforter, Guider to Truth, Glorifier of Jesus, and Revealer of Things to Come (see John 14:26 and 16:13-14). The pages concerning the Holy Spirit would be especially user-friendly because of our constant need for the energy it takes to live this Christian life. Once you got used to using the site, chatting with the Spirit would become as natural as breathing. It would be like a constant, internal conversation with the best life coach ever.

The three—Father, Son, and Spirit—are one: eternal and inseparable yet distinct. The best human metaphor to explain the phenomenon of the Trinity is that of the sun. The sun is a real thing; it exists and has mass. That's God the Father. The sun gives off light. That's Jesus, God the Son, the light of the world. The sun gives off heat. That's the power of God the Holy Spirit.

But since God doesn't have a website, we can access all of Him—as Father, as Son, and as Holy Spirit—via the longest running best seller on the market, the Bible. And here's the great news: not only is the Bible available as an actual book you can hold in your hands, but it can also be accessed via the web (start at Biblegateway.com) and in many free, downloadable versions for your computer, iPad, iPhone, Kindle, Nook, etc.

No excuses. Download God's Word into your brain and heart. It's easy. Just read it.

#348
December 13: On Trusting God

I attended two funerals within two weeks. In both cases, one of the messages of the eulogy was that the deceased knew the Lord and were indeed still alive, in fact, very much more alive than they had ever been here on earth. Those men are living in Heaven and will do so forever. They had trusted in Christ and that trust has now paid off.

Do we really trust God and what does that mean? Unfortunately, our human nature and our staunch enemy (Satan) team up to challenge our trust in God on a daily basis. The Bible tells us over and over again that we can find ourselves wrongly putting our trust in:

- Our own riches – see First Timothy 6:17-19
- Our ability to protect ourselves – see Psalm 44:5-6
- Our ability to oppress others and take from them to increase our bank accounts – see Psalm 62:10
- The lying words of those pretending to be from God – see Jeremiah 7:4-7
- Neighbors and brothers who are deceivers and slanderers of our faith – Jeremiah 9:4 and Jeremiah 12:6
- Our friends, children, and other family members over the words of God – Micah 7:5-7
- Our own understanding – see Proverbs 3:5

However, the benefits of putting our trust in God abound.

- We'll have a place to live and food to eat. "Trust in the LORD, and do good; so shalt thou dwell in the land, and verily thou shalt be fed" Psalm 37:3 (KJV).
- God will cause to happen whatever it is we need. "Commit thy way unto the LORD; trust also in him; and he shall bring it to pass" Psalm 37:5.
- God gives us peace of mind and heart; even as we watch others seemingly prosper by doing wrong. "Rest in the LORD, and wait patiently for him: fret not thyself because of him who prospereth in his way, because of the man who bringeth wicked devices to pass" Psalm 37:7. And "Thou wilt keep him in perfect peace, whose mind is stayed on thee: because he trusteth in thee" Isaiah 26:3.
- We have a place to go – a refuge – when we need to pour out our hearts. "Trust in him at all times; ye people, pour out your heart before him: God is a refuge for us. Selah" Psalm 62:8.
- We have help and protection. "Ye that fear the LORD, trust in the LORD: he is their help and their shield" Psalm 115:11.
- We'll have strength to stand in the face of any trial or opposition. "They that trust in the LORD shall be as mount Zion, which cannot be removed, but abideth forever" Psalm 125:1.
- God gives us not only strength when we're afraid, but a song and the reminder that He is our salvation, the source of our rescue. "Behold, God is my salvation; I will trust, and not be afraid: for the LORD JEHOVAH is my strength and my song; he also is become my salvation" Isaiah 12:2.
- We are blessed when our trust and hope is in God. "Blessed is the man that trusteth in the LORD, and whose hope the LORD is" Jeremiah 17:7.
- We are the praise of His glory. "That we should be to the praise of his glory, who first trusted in Christ" Ephesians 1:12.

We don't know when our appointed time to die will come. One of the gentlemen I spoke of earlier who passed away was an older man who had been very sick and in the hospital for a long time. We had time to get ourselves prepared for the probable news of his death. The other man was singing in the choir on Sunday and didn't wake from his sleep on Monday. If we want to know for sure that we'll be in Heaven when the time comes for us to die, we need to be living now like we really trust the God of Heaven. They did; let's do the same.

#349
December 14: God Our Enlistment Officer

The Merriam Webster online dictionary says that "enlist" means "to enroll oneself in the armed forces, to participate heartily as in a cause, drive, or crusade." Enlisting goes beyond merely joining. When we join something, we can simply add our name to the roll and never do another thing. When we enlist, we jump in with both feet, take off running, and look for ways in which we can add all our energies to the furtherance and betterment of the organization.

Second Timothy 2:4 puts something of a twist on enlistment. It says, "No one engaged in warfare entangles himself with the affairs of this life, that he may please him who enlisted him as a soldier" (NKJ). We generally think of enlistment as something we do voluntarily. We go down to the recruitment office and sign up – we enlist – in the Army, Navy, Air Force, Marines, or Coast Guard. However, this verse flips the script. It speaks of being enlisted in the way we speak of being drafted.

Paul is using this analogy to encourage Timothy, the young preacher, to hang in there in his walk with Christ. Paul's saying that Timothy has been enlisted in the sense of being chosen for this life. The Greek word translated as "enlisted" in this verse is the word "stratologeo" (strat-ol-og-eh'-o) from which we get our English word "strategy and strategic". In other words, Timothy has been strategically hand-picked for his job in the ministry, and like a soldier or warrior, it is expected of him to internalize that selection as if he had chosen the job for himself.

So too with us. We have been enlisted by the Master into this job as Christians, ambassadors of Heaven. Now it's expected of us to enlist our bodies, minds, and spirits – our every energy – to the work. It's time to internalize our selection into God's service and hit the ground running, using our gifts and talents for the furtherance of the Kingdom. As enlisted soldiers in God's service, our only answer to whatever He commands must be, "Yes sir!"

#350
December 15: God is Omnipresent

If you've ever played Peek-a-Boo with babies, it's funny to realize that in their minds, you have really gone away when you cover your face. Then they think you actually reappear when you uncover it, open your eyes really wide, smile and say, "Peek-a-Boo!" Their perception has not matured to understand that you are still very present.

In Ezekiel's day, God's people acted like these little children. In Ezekiel chapter eight, God carried the prophet into the spiritual realm so he could see all the abominations that the people were doing. Seventy men of the elders of the house of Israel were secretly offering incense to idols (verses 9 – 12), the women were secretly weeping for the idol goddess Tammuz (verse 13), and he saw "about twenty-five men with their backs toward the temple of the LORD and their faces toward the east... worshiping the sun toward the east" (verse 16, NKJ). These three groups represented the apostasy of the entire nation, acting in secret as if God couldn't see what they were doing.

And what was God's reaction to what He could clearly see His people doing? "Have you seen this, O son of man? Is it a trivial thing to the house of Judah to commit the abominations which they commit here? ...they have returned to provoke Me to anger... Therefore I also will act in fury. My eye will not spare nor will I have pity; and though they cry in My ears with a loud voice, I will not hear them" Ezekiel 8:17-18 (NKJ).

Consider the babies playing Peek-a-Boo and the people of Ezekiel's day. How like them are we? Do we think we're secretly committing our sins? Not even our thought life is hidden from our God. Hebrews 4:12-13 says, "For the word of God is living and powerful, and sharper than any two-edged sword, piercing even to the division of soul and spirit, and of joints and marrow, and is a discerner of the thoughts and intents of the heart. And there is no creature hidden from His sight, but all things are naked and open to the eyes of Him to whom we must give account" (NKJ).

Let's grow up and stop playing Peek-a-Boo with God. He's not gone simply because we are not looking at His face. Perhaps it's because we're not looking at His face that we think He's not around. We must mature in the understanding of His omnipresence, and operate realizing we are always in full view of the Master.

#351
December 16: The Encourager

Not long ago, I was feeling anxious and a bit discouraged. The career I had loved for 27 years had ended when the Christian high school I taught at closed its doors. I launched Life That Matters Ministries with high hopes and initial contributions from benevolent donors. The website was up; beautiful brochures, business cards, and other advertising items were printed; the publicist was hired; and social networks were connected.

Then I guess I panicked. What would happen when this initial money ran out? Why isn't anyone calling to book my seminars? Would I get another book contract? When would donations to the ministry pick up? Is anyone going to invite me to speak?

God wasn't answering and the days dragged on. I did, however, have one women's conference for which to prepare, so I dove into the task of getting my workshops ready for those ladies. Women's retreat and conference junkie that I am, I couldn't wait to get there to fellowship with the women of God.

Sure enough, the camaraderie immediately began to lift my spirits, but the strain must have still been evident on my face. As we moved about in the worship time to pray for one another, my friend Rosalind, the pastor's wife, caught my eye and drew me into a hug. She whispered to me, "God has not forgotten your faithfulness and He will be faithful to reward you." Later in the conference, I also received a prophetic word from the keynote speaker which started, "Do not worry about another dime." God went on to speak more support into my flagging spirit. How those ladies' words ministered to me!

The people receiving the letter to the Hebrews must have been in my same dispirited boat. The writer encourages them by saying, "For God is not unjust to forget your work and labor of love which you have shown toward His name, in that you have ministered to the saints, and do minister... do not become sluggish, but imitate those who through faith and patience inherit the promises. For when God made a promise to Abraham... He swore by Himself, saying, 'Surely blessing I will bless you, and multiplying I will multiply you.' And so, after he had patiently endured, he obtained the promise" Hebrews 6:10-15 (NKJ).

God won't forget what we are doing for the Kingdom. He's got our backs. I'm so busy with coaching writers, editing jobs, upcoming seminars, planning for a new book's release events and a new book contract, that my days were very full. There were still enough open squares in my Daytimer to keep me trusting God, but I refused to "become sluggish" and continued to believe and "imitate those who through faith and patience inherit the promises."

Surely God will bless and multiply the work of our hands. Be encouraged and patiently endure. The fulfillment of the promises is just around the corner.

#352
December 17: What is Jesus Waiting For?

Sometimes our troubles may seem so burdensome that we may think it would sure be nice if Jesus would just return. Let's just get this earthly life over with and start the everlasting Paradise party. After all, we hear about a glorious future with God when there will be no more strife, no more wars, no more pain, sorrow, sickness, or death. There will be no more heartbreaks and bad news, bills and creditors, recession and depression, arguments and misunderstandings. We want to throw our hands in the air, raise our faces toward heaven and shout, "Come on, Jesus. What are you waiting for?"

Hebrews 10:12-13 answers, "But this Man, after He had offered one sacrifice for sins forever, sat down at the right hand of God, from that time waiting till His enemies are made His footstool." (NKJ).

Okay, so He's waiting for His enemies to be made His footstool. The words "to be made" come from the Hebrew word *tithēmi* which is translated "to set, fix, establish, to set forth, ordain." So, He's waiting for a time when, without a shadow of a doubt, it will be definitely established who His enemies are. The Matthew Henry Commentary suggests, "One would think such a person as Christ could have no enemies except in hell; but it is certain that he has enemies on earth, very many... But Christ's enemies shall be made his footstool; some by conversion, others by confusion; and, which way soever it be, Christ will be honoured."

So, if we would like to participate in hastening the time along when Christ returns (so we can get on with that Paradise party), we need to be actively witnessing – sharing our faith with all who will listen. You see, it's those who don't know Christ who are His enemies. As we share Christ with people, they have two choices. They will either accept or reject His claims. If they accept His claims, they are made His footstool by conversion; if they reject His claims, they become His footstool by confusion. Those converted are gladly at His feet in worship; those confused are under His feet, condemned by their own decision.

Jesus is patiently waiting; let's get to work on those enemies.

#353
December 18: On Creativity

On October 5, 2011, at only 56 years old, Steve Jobs, co-founder of the mega-universally famous Apple company, died. The creative mastermind behind the MacBook, iPod, iPhone, and iPad is being compared to Thomas Edison, who until just recently, held the creative mastermind record with 1,093 U.S. patents for his inventions. Another name on the same great-ones list would be Benjamin Franklin whose kite and key experiment opened the door to the harnessing of the electricity we use to access Jobs' creations. Indeed we can be grateful for the creativity of Franklin, Edison, Jobs, and many others who carried their interesting thoughts into reality and fashioned products that make our lives more enjoyable.

According to Wikipedia (an on-line site I can google on my iPad), "creativity refers to the phenomenon whereby a person creates something new (a product, a solution, a work of art, a novel, a joke, etc.) that has some kind of value." Interestingly enough, Wikipedia goes on to tell us "it is commonly argued that the notion of "creativity" originated in Western culture through Christianity, as a matter of divine inspiration. According to the historian Daniel J. Boorstin, 'the early Western conception of creativity was the Biblical story of creation given in the Genesis.' …In the Judaeo-Christian tradition, creativity was the sole province of God; humans were not considered to have the ability to create something new except as an expression of God's work." Hebrews 11:3 says, "By faith we understand that the worlds were framed by the word of God, so that the things which are seen were not made of things which are visible" (NKJ).

What I get from all of this is simply the following: once God's word, the creative involvement of Jesus Christ, and the power of the Holy Spirit put everything in motion ("In the beginning God created the heaven and the earth" Genesis 1:1), He continued to pull new "creations" out of the matter He placed in our universe. The Hebrew word "bara" (creation) is used to denote the something-out-of-nothing or ex nihilo creation; the word "asah" (made) is used to describe the forming of something out of matter that already exists. Both words are used of God's action in the beginning of time as indicated in Genesis 2:3 when the writer indicates that God "rested from all His work which God had created and made" (NKJ). God, using the minds and the hands of man, His highest creation, allowed Franklin, Edison, and Steve Jobs to use His raw materials and participate in "asah" creation, whether they gave God the glory or not.

Just by thinking things out and carrying things through, look what human inventors—Christian or not—have accomplished. Just think what could be possible if we, who have a personal relationship with the Author of creativity, actually "take captive every thought to make it obedient to Christ" Second Corinthians 10:5 (NIV).

#354
December 19: The Invisible Creator of the Visible

Every few years, another round of the debate comes up between Creation and evolution. Ever since Darwin's *Origin of Species*, Christians have been in the fight of their lives over whether or not God created the universe. The definitive answer takes faith no matter what side of the debate you are on.

It takes much more faith to believe in evolution than it does to believe in Creation. Evolution takes chance after chance after far-fetched chance to believe that the chain of events it claims actually happened that way. First of all, there's this big bang, an incredible explosion of gasses that ends up forming galaxies, universes, the heavens, planets, stars, and a highly organized single-cell structure. That single cell eventually multiplies, forming a multi-celled organism that again begins to differentiate up the chain until you ultimately get to man. To believe this theory (and it is still called a theory today) is to truly have a great amount of faith in chance. If just one thing went wrong anywhere along the way of these supposed millions of years of changes, the whole theory would be shot. What are the mathematical chances of every single change happening just that way to form the universe and the living creatures we know to exist today? Such faith!

On the other hand, a far simpler – and I dare say a much more logical – answer to the where-did-it-all-come-from question exists. Two Bible verses – one in the Old Testament and the other in the New – make it crystal clear. Genesis 1:1 says, "In the beginning God created the heavens and the earth" (NKJ). And Hebrews 11:3 proclaims, "By faith we understand that the worlds were framed by the word of God, so that the things which are seen were not made of things which are visible" (NKJ).

God, the invisible One to us until Jesus' incarnation, created the visible. There's no believing in chance involved. All that's necessary is belief and faith in God. Start there, and everything else – from how the world was created to knowing our purpose in it – falls in line. It's a faith thing; have faith in God.

And by the way, if there was nothing to begin with, what exploded?

#355
December 20: His Real Presence

I remember orientation night at a school at which I taught. Parents and students rotated from class to class to meet each teacher and become acquainted with the school's policies and procedures. I let the parents know that they could visit my class at any time. I emphasized that I literally meant for them to come and sit in on the lectures and discussions. It was funny watching the students cringe at that particular invitation because the last thing they wanted was their parents to be really present with them in the class.

In Hebrews 13:5, the writer reminds us that God has said, "I will never leave you nor forsake you" (NKJ). It's interesting to note that those words are at the end of a verse that says, "Let your conduct be without covetousness; be content with such things as you have." This verse is saying since you know God is with you at all times, act right. You see, I put my students on notice that their parents might walk in at any time, so they should conduct themselves all the time as they would if their parents were physically seated beside them.

The real presence of God is literally with us. Oswald Chambers puts it this way, "Suppose Jesus suddenly lifted the veil from our eyes and let us see angels ministering to us, His own Presence with us, the Holy Ghost in us, and the Father around us, how amazed we should be!" Our deportment and character should reflect the fact that we are aware of God's actual presence.

So for practical purposes, let's dub this "Take Your Savior to Work Day." If you're a police officer, it's "Ride Along Day." If you're a homemaker, retired, or on vacation, walk through your day actually realizing God is accompanying you in everything you do. This evening, I promise you there will be a new meaning to your answer to the question, "How was your day?"

#356
December 21: It is Not God's Fault

Comedian Flip Wilson made a fortune dressed as his comic character Geraldine. He had her deny all culpability for her outrageous behavior by proclaiming, "The devil made me do it!" If we could get away with it, most of us wouldn't mind finding someplace else or someone else on which to place the blame for our wrongdoing. We hear excuses being bantered about all the time. "My workaholic mother neglected me, choosing the power of the boardroom over the peace of a bedtime story," or "My father was an alcoholic who abused me," or "teachers never took the necessary time to help me," etc., ad infinitum.

What's even worse than placing the blame for our screwed-up thinking on other people, is when we have the unmitigated gall to place the blame on God.

- "I couldn't reach my dream of playing in the NBA because God made me too short. That's why I've been forced to throw my life away to drug abuse."
- "God knows my body has needs, so that's why I'm promiscuous and dependent upon government subsidy to feed my six kids."
- "I didn't make this society so hard to live in. That's why I cheat on my taxes, tap into my neighbor's cable line,

purchase bootleg CD's, and lie about where I live so my kids can go to a better school. God knows I just have to beat the system.

This place-the-blame-on-God phenomenon is nothing new. Our first ancestor, Adam, started it in the Garden of Eden. The minute he was caught doing the first sin, instead of 'fessin' up, he threw Eve under the bus, and blamed God all in one sentence. (Okay, so buses weren't invented yet, but you get the picture.) When directly asked by God if he had eaten of the tree he had been told not to eat from, Adam answered, "The woman whom You gave to be with me, she gave me of the tree, and I ate" Genesis 3:12 (NKJ).

Yes, it seems fewer and fewer of us want to step up to the plate and take responsibility for our own actions. James 1:13-15 shows clearly that our sinfulness is not God's fault. "Let no one say when he is tempted, 'I am tempted by God'; for God cannot be tempted by evil, nor does He Himself tempt anyone. But each one is tempted when he is drawn away by his own desires and enticed. Then, when desire has conceived, it gives birth to sin; and sin, when it is full-grown, brings forth death" (NKJ).

God does not tempt us to sin. Our own flesh is our problem; it lures us toward evils. Spending time desiring those evils causes us to start planning to make those desires reality. When we make our sinful desires into realities – when we do the deed – sin happens. And sin always, always leads to death.

Today, let's stop blaming God for our sin, realize the enticement lies within, and turn to God for the strength to avoid yielding to temptation.

#357
December 22: Demons Believe

Halloween seems to have become as big a holiday in the United States as Christmas. Millions of dollars are spent on costumes, decorations, and candy. Stores dedicated to the day have even sprung up at shopping malls. The most preferred costumes by far are the scary, bloody, ghastly, and ghostly variety. Hollywood cashes in too. Movies celebrating the paranormal released around this time of year can be assured of huge payoffs at the box office.

Many of us accept the depictions of the mystical in costumes and the movies as mere entertainment, when in actuality, the spirit world exists. If Satan can get us to relax about his existence, he can worm his way into our lives and negatively affect our marriages, our children, our workplaces, our churches, and our communities.

Although the demonic is nothing to be feared if we know our place in Christ, it is also nothing to play around with. Demons are all about havoc and the creation of mayhem, but they know Jesus and must bow to Him. Consider the following events of Scripture:

> Mark 1:23-24 "Now there was a man in their synagogue with an unclean spirit. And he cried out, saying, 'Let us alone! What have we to do with You, Jesus of Nazareth? Did You come to destroy us? I know who You are-- the Holy One of God!'" (NKJ)

> Mark 5:1-7 "Then they came to the other side of the sea, to the country of the Gadarenes. And when He had come out of the boat, immediately there met Him out of the tombs a man with an unclean spirit... And always, night and day, he was in the mountains and in the tombs, crying out and cutting himself with stones. When he saw Jesus from afar, he ran and worshiped Him. And he cried out with a loud voice and said, 'What have I to do with You, Jesus, Son of the Most High God? I implore You by God that You do not torment me'" (NKJ).

> James 2:19 "You believe that there is one God. Good! Even the demons believe that-- and shudder" (NIV).

There is something in every day of the year that can turn our thoughts toward God. Halloween is a strong reminder of Jesus' victory over demonic forces which war against us. Be reminded that Satan is fighting from a place of defeat; we from a place of victory. We can operate in confidence when demonic forces of discouragement, illness, and obstacles raise their ugly heads because we know how the story ends; we've read the end of the book. Facing our demonic foe is like watching the rebroadcast of a football game that we won. We're not concerned at all during the times when our team is behind because we already know the outcome.

#358
December 23: God Answers Prayer for the Sick

James, our Lord's brother, knew all about Jesus both as his natural relative and as the Savior. The unique perspective James gives in his epistle shows Jesus' ways to be quite practical. When speaking of prayer, James says, "Is anyone among you sick? Let him call for the elders of the church, and let them pray over him, anointing him with oil in the name of the Lord. And the prayer of faith will save the sick, and the Lord will raise him up. And if he has committed sins, he will be forgiven. Confess *your* trespasses to one another, and pray for one another, that you may be healed. The effective, fervent prayer of a righteous man avails much" James 5:14-16 (NKJ).

Simply put, James tells us that when we're sick, we ought to go to God in prayer and we ought to take others with us. Once we ask in the name of the Lord, the Lord will move on behalf of the one needing help. How encouraging and how practical!

Over and over again while traveling around with Jesus, James saw this played out. People were sick; they went to Jesus. Some were so sick that they couldn't get to Jesus on their own, so their parents or friends either took them or sought Jesus out on their behalf. No matter what the illness—physical, spiritual, or mental—the result was the same; taking the problem to Jesus meant He made a difference in the life of the sick person.

Are you hurting? Go to Jesus with the problem and take some friends along. Do you know people who are hurting? Take them to Jesus or go to Him on their behalf. Don't give up. Be encouraged with the knowledge that your prayers as one of God's righteous ones are extremely effective. In other words, God is listening. He hears. He touches. He heals.

#359
December 24: God's Patience and Promises

In his second epistle, the apostle Peter found it necessary to correct a false view espoused by antinomian philosophy. "Antinomians believe that since salvation was by grace alone, the requirements of the moral law were irrelevant."* The problem with that view should be obvious: grace does not erase the moral standards set out in Scripture. Grace does not give us license to sin; instead, it has provided us with all the power of Heaven to stand against sin, and it also provides forgiveness when we do sin. It was tough for these new, first century believers to cling to their faith walk in the face of strong persecution and damaging false philosophies. Peter had to help them understand and encourage them to hold on as they questioned why it was taking Christ so long to return and end all the misery in which they found themselves. Peter told them:

> "...scoffers will come in the last days, walking according to their own lusts, and saying, "Where is the promise of His coming? ...But the heavens and the earth which are now preserved by the same word, are reserved for fire until the day of judgment and perdition of ungodly men.
> But, beloved, do not forget this one thing, that with the Lord one day is as a thousand years, and a thousand years as one day. The Lord is not slack concerning His promise, as some count slackness, but is longsuffering toward us, not willing that any should perish but that all should come to repentance.
> But the day of the Lord will come as a thief in the night... Therefore, since all these things will be dissolved, what manner of persons ought you to be in holy conduct and godliness, looking for and hastening the coming of the day of God...
> Therefore, beloved, looking forward to these things, be diligent to be found by Him in peace, without spot and blameless; and account that the longsuffering of our Lord is salvation..." Second Peter 3:3-15 (NKJ).

As it was then, so it is now. People who question our faith and mock our God will attempt to cast doubt by pointing out that Christ still has not returned. His patience and longing for the souls of even those who are mocking are the very reasons why He's waiting. We want to see things changed right now. We want Him to return right now. But what about those people who need a little more time? What about those who are just about to see the light?

God's patience is not eradicating His promise. God's patience is merely telling His promise to wait a bit longer for the salvation of as many as possible. He is going to return and all His promises will indeed happen. May we learn to rest in God's patience as we wait not only for His return, but also for all His promises to manifest in our lives.

#360
December 25: God is Light

There is something wonderful about light. Light chases away the Boogie Man in a young child's imagination as she lays wide awake and in fear at night. Light helps us creep along a highway through a rainstorm. Light enables us to find what we're looking for. We even use the word apart from physical illumination. When we want to understand a mystery, we ask to be enlightened.

In First John 1:5-7, the apostle gives us some enlightenment about light. He writes, "This is the message which we have heard from Him and declare to you, that God is light and in Him is no darkness at all. If we say that we have fellowship with Him, and walk in darkness, we lie and do not practice the truth. But if we walk in the light as He is in the light, we have fellowship with one another, and the blood of Jesus Christ His Son cleanses us from all sin" (NKJ).

Light, this amazing thing, was the very first thing created. The very first words spoken over nothingness were, "Let there be light," and bang, there was light (Genesis 1:3). (Now that indeed is the big bang!) Since God is light, those phenomenal four words were as if He was saying, "Look out emptiness, I've arrived," and the void—the barrenness, the blankness, the nothing, the dark—had no choice but to get up out of there.

Light works the same way in our lives as it did at Creation. Light and darkness cannot take up the same space. If we are God's children, we are lying to ourselves and to the world if we are trying to walk in darkness. It is also a lie from the pit of hell if some "dark" label has been placed upon our life.

- We are not ignorant; all wisdom comes from God. (James 3:17)
- We are not empty; every good and perfect gift come from God. (James 1:17)
- We are not lost in sin; we are the righteousness of God in Christ. (Second Corinthians 5:12)
- We are not gay; God created male and female to complement each other in relationship, and to reflect the union between Christ and the Church. (Mark 10:6-8, Ephesians 5:21-33)
- We are not unloving; the love of God is shed abroad in our hearts. (Romans 5:5)

We cannot allow Satan to sell us a "dark" bill of goods. It's time to recognize who we are as children of light, children of the Most High God, in whom is "no darkness at all." Since there's no darkness in Him, He has paved the way for us to "walk in the light as He is in the light." We are to maintain "fellowship with one another," and continuously allow "the blood of Jesus Christ His Son [to cleanse] us from all sin."

#361
December 26: When God Says No

If my toddlers would ask me to let them play with a buzz saw, I would obviously say, "No." No explanation would be necessary; they wouldn't understand it anyway. My negative response would just have to be sufficient because of my authority and what I know about the tragic outcome of granting their request. However, if they were to ask me for more vegetables and less sweets, I would eagerly and quickly give them exactly what they asked for. Why? Because they would be asking for something that was in accordance with my will for them.

Our prayers are never ignored, nor do they go unanswered. When it comes to prayer, we have a tendency to forget that "no" is an answer. First John 5:14-15 is pretty clear, "Now this is the confidence that we have in Him, that if we ask anything according to His will, He hears us. And if we know that He hears us, whatever we ask, we know that we have the petitions that we have asked of Him" (NKJ). God fulfills for us those things we ask in accordance with His will for us. When we ask for stuff He doesn't want for us, He says, "No."

Prayer is more about getting into God's head than about letting God get into ours. He already knows what we think, want, and need. When we pray, let's be about the business of finding out what God wants for us in every situation of life. Once we know His outlook on a subject, our prayer-confidence meter will soar. We will see prayer answered in the positive left and right because we'll spend much less time asking for what we want, and much more time asking for what He wants for us.

#362
December 27: Snapshots of Jesus

It's probably a good thing that cameras were not yet invented when Jesus physically walked the earth. You know how we are. We would have taken His picture and then worshipped the photographs after His death and resurrection. We would have formed prejudicial views against Him because of the color of His skin, His height, His weight, His looks. Everyone of His same pigment and outer characteristics would have felt superior to everyone who did not look the same.

God allowed the record of His deeds to last through the written record of eyewitness accounts. The few physical descriptions we have show Him exactly as God wanted us to see Him.

- At His initial appearance on earth, we first see Jesus as a baby, wrapped in cloths. "And she brought forth her firstborn Son, and wrapped Him in swaddling cloths, and laid Him in a manger, because there was no room for them in the inn" Luke 2:7 (NKJ).
- God purposely gave Jesus a very ordinary physical appearance while He did His work on earth with us. Isaiah 53:2 records, "He grew up before him like a tender shoot, and like a root out of dry ground. He had no beauty or majesty to attract us to him, nothing in his appearance that we should desire him" (NIV).

- Throughout the accounts of Jesus' activities, starkly absent are descriptions of His looks. We're only apprised of His clothing when it matters to His ministry. For example, we know He wore a robe because the woman with the issue of blood reached out to touch the hem of His garment and she received her healing (see Matthew 9:20ff). It was also significant when the soldiers mocked Jesus, pushing Him forward in a robe with a crown, sarcastically presenting Him to the crowd as their king. "When Jesus came out wearing the crown of thorns and the purple robe, Pilate said to them [the crowd], 'Here is the man!'" John 19:5 (NIV).

- We then see Jesus on the cross. Isaiah 52:14 foretells, "Just as there were many who were appalled at him-- his appearance was so disfigured beyond that of any man and his form marred beyond human likeness..." (NIV).

God wanted us to see Jesus not as a celebrity, but as "the Son of Man came to seek and to save what was lost" Luke 19:10 (NIV), and as the one who "did not come to be served, but to serve, and to give His life a ransom for many" Mark 10:45 (NKJ).

But like any parent, God not only displays photos of His Child as things were happening through the growing years, but He also proudly exhibits memories of His Child's crowning achievements in the most ornate frame. Such is the picture we see in the Revelation of John. God didn't end the Book without one last snapshot, one quite different from all the others. John sees:

One like the Son of Man, clothed with a garment down to the feet and girded about the chest with a golden band. His head and hair were white like wool, as white as snow, and His eyes like a flame of fire; His feet were like fine brass, as if refined in a furnace, and His voice as the sound of many waters; He had in His right hand seven stars, out of His mouth went a sharp two-edged sword, and His countenance was like the sun shining in its strength. [And this Man says] "Do not be afraid; I am the First and the Last. I am He who lives, and was dead, and behold, I am alive forevermore. Amen. And I have the keys of Hades and of Death" Revelation 1:13-18 (NKJ).

Look through the entire "photo album" for a clear picture of who Jesus really is. Don't get it twisted. The helpless baby, suffering servant, and condemned man on the cross is none other than our conquering King, Jesus the Christ.

#363
December 28: Jesus' Facebook Photo

If the apostle John had had an iPhone while exiled on the isle of Patmos, he surely would have taken a picture of Jesus and posted it on Facebook for all to see. Here's what the photo would have looked like:

- Someone "like a son of man," dressed in a robe reaching down to his feet and with a golden sash around his chest
- His head and hair were white like wool, as white as snow
- His eyes were like blazing fire
- His feet were like bronze glowing in a furnace
- His voice was like the sound of rushing waters
- In his right hand he held seven stars
- Out of his mouth came a sharp double-edged sword
- His face was like the sun shining in all its brilliance

Accompanying the photo, Jesus would probably have added in His profile:
- Do not be afraid. I am the First and the Last
- I am the Living One
- I was dead, and behold I am alive for ever and ever!
- And I hold the keys of death and Hades.

No need to have a Facebook account, though, to get this snapshot and this profile. It's recorded for us in the original Facebook—the Book that shows us Jesus face-to-face—the Bible. The description is found in Revelation 1:13-18 (NIV). We may not have any paper or digital photos of Jesus, but the Bible is full of explanatory snapshots showing us in no uncertain terms what Jesus is like, and making clear to us who He is.

John may not have had an iPhone or Facebook, but He had something far more important, a heart-to-heart and face-to-face relationship with Jesus that made him know that Christ was real and that Christ was who He said He was. Thanks to the five Bible books John wrote (St. John; First, Second, and Third John; and The Revelation), combined with the 61 other books of the Bible, we too can know Jesus heart-to-heart, and eventually, face-to-face.

#364
December 29: God: The One to Hang Onto

Many of us may have seen the cute poster of a cat hanging by its front paws, clinging on for dear life. The caption reads: When you come to the end of your rope, tie a knot and hang on in there.

Sometimes so much seems to be bombarding us at the same time that we may well feel like that little cat. At those times, remember Revelation 3:10-11 which says, "Because you have kept My command to persevere, I also will keep you from the hour of trial which shall come upon the whole world, to test those who dwell on the earth. Behold, I am coming quickly! Hold fast what you have, that no one may take your crown" (NKJ).

The King James Version begins verse 10 by saying, "Because thou hast kept the word of my patience..." So this command to persevere, as translated in the New King James version of the Bible, comes from the Greek word "hupomone" (hoop-om-on-ay') which means "cheerful or hopeful endurance, constancy, and enduring patience in waiting." In other words, God is telling us to hang on in there. We can do this waiting not only patiently, but also cheerfully and hopefully patiently because we have the assurance that He has our backs. The trials that are consuming the whole world won't consume us. In fact, He is coming quickly. Just hold tight.

Remember, miracles don't occur until we can do nothing else for ourselves. Hold on. As we live and give our all for God, He will not let us go under. David, one of God's main men, said it best: "I was young and now I am old, yet I have never seen the righteous forsaken or their children begging bread" Psalm 37:25 (NIV).

#365
December 30: Lukewarm? Yeech!

The breakfast buffet in a fine hotel offered many scrumptious items to delight the palette. I decided to visit the omelet bar, and while the chef prepared my spinach-mushroom-tomato-onion-cheese masterpiece, I surveyed the rest of the counter. Since it was a cold, snowy morning outside, the hot oatmeal called my name. I filled a bowl with the steaming delight, added butter and brown sugar, retrieved my omelet, and headed for my table where the fresh orange juice was already awaiting my arrival. Ahhh, what a pleasure to take those first, hot spoonfuls of that creamy, sweet oatmeal! Even so, after several times back and forth between bites of omelet and bites of oatmeal, that oatmeal began to cool. The last few spoonfuls were nowhere near as satisfying as the first few because it had become lukewarm.

Nothing is good when it's lukewarm. We'd prefer our food or drink to be either hot or cold. We feel about our food as God feels about our spiritual walk. Although specifically speaking to the church at Laodicea, God's words ring true for us as well. "I know your works, that you are neither cold nor hot. I could wish you were cold or hot. So then, because you are lukewarm, and neither cold nor hot, I will vomit you out of My mouth. Because you say, 'I am rich, have become wealthy, and have need of nothing'-- and do not know that you are wretched, miserable, poor, blind, and naked-- I counsel you to buy from Me gold refined in the fire, that you may be rich; and white garments, that you may be clothed, that the shame of your nakedness may not be revealed; and anoint your eyes with eye salve, that you may see" Revelation 3:15-18 (NKJ).

God shows us here that we become lukewarm when we think we have it all together. Let a few things go right for us – there's money in the bank, the job's secure, we own a fine car, the kids are healthy – and we forget just how dependent upon God we really are. We start to take the credit for our good fortune and leave God out of the mix. Suddenly, we have no time to go to church, Sunday school, or Bible study, and we certainly don't want to tithe. We rationalize that we have to get our rest so we can do our best on the job, and we have to hold onto our money so we can keep up with our bills and current lifestyle.

God hates those actions and that attitude. He counsels us to buy gold from Him. His gold is righteous living (white garments) and spiritual understanding (anointed eyes): that's what makes us truly rich.

So we have a choice. We can either be cold by walking away from God and turning to total dependence upon ourselves (after all, that's how we may be living anyway), or we can be hot and live our lives completely as God would have us live them. The cold have sealed their own doom, and to the lukewarm, He says, "Yeech!" Hot is all He accepts.

#366
December 31: Reacting to God's Correction

In the sixteenth chapter of The Revelation, seven angels are allowed to pour the wrath of God upon the earth and all kinds of bad stuff starts happening:

- foul and loathsome sores break out on those who have taken the mark of the beast upon themselves,
- the sea becomes blood and all the sea creatures die,
- the rivers and springs become blood so there's no water to drink,
- the sun is affected so that it scorches people with its heat,
- etc.

God is obviously perturbed and you would think the people on earth would get the message; yet, not so. Read their reaction, "They blasphemed the God of heaven because of their pains and their sores, and did not repent of their deeds" Revelation 16:11 (NKJ).

Not much had changed in hundreds of years. Just a few generations after Adam and Eve plundered mankind into sin, humans had gotten so rotten that we hear God saying, "My Spirit shall not strive with man forever, for he is indeed flesh..." And the LORD was sorry that He had made man on the earth, and He was grieved in His heart" Genesis 6:3 and 6 (NKJ). God's next thought was to just wipe everybody out. After all, He was well capable to start all over again. "So the LORD said, 'I will destroy man whom I have created from the face of the earth, both man and beast, creeping thing and birds of the air, for I am sorry that I have made them'" Genesis 6:7 (NKJ).

To what lengths do we push God before we decide to repent? Our maturity as children of God can be measured by the length of time it takes us from the recognition of our sin to our repentance. The shorter the time, the more mature we are becoming. Rather than going through levels of denial and arguments of justification, once we become aware we have sinned, our commitment to Christ ought to compel us to immediately confess it before God and turn from it. And if God is trying to get our attention through some form of discipline He's sent, it's a great idea to submit to His chastening quickly.

Let's not be the ones who fall under God's wrath or move Him to say He's sorry He made us.

About The Author

A Biola University graduate, 30-plus year career educator, award-winning multi-published author, astute Bible teacher, compelling preacher/speaker, and religious broadcaster Rev. Sharon Norris Elliott excitedly realizes her life calling involves sharing the good news of the Gospel in and with every aspect of her life. Sharon and her husband James share their comfortable Southern California home, and enjoy participating in their church activities, exploring the sites of the Underground Railroad, and traveling to spend time with their children and grandchildren.

This is what the Lord says:
"Don't let the wise boast in their wisdom, or the powerful boast in their power, or the rich boast in their riches. But those who wish to boast should boast in this alone: that they truly know me and understand that I am the Lord who demonstrates unfailing love and who brings justice and righteousness to the earth, and that I delight in these things. I, the Lord, have spoken!
Jeremiah 9:23-24 (NLT)

___

In his classic work *Knowing God*, Christian theologian J. I. Packer astutely asks, "What makes life worthwhile is having a big enough objective, something which catches our imagination and lays hold of our allegiance, and this the Christian has in a way that no other person has. For what higher, more exalted, and more compelling goal can there be than to know God?"

Indeed. Life is worthwhile and our imagination is captured by the fascination we experience upon gaining familiarity with our eternal, all-encompassing, omniscient God. Just to embark upon the journey itself gives our very existence new meaning. This is the lofty goal of the book you hold in your hands. Author Sharon Norris Elliott invites you to become a part of a movement of the faithful who insist upon growing closer to God through gaining a deeper knowledge of Him. By glimpsing a tiny bit of His glory every day, you will:

➢ Discover something amazing about God every day
➢ Increase your understanding of Scripture in general

➢ Enjoy engaging contemporary stories that point out God's attributes
➢ Be encouraged in your walk with the God
➢ Be challenged to make necessary, positive changes
➢ Develop a new love for the Bible

Again, J. I. Packer seems to speak directly to Elliott's aim for her readers. "There is no peace like the peace of those whose minds are possessed with full assurance that they have known God, and God has known them, and that this relationship guarantees God's favor to them in life, through death and on for ever." Join the movement and get to know the God who already knows you by taking 366 glimpses of God.

Glossary

<u>Part 1: Glimpses of God in the Books of Moses and the Books of History</u>

1. A New Year, a new Focus, a New Challenge — Psalm 149:4
2. Living Outside of Time — Genesis 1:1, Romans 8:28, John 3:16
3. God in the Beginning — Genesis 1 – 2
4. God and the Miracle of Birth — Genesis 4:1
5. Compassion Trumps Pain — Genesis 6:5-8
6. Remember as God Remembers — Genesis 9:14-16
7. God, the One Who Blesses — Genesis 12:1-3, Psalm 25:12-13
8. The Call of God — Genesis 12:1-3, Proverbs 1:33
9. Been Waiting Long? — Genesis 15:1
10. The God Who Sees — Genesis 16:7-13, Matthew 6:8b
11. Nothing Too Hard for God — Genesis 18:14
12. God as Judge — Genesis 18:23-25, 19:29
13. God the Promise Keeper — Genesis 21:1
14. God Hears Our Children's Cries — Genesis 21:14-19
15. Take Your G.O.D.'s — Genesis 22:1-2, 11-12; Job 1:9-11
16. God of Extended Blessings — Genesis 22:18, 30:30, 30:3-6a
17. Nothing Left Undone — Genesis 24:1, Colossians 2:8-10
18. Commander of the Angels — Genesis 24:7
19. God Thought of it First — Genesis 25:22-24, Psalm 139:13-17

Part 2: Glimpses of God in the Books of Poetry

100.	God's Ownership	Job 41:11b
101.	One Thing I Know For Sure	Job 42:2
102.	God's Excellence	Psalm 8:1
103.	Purpose Fulfiller	Psalm 20:4
104.	Why Serve Any Other God?	Psalm 23
105.	On the Voice of God	Psalm 29:3-5, 7-9
106.	God is Extol-able	Psalm 30:1-4
107.	Momentary Anger	Psalm 30:5
108.	God in Prosperity	Psalm 30:6-7a
109.	God's Great Goodness	Psalm 31:19
110.	Not Holding It Over Me	Psalm 32:1-2
111.	The Life Coach	Psalm 32:8
112.	God and Beautiful Music	Psalm 33:1-3
113.	International Politician	Psalm 33:10-19
114.	When God Hears, Results Follow	Psalm 34:4 & 6
115.	God's Hearing is Listening	Psalm 34:4 & 6
116.	God Likes Us	Psalm 37:23-24
117.	God Knows	Psalm 44:20-21
118.	Present Help	Psalm 46:1
119.	Still on the Throne	Psalm 47:2, 7-8
120.	Creator and Renovator	Psalm 51:10
121.	Wanted Alive, Not Dead	Psalm 51:15-17
122.	My Box, God's Bottle	Psalm 56:8
123.	Hiding Place	Psalm 57:1
124.	De-Fense!	Psalm 62:5-6, 94:22-23
125.	See God in the Sanctuary	Psalm 63:2
126.	Like Momma	Psalm 66:13
127.	When God Rises Up	Psalm 68:1 and 3
128.	Only Wondrous Things	Psalm 72:18
129.	Thanks Due to God	Psalm 75:1
130.	God is Known	Psalm 76:1a
131.	God Responds to Our Voice	Psalm 77:1
132.	When Life Deals a Bad Hand	Psalm 77:1-15
133.	Pain Relief	Psalm 77:10-12
134.	God is at Church	Psalm 77:13a, Hebrews 10:25

Part 5: Glimpses of God in the Letters (Epistles) and The Revelation

MINISTRY CONTACT INFORMATION

Sharon Norris Elliott
www.LifeThatMatters.net

Sharon's on Internet TV & Radio

Watch The Holy Spirit Broadcasting Network (**www.HSBN.tv**)
for Sharon's new shows:

"Life That Matters"

and

"A View from the Upper Room"

Find me as **SaneWriter** on Facebook and Twitter

Subscribe **to "A Heart for the Word," the daily devotional blog:**
www.sanewriter.wordpress.com

<u>NEW BOOK! Be sure to obtain a copy of Sharon's newest book *"Why I Get Into Trouble"*. Available at www.createspace.com/5131814</u>

<u>Sharon's other available books include:</u>

Boomerangs to Arrows:
A Godly Guide for Launching Young Adult Children
Judson Press

Power Suit: The Armor of God Fit for the Feminine Frame
New Hope Publishers

Raising Boys to be Like Jesus, Judson Press

Living a Milk & Honey Life:
Letting Go of What's Holding You Back,
Beacon Hill Publishers

What? Teenagers in the Bible? Redemption Press

(Available from the publishers, in bookstores, and online via Amazon.com, ChristianBook.com, BarnesAndNoble.com, & <u>www.hsbn.tv</u> in the webstore)